The Social Life of Money in the English Past

In an age when authoritative definitions of currency were in flux and small change was scarce, money enjoyed a rich and complex social life. Deborah Valenze shows how money became involved in relations between people in ways that moved beyond what we understand as its purely economic functions. This highly original investigation covers the formative period of commercial and financial development in England between 1630 and 1800. In a series of interwoven essays, Valenze examines religious prohibitions related to avarice, early theories of political economy, an experimental workhouse banning money, and exchange practices of the Atlantic economy. In applying monetary measurements to women, servants, colonial migrants, and local vagrants, this era was distinctive in its willingness to blur boundaries between people and things. As money became identified with a new notion of the self, more modern attitudes emerged. Lucid and highly readable, the book revises the way we see the advance of commercial society at the threshold of modern capitalism.

Deborah Valenze is Professor of History at Barnard College, Columbia University, in New York City. She has been awarded fellowships by the American Council of Learned Societies, the National Endowment for the Humanities, the Bunting Institute of Radcliffe College, and the Yale Center for British Art. She is the author of *The First Industrial Woman* (1995), *Prophetic Sons and Daughters: Female Preaching and Popular Religion in Industrial England* (1985), and numerous scholarly articles. She lives in Cambridge, Massachusetts, with her husband and two daughters.

T0345053

THE SOCIAL LIFE OF MONEY IN THE ENGLISH PAST

Deborah Valenze
Barnard College, Columbia University

CAMBRIDGE
UNIVERSITY PRESS

CAMBRIDGE
UNIVERSITY PRESS

University Printing House, Cambridge CB2 8BS, United Kingdom

Cambridge University Press is part of the University of Cambridge.

It furthers the University's mission by disseminating knowledge in the pursuit of education, learning and research at the highest international levels of excellence.

www.cambridge.org
Information on this title: www.cambridge.org/9780521617802

© Deborah Valenze 2006

First published 2006

A catalogue record for this publication is available from the British Library

Library of Congress Cataloguing in Publication data

Valenze, Deborah M.
The Social life of money in the English past / Deborah Valenze.
    p. cm.
Includes bibliographical references.
ISBN 0-521-85242-0 (hardback) – ISBN 0-521-61780-4 (pbk.)
1. Money – Social aspects – England – History – 18th century.
2. Money – Social aspects – England – History – 17th century.   3. England –
Economic conditions – 18th century.   4. England – Economic conditions –
17th century.   5. England – Social conditions – 18th century.   6. England – Social
conditions – 17th century.   I. Title.
HG950.E54V35   2006
306.3′4094209032 – dc22   2005028143

ISBN 978-0-521-85242-5 Hardback
ISBN 978-0-521-61780-2 Paperback

For Eric and Marlene Hobsbawm

Contents

Illustrations

Acknowledgments

This book emerges from a long gestation during which the field of British history, reflecting the turmoil of world politics, has undergone enormous changes. Perhaps this accounts for why I turned my attention to the subject of money after having explored the subjects of religion, gender, and work. If I remember correctly, the idea originated in a conversation with Tom Laqueur, who, knowing my inclinations as a historian of economic culture, said he thought I should consider returning to where R. H. Tawney left off in order to think more about social ethics during the rise of capitalism in late seventeenth-century Britain. For some time, I believed that the subject of my new project was eighteenth-century poverty. Then, in the midst of a trawl through the archives of the Greater London Record Office, I began to take note of a persistent intrusion of money, not just in places where it belonged, but also within reports of the most ordinary social administration. Admittedly, the topic of money was multifaceted in the most daunting sense. Many friends expressed skepticism, perhaps thinking that I had drifted misguidedly into the thickets of business history. It was only after several more years of adjusting my purview that the work finally assumed its present frame, which may or may not set to rest their suspicions of a certain intellectual hubris.

I owe thanks to many people who read or listened to my ideas and responded with thoughts of their own. Peter Weiler and Susan Amussen helped to launch this project into a serious pursuit by asking me to give a plenary talk at a meeting of the Northeast Conference on British Studies some years ago. They and other friends intervened at critical moments and kept me on track. Tim Hitchcock shared his knowledge, works-in-progress, and files with unstinting generosity. Margot Finn understood my intentions and cheered me on from the beginning. Bernard Bailyn gave me a bibliographical lead that brought an entire chapter into being. Carl Wennerlind's own work on the intellectual history of money and his readings of several chapters were an important source of encouragement. I am grateful to two anonymous readers for Cambridge University Press, who offered expert advice and guidance twice during the writing of the manuscript; all remaining oversights and errors are my own. The following colleagues and friends also gave considerable time to reading and commenting on sections, and in some cases, all of the manuscript: John Beattie, Nick Dirks, Jim Obelkevich, Peter Onuf, Steve Pincus, Tom Laqueur, Nick Rogers, Ruth Smith, Lisa Tiersten, John Walsh, and Peter Weiler. Others who offered helpful conversation, suggestions, and friendship over the years were Tim Alborn, Donna Andrew, Jim Basker, Brad Bateman, Judith Bennett, Virginia Berridge, David Bindman and Frances Carey, Ann Blair, David Cannadine, Nancy Carney, Penny Corfield, Lee Davidoff, István Deák, Amy Froide, Catherine Gallagher, Merav Gold, Cynthia Herrup, Carla Hesse, Kaia Huseby, Anne Janowitz, Martin Jay, Maryanne Kowaleski, Peter Linebaugh, Peter Mandler, Rachel Manley, Michael McKeon, Sandra Sherman, Herb Sloan, Susan Staves, Philip Stern, Pat Thane, David Underdown, Wendy Urban-Mead, Frances Walsh, and Nancy Woloch. Seth Rockman and Joseph Dineen assisted me with the State of Maryland Archives. I am also especially grateful to Nancy Carney, Kim Hays, Janna Malamud Smith, Ruth Smith, Donna Vinter, and Irene Briggin. And I owe thanks to Donna and Richard Vinter and family and Jim Obelkevich for offering hospitality, music, and cheer in London.

I am grateful to my students at Barnard College, Columbia College, graduate students at Columbia University, and especially my colleagues in the History Department at Barnard, who have been a source of intellectual companionship during the writing of this book, as well as the administration of Barnard College and Ms. Sully Rios for their enduring assistance. I have also received support from the American Council of Learned Societies, the Bunting Institute of Radcliffe College (now the Radcliffe Institute for Advanced Research), the National Endowment for the Humanities, a Barnard College Research Grant, the Society for Eighteenth-Century Studies, and the Yale Center for British Art. Frank Smith gave me the best of guidance at Cambridge University Press, along with Eric Crahan and Gillian Linden.

The following libraries offered the resources without which this book could not have been written: the British Library; Corporation of London

Record Office; Folger Shakespeare Library; the Friends Library; Greater London Record Office; Guildhall Library; Harvard Law School Library; the Houghton Library of Harvard University, with special thanks to Susan Halpert; Butler Library of Columbia University and Wollman Library of Barnard College; the Yale Center for British Art, with thanks to Susan Brady; the Beinecke Library and Sterling Library of Yale University; the Lewis Walpole Collection of Yale University, with thanks to Joan Sussler; and Widener Library of Harvard University. For help with and permission for the illustrations, I am indebted to Janet Larkin and the Department of Coins and Medals of the British Museum; the Guildhall Library, Corporation of London; the Houghton Library of Harvard University; the National Gallery of Ireland; the Norwich Castle Museum and Art Gallery; and the Tate Gallery, London.

My family made this project possible in a fundamental way. They willingly relocated to London for the first half-year of research and for intermittent months after that. My husband, Michael Timo Gilmore, set aside his own writing to read successive drafts and never flagged as my best critic and support. Emma and Rosa Gilmore have provided their incomparable companionship, commentary, and illumination every step of the way. Along with my love, I offer them endless thanks.

My final debt is shown in the dedication of this book. I have been supremely fortunate to know personally my favorite historian, Eric Hobsbawm, who has been an intellectual mentor to me for more than thirty years. Together, Eric and Marlene have supplied not only this historian, but an entire network of lucky friends, with camaraderie, hospitality, and moral support. Without them, it would have been impossible for me to mount the same line of vision or muster the same endurance. This book is a small measure of ongoing gratitude and affection.

Abbreviations

CLRO	Corporation of London Record Office
EHR	Economic History Review
GL	Guildhall Library, London
GLRO	Greater London Record Office
FSL	Folger Shakespeare Library
HJ	Historical Journal
JEH	Journal of Economic History
P&P	Past and Present
PMLA	Proceedings of the Modern Language Association
SH	Social History

Introduction: The Social Life of Money, ca. 1640–1770

In September of 1688, Samuel Pepys made his way to Bartholomew Fair in search of pleasure after a day's work. There he chanced upon an amusing demonstration in the form of "a Mare that tells money," probably by a stamp of the hoof or shake of the head. The spectacle cost Pepys twelvepence. Given his careful recording of the performance, the energetic naval secretary could not have been dissatisfied. Perhaps he had perceived an affinity between his own line of work, which entailed sorting out money matters, and that of the winsome, four-legged accountant.[1]

Everybody in seventeenth-century London recognized the worth of money and knew that it would be folly to try to navigate the city without some of it in their pockets. The apparent similarities between early modern assumptions and our own must stop there, however. Coins in the past may have met with universal approbation, particularly in urban settings, but they were hardly standardized or ubiquitous. The British state would not issue small coins for the masses until the early nineteenth century, and shopkeepers in London were accustomed to making do with poor substitutes. Coins commanded none of the same respect that modern money now enjoys: they were too often clipped, bitten, counterfeited, chucked, and generally abused. A bewildering variety jostled for recognition; like struggling dialects, some managed to retain their value despite changing standards in a multilingual universe. Indeterminacy characterized paper money in an equally pronounced way, though with greater consequences for a more elite world of finance. In the form of bills and notes, new varieties evolved to fill new needs and desires.

---

[1] Robert Latham and William Matthews, eds., *The Diary of Samuel Pepys*. 11 vols. (Berkeley, 1976) 9 (1668–9):297.

Experimentation with investments was unprecedented from the late seventeenth century through the first third of the next century and would not be repeated to such an extent until our own era. Money during the early modern period could best be described as functionally unstable: to paraphrase the monetary theorist, money was what money could do.[2]

Our modern-day vantage point, then, offers limited help in recovering the meanings and functions attributed to money in the past, and the long eighteenth century presents a particularly problematic phase of history in Britain. No single institution claimed an absolute monopoly over money from the late seventeenth century to the beginning of the nineteenth century, and public opinion had not yet developed a consensus on what constituted appropriate applications of its properties. For the twenty-first-century investigator, the study of money requires a critical alertness to the unexpected variety of elements contributing to economic life. With these points established, I wish to disengage this book from the task of providing a systematic account of the history of money. If such a treatment of money is even possible, it is not what I have set out to do in the following pages. Instead, I hope to extend our grasp of the subject by presenting a series of interwoven investigations into what might be called the social life of money, its propensity to become involved in relations between people in ways that move beyond what we understand as its purely economic functions.

My basic premise is that English people of the period from roughly 1640 to 1770 carried with them a wide repertoire of concepts and techniques for understanding and using money, a fact that had important implications for personal lives and society at large. In the course of their daily activities, early modern people regarded the money they encountered as laden with qualities that indicated its character and connections within broad social networks of meaning. Its powers defined by historically variable contingencies, money might signal an awareness of political or moral boundaries that delimited its use, or ignited the

---

[2] Geoffrey Ingham, "On the Underdevelopment of the 'Sociology of Money'," *Acta Sociologica* 41, no. 1 (1998): 1; Thomas J. Sargent and Francois R. Velde, *The Big Problem of Small Change* (Princeton, 2002); Andrea Finkelstein, *Harmony and the Balance: An Intellectual History of Seventeenth-Century English Economic Thought* (Ann Arbor, 2000); Sir John Craig, *The Mint: A History of the London Mint from A.D. 287 to 1948* (Cambridge, 1953); P. G. M. Dickson, *The Financial Revolution: A Study in the Development of Public Credit, 1688–1756* (repr., Aldershot, 1993); Bruce G. Carruthers, *City of Capital: Politics and Markets in the English Financial Revolution* (Princeton, 1996).

hope of disrupting or transcending established hierarchies of value and rank. Money also regulated areas of social life at variance with what we think of today as its rightful province: as "blood money" in encouraging the apprehension of thieves and vagrants, for example, or as a payment that legitimated the sale of wives in a plebeian form of divorce. Such social uses of money, as historians have argued in the study of other societies, tend to enhance the degree to which its measuring and evaluative functions may seep into other areas of life, thus becoming generalized in common practices outside economic activity.[3] As the following chapters will attempt to argue, such monetary measurements and evaluations were ubiquitous throughout early modern English society, though we have yet to assess their significance.

My argument has a second thread, which grows out of the first: in its early modern, protean form, eighteenth-century money evolved through mutually defining relationships with elements of human life. The abstracting power connected to money, particularly as it related to imaginative activity and self-fashioning, seems to have had a marked impact on British culture in its widest sense.[4] Literary critics have led the way in illuminating this subtle reticulation of economy and culture, revealing how, for example, a conceptual distinction between persons and commodities was highly permeable in an age when language and custom elided the two. This was particularly true in the case of women, whose legal persons were surrendered upon marriage, as wealth, goods, and identities were transferred from household to household within a culturally specific system of exchange.[5] In the imaginative world of literature, the free flow of images of persons and things was particularly evident, through narratives, for example, which animated coins

---

[3] See, for example, the collection of essays in Jane I. Geyer, ed., *Money Matters: Instability, Values and Social Payments in the Modern History of West African Communities* (Portsmouth, NH, 1995); cf. Keletso Atkins, *The Moon is Dead! Give Us Our Money!: The Cultural Origins of an African Work Ethic, Natal, South Africa, 1843–1900* (Portsmouth, NH, 1993).

[4] I am thinking of a definition of culture that incorporates multiple forms of consciousness and the possibility of conflict, such as that employed by Jean and John L. Comaroff, described as "the space of signifying practice, the semantic ground on which human beings seek to construct and represent themselves and others." *Of Revelation and Revolution, Vol. 1: Christianity, Colonialism, and Consciousness in South Africa* (Chicago, 1991), 21, as cited in Sally Engle Merry, "Hegemony and Culture in Historical Anthropology: A Review Essay on Jean and John L. Comaroff's *Of Revelation and Revolution,*" *American Historical Review* 108, no. 2 (April 2003): 466–7.

[5] Susan Staves, *Married Women's Separate Property in England, 1660–1833* (Cambridge, MA, 1990); Margot C. Finn, *The Character of Credit: Personal Debt in English Culture, 1740–1914* (Cambridge, 2003), esp. Part I.

or objectified persons.[6] Such works released countervailing impulses into the psychological lives of readers: the possibilities of freedom, as well as subjection, were commonly identified with money and these linkages emerged as important features of literary and popular culture.

The subject of money in England, in particular, presents a problem worth investigating for several reasons. Boasting an early example of a centralized nation state, England appears on the European stage as a hospitable setting for a precocious and sophisticated market society. The early decay of feudalism, the commutation of tenant obligations to monetary payments, the use of money, not produce, for the payment of rents, and flourishing trade in both country and town nourished a complex involvement with money across England.[7] From early medieval times, money made its presence felt in legal dealings and theological considerations.[8] Historians of England have long since recognized that some version of market values, such as the goal of systematic profit-making and the maximization of potential in land and its produce, played a role in the development of the society and culture in general.[9]

The development of commerce since medieval times allowed for an unprecedented expansion in the circulation of people and the exchange of goods, which provided an obvious context for the use of money.

[6] For literary studies of women and money in eighteenth-century England, see Deidre Shauna Lynch, *The Economy of Character: Novels, Market Culture, and the Business of Inner Meaning* (Chicago, 1998); Catherine Gallagher, *Nobody's Story: The Vanishing Acts of Women Writers in the Marketplace, 1670–1820* (Berkeley, 1994); Edward Copeland, *Women Writing About Money: Women's Fiction in England, 1790–1820* (Cambridge, 1995), Harriet Guest, *Small Change: Women, Learning, Patriotism, 1750–1810* (Chicago, 2000).

[7] For a helpful survey of these developments, see Peter Spufford, *Money and its Use in Medieval Europe* (Cambridge, 1988), esp. Chap. 11. Contributors to the identification of money as an important aspect of early modern history include Max Weber, Marc Bloch, and Carlo Cipolla; see also Raymond de Roover, *Business, Banking and Economic Thought in Late Medieval and Early Modern Europe*, ed. Julius Kirshner (Chicago, 1974); H. A. Miskimin, *Cash, Credit and Crisis in Europe, 1300–1600* (London, 1989) and Pierre Vilar, *A History of Gold and Money, 1450–1920*, trans. Judith White (1969; London, 1976).

[8] The literature on medieval markets and the use of money is extensive: see, for example, Maryanne Kowaleski, *Local Markets and Regional Trade in Medieval Exeter* (Cambridge, 1995); R. H. Britnell, *The Commercialisation of English Society, 1000–1500*, 2nd ed. (Manchester, 1996); Joel Kaye, *Economy and Nature in the Fourteenth Century: Money, Market Exchange and the Emergence of Scientific Thought* (Cambridge, 1998).

[9] Paul Sweezy et al., *The Transition from Feudalism to Capitalism* (London, 1976); T. H. Aston and C. H. E. Philpin, eds., *The Brenner Debate: Agrarian Class Structure and Economic Development in Pre-Industrial Europe* (Cambridge, 1985); Alan Macfarlane, *The Origins of English Individualism: The Family, Property and Social Transition* (Oxford, 1978).

Emphasis needs to be added to the simple fact of geographical mobility: England was a nation of people on the move.[10] The magnetism of London as a destination of migrants, both English and foreign, established a demographic trend that was remarkable by the early sixteenth century.[11] The apparent restlessness of the English population generated movement outside this predictable pattern. Studies have revealed that various forms of internal migration before the Civil War reached as high as 82 percent of the population in selected counties; in the post-Restoration period, rates declined in some areas but still remained higher than in most European countries. Movement to North America and the West Indies from the 1630s onwards represented "a very considerable leakage of population," which constituted a new and significant expansion of the English predilection for changing places of residence.[12] Laws of settlement more likely regulated rather than deterred migration after 1660. Furthermore, as a new generation of studies has argued, the history of migration must take into account every category of geographical movement, including that of unfree labor. From the vantage point of the history of indentured servitude, convict transportation, as well as the voluntary emigration of English laborers, David Eltis has argued, "the British were preeminent in the business of free as well as coerced long-distance migration." The salience of this phenomenon in English social life provides one of the distinctive backdrops for this study.[13]

Given the propensity of English people to move from place to place, local governments and Parliament were drawn into the business of

---

[10] This is one of many insights offered by an early collection of studies, Peter Clark and David Souden, eds., *Migration and Society in Early Modern England* (London, 1987), esp. 33; see also K. D. M. Snell, *Annals of the Labouring Poor: Social Change and Agrarian England, 1660–1900* (Cambridge, 1985); Alison Games, *Migration and the Origins of the English Atlantic World* (Cambridge, MA, 1999); Colin G. Pooley and Ian D. Whyte, *Migrants, Emigrants and Immigrants: A Social History of Migration* (London, 1991); Ida Altman and James Horn, eds., *'To Make America': European Emigration in the Early Modern Period* (Berkeley, 1991).

[11] Vanessa Harding, "The Population of London, 1550–1700: A Review of the Published Evidence," *London Journal* 15 (1990), 111–28; R. Finlay, *Population and Metropolis: The Demography of London, 1580–1650* (Cambridge, 1981).

[12] Clark and Souden, "Introduction," *Migration and Society,* 29, 32, 37.

[13] "Seventeenth Century Migration and the Slave Trade: The English Case in Comparative Perspective," in Jan Lucassen and Leo Lucassen, eds., *Migration, Migration History, History* (Bern, 1997), 87. See also Michael P. Hanagan, "Labor History and the New Migration History: A Review Essay," *International Labor and Working-Class History* 54 (Fall 1998): 57–79; for relevant revisionist arguments, see Dirk Hoerder and Jorg Nagler, eds., *People in Transit: German Migrations in Comparative Perspective, 1820–1930* (Cambridge, 1995); Games, *Migration.*

regulating their passage in ways that involved the use of monetary payments and fines attached to human bodies. The poor laws of the sixteenth
century can be seen in this light, along with various local mechanisms
to deter illicit traffic across even longer distances. In such cases, the
state sometimes jostled for authority with merchants and adventurers.
As David Harris Sacks showed in his study of mid-seventeenth-century
Bristol, the transport of labor to the colonies became a complex, competitive enterprise involving questionable practices with money and people,
including "the inveigling purloining carrying and Stealing away boyes
Maides and other persons" to fill out holds and render a profit by trading
in people. As a result, Bristol's local government initiated a somewhat
successful method of registering servants, though this did not eliminate
the market for "spirited" and kidnapped servants entirely.[14] In addition
to indentured or coerced migration of servants, the transport of convicted criminals employed language and conceptual categories marked
by monetary amounts. Following the Transportation Act of 1717, "an
unprecedented commitment of government resources" went into this
project and, in so doing, further elaborated the way in which monetary
thinking and bureaucratic control of subjects became allied.[15] Developments such as this constitute one part of this study, namely, the emergence of administrative practices that employed money in ways that
effectively categorized and "priced" people.

My interest in this project originated in one particular aspect of the
harnessing of money by the state, the administration of laws relating
to vagrancy and the poor in eighteenth-century London. In examining
the Middlesex Sessions Reports for the first half of the century, I was
struck by the number of ways in which money was involved in the

---

[14] *The Widening Gate: Bristol and the Atlantic Economy, 1450–1700* (Berkeley, 1991), 252.

[15] On transportation, see A. Roger Ekirch, *Bound for America: The Transportation of British
Convicts to the Colonies 1718–1775* (Oxford, 1987), 18; Peter Wilson Coldham, *Emigrants
in Chains: A Social History of Forced Emigration to the Americas, 1607–1776* (Stroud,
Gloucestershire, 1992); on indentured service, see Kenneth Morgan, *Slavery and Servitude in North America, 1607–1800* (Edinburgh, 2000); Stanley L. Engerman, "Coerced
and Free Labor: Property Rights and the Development of the Labor Force," *Explo-
rations in Economic History* 29 (1992), 1–29; David Galenson, *White Servitude in Colonial
America: An Economic Analysis* (Cambridge, 1981); on kidnapping, see John Wareing,
"Preventive and Punitive Regulation in Seventeenth-Century Social Policy: Conflicts
of Interest and the Failure to Make 'Stealing and Transporting Children, and Other
Persons, a Felony, 1645–73,'" *Social History* 27, no. 3 (October 2002): 288–308; and
"'Violently Taken Away or Cheatingly Duckoyed'. The Illicit Recruitment in London of
Indentured Servants for the American Colonies, 1645–1718," *London Journal* 26 (2001):
1–22.

regulation of people found on the streets in London. These decades witnessed the reissuing of acts calling for the apprehension of vagrants, and with each proclamation, monetary rewards became part of a standard repertoire of a call to citizens for assistance in maintaining public order and police.[16] The notorious use of rewards in the eighteenth century is well known, though the various social meanings and significance of such incentives have not been sufficiently explored. It is worth pointing out that the laws applying rewards to vagrancy apprehension coincided with the career of thief catchers like Jonathan Wild, alongside a rising concern about crime against property in London. In this age of rudimentary policing of the metropolis, rewards were part of a larger artillery of stopgap measures used by an understaffed constabulary.[17] They also contributed to a conjunction of draconian laws aimed at violators of property and a rising awareness of the problem of poverty.

The methods set out to handle the movements of the wandering poor entailed monetary transactions at every turn. Studded with perquisites, fines, and forfeits, the laws apparently took as their starting premise the effectiveness of money payments as both carrot and stick. Persons who obstructed the execution of the law pertaining to the apprehension of rogues, dating back to Elizabethan times, might be fined £5; if constables between the place of apprehension and the rogue's parish of origin failed to cooperate, they might be fined £5; and if the Churchwardens and Overseers at the parish of origin refused to accept the rogue as their responsibility, they, too, were required to forfeit £5. A statute from the early seventeenth century declared that rogues were to be "Branded in the left Shoulder with a burning Iron, having a great Roman R upon it as broad as a Shilling," giving tangible meaning to the power of money to seal these rituals with the authority of the Crown.[18] Of course, the administration of the poor law, of which settlement law was a part, differed from parish to parish, between regions, and in

---

[16] Nicholas Rogers, "Policing the Poor in Eighteenth-Century London: The Vagrancy Laws and Their Administration," *Histoire Sociale – Social History* 24 (May 1991): 127–47; "Vagrancy, Impressment and the Regulation of Labour in Eighteenth-Century Britain," in *Unfree Labour in the Development of the Atlantic World*, ed. Paul E. Lovejoy and Nicholas Rogers (London, 1994), 102–113.

[17] J. M. Beattie, *Policing and Punishment in London, 1660–1750: Urban Crime and the Limits of Terror* (Oxford, 2001), esp. 401–17.

[18] *The Laws Concerning the Poor* (1705), 161–70. The handbook refers to 39 *Eliz.* along with several laws passed by the Stuarts, including 14 *Car.* 2. c. 12.

town and country. Historians have argued over the extent of migration and the degree to which parishes monitored the traffic of laborers.[19] While administration of the law followed an irregular pattern in this period, the concern generated by the obvious problem of the poor resulted in repeated issuance of recommendations, copies of statutes, and manuals on how to deal with migration and settlements. In the drive toward delineating solutions, the measure of money assumed a facilitating part.[20]

By the eighteenth century, the system of poor law and vagrancy administration had generated a metalanguage of procedures mirroring market practices. Certificates and passes, accompanied by payments, marked each parochial duty, and officers referred to people in transit with monetary nomenclature. "Certificate women" and "certificate men" were passed along a network of constables, and those who transported vagrants eventually redeemed actual certificates for the cost of haulage. The letter of the law advised administrative legibility of the most painstaking kind as numerous petty layouts of cash, strung across several counties, were at stake. Recommendations in *The Complete Parish Officer* (1734) were typical of the many handbooks available for those new to the job:

> When a Petty Constable has convey'd the Vagrant to the Place ordered by the Pass, on his bringing to the High Constable such Certificate as aforesaid, with the Receipt from the Constable or other Officer to whom the Vagrant was delivered, the Chief Constable shall pay such Petty Constable the Allowances ascertained in the Certificate, and no more, taking the said Certificate and his Receipt, which is to be allowed the Chief Constable by the Treasurer of the County.
>
> Justices in Sessions are to appoint Allowances for passing Vagrants at so much a mile, or otherwise; and make Orders for raising Money for that Purpose, to be paid quarterly to the High Constables. And Rates for reconveying, being likewise appointed by Justices of Peace in the Sessions,

---

[19] The literature on the Settlement Acts is extensive and, by now, rather dated. See one such debate in Norma Landau, "The Laws of Settlement and the Surveillance of Immigration in Eighteenth-Century Kent," *Continuity and Change* 3, no. 3 (1988): 391–420; K. D. M. Snell, "Pauper Settlement and the Right to Poor Relief in England and Wales," *Continuity and Change* 6, no. 3 (1991): 375–415; Norma Landau, "The Eighteenth-Century Context of the Laws of Settlement," *Continuity and Change* 6, no. 3 (1991): 417–39.

[20] Stephen Macfarlane, "Social Policy and the Poor in the Later Seventeenth Century," in *London, 1500–1700: The Making of the Metropolis*, ed. A. L. Beier and Roger Finlay (London, 1986), 252–77; James Stephen Taylor, *Poverty, Migration and Settlement in the Industrial Revolution: Sojourners' Narratives* (Palo Alto, CA, 1989).

the Constable must make Oath before a Justice of what Expences he is at in reconveying Vagrants to *Ireland*, or any Place abroad; whereupon the Justice is to direct the Payment by an Order under hand and Seal.[21]

At times, apprehension was carried out by ordinary citizens, and Giles suggested that Justices might "pay 2s. to the Person apprehending, ... [as] a Recompence for Trouble and Loss of Time is to be satisfied."[22] The law thus conceived shed an aura of commodification on displaced laborers, who were, as it happened, penniless people captured in a system of monetary measurement.

Given the legacy of vagrancy statutes dating back to Tudor times, these uses of money reinscribed the poor within a distinct transactional order related to a long-standing administration of relief. One might argue that rather than objectifying people by treating their bodies as commodities, this self-contained system worked towards preserving social cohesion and should not be confused with other, more commercially oriented spheres of monetary exchange.[23] Such practices may have stigmatized the poor, but, as Thomas Sokoll has argued, eighteenth-century letters to parish officers show paupers as fully engaged participants, asserting their rights to the full extent of their entitlements through persistent negotiations.[24] In the case of payments for apprehension and conveyance of the wandering poor, we might consider local parishes as substitutions for patriarchal households, which were empowered to exercise jurisdiction over the lives of their members. Parallels exist between such transactions and transfers occurring in colonial societies in Africa, where "rights-in-people" passed from one household to another when wives, wards, and offspring were exchanged for specified payments.[25] As money passed between parties, family heads exchanged rights *over* the individuals in question rather than rights *to* their existence. Money accompanied these passages, offering material benefits to participants; but more importantly, such payments served

---

[21] Giles Jacob, *The Complete Parish Officer* (London, 1734), 73–4.   [22] Ibid., 72.

[23] Maurice Bloch and Jonathan Parry, "Introduction: Money and the Morality of Exchange," in *Money and the Morality of Exchange*, ed. Maurice Bloch and Jonathan Parry (Cambridge, 1989), 23–30.

[24] Thomas Sokoll, "Old Age in Poverty: The Record of Essex Pauper Letters, 1780–1834," in *Chronicling Poverty: The Voices and Strategies of the English Poor, 1640–1840*, ed. Tim Hitchcock, Peter King, and Pamela Sharpe (Basingstoke, 1997), 127–54; Thomas Sokoll, ed., *Essex Pauper Letters, 1731–1837* (Oxford, 2001).

[25] Igor Kopytoff, "The Cultural Biography of Things: Commoditization as a Process," in *The Social Life of Things: Commodities in Cultural Perspective*, ed. Arjun Appadurai (Cambridge, 1986), 71.

to mark the identities of transferred people as dependent members of a network of families, not as people dehumanized through commodification.[26]

As our example of priced vagrants can show, attributes of "modern" and "traditional" may operate side by side as they compete for dominance in the course of historical developments. This lack of synchrony needs to be recognized, as Natalie Zemon Davis's work on gift exchange shows, as a way of cautioning us against seeing modern, contractual relations (often associated with money) as automatically canceling out more customary social relations of gifting. Just as "gift exchange persists as an essential relational mode, a repertoire of behavior, a register with its own rules, language, etiquette, and gestures" in modern settings, so too can relationships established around the use of money create their own customary rituals, which, to us, seem out of keeping with a more standard contractual model of eighteenth-century social relations.[27] Such a revisioning of social relations is in keeping with recent work in anthropology, which has attempted to break out of the dichotomous thinking engendered by polarizing the features of western and "'traditional' non-Western" societies, imputing rationality of means and ends to western societies while attributing "embedded" characteristics to traditional settings.[28]

Money in these cases acted as a red flag calling attention to the dependent and subordinated status of certain classes of people, whose objectified state resulted in physical constraint and sometimes abuse, or, put another way, marked vulnerability to the wills of others. Imbricated within the structures of eighteenth-century political power, money could reinforce hierarchical social obligations; yet it might also introduce

---

[26] Chapter 6 proposes a different view of this process.

[27] Natalie Zemon Davis, *The Gift in Sixteenth-Century France* (Madison, 2000), 33 and passim. See also the classic work of Marcel Mauss, *The Gift: The Form and Reason for Exchange in Archaic Societies*, trans. W. D. Halls (New York, 1990). Mauss introduced an important notion that modifies a strictly economic approach to exchange: in archaic settings, things could possess "personality," "force," or "spirit." Unlike the commodity under capitalism, the gift could acquire humanlike attributes. The literature on gift relations is considerable: for a synthetic approach, see James Carrier, *Gifts and Commodities: Exchange and Western Capitalism Since 1700* (London, 1995); Bruce Kapferer, ed., *Transaction and Meaning: Directions in the Anthropology of Exchange and Symbolic Behavior* (Philadelphia, 1976).

[28] Agnar Helgason and Gisli Pálsson, "Contested Commodities: The Moral Landscape of Modernist Regimes," *Journal of the Royal Anthropological Institute* 3, no. 3 (September 1997): 451; James G. Carrier, ed., *Meanings of the Market: The Free Market in Western Culture* (Oxford, 1997), esp. his "Introduction," 1–67.

competing suggestions of opportunity invested in circulation, evident in the common notion of "selling" oneself into service of limited duration in the colonies. The tension was not lost on contemporaries, who witnessed daily contradictions of market mentalities and the persistence of traditional obligations: poor mothers leased their babies as emblems of worthiness to beggars on the streets of London, for example, and pregnant servants turned to the courts to swear their babies to the responsible men, from whom they might receive paternity payments. The era was marked not only by restrictive forms of governance but also by the demonstrated desire for goods, money, and freedom that recent historians have recognized as universal and increasing in intensity during this period.

It is within this spirit of reinterpretation that the following chapters address the mid-seventeenth to the late eighteenth century, which remains well trodden as the site of the origins of market society.[29] The arguments presented many years ago by Karl Polanyi remain no less compelling today for historians interested in money. Polanyi directed attention to the question of whether modern economic life significantly altered the fundamental terms of social relations as they had existed in preindustrial contexts. His provocative thesis argued that economic activity originally assumed a subordinate role within a larger system of social life, but later, through the process of industrialization, a new species of activity (specifically belonging to "market economy") vanquished dominant forms of sociality. Though Polanyi did not pursue the subject in detail, money played a key role in the triumph of the artifice of market relations, as the following passage from *The Great Transformation* implies:

> The transformation implies a change in the motive of action on the part of the members of society: for the motive of subsistence that of gain must be substituted. All transactions are turned into money transactions, and these in turn require that a medium of exchange be introduced into every articulation of industrial life.[30]

---

[29] Thomas L. Haskell and Richard F. Teichgraeber III, eds., *The Culture of the Market: Historical Essays* (Cambridge, 1993); Albert O. Hirschman, *Rival Views of Market Society and Other Recent Essays* (Cambridge, MA, 1992); John Brewer and Roy Porter, eds., *Consumption and the World of Goods* (London, 1993); Roger Friedland and A. F. Robertson, eds., *Beyond the Marketplace: Rethinking Economy and Society* (New York, 1990); William M. Reddy, *The Rise of Market Culture: The Textile Trade and French Society, 1750–1900* (Cambridge, 1984).

[30] *The Great Transformation* (1944; Boston, 1957), 41.

Market activity created what anthropologists and historians have identified as monetization, a process that involves more than simply the adoption of specie as tokens of exchange. This larger definition views money as permeating social thought, introducing a new "way of organizing and of thinking about many crucial matters." In particular, money imbues all things with its trademark characteristic of fungibility, suggesting interchangeability with anything else.[31] Polanyi also identified a propensity to create "commodity fiction[s]" out of land, labor, and money, which "are obviously *not* commodities" and therefore not intended for sale.

In what has become known as a substantivist interpretation of history, Polanyi situated these changes within a much larger context of transformation, too extensive to be recounted here, involving new methods of exchange and distribution. Once embedded in society, economic activity became reorganized by market mechanisms, and "human society [became] an accessory of the economic system."[32] Imprinted by philosophical traditions of the first half of the twentieth century, which strove for a holistic approach to human society, Polanyi's argument inspires a return to the study of economic life within a larger frame of early modern English culture. Though based on evidence from the years between Speenhamland in the 1790s and the New Poor Law of 1834, his general theory concerning the power of monetary transactions may yield valuable insights into the long century preceding industrialization as the birthplace of important shifts in conceptualizing commerce and labor.

Another canonical theorist of market society, C. B. Macpherson, identified a similar predisposition for a "transformation" of English culture in the early modern period. Macpherson argued that the basic assumptions informing seventeenth-century political theory were artifacts of a contemporary predilection for exchange. The very attributes of a man's power in society as described by Thomas Hobbes consisted of behavior already adapted to the social arrangements and political institutions of a market economy. The famous passage of *Leviathan*, which attempted to describe how people related to one another, illustrated the mentality in vivid terms:

> The *Value*, or WORTH of a man, is as of all other things, his Price; that is to say, so much as would be given for the use of his Power: and therefore is not absolute; but a thing dependant on the need and judgement of another.... And as in other things, so in men, not the seller, but the buyer determines

---

[31] David M. Schaps, *The Invention of Coinage and the Monetization of Ancient Greece* (Ann Arbor, 2004), vi, 31. See also his helpful discussion of Polanyi, 22–5 and 31–3.

[32] *Great Transformation*, 72, 73, 75.

the Price. For let a man (as most men do,) rate themselves at the highest Value they can; yet their true Value is no more than it is esteemed by others.[33]

Macpherson underestimated the degree to which older, more feudal values, such as honor, also informed Hobbes's perspective, existing "side by side" with his recognition of the influences of capitalism on his immediate environment.[34] Yet Hobbes's keen eye for particular signs of the permeation of market thinking are nevertheless helpful. Prices, human worth, and honor together shaped social interactions of the early modern period as individuals behaved rationally in their dealings, acting according to objectives aimed at maximizing their own power and advantages.[35]

It should come as no surprise that early modern people often measured their world and even themselves in monetary terms. The commitment of enormous resources to commercial and colonial ventures, the creation of capital markets, and the birth of consumer society tapped into a marked propensity to use and think about money and financial instruments for personal gain. These were the very years of the Financial Revolution in England, as well as the rise of the "fiscal-military state," a series of developments involving the transfer of government debt to long-term obligations spread across newly founded private companies and a national bank.[36] The effects of these developments were felt across every level of society, as well as within the English government, where revenue departments grew in size and importance, particularly in relation to the collection of taxes. English people came to think of themselves as rate payers and investors, as well as regular spenders.[37]

A concurrent wellspring of consumer commodities indicated a growing participation in exchange relations advanced by the use of money

---

[33] Thomas Hobbes, *Leviathan* (Oxford, 1929), 67, as quoted in C. B. Macpherson, *The Political Theory of Possessive Individualism: Hobbes to Locke* (Oxford, 1962), 37. For another contribution to this discussion, see Samuel Bowles, "Endogenous Preferences: The Cultural Consequences of Markets and Other Economic Institutions," *Journal of Economic Literature* 36 (March 1998): 75–111.

[34] Keith Thomas, "The Social Origins of Hobbes's Political Thought," in *Hobbes Studies*, ed. K. C. Brown (Cambridge, MA, 1965), 191.

[35] *Political Theory of Possessive Individualism*, 54–5.

[36] John Brewer, *The Sinews of Power: War, Money and the English State, 1688–1783* (London, 1989), xvii; Carruthers, *City of Capital*; H. Roseveare, *The Financial Revolution, 1660–1760* (London, 1991); L. Neal, *The Rise of Financial Capitalism: International Capital Markets in the Age of Reason* (Cambridge, 1990); Dickson, *Financial Revolution*.

[37] P. K. O'Brien, "The Political Economy of British Taxation, 1660–1815," *Economic History Review*, 2nd ser., 41, no. 1 (1988):1–32; Michael J. Braddick, *The Nerves of State: Taxation and the Financing of the English State, 1558–1714* (Manchester, 1996).

and credit in the seventeenth century. According to Carole Shammas, data demonstrate a significant uptick in spending, and Joyce Appleby has suggested that a "barrier" was crossed "[s]omewhere around 1650," when "the English moved beyond the threat of famine."[38] As part of an "industrious revolution," Jan de Vries noted that "[c]onsumer demand grew, even in the face of contrary real wage trends, because of real-locations of the productive resources of households." Important sectors of English and European society oriented their labor toward the goal of increasing their purchasing power, a "demand-side" revolution well in advance of the technological changes of the later eighteenth century.[39] Popular commodities like tobacco, sugar products, coffee, tea, and chocolate joined a list of household and personal durables that were declining in price and broadening in availability over the course of roughly a century after 1650.[40] Through the use of both money and credit, early modern people participated in a sweeping upsurge in spending in what historians now call "the consumer revolution."

By focusing on these developments, however, we inadvertently give money a natural gloss, handing it a triumph that emerges organically from English soil. Many problems exist with such an approach, including the question of how money became firmly attached to self-serving behavior in economic and social life in the first place. The following chapters contend that money was stubbornly attached to many other sentiments and processes, even as it supported a competitive, individualist strain of economic behavior. The multiplicity of paths available to money stands as the most powerful aspect of its very active social life in the English past.

THE LOCATION OF THE HISTORY OF MONEY IN SOCIAL LIFE

I have started from the premise that money cannot be understood apart from its social context in history.[41] While anthropologists and

---

[38] Carole Shammas, *The Pre-Industrial Consumer in England and America* (Oxford: Clarendon Press, 1990), 291; Joyce Appleby, "Consumption in Early Modern Thought," in *Consumption and the World of Goods*, ed. John Brewer and Roy Porter (London, 1993), 162. See also Joan Thirsk, *Economic Policy and Projects: The Development of a Consumer Culture in Early Modern England* (Oxford, 1978).

[39] Jan de Vries, "Between Purchasing Power and the World of Goods: Understanding the Household Economy in Early Modern Europe," *Consumption*, 107.

[40] Carole Shammas, "Changes in English and Anglo-American Consumption from 1550 to 1800," *Consumption*, 193, 199.

[41] Bloch and Parry, "Introduction," *Money and Morality of Exchange*, 1.

sociologists have attempted to come to terms with this simple fact, historians have understated its significance. Faced with a plethora of monetary activities, most studies understandably have focused on a single aspect, such as coinage or taxation, but they have often placed their subjects within a modernizing narrative. By emphasizing the centralizing power of institutions, histories have pared away evidence of unorthodox or extraneous uses of money. Drawing their assumptions from empirically oriented disciplines, especially the field of economics, scholars have unwittingly imported methodological and theoretical biases that point toward rationalization.[42] The protean aspect of money – its symbolic capacity, for instance – has been quarantined as a subject non grata, even by those who recognize its fascinating potential. Summed up eighty years ago by Luigi Einaudi as the conflict between *"moneta imaginara"* and *"moneta real"* – money as a conceptual system of abstractions and money as a store of "real" metal wealth – the topic has been saddled with an unfortunate strain of dualism.[43] Thus, in the late twentieth century, the investigation of the imaginary or abstract qualities of money has been left almost entirely to literary and cultural studies.[44]

An early exception to this disciplinary dilemma was William Reddy's provocative synthesis, *Money and Liberty in Modern Europe: A Critique of Historical Understanding* (1987). Reddy's main objective was not money itself but the disruption of a narrative of European social history based on class identities and class conflict. The constant involvement of money in determining social relations, he pointed out, undermined the basic assumptions beneath a pet narrative of European historians, the progress-oriented struggle to realize individual freedom and equality. He argued that money and exchange relations provided the true generators of "this-worldly interaction" through the struggle for subsistence that took precedence over collective considerations. Rather than offering an arena in which all participants dealt with one another on an equal footing, as models of market society would suggest, such relations reinforced existing social distinctions. "[A] very local, very

---

[42] Ingham, "On the Underdevelopment of the 'Sociology of Money'," 4–6; Keith Hart, "Heads or Tails? Two Sides of the Coin," *Man* 21 (December 1986): 643–7.

[43] Ingham, "On the Underdevelopment of the 'Sociology of Money'," 5–6; Luigi Einaudi, "The Theory of Imaginary Money from Charlemagne to the French Revolution," trans. and repr. in *Enterprise and Secular Change*, ed. Frederic C. Lane and Jelle C. Riemersma (Homewood, IL, 1953), 229–61.

[44] Lynch, *Economy of Character*; Sandra Sherman, *Finance and Fictionality: Accounting for Defoe* (Cambridge, 1996); James Thompson, *Models of Value: Eighteenth-Century Political Economy and the Novel* (Durham, 1996).

concentrated form of power" evolved from monetary "exchange asymmetries," in which "the poor's need to get money and to spend it quickly again" ensured that their social disadvantages would persist. These exchange asymmetries acted as crucial determinants in political formations because they affected the day-to-day calculations informing larger allegiances. Reddy thus showed how "certain kinds of exchange relationships resemble coercion in that they create a potential for social discipline." That is, monetary considerations may have created their own distinctive regimes of power.[45]

Reddy's second aim, to demystify the idea of money as an instrument of freedom, realized an important aim of social historians, the need to ground enlightenment debates about the nature of capitalism in contemporary social conditions. His account of the "growth of the liberal illusion" – the sense that money stood in as a fair and precise "medium of exchange between legal equals"[46] – is especially useful in reorienting discussion of money away from a whiggish teleology. Economic theory since its birth in the eighteenth century has infused the history of economic thought with universalizing tendencies. Early modern assumptions about exchange lay the cornerstones of modern economics: that all exchanges were somehow "similar both in their social causes and in their social effects" and that all motives stemmed from the same fundamental impulses, which usually had to do with vanity and self-interest. Money even became bound up in a belief in a measurable, universal motivation for human action.[47] Its central place in the emerging capitalist economy seemed to ensure that the outcome of exchanges, by virtue of the transparency of money, would promise justice and opportunity. As Reddy argued from the theories of Locke, Montesquieu, and Adam Smith, the social historian can detect "a pivotal confusion of the period ... in the notion that unregulated monetary exchange was perfectly compatible with – indeed, was an essential precondition for – personal freedom. This," he added, "is a most profoundly erroneous idea."[48]

Reddy's work underscored the gap between the theoretical description of exchange relations and their social embodiment, opening up the

[45] *Money and Liberty in Modern Europe: A Critique of Historical Understanding* (Cambridge, 1987), 60, 116.
[46] *Money and Liberty*, 73 and Chap. 3, passim.
[47] *Money and Liberty*, 63; see also 73–81; Albert O. Hirschman, *The Passions and the Interests: Political Arguments for Capitalism before Its Triumph* (Princeton, 1997).
[48] *Money and Liberty*, 81.

need for a history of the social relations surrounding money. For the early modern period, historians have focused on the displacement of customary social ties by the intrusion of capitalist practices; yet these endeavors, as Reddy pointed out, presumed that money was an accessory to other objectives and was not determinative of the narrative of history itself. Not until Craig Muldrew offered a systematic analysis of credit and community relations did British historians begin to pay attention to the "dyadic" and even more extensive networks of relationships at the point of exchange.[49] Muldrew's study uncovered the pervasive use of credit, not ready money, in the day-to-day financial relations of early modern England, which arose at least in part from a fundamental shortage of coin. Without focusing on money itself, Muldrew directed attention to "the complex motivations and practices of agents acting out relationships of economic exchange," which did not follow a model of self-interest. Like Reddy, he demonstrated how theories of market individualism did not adequately represent commercial activity of the past. Alongside motivations of self-interest, Muldrew identified an early modern sensibility informed by "reciprocal obligations of neighbourliness" and mutual confidence.[50]

Muldrew depicted credit in the early modern period as the embodiment of embedded social relations, as a rich panoply of contractual obligations evoked a moral equality that cut across class lines and cushioned the inequities of status. The social import of contractual obligation was so great that all social life was practically indistinguishable from the enforced relationality of trust generated by credit.[51] Muldrew ended his study by pointing to the modernizing influence of "utilitarian economics and a social theory of individualism," which enforced a broad acceptance of individual responsibility lifted out of social contexts. His conclusion revealed an underlying premise common to many interpretations of the eighteenth century: the rationalizing influence of legal and

---

[49] The emphasis on "dyadic" comes from Reddy. For an early explication of the arguments of Craig Muldrew, see his "Interpreting the Market: The Ethics of Credit and Community Relations in Early Modern England," *Social History* 18, no. 2 (1993): 163–8; *The Economy of Obligation: The Culture of Credit and Social Relations in Early Modern England* (London, 1998).

[50] Muldrew, "Interpreting the Market," 163, 178. For a critique of too heavy a reliance on the positive features of credit relations, see Julian Hoppit, "The Use and Abuse of Credit in Eighteenth-Century England," in *Business Life and Public Policy: Essays in Honor of D. C. Coleman*, ed. Neil McKendrick and R. B. Outhwaite (Cambridge, 1986), 64–78.

[51] *Economy of Obligation*, 321–5.

financial institutions, which allegedly swept away the archaic features of early modern social relations.

Yet the persistence of relations of a more hierarchical, adversarial nature was the subject of Margot C. Finn's *The Character of Credit: Personal Debt in English Culture, 1740–1914*. Setting out the literal "limited operation of the cash nexus" over an extended period of cultural history, Finn started from the premise that credit relations were characterized by aspects of gifting and obligation between people of unequal status. Distinctions of status and gender left their imprint on such ties, undermining the "primacy of contractual and monetary transactions," which historians have associated with the development of modern consumer society.[52] Finn was less sanguine than Muldrew in her evaluation of the impact of indebtedness on English culture. Citing Bourdieu, she saw credit as crucial in the "exercise of gentle violence" as it continued to reinforce social distinctions from the eighteenth through the nineteenth centuries, even surviving the efforts of courts to enforce standardized contractual obligations.[53] Though Finn restricted her focus to the history of credit relations within the chronological framework of older modernizing treatments, her analysis of the complex social relations radiating from exchange practices provides a model for the further investigation of early modern money.

Did exchange relations using credit, then, succeed in strengthening a mentality of social cohesion in early modern Britain? The development of monetary relations can claim an important lineage in the venerable historiography of popular *mentalités*. Enriched by intersecting strands of Braudelian and English Marxist historiography, the study of popular attitudes and beliefs has produced a useful complement to treatments of money based on the evolution of the role of the state, such as John Brewer's *The Sinews of Power: War, Money and the English State, 1688–1783*.[54] It is no coincidence that one of the best examples of this approach, Malcolm Gaskill's *Crime and Mentalities in Early Modern England*, focused on contesting practices of coining during the very period of Muldrew's study, when money was in short supply. Gaskill's originating premise, rather more skeptical than that of Muldrew, was that the historian must expect and look for "alterity" when investigating aspects of the past that seem familiar. In searching for "a history of social meanings" lying beneath evidence too quickly assimilated into contemporary

---

[52] (Cambridge, 2003), 76, 81.   [53] Ibid., 9–10.   [54] (Cambridge, MA, 1988).

perspectives, Gaskill deliberately exposed a chaotic maelstrom of historical material. Seventeenth-century coining offered the perfect example of a nexus of contradictory beliefs and practices: coiners broke the law with impunity when they counterfeited coin because statutes against the practice, which decreed coining as treasonous, were founded on "flawed" logic in the eyes of common people. No overarching Christian or moral justification for seeing coins of the state as inviolable existed, leaving the law exposed as the naked construct of the state. Gaskill set out the plethora of contemporary denunciations of the practice alongside an equally profuse array of common violations, which were performed by artisan amateurs as well as high-class professionals dedicated to the task. The paradoxical nature of his findings convinced him that the study of *mentalités* can lead to no clear evolution at all but rather an interwoven advance of prescriptive and experiential strands of history. In the early modern period, as a result, neither institutions nor individuals predominated in determining the use of money.[55]

MONEY IN THE AGE OF THE FINANCIAL REVOLUTION

The indeterminacy of money at the turn of the eighteenth century raises questions about the framework of institutions, bodies of law, and social practices surrounding the everyday use of coin and currency. Given this reorientation, one of the major stumbling blocks in studying money becomes its tightly bound connection to functionalist market behavior. Modern-day monetary theorists rely on standard definitions of money determined by its uses in economic life: as a means of payment (or a medium of exchange), a store of value, and a unit of account.[56] Contingencies of historical context compromise the universalizing tendency suggested by each of these functions; mediating institutions (such as government sanctions, banks, and mints) mark out the domain of money and considerable community consensus must lend institutions their authority. As several recent studies of the financial revolution have

---

[55] Gaskill, *Crime and Mentalities in Early Modern England* (Cambridge, 2000), 4, 9, 127–8, 132; J. A. Sharpe, *Crime in Early Modern England, 1550–1750*, 2nd ed. (New York, 1999).

[56] I have drawn my conceptualization of these definitions from Thomas Crump, *The Phenomenon of Money* (London, 1981), 10–11, and Peter Newman, Murray Milgate and John Eatwell, eds., *The New Palgrave Dictionary of Money and Finance*, 3 vols. (London, 1992), 2: 770–2.

shown, the now familiar polestars of monetary life were as yet imperfectly constructed in the seventeenth century. State finance, commercial ventures, and private investment strategies were heavily contested matters, resolved, sometimes only fleetingly, in a flurry of debate over money that was taking place across the boundaries of established institutions from the time of the Glorious Revolution.[57]

Seventeenth-century people recognized that money sustained an abundance of representations and practices, and within the nascent discipline of political economy the "idea" of money was a matter of considerable discussion. At least three writers during the second half of the century cited *Ecclesiastes* in reminding readers that "Money answers all things," and the proverb was echoed again in 1734 with Jacob Vanderlint's audacious tract by that title.[58] As one of these authors, John Locke devoted much attention to the problem of money not only in *Two Treatises of Government* and his *Essay Concerning Human Understanding* but in several works focusing directly on the topic.[59] Defending the notion of intrinsic value of coin against the tide of trade, he fully recognized the need for the state to assert absolute sovereignty over the use of money. He maintained this position in the face of fierce opposition, which argued that a strict approach to value would deprive a broad public of necessary coin that remained scarce in spite of the broad license enjoyed in current usages.[60]

Josiah Child, Nicholas Barbon, and Dudley North contributed to practical discussions about trade, interest, and coinage during the 1690s, but it was not until George Berkeley's later discussion of money in *The Querist* that the more philosophical aspects of money usage were once again addressed. Berkeley's insights can be explained, according to Constantine George Caffentzis, by referring to the social context in

---

[57] For state administrative aspects of this discussion, see Brewer, *Sinews of Power*, Chap. 4; on other forms of financial activity, Carruthers, *City of Capital*; Roseveare, *Financial Revolution*; Antoin Murphy, *John Law: Economic Theorist and Policy Maker* (Oxford, 1997).

[58] The authors were William Potter (in *The Tradesman's Jewel* [1650], 5), John Locke (*Further Considerations* [1695], 313), and John Briscoe (*Discourse of Money* [1698], 70). Vickers, *Theory of Money*, 30n.

[59] "Some Considerations of the Consequences of the Lowering of Interest, and Raising the Value of Money" (1691) and *Further Considerations Concerning Raising the Value of Money* (1695). See Patrick Hyde Kelly, ed., *Locke on Money*, 2 vols. (Oxford, 1991).

[60] Constantine George Caffentzis, *Clipped Coins, Abused Words and Civil Government: John Locke's Philosophy of Money* (New York, 1989), 75. See also Carl Wennerlind, "Credit-Money as the Philosopher's Stone: Alchemy and the Coinage Problem in Seventeenth-Century England," *History of Political Economy* 35 (2003, suppl.): 235–62.

which he lived, an era famous for opportunities in risk-taking investments, gambling, and lottery tickets. Money, according to Berkeley, acted
as a principal stimulant of the imagination and an aid to mental powers
of abstraction. "This making and unmaking of ideas," the work of the
imagination, could be tracked through daily experience, not just through
aesthetic appreciation of music and art but even at the gambling table
and in 'Change Alley. Financial catastrophes like the South Sea Bubble
only reinforced Berkeley's apprehension that overstimulated imagina-
tions enabled enthusiasm to run out of control and wreak destruction in
the real world of public wealth. That Locke and Berkeley were absorbed
in analyzing the relationship between money and the signifying powers of the mind alerts us to the fact that the meaning of money passed
through a period of epistemological *and* social flux at this time.[61]

Institutional history, with its attention to fixed practices and regulation, cannot account for the entire social life of money and its connection to psychological habits of early modern people. Unrecognized in
the typical account of money is the shadowy persistence of an abstract
quality projected onto money, which is rendered particularly powerful
by factors such as a user's distance from centers of power, or the legitimacy conferred upon a particular practice by the weight of custom. This,
according to Georg Simmel, constituted the "dual nature of money, as
a concrete and valued substance and, at the same time, as something
that owes its significance to the complete dissolution of substance into
motion and function."[62] Money can move between concrete form and
abstract idea at any time, entering into intellectual tasks, such as measuring and comparing things along a numerical scale, or relating different
objects involved in transactions to a common scale of value. In the final
analysis, as sociologist Geoffrey Ingham has argued, money becomes
simply "a *conceptual scheme* for the measurement of value, which lies
behind any particular *form* that it might take as a means of payment."[63]

Our resistance to dwelling on the shadowy side of money stems from
a century of disciplinary constraints dating back to the *Methodenstreiten*,

---

[61] *Exciting the Industry of Mankind: George Berkeley's Philosophy of Money* (Dordrecht, 2000),
306; Douglas Vickers, *Studies in the Theory of Money, 1690–1776* (Philadelphia, 1959),
141–52. On the parallels between the dangers of the mental world of finance and other
uses of the imagination, see Thomas W. Laqueur, *Solitary Sex: A Cultural History of
Masturbation* (New York, 2003), 292–6.

[62] Georg Simmel, *The Philosophy of Money*, trans. Tom Bottomore and David Frisby (Boston,
1978), 176.

[63] Ingham, "On the Underdevelopment of the 'Sociology of Money'," esp. 10.

the methodological disputes that occupied influential German monetary theorists from the end of the nineteenth century. The outcome was decisive for the field of economics: by the beginning of the twentieth century, a natural science model had triumphed over more interpretative or cultural methods, enabling the field of economics to claim a basis in general laws and positivist theories, including "axioms of individual rational choice and the associated equilibrium model of the perfectly competitive market." As Ingham points out, "[S]ocial relations . . . form no part of the model; in this pure theory of exchange, human agents are literally only the 'carriers' of commodities." Thus, "this metatheory . . . renders money epiphenomenal," obscuring its importance beneath a "veil" of neutrality. Further discussion about money henceforth focused on economic actors pursuing self-interest in market exchange, leaving the phenomenon of constantly evolving understandings of money at the sidelines.[64]

In contrast, Ingham proposed "modern bank and state credit-money" as *the* significant breakthrough in the conceptualization of money. Ingham's perspective no doubt benefits from a late twentieth-century vantage point on credit money, which has demonstrated the powers of abstract thinking with money in the contemporary world beyond any doubt. The germ of his theory, however, springs from a specific historical context: institutional changes in finance, which he dates from "around the mid-sixteenth to the mid-eighteenth centuries." The use of bills as autonomous media of exchange and means of payment at this time was "a critically important 'mutation'" in the history of banking networks.[65] New forms of promissory notes, for example, signaled the ability of parties to carry out exchanges at greater geographical distances and transfer debt to unknown third parties. This set the stage for greater liquidity of all forms of debtor/creditor relationships.[66] Thus, from the late seventeenth through the eighteenth centuries, "money form in western Europe underwent a significant evolutionary transformation: it became progressively 'dematerialized'."[67] Harking back to the dualistic notion

---

[64] Ibid., 4.   [65] Ibid., 10.

[66] Carruthers, *City of Capital*, 130, 128, 135. Dyadic, or two-party, promises became legitimated by law as transferable bills through the Promissory Notes Act of 1704 (3 & 4 Anne, c.9).

[67] "On the Underdevelopment of the 'Sociology of Money'," 10. Ingham cites Simmel as the source of the "dematerialized" condition of money, but he also acknowledges the German "historical school" of economic theory, which posited an evolutionary account of monetary use, "from barter, to commodity-money, to credit-money" (16n.)

of money as "imaginary" or "real," Ingham posits that "[i]f money is essentially an abstract measuring system, then all 'money' (as opposed to simple media of exchange) is 'virtual,' including not just 'modern' or even 'postmodern' money."[68]

Ingham's theory about money helps us to de-center our sense of what gave money its legitimacy in the past. In contrast to early twentieth-century theories that laid emphasis on the power of the state in centralizing authority concerning money usage, Ingham's model relies on extensive and diverse relationships chaotically emerging from the circulation of money. Like Finn and Muldrew, Ingham sees a web of ties evolving from such activity, but his are less formal and more fleeting (in other words, more modern) than those of a strict contract-model society. The development of greater liquidity and more transferable abstractions representing wealth suggests a more permissive *mentalité* having to do with money itself that may also date from the late seventeenth century. It seems clear that British society was capable of stretching the abstract representations of money to greater lengths. This willingness to "play with money" was evident in the early eighteenth-century predilection to purchase lottery tickets, to gamble, and to invest in insurance against parties unknown to the buyer simply as an investment that might generate income. As Geoffrey Clark discovered in his research on insurance, "proliferating forms of risk being manufactured by finance capital in late Stuart London . . . offered consumers of these financial instruments unprecedented freedom to dabble in contingencies and to refashion their personal and social affairs accordingly."[69]

Eighteenth-century investment and finance have been seen as an early evocation of "rational man" demonstrating unfettered self-interest when seduced by risky ventures. But a more money-centered approach yields different impressions. Clark's example of gambling with insurance suggests that forms of money (including credit) violated the boundaries between objects and people, which were dimly demarcated in the early eighteenth century. The point is often lost in the eagerness to focus on prescient capitalist behavior, when in this case, commercial capitalism was giving permission to activities that were closely wedded to existing social hierarchies. Insurance provided the basis for claiming

---

[68] Ibid., 8–9.

[69] Geoffrey Clark, "Life Insurance in the Society and Culture of London, 1700–75," *Urban History* 24, pt. 1 (1997): 18; *Betting on Lives: The Culture of Life Insurance in England, 1695–1775* (Manchester, 1999).

"rights" – in this case, monetary ones – over the lives of others. The objectification of people through betting on lives was possible because money was assuming the function of "the primary mediating term between individual and society," in this case, within a burgeoning capitalist culture.[70] The signification of money was indeterminate: it could move from being an abstraction that measured any kind of value to an actual measure of currency value at any time. Its distinctive identity lay in its lability and, more specifically, its use as a "means for the calculation and transportation of value through time and space."[71]

In an attempt to theorize what happens to "things" (whether commodities or people) when pulled into the market, anthropologists have sought to expand the types of exchange that can be considered as imbuing goods (and by implication, people who might be treated as commodities) with "commodity" status. Arguing from Marx's broader theoretical definition of the commodity, Arjun Appadurai aimed to elucidate exactly what made commodities special. He concluded that the set of practices associated with exchange – pricing, the use of money, the movement of objects from one place to another – introduce their own dynamics worthy of theoretical attention. Circulation, in particular, may generate what Appadurai called the "spirit" of the commodity, which may become invested in activities and "any thing" that might fall in the way of situations involving exchange. Thus, it is the *context* that determines the tendency to create the circumstances of "commoditization."[72]

Keith Hart theorized an evolutionary model of this process, which enables us to imagine people becoming "like" commodities, depending on their place in a particular set of changes over time and space. The commodity may move through many phases of exchange, establishing other identities along the way. At some point, the commodity may be "crystallized as pure exchange value, i.e., money." Ultimately, it may become an "abstract cipher," as in the case of human

---

[70] William Outhwaite and Tom Bottomore, eds., *Blackwell Dictionary of Twentieth-Century Social Thought* (Oxford, 1993), 397. Simmel was convinced, e.g., that "money is entirely a sociological phenomenon, a form of human interaction." *Philosophy of Money*, 172.

[71] Ingham, "On the Underdevelopment of the 'Sociology of Money'," 14–15.

[72] Arjun Appadurai, "Introduction," in *Social Life of Things*, esp. 6–13. Distinguished from Marx's more commonly understood "commodification," commoditization demands a consideration of the institutions and mechanisms that make circulation and exchange possible. Commoditization thus entails progressive abstraction away from the originating activity of labor. Whereas Marx's concept depended on producers and the objects they bring to market, commoditization depends upon historical forces in a grand sense, those that draw the commodity into a seemingly irresistible press of market activity.

services that are represented by "numbers in information-processing machines."[73] Seeing the exchange of commodities as part of "human social evolution," Hart argued that, over the course of history, "ever-widening circles of humanity" naturally become involved in "commodity production and exchange."[74] The process thus acquires increasing power through the multiplication of social relations involved in its technologies.

Money plays a key role in this process, ensuring its own overwhelming and even hegemonic influence on societies. Igor Kopytoff has underscored the striking nature of this impact in places where exchange previously had taken other forms, pointing to "the uniform results of the introduction of money in a wide range of otherwise different societies: more extensive commoditization and the merger of separate spheres of exchange. It is as if the internal logic of exchange itself pre-adapts all economies to seize upon the new opportunities that wide commoditization so obviously brings with it."[75]

Other anthropologists have challenged the way in which such arguments endow money "with an *intrinsic* power to revolutionise society and culture," pointing out that "[m]oney . . . is in nearly as much danger of being fetishised by scholars as by stockbrokers."[76] Mindful that other factors entered into the transformation of the legendary case of the Tiv of Northern Nigeria studied by the Bohannans, Jonathan Parry and Maurice Bloch argued for the variability of adaptations to money use. The struggle "for the maintenance of the long-term order" must allow for "some ideological space within which individual acquisition is a legitimate and even laudable goal," they insisted, and money may not be reduced to either a "devilish acid or . . . [an] instrument and guarantor of liberty."[77]

The following studies of the social life of money from roughly 1640 to the late eighteenth century demonstrate similarly contradictory impulses. In order to establish the framework within which money enjoyed its particular purchase on social relations during this period, I have begun by surveying the variety of money forms and, in particular, the practices emanating from a pronounced shortage of coin in the

[73] Keith Hart, "On Commoditization," in *From Craft to Industry: The Ethnography of Proto-industrial Cloth Production*, ed. Esther N. Goody (Cambridge, 1982), 38–49.

[74] Hart, "On Commoditization," 38, 40.

[75] Kopytoff, "Cultural Biography," *Social Life of Things*, 72.

[76] Bloch and Parry, "Introduction," *Money and the Morality of Exchange*, 3.

[77] Ibid., 26, 30.

seventeenth and eighteenth centuries. Touching briefly on the debate over intrinsic value and the Recoinage of 1696, this discussion sets out the problems of social distinctions and geographical distance, which gave license to a wide variety of unorthodox monetary practices, including paper and commodity currencies in the colonies. Personal liberties in fashioning exchange media contributed to a more general sense of affinity between coins and people. In Chapter 2, this tendency becomes clearer through an examination of the tropes and metaphors used to understand the functions of money in early modern England. In particular, a sense of the animation or "life" embedded in money itself came to dominate theoretical and popular concepts of the medium, apparent in three different forms of expression: formal texts within the new science of political economy; proverbial wisdom and everyday speech; and print culture, including literary works depicting coins as central characters who speak of their own experiences.

A second part of the study moves to more specific examples of personal involvement with money, first through two seventeenth-century diarists, Nehemiah Wallington and Ralph Josselin, and then through an examination of the ideas of John Bellers, the Quaker reformer, and his experiment in a community removed from the "mischiefs" of money, the Clerkenwell Workhouse. These chapters engage with a central issue of the time, the threat of money as a symbol of avarice and worldly corruption. Wallington and, to a lesser extent, Josselin wrestled against the blandishments offered by money mounting in their boxes and drawers, aiming to preserve personal funds from the taint of greed and injustice that they believed characterized the natural domain of money.

A similar perspective is evident in the thought of John Bellers, whose writings on the subject of money stand as singular contributions to political economy at a formative juncture in its development as a body of knowledge. Bellers proposed an extraordinary practical application of his convictions: in an experimental workhouse for the poor, he tried to eliminate the pernicious effects of money by excluding it from the lives of the inhabitants. Such a plan was ultimately unrealistic, given the day-to-day needs of the inmates and the maintenance of the institution itself. More revealing, however, were the attitudes of the inmates themselves. Set against the counterpoint of the emergent consumer society of London, the collection of people gathered at the Clerkenwell Workhouse proved to be thoroughly habituated to the use of money as an instrument of freedom and a measurement of multiple forms of value. Bellers's condemnation of money as the "Mammon of unrighteousness" was extraneous to the quotidian applications of its powers by ordinary and even poor Londoners.

An explosion of printed works on the subject of money at the turn of the seventeenth century attested to growing public interest in reconsidering its place in a society oriented toward commerce and consumption. Coinciding with the Financial Revolution, this fulsome debate took advantage of a distinctive public sphere of print, which was particularly attuned to problems of politics, political economy, and morality. At every level of society, "quarrels over money" exposed the pragmatic link between money and free movement. Expanding on earlier discussions of popular literature and proverbial knowledge of money, this evidence suggests that customary arguments linking individual freedom to money were advanced before the appearance of Bernard Mandeville's *Fable of the Bees* in 1714.

Yet the early eighteenth century was not yet prepared to witness the advance of autonomous agency through money as imagined by popular balladry and proverbial wisdom. In fact, the eighteenth-century state employed money to regulate the movements of its laboring population, and the third part of this study examines the role of money in a contradictory process, that of controlling vagrancy and in accompanying the passage of migrants, servants, and convicts across geographical distances. These practices gave rise to both dominating and dominated identities; or, to paraphrase C. B. Macpherson, this age of possessive individualism may have witnessed the simultaneous advance of "possessed individuals," made possible by a regulatory regime mediated by money.

The end of this study will present a number of coinciding shifts in regulating the use of money as it involved people – the abrogation of rewards for apprehension of those accused of crimes and the modernizing of apprenticeship law, for example – that occurred beyond the boundaries of this study, at the beginning of the nineteenth century, which may have worked to curb the "possessive" power of money. Attitudes condemning wife sale and slavery suggested mounting resistance to the subjection of people to a regime in which monetary measurements and interests called the tune. A final chapter will explore the way in which money's potential for the expansion of personal experience and freedom came of age in the late enlightenment.

Sketching out the social life of money leaves us with a persistent dilemma: given that the use of money included innovative, highly abstract techniques of measuring value in an increasingly complex world of capitalism, did the tendency of money to seep into a wide range of activities beyond the economic mean that it acted as a purveyor of modern life? Or, given its colorful past, was the social life of money a marker of its archaic nature, an atavism of former social structures and values that later became irrelevant to users? Viviana Zelizer's definitive sociological study, *The Social Meaning of Money*, laid out plentiful evidence of our indefatigable efforts to personalize the onslaught of generic funds that come our way in the shape of paychecks and inheritances.[78]

Whatever it may mean to the treasuries of modern governments, money sheds and acquires definitions and personal meaning through the ingenuity of determined users. More important to historians is the question of how boundaries were established by the state and public opinion in the past. The conclusions of this study suggest that because the identification between users and money was so close in the early modern world, individuals, as well as the state, did not hesitate to use the power of money, in the words of the proverb, "to make masteries." It would take further developments in the psychological and moral realms of social thought to make possible the construction of wholly new boundaries between people and things, a project that would begin in England only at the end of the eighteenth century.[79]

---

[78] *The Social Meaning of Money* (New York, 1994).

[79] See G. R. Searle, "Selling People is Wrong: Slavery and Political Economy," in *Morality and the Market in Victorian Britain* (Oxford, 1998), 48–76.

PART I

THE RELATIONSHIP BETWEEN MONEY AND PERSONS

CHAPTER 1

Coins of the Realm: The Development
of a Demotic Sense of Money

The late seventeenth century arguably constituted one of the most important watersheds in English economic history.[1] Extraordinary achievements in finance, both public and private, enabled the nation to emerge as a supreme mercantile and naval power. With the accession of William and Mary, the state redoubled its efforts in bolstering trade and superseding commercial rivals. Of particular significance were the innovations in the administration of the wealth of the state. Along with more systematic collection of excise and land taxes, the founding of the National Debt and the establishment of the Million Lottery in 1693 promised the government increased revenue. Authorization of the Bank of England in 1694 inspired public confidence by asserting central control over various ad hoc arrangements providing the nation with capital.[2] The Board of Trade reemerged in 1695, staffed by celebrated luminaries and seasoned men of finance. A major reform of coinage in 1696, though controversial, restored confidence in the currency of everyday exchange. And throughout the country, the administration of

---

[1] The literature on the financial revolution is extensive and growing; a few examples are H. Roseveare, *The Financial Revolution in England, 1660–1760* (London, 1991); John Brewer, *Sinews of Power: War, Money and the English State, 1688–1783* (Cambridge, MA, 1988); P. G. M. Dickson, *The Financial Revolution: A Study in the Development of Public Credit, 1688–1756* (repr., Aldershot, 1993).

[2] M. J. Braddick, *The Nerves of State: Taxation and the Financing of the English State, 1558–1714* (Manchester, 1996); Patrick K. O'Brien, "The Political Economy of British Taxation, 1660–1815," *Economic History Review*, 2nd ser., 41, no. 1 (1988): 1–32; Charles Wilson, *England's Apprenticeship, 1603–1763*, 2nd ed. (London, 1984), 219; on the Bank of England, a classic study remains Sir John Clapham, *The Bank of England: A History* (Cambridge, 1944); see also Richard Roberts and David Kynaston, eds., *The Bank of England: Money, Power and Influence, 1694–1994* (Oxford, 1995).

the fiscal machinery of government underwent reform and expansion. In a relatively brief period, classically defined as the Financial Revolution, institutions dealing with money came of age.[3]

Yet to what extent did these changes usher in a "modern" age with regard to money? Recent historians of political economy have begun to question the whiggish direction of this line of argument, which exaggerates the degree of change coinciding with the Glorious Revolution.[4] If, as Max Weber argued, institutions impose bureaucratic order over irregularity, it is obvious that much remained to be achieved in the administration of coinage. The English state did not exert complete control over dealings with money, even though the mercantilist age held that the flow of precious metals was of utmost concern. A more difficult question to answer is the nature of the linkages between the development of financial institutions and everyday exchange relations. Government policies necessarily impinged on the terms of ordinary trade: strictures on the supply of silver coin, for example, forced the English population to rely to an even greater extent on credit for ordinary exchanges. As one financial historian put it, credit became a "money-substitute" after the Great Recoinage of 1696.[5] The ubiquity of lending and borrowing militated against "modern" money relations. Instead of engendering impersonal transactions, or rampant self-interest, according to Craig Muldrew and Margot Finn, credit relations persisted in fostering relationships of mutual obligation.[6]

Historians of credit have corrected the dichotomy that associates personal financial relations with the intimacy of village life while projecting modern behavior onto urban commerce. The web of joint indebtedness that Muldrew traced in seventeenth-century King's Lynn was not unlike business in eighteenth-century London. In order to facilitate

---

[3] A flood of pamphlet literature followed in response to the question of recoinage; see Joyce Oldham Appleby, *Economic Thought and Ideology in Seventeenth-Century England* (Princeton, 1978), 219–41; A. E. Feaveryear, *The Pound Sterling: A History of English Money* (London, 1931), 86–90; 148–9; Wilson, *England's Apprenticeship*, esp. 219; Geoffrey Holmes, *The Making of a Great Power: Late Stuart and Early Georgian Britain, 1660–1722* (London, 1993), 266–77.

[4] See, for example, Patrick K. O'Brien, "Fiscal Exceptionalism: Great Britain and Its European Rivals from Civil War to Triumph at Trafalgar and Waterloo," in *The Political Economy of British Historical Experience, 1688 – 1914*, ed. Donald Winch and Patrick K. O'Brien (Oxford, 2002), 245–65.

[5] J. Keith Horsefield, *British Monetary Experiments* (Cambridge, MA, 1960), 15–16.

[6] Margot C. Finn, *The Character of Credit: Personal Debt in English Culture, 1740–1914* (Cambridge, 2003); Craig Muldrew, *The Economy of Obligation: The Culture of Credit and Social Relations in Early Modern England* (London, 1998).

brisk exchange in commodities and services, from the barber's shop to Thomas Chippendale's cabinetry business, credit regularly replaced money in many daily transactions. As Peter Earle has shown, "'trusting' was essential in a world where the majority of customers had no regular income," and those who denied credit to customers usually lost business even from those who could pay up front. Earle points out that Daniel Defoe underwent a change of heart on this subject, from his condemnation of retail credit in 1709 to his affirmation of its ubiquity in the 1720s. Defoe's acceptance gave proof of the lively expansion of London commercial life alongside his awareness of an inescapable reality: the spending power of common consumers was fueled by erratic payments of money for their goods and labor. At the upper end of the social scale, even aristocrats might be hard-pressed for ready money in a great chain of debt and credit entanglement. "As I receive my rents once a year," reported one of Chippendale's customers, "so I pay my tradesmen's bills once a year which is not reckoned very bad as ye world goes."[7] Modernizing financial administration did not necessarily mean an analogous development in the social relations of money.

Customary exchange relations were slow to change and much interaction remained outside the purview of institutions. What has been curiously absent from many historical accounts of money in the financial revolution is the aptitude on the part of individual users for thinking about and employing money in uniquely early modern ways. While aware of the latent civic authority invested in money, many English people, at home and in the colonies, moved outside the bounds of what we might consider a conventional or fixed use of currency. By enlisting the unstable properties of money – its fungibility, or capacity for changing form – in the social relations of exchange, they involved currency in a critical cultural process of drawing boundaries that established distinctions between persons and things, and between categories of people across society. Money's trademark came to be its unsettling power, its tendency to introduce categorical instability into many areas of social and personal life. How and why this should have occurred can be explained, in part, by looking at the development of coinage in the seventeenth and eighteenth centuries. It is this evolution that we must examine in order to understand the complex life of money within British culture.

---

[7] Peter Earle, *The Making of the English Middle Class: Business, Society and Family Life in London, 1660–1730* (Berkeley, 1989),115–18.

THE SOCIAL AND CULTURAL IMPACT OF A SHORTAGE
OF COIN

The ubiquity of retail credit – that is, the use of credit for small daily purchases – indicates the pervasive social impact of the shortage of coin. The
absence of a central banking system, combined with the effects of significant inflation, forced early modern states throughout Europe to grapple
with the same difficulty from the sixteenth century. In a commercially
advanced nation such as England, where urban markets and wage labor
demanded a considerable supply of coin, the problem was particularly
acute.[8] Craig Muldrew has estimated that an increase in the demand for
coins by about 500 percent was hardly matched by an increase in supply
of 63 percent between 1540 and 1600.[9] The dilemma persisted throughout the seventeenth and eighteenth centuries. All accounts agree that
the English state retreated from the job of providing sufficient coinage
to sustain a growing commercial economy.[10]

At the heart of the issue lay a resolute adherence, grounded in Tudor
and Stuart policies, to the principle of "intrinsick value": the belief that
the value of coin must be backed by an equivalent value of the precious metal it contained. Gold and silver embodied characteristics of
durability and scarcity that gave them universal appeal over lesser metals; such qualities converged with an overarching theory of the cosmos
and warranted their use as monetary standards.[11] Small change posed
a dilemma because fractional amounts of silver suffered from excessive
wear and consequent loss; as one contemporary attested, "by experience

---

[8] B. E. Supple, "Currency and Commerce in the Early Seventeenth Century," *Economic History Review*, 2nd ser., 10 (1957): 239–55.

[9] Craig Muldrew, *Economy*; "'Hard Food for Midas': Cash and its Social Value in Early Modern England," *Past and Present*, no. 170 (Feb. 2001), 78–120.

[10] William Boyne underscored the tendency in a survey of the eighteenth century, calling the government's inaction "most extraordinary." (*The Silver Tokens of Great Britain and Ireland, The Dependencies, and Colonies* [London, 1866], iv.) See also Sir John Craig, *The Mint: A History of the London Mint from A.D. 287 to 1948* (Cambridge, 1953), 128; Peter Mathias, "The People's Money in the Eighteenth Century: The Royal Mint, Trade Tokens and the Economy," in *The Transformation of England: Essays in the Economic and Social History of England in the Eighteenth Century* (London, 1979), 190–208.

[11] As Andrea Finkelstein has written, "intrinsic (or objective) value was the cement hold-ing the finite universe together. It was the axis running through the center of each cosm and linking them all in the Great Chain of Being." *Harmony and the Balance: An Intellectual History of Seventeenth-Century English Economic Thought* (Ann Arbor, 2000), 41–44, 88.

we find of our half-pence, who are so small and thin, that many cannot feele them between their fingers."[12] Yet the prospect of compromise did not appeal to Tudor monarchs, who felt that coinage of alloys diluted royal authority. Elizabeth I rejected a practical-minded proposal to mint copper coinage in small denomination, insisting on the exclusive use of precious metals for royal coin, and she later instated a system of minimum legal weights for English gold and silver coins.[13] Only on occasion did the Crown authorize the use of base metal tokens, usually made out of copper or lead, which could serve the purposes of small change necessary for "small measures and little purchases," as well as adequate alms for beggars.[14]

James I was not unaware of the practical impediments created by a short supply of small change. When he decided to issue farthing tokens in 1613, his proclamation indicated an awareness of the social value of coins made of base metal:

> Whereas [it said] there hath been in times past some toleration in this Our Realm of Tokens of Lead, commonly known by the name of farthing tokens, to pass between Vintners, Tapsters, Chandlers, Bakers and other the like Tradesmen and their Customers, whereby such small portions and quantities of things vendible as the necessity and use specially of the poorer sort of People doth oftentimes require may be conveniently bought and sold without enforcing men to buy more ware than will serve for their use and occasions; inasmuch therefore as the use of Farthing Tokens hath in itself a good end, tending to parsimony and to the avoiding of waste in petty contracts and pennyworths; in which respect it cannot be but a great comfort to the poorer sort of the People.[15]

Yet the concession to public need went only part of the way. The Mint was not involved in the decisions regarding the new farthings, or in their production, and by royal decree, acceptance of these farthings was not compulsory. Political instability introduced further difficulty, particularly as monopoly production of farthings led to their curtailment by Puritans in 1644. Thus a contradictory situation persisted, best described

---

[12] "A Remedy against the Losse of the Subject by Farthing-Tokens," (1644), reprinted in George C. Williamson, *Trade Tokens Issued in the Seventeenth Century in England, Wales, and Ireland, by Corporations, Merchants, Tradesmen, Etc., A New and Revised Edition of William Boyne's Work*, 2 vols. (London, 1889), 1:513.

[13] Craig, *Mint*, 128–9.   [14] Ibid., 82.

[15] Ibid., 140; see also Peter Mathias, "The People's Money," 191–2.

by a twentieth-century historian as a system "based on a dual coinage of so-called 'real' and 'imaginary' money."[16]

The prestige of silver coin, coupled with the haphazard oversight of lesser coinage, posed a persistent problem for the English state: competitors in the form of counterfeiters and coin-clippers, sometimes working in tandem, entered the arena. Before the introduction of milled edges by mechanized means in 1662, clipping from good coin to make bad was particularly widespread, and the practice continued long after improved technology declared war on the crime.[17] The populace were so accustomed to sorting their change in this way that when the government issued new copper halfpennies in 1672, they treated them as medals rather than coin, hoarding rather than using them. (The design of the coin compounded the problem: the image of the king looked to the left, rather than the customary right, presumably to register the exceptional nature of such small change, and in the world of coinage, such an anomaly rendered the piece "collectable."[18]) Tradesmen and consumers alike accepted odd and deficient coins as tender. The situation left much room for counterfeiting, particularly as the contracting of private coiners for small change made regulation of imposters difficult. Punishment was notoriously inconsistent because most people accepted and paid out expenses with bad coin. Flagrant assaults on royal authority faced reprisal, and, as head of the Mint, Newton zealously sought out offenders, ordering coiners from every walk of life, including one respectable and successful businessman, hanged. Statutory punishments for counterfeiting copper coin, meanwhile, remained relatively lenient until as late as 1742, when the crime was upgraded from misdemeanor to two years' imprisonment.[19]

---

[16] Craig, *Mint*; Supple, "Currency and Commerce," 239.

[17] As Malcolm Gaskill points out, clipping and counterfeiting were carried on throughout the seventeenth century and were not a "peculiarity" of the eighteenth-century "yellow trade" studied by John Styles. Gaskill also points out that able counterfeiters even clipped coins in order to make them look more authentic. *Crime and Mentalities in Early Modern England* (Cambridge, 2000), 132; John Styles, "'Our Traitorous Money Makers': The Yorkshire Coiners and the Law, 1760–83," in John Brewer and John Styles, eds., *An Ungovernable People? The English and Their Law in the Seventeenth and Eighteenth Centuries* (London, 1980), 172–249.

[18] Craig, *Mint*, 174. The king's title appeared as "Carolus a Carolo," which again differed from that on gold and silver coins.

[19] Carl Wennerlind, "The Death Penalty as Monetary Policy: The Practice and Punishment of Monetary Crime, 1690–1830," *History of Political Economy* 36, no. 1 (Spring 2004): 129–59; Craig, *Mint*; Mathias, "The People's Money," 205. Gaskill cites Dryden's "Prologue from King Arthur" (1691) as additional testimony to the undersupply of

During the seventeenth century, most other European nations were producing such money to satisfy commercial and popular needs,[20] but the English Crown believed that divorcing coin from intrinsic value introduced too many hazards, including the potential for counterfeiting. Thus the stage was set for a subtle contretemps between royal inertia and private initiative, which would create, in effect, a two-tiered system of coinage. Given the needs of urban commercial life, popular initiative rose to fill the breach: from 1648, independent manufacturers turned out a "vast variety of private tokens, mostly for halfpence" to take the place of royal farthings.[21] Town councils authorized their own token production and business establishments boasted their own coin presses. The self-styled metal pieces passed as local or simply neighborhood tender. Makers sold packs of tokens at a profit to tradespeople and shopkeepers, who then offered them as change in transactions. Town councils also contracted with tokeners, selling halfpence and farthings to those who needed them, sometimes for the best price offered. Their value rested simply on the assumption of continuing neighborhood custom and popular trust.[22]

According to one count, the City of London, Westminster, and the suburbs of London boasted 3,543 tokeners in the 1660s, who offered coins of various sizes, shapes, and alloys.[23] Similar operations appeared in provincial towns throughout England, Scotland, and Ireland. A certain amount of unscrupulous dealing went on, wrought by "Projectors," "the very Caterpillers of this Kingdome," according to a pamphleteer of the 1640s.[24] In some localities, a flood of different tokens, demonstrating Gresham's Law, drove out good silver and left people with a surfeit of money of limited value and usefulness. In such instances, local authorities declared only particular token farthings valid, leaving

---

coin: "when clipp'd money passes, 'tis a sign/ A nation is not over-stock'd with coin." *Crime*, 188.

[20] Appleby, *Economic Thought*, 228.

[21] Craig, *Mint*, 142. Craig's sparse coverage of token history follows from the orthodox view that they fall outside the purview of a formal currency system and certainly beyond the jurisdiction of the Mint.

[22] J. R. S. Whiting, *Trade Tokens: A Social and Economic History* (Newton Abbot, 1971), 17–20.

[23] Figures from Liza Picard, *Restoration London* (New York, 1997), 144; see also Craig, *Mint*, 140.

[24] "A Remedy against the Losse of the Subject by Farthing-Tokens," 1644, reprinted in George C. Williamson, *Trade Tokens Issued in the Seventeenth Century in England, Wales, and Ireland, by Corporations, Merchants, Tradesmen, Etc., A New and Revised Edition of William Boyne's Work*, 2 vols. (London, 1889), 1:510–14.

holders (often poor women working in petty trade) at a loss. Yet the plea for government-issued farthings of copper or brass met with resistance until after the Restoration, and then, only with great difficulty were private and local tokens suppressed from circulation.[25]

Seventeenth-century tokeners struck their own way through a thicket of prerogatives and obstacles: what one historian has termed "the people's money" provided a revealing stage upon which tradesmen, innkeepers, artisans, and even the occasional poor widow made a plea for custom.[26] Made of copper, leather, tin, or lead, most tokens were round, but some appeared in more creative shapes, including hearts and hexagons. Many were particularly personal; images might be crude or finely wrought and frequently offered punning inscriptions: "Square dealing is best" appeared imprinted on a square token.[27] Pictures genially invoked physical experience: a coffeehouse attendant, for example, pouring coffee from a steaming samovar, issued by "Howard Coffee House in New Street, 1671." Slogans were often tongue-in-cheek: "Although but brass yet let me pass" and "Welcome you be to trade with me." Vernacular language and inventive spelling abounded; one collector noted ten spellings of Peterborough in as few as twenty-five tokens.[28] The variety of small change necessitated distinctive equipment and ritual: shopkeepers sorted them into compartmentalized boxes and regularly exchanged them for other currency at the site of their issuers.[29]

A heterogeneous money supply schooled a commercially active population in a particular form of technical virtuosity in exchange relations. Underweight coins dating from earlier decades circulated alongside newer issues, requiring users to discern denominations of all sizes and metals. Sometimes people simply adapted to what was available, as in coastal towns in Kent, Sussex, and Hampshire, where foreign coins, such as Spanish pieces of eight and "divers sorts of Dollers," passed as tender.[30] The mixture of coinage was not unique to England. Barry Supple

---

[25] Whiting, *Trade Tokens*, 18–19.

[26] According to one authority, "a goodly number were of the gentler sex... probably strong-minded widows, who were endeavouring by honest industry to support and bring up their fatherless children." Williamson, *Trade Tokens*, 1:131. His volume shows several examples of tokens inscribed with "widow."

[27] Ibid., xxix–xxxi.   [28] Ibid., xxx.

[29] William Boyne, *Trade Tokens Issued in the Seventeenth Century in England, Wales, and Ireland* (London, 1858); Picard, *Restoration London*, 144–5.

[30] "A Remedy against the Losse of the Subject by Farthing-Tokens," 513.

points out that in 1614 "it was claimed that 400 types [of coin] circulated in the Low Countries, and 82 in France." A proliferation of handbooks for merchants testified to the need to translate one coin's value into that of another.[31] Users learned to rely on the varying sounds of "chink" that helped to identify coins and on gradations of color, thickness, design, and relief. They also recognized the need to distinguish between "good" and "bad" coins, as Samuel Pepys did, saving the good ones for important transactions.[32] Milled edges and circumscription made clipping more difficult in the later years of the seventeenth century (the "Inventor [whoever he were] worthy [*sic*] the Honor of *Medal* himself," according to diarist John Evelyn[33]), but the more ingenious practitioners of the art of clipping managed to persist even after these innovations. Thus, a great deal was left up to the individual in determining the actual value of any given coin.

The Great Recoinage of 1696 represented a late chapter in this struggle over rightful public authority over circulating coin. As the government finally determined to call in silver coinage and remint it at value, roughly 400 pamphlets from a wide-ranging roster of authors demonstrated the extent of public awareness and concern over the subject.[34] Opinion lined up along two sides: those like Locke (and ultimately, the Treasury) favored maintaining the value of silver coins according to the intrinsic value of the precious metal itself, established at the time of Elizabeth; their opposition favored uncoupling the value of coinage from the standard of silver and gold, allowing the relative value of goods on the market to find their own levels. The debate was not simply about the technicalities of maintaining a sound money supply. From every side, voices weighed in with social and moral judgments that revealed just how directly the question of currency impinged on more general concepts of the polity and its future governance.[35]

Many writers cherished the principle of intrinsic value as the polestar within a vast, crowded vista of possibilities. "Intrinsical" value

---

[31] Supple, "Currency and Commerce," 240n.   [32] Muldrew, *Economy*, 100.

[33] *Numismata: A Discourse of Medals, Antient and Modern* (London, 1697), 225.

[34] Appleby, "Locke, Liberalism and the Natural Law of Money," *Past and Present* 71 (1976): 48; *Economic Thought*, 220ff; Peter Laslett, "John Locke, the Great Recoinage, and the Origins of the Board of Trade," *William and Mary Quarterly* 14 (1957): 368–402.

[35] Tracts issuing from the pamphlet debate over recoinage educated the general public about "Intrinsick Value" and other definitions of early political economy; see, for example, Anon., *A Discourse of Money* (London, 1696), 97–102; A Merchant, *A Discourse of the General Notions of Money, Trade, and Exchanges* (London, 1695); Horsefield, *British Monetary Experiments*.

transcended the "local value they call Extrinsical, as depending upon the impression of the mark and ordinance of the State," Rice Vaughan had argued in 1675. Regardless of the attempts by princes, he pointed out, "in truth Gold and Silver will retain the same proportion towards other things, which are valued by them, which the general consent of other Nations doth give unto them, if there be a Trade and Commerce with other Nations."[36] Intrinsic value promised order over confusion, stability in the face of flux, and reliable standards across kingdoms and expanses of space. "[W]ithout this Rule, Trading People would be ever in the dark, and not know how to make one regular step in their Business," argued a typical pamphlet.[37] Vaughan's tract reminded readers of the tale of Lycurgus, who succeeded in isolating his subjects from commerce with strangers only by prohibiting gold and silver from his city.[38] Reliance on the principles attached to intrinsic value promised to harmonize public interests with a particular notion of the public good of England that extended on a grand scale to the entire universe. Only then could English "men in God's Name traffick freely" with money and "never prejudice the State."[39]

So embedded was intrinsic value in other systems of thought and calculation that English commentary (and monarchs) dismissed alternatives as unrealistic, distasteful, and thoroughly alien to English customs. (Ireland, however, was a different matter: copper coins of pence, halfpence, and farthings were introduced there in 1601.[40]) John Evelyn lauded the convictions of Edward VI and Queen Elizabeth, who helped to make "*England* only of all the Kingdoms, not of *Europe* alone, but of all the World besides," a state that "preserve[d] the Standard, intrinsically valuable, by a Law as Sacred and Inviolable as that of the *Medes* and *Persians*." As a result, he pointed out, "we may esteem as *Medals*" their coinage.[41] Dangers lurked in debasing the coinage, more than simply risking the reputation of the nation. According to Vaughan, mixing metals confounded the powers of discrimination of "Colour, Sound, Weight, and other more hidden Qualities of the different mettals," enabling

---

[36] Rice Vaughan, *A Discourse of Coin and Coinage* (London, 1675), reprinted in *Old and Scarce Tracts on Money*, ed. J. R. McCulloch (London, 1933), 12. Vaughan's understanding of intrinsic value was subtler than that of his contemporaries, according to Supple, because he recognized the extent to which enhancements of value at home could determine the movements of the money supply abroad. "Currency and Commerce," 254.

[37] *Discourse of Money*, 102.   [38] Vaughan, *Discourse*, 12.

[39] The last two phrases are from Evelyn, *Numismata*, 230.   [40] Craig, *Mint*, 128–9.

[41] Evelyn, *Numismata*, 230.

"Strangers" as well as "Natives," rather than the state, to produce "the greatest part" of the money of the kingdom.[42] The defense of intrinsic value was the obligation of the state, imbued with moral significance and promising the preservation of supremacy over bankers, merchants, and rogue coiners everywhere.[43]

According to Joyce Appleby, John Locke's belief that a coin's value must be equal to the value of its precious metal content triumphed mainly because it happened to coincide with the "interests of the parliamentary magnates."[44] The contradiction between his authoritarian stance on money and his otherwise liberal notions of the role of the state can only be explained by looking at the social relations of money. As Constantine George Caffentzis has pointed out, Locke's argument can be seen as an attempt to bring under control multiple social orders of exchange. While illicit coin production threatened to undermine the power of the Mint in matters of currency, he saw the need to assert the supremacy of fixed principle and pure metal. "The use and end of the public stamp is only to be a guard and voucher of the quality of silver which men contract for; and the injury done to the public *faith*, in this point, is that which in clipping and false coining heightens the *robbery* into *treason*," Locke wrote in his second pamphlet on the need for recoinage.[45] Though his defense of silver was not novel, Locke's forceful language and legal strategy counted as such. By joining the Crown's authority to coinage and applying the penalty of death to counterfeiting, he introduced a new emphasis on state control in the face of the permissive disorderliness that had characterized the previous half-century.[46]

Nicholas Barbon, an indefatigable designer of financial schemes, offers a window into competing vernacular practices of the times, soon to be eclipsed by the more systematic theorizing of political economists who followed Locke.[47] Barbon has been characterized by historians as "a polished and unscrupulous man of business," "something of a buccaneer," the author of tracts "neither disinterested nor systematic."[48]

---

[42] Vaughan, *Discourse*, 31.   [43] Finkelstein, *Harmony*, 43–44.

[44] Appleby, *Economic Thought*, 230; "Locke," 65.

[45] *Further Considerations*, 144, quoted in Caffentzis, *Clipped Coins, Abused Words and Civil Government: John Locke's Philosophy of Money* (New York, 1989), 46–7.

[46] Caffentzis, *Clipped Coins*; see also Wennerlind, "Death Penalty," 129–59.

[47] Appleby, *Economic Thought*, 252, 258.

[48] P. G. M. Dickson, *The Sun Insurance Office, 1710–1960* (London, 1960), ix, 7–8; William Letwin, *Origins of Scientific Economics: English Economic Thought, 1660–1776* (Westport, CT, 1975), 48. Barbon is credited with the founding of British fire insurance, originating in his "Insurance Office for Houses" near the Royal Exchange in 1681.

Yet Barbon nevertheless expressed various points of view that contested the strict control of monetary value. His pamphlet salvo against Locke brings to life the social dynamics of his time, revealing the realpolitik of finance and its distinctive world of judgments and considerations. Barbon complained that Locke adhered to a quaint but obsolete notion of value. "There is nothing that troubles this Controversy more, than for want of distinguishing betwixt Value and Vertue," he pointed out. So pervasive was fungible market value in late seventeenth-century England, Barbon contended, that "nothing can have an Intrinsick Value."[49]

There is no question that beneath this war of words lay tensions relating to social rank and status. Intrinsic value accorded with aristocratic notions of inherent worth and the preservation of hierarchy, while a more fungible notion of money belonged to the meretricious world of 'Change Alley and financial schemes. The real victims of the Great Recoinage were the common people who suffered from a stringent shortage of circulating coin, which was reduced by £1 million at the end of the seventeenth century; moreover, the smallest denomination reminted at the time of the recoinage was the sixpence.[50] Prices fell dramatically, but so did wages and employment. In the words of one historian, recoinage was a "drastic bloodletting operation," acceptable only because the wealthier members of society were able to depend on their use of various forms of paper currency.[51] Malcolm Gaskill's research has shown that popular unrest was considerable just before and for some time after the transition to new money in the spring of 1696. From most parts of England, reports of protest and disorder were arriving at the Treasury, indicating that an insufficient supply of coin had left soldiers unpaid and common people without the currency to buy bread. Justices of the Peace expressed anxiety over the simmering discontent and called for help from the government.[52]

The thrust of commercial life worked against strict metal standards, encouraging a double standard with regard to understanding what money stood for. Common assumptions about economic life simply

---

[49] Nicholas Barbon, *A Discourse Concerning Coining the New Money [L]ighter* (1696), 6.

[50] Muldrew, "'Hard Food for Midas'," 99.

[51] The quotation is from Wilson, *England's Apprenticeship*, 224, but see also 220–1; Caffentzis, *Clipped Coins*, 45–76; Appleby, "Locke, Liberalism and the Natural Law of Money," 64–9.

[52] Gaskill, *Crime*, 194–7.

assumed that extrinsic standards of value existed apart from the stated value of money.[53] Bad coin continued to pass for good, as coin-clipping and counterfeiting persisted, and the criminal aspect of tampering with the money supply found irregular support. Attitudes toward violations having to do with the money supply, from both official and popular ends, remained wedded to principles of expediency and necessity.[54] Even vernacular language, in its own haphazard way, demonstrated the same drift away from intrinsic value. The late seventeenth century used "quid" as slang for "guinea," derived from "quiddity," meaning the "real nature or essence of a thing; that which makes a thing what it is." As gold coin, the guinea stood for the "essence" of money. But by 1700, canting language had appropriated the term more generally, using "quids" to refer to any kind of money or cash.[55]

Defenders of intrinsic value correctly suspected that the commercial life of the nation had somehow pried open a Pandora's box of monetary associations: the alchemy of money, via the nexus of economic activity, was influencing all areas of English society, destabilizing customary notions of order. Evelyn's panegyric to medals, the elite of coinage, par excellence, comprehended this, largely because of the way he understood the poisonous effects of departing from strict monetary standards. Helped along by an organic conception of the fiscal nation, he traced the lengthy chain of connective tissue that maintained the health of the body politic. "[W]hatever pretends to add or detract from the value of Money, must of necessity Influence, and insensibly Affect all that's necessary, not only to the well-being, but to the very *Form* and *Essence* of a Kingdom. All Pacts and Covenants, Bargains, Obligations, Estates, Rents, Goods, Credit and Correspondences whatsoever (becoming dubious and uncertain) must sink and be at an end," he intoned. Though histrionically pessimistic, Evelyn's sociology of money described a pervasive circulatory network of money. What he did not realize was the limitations of a precious metals standard and the authority of the state in the face of such a complex system of interaction.[56]

---

[53] See Appleby on this point: *Economic Thought*, 228–30.
[54] Gaskill, *Crime*, 174–99, esp. 186.
[55] B. E., *A New Dictionary of the Terms Ancient and Modern of the Canting Crew, In its Several Tribes, of Gypsies, Beggers, Thieves, Cheats, &c.* (1699), "Quidds" *Oxford English Dictionary*, "quid."
[56] Evelyn, *Numismata*, 233.

MONEY ACROSS THE ATLANTIC: EXPERIMENTS BREED
HETERODOXY

The monetary life of England existed within the larger realm of empire, as advocates of an expansionist approach to British history have shown through considerable scholarship. No study of the evolution of economic institutions can ignore the extension of the life of money into the remote laboratories of the North American colonies, where mercantilist policies and geographical distance led to alternative methods of establishing a money supply. The "double-ended process connecting metropolitan and dependent worlds was most evident" in "the economic arena," revealing mutual influences and borrowings in monetary practices and actual coin.[57] In a slightly later period, John Wright's *American Negotiator* (1761–1765) documented the different types of money found in the colonies, and, as historian Jacob Price has shown, the subscription lists for this rather costly publication nearly reached 3,700 people. Such evidence indicates an interdependency built on considerable industry and commerce.[58]

As part of the larger system of trade, the colonists were subject to the regulatory authority of the Crown, which forbade the export of precious metal. Coins were therefore in short supply, and colonists were forced to devise other means of carrying on internal trade. Initially, they set up their own mints, but the English government objected and in 1684 explicitly prohibited their operation.[59] The subsequent phase of the history of money has become legendary: Americans then resorted to *wampum* and "commodity-currencies," goods selected as viable counters and as independent means of exchange. Most frequently, tobacco fit the bill, though predictable problems arose as colonial governments struggled to maintain a semblance of authority over rogue producers and low-grade counterfeits. Such commodities did not simply constitute "truck" payments but bonafide currency, which could be passed along as money in further negotiations for other items. By means of acts passed by colonial governments, timber, cattle, furs,

---

[57] Bernard Bailyn and Philip D. Morgan, "Introduction," in *Strangers within the Realm: Cultural Margins of the First British Empire*, ed. Bernard Bailyn and Philip D. Morgan (Chapel Hill, NC, 1991), 24.

[58] Jacob M. Price, "Who Cared about the Colonies? The Impact of the Thirteen Colonies on British Society and Politics, circa 1714–1775," *Strangers*, 406–12.

[59] C. P. Nettels, *The Monetary Supply of the American Colonies before 1720* (Madison, 1936), 212; Paul Einzig, *Primitive Money*, 2nd ed. (Oxford, 1966), 278; Craig, *Mint*, 377.

dairy produce, musket balls, oats, pork, and many other items became authorized as legal tender.[60]

The "irregularities of colonial currencies," as a late Victorian historian put it, continually provoked conflict between the crown and the North American colonies. "The early years of the 18th century were marked by a serious effort in England to grapple with the grave inconveniences and anomalies of colonial currency as a whole, and to introduce law and order perforce," wrote William Chalmers.[61] Trade with merchants abroad led to the first issue of paper money (for amounts as small as a penny) among the colonies. But direct conflict erupted over the practice by the colonies of setting their own rates in accepting Spanish pieces of eight. A Royal Proclamation of 1704 established a maximum rate for them and, more importantly, insisted upon rating other silver coins "according to intrinsic content," a practice the colonists had strictly avoided. "From the Imperial legislation of 1704," according to Chalmers, "may be dated the traditional preference for paper which characterises the currency of the United States."[62] The British Board of Trade saw paper money "perhaps as unfit as anything can possibly be" and favored silver and gold as the currency of choice.[63] The colonists nevertheless came to understand that a shortage of currency linked to precious metals made prices for their goods fall, while an increase in any medium accepted as currency resulted in higher prices and brisker trade. As the governor of New York attested to British authorities in 1718, "I do affirm, that since the circulation of these bills [of paper money issued in 1715] the trade of this place has increased at least above one half of what it was."[64] The practical advantages of circulating sufficient amounts of

---

[60] Einzig, *Primitive Money*, 278–86. Nettels, *Monetary Supply*; Robert Chalmers, *A History of Currency in the British Colonies* (London, 1893); see also Richard A. Lester, *Monetary Experiments: Early American and Recent Scandinavian* (Princeton, 1939). Einzig notes that in 1690, Massachusetts colonists used "wheat, Indian corn, barley, peas, oats, pork and beef" as money, while Connecticut used "wheat, peas, Indian corn, rye, pork, and beef." *Primitive Money*, 282.

[61] Chalmers, *History*, 11.

[62] Craig, *Mint*, 377; Chalmers, *History*, 11. In effect, the colonists had devalued the shilling by raising the value of pieces of eight as a way of attracting foreign coin into their hands. Lester, *Monetary Experiments*, 21–2. Tensions only increased after a Parliamentary ruling of 1708, which forbade the colonies to set their own rates in accepting Spanish pieces of eight.

[63] *Archives of the State of New Jersey*, First Series, Vol. IX, 411, 412, cited in Lester, *Monetary Experiments*, 23.

[64] B. Fernow, "Coins and Currency of New York" in *The Memorial History of the City of New-York*, ed. J. G. Wilson (1893) 4:318, cited in Lester, *Monetary Experiments*, 19.

improvised money convinced colonists of the benefits of taking matters into their own hands.[65]

The resort to commodity money raises interesting questions related to the inventiveness associated with exchange practices. Einzig and others have cataloged reasons that American colonists may have turned to commodities in place of precious metal coinage; as one historian pointed out, they found that "[t]hey could not have both a metallic currency and an axe."[66] Silver was not completely unobtainable, but it seems to have been reserved for particular kinds of exchange. Most colonists could not have paid taxes unless commodities had been accepted, and even the salaries of colonial officers necessitated the use, at least in part, of commodity money. But clearly, necessity was not all that inspired North Americans in choosing their methods. John Kenneth Galbraith may have hit closer to the mark when he pointed out that the colonists boasted "an instinct for monetary experiment," along with a resistance to paying taxes, which the manufacture of paper money enabled them to exercise. The two tendencies may have gone hand in hand, as in the case of Virginia, where tobacco money came into being as legal tender in 1642 as a by-product of a rather odd law against contracts requiring payment in gold or silver.[67] Precious metals remained associated with rule from above, while commodity money was capable of representing the *vox populi* as a gesture of defiance against excessive limitations imposed by colonial authority.

The choice of commodity expressed a kind of common denominator, as in the case of sugar in the West Indies. In the first decades of English involvement with Barbados, values were measured according to amounts of cotton and tobacco, but in later years, these were superseded by the rise of sugar. Along with market prices, fines for violating laws concerning behavior were also expressed in commodity money. Chalmers cited an "Act concerning morning and evening prayer in families," which decreed that "whosoever shall swear or curse, if a master or a freeman, he shall forfeit for every such offence four pounds of sugar; if a servant, two pounds of sugar."[68] Not even property was exempt from

---

[65] Chalmers, *History*, 11.

[66] Horace White, *Money and Banking* (New York, 1908), 14, quoted in Einzig, *Primitive Money*, 279.

[67] John Kenneth Galbraith, *Money: Whence It Came, Where it Went*, rev. ed. (Boston, 1995), 47–8.

[68] Chalmers, *History*, 47, also cited in Einzig, *Primitive Money*, 291. Chalmers reckons that this law dates from 1645.

the hegemony of sugar: on the island of St. Christopher, where an estate of "600 akers" was estimated in 1698 to be worth "att least att 1,000 li. Sugar" per acre, "the usual price the Sugar att 12s. 6 d. per hundred----£. 3,750."[69]

The spread of paper money issued by colonial governments led to the gradual phasing out of commodity money, though not its extinction. It is possible to see the move from commodity money to paper money in the case of tobacco, a commonly used currency in Virginia, Maryland, Carolina, and other neighboring states. During the seventeenth century, the spread of tobacco money led to the need for some kind of regulation, as private production enabled everyone to enter the fray and prices fell accordingly. By the 1720s, colonial officials had established control over warehouses, inspecting the crops for quality and issuing certificates of deposit that could be used as currency in the surrounding regions. These certificates acted as legal tender throughout the eighteenth century.[70] Yet in the Leeward Islands, commodity money continued to play a part in exchange. In Antigua and Nevis, for example, an "unexplained . . . influx of metallic money" displaced sugar as the major currency around 1699, but "disputes and controversies" forced the passage of an act, the following year, setting standard rates for the conversion of sugar, indigo, cotton, tobacco, and ginger into silver amounts. With the accession of Queen Anne and a shift to a standard of gold, further confusion ensued, and parties regularly appointed "viewers" to estimate the worth of commodities used as currency. "[I]n case of disagreement the Viewers called in an umpire." As late as the 1750s, local authorities in Nevis were still refereeing disputes, and in 1760, Antigua passed an act that ruled out paying taxes in commodities. The opposite occurred in St. Christopher in 1784, where the government recognized that because the use of specie "may be burthensome and oppressive," taxes "may be in cash, sugar, or rum, at the option of the person or persons liable."[71]

Fiscal emergencies brought on more creative solutions to a shortage of money. Economic historians frequently point out that military needs usually prompted extraordinary measures in the line of currency production; the need to pay soldiers and requisition supplies almost always forced the hand of governments reluctant to inflate their money supply. When authority was divided between crown and officer, with an ocean in between, as was the case in colonial North America, expedience might

[69] Chalmers, *History*, 61.   [70] Einzig, *Primitive Money*, 281.
[71] Chalmers, *History*, 62–3.

trump precedent. In French Canada, for example, the intendant found he had little recourse but to invent his own currency in 1685. He had already drawn upon his own funds and borrowed from friends in order to pay troops and expenses. In desperation, the commanding general ordered troops "to hire themselves out to the inhabitants...until His Majesty sends us new funds." This method failing (it was the wrong time of the year and farmers had no need for additional hands), the intendant issued notes on playing cards and ordered "all the inhabitants to receive this money in payments" until he might redeem them when the resources arrived from France. Because many inhabitants were illiterate, the cards needed to be readily identifiable as different denominations; they also needed to look official. To these ends, the intendant cut them into different sizes and shapes, colored them, and signed them, together with his treasurer and the governor general. The French colony was able to make do until the next shipment of funds arrived from France; the Canadian colonists witnessed the beneficial effects of exchange in the meantime. Despite the condemnation of the king, card money was then issued annually from 1690 to 1719.[72]

Canadian card money, more than commodity-currency, represented a conceptual advance over and above its practical success as a solution to the problems of colonial money supplies. It was in this instance that user and issuers alike recognized the *abstract* aspect of money: its representation of potential, not actual value. Commodity-currency laid claim to such status, but its unregulated availability meant that individuals, not just governments, could issue it. Card money, however, constituted a "modern" form of currency in the nature of its authorized and fixed value.[73]

From the 1690s through the first decades of the eighteenth century, conceptions of money in England and within the English North American colonies fluctuated between concrete and abstract poles. Forms of credit became more popular and necessary following recoinage of the late 1690s, when notes of all kinds became effective "money-substitutes." In London, monetary experiments took the form of promissory notes, bank notes, and other forms of paper credit.[74] The

---

[72] Adam Shortt, ed., *Documents Relating to Canadian Currency, Exchange and Finance during the French Period* (1925) 1:75, cited by Lester, *Monetary Experiments*, 36–41.

[73] I am following the definition provided by Craig in *Mint*, xiv. It was not until the nineteenth century that paper money became accepted as reliable, "inconvertible" money. Einzig, *Primitive Money*, 312.

[74] Horsefield, *British Monetary Experiments*, 15–6.

number of forms of credit money was increasing, along with a wider understanding of the fungible nature of investments; hence, the popular fascination with insurance policies, stocks, and 'tickets' of all kinds. At the same time, on the peripheries, commodities continued to take the place of more formal (i.e., institutionally produced) forms of money well into the eighteenth century. Leather money persisted in the Isle of Man, while Scottish villagers used iron nails as money in the eighteenth century. As Einzig points out, "[s]mall and remote communities possessing little money are apt to revert to the use of produce for monetary purposes."[75]

From the point of view of the English treasury, currency in the colonies verged on chaos, but the perspective from below was simply practical. No one currency fulfilled all the functions of money as we know it, but eighteenth-century people were accustomed to having to master different monetary media, each with its requisite techniques of exchange. Using money schooled people in more than just the art of making payments; individuals became adept at translating from one unit of account to another, and reckoning from different standards of value. Sometimes they were forced to compare the value of one commodity to that of another or to relative amounts of silver or paper money. They also learned to approach the act of exchange with an eye to both the past and future values of certain items, understanding that in some cases, the "store of wealth" represented by money might change over time.[76] Finally, and most contradictorily, they were forced to reserve a certain degree of flexibility in their financial dealings, remaining prepared to offer or accept commodities they would then have to pass on to someone else before attaining satisfaction. Over time, colonial governments worked toward establishing stable, institutionalized currencies, but as long as trade continued across borders, states were forced to handle primitive money alongside more conventional forms.[77] The situation bred a hybrid mentality, along with an apparent lack of deference toward centralized authority and its solutions to the problem of currency.

---

[75] Ibid., 287; Adam Smith, "Of the Origin and Use of Money," *An Inquiry into the Nature and Causes of the Wealth of Nations*, ed. Edwin Cannan (Chicago, 1976), 1:27.

[76] To a surprising degree, eighteenth-century people were familiar with the idea of price indices. See John J. McCusker, *How Much Is That In Real Money? A Historical Commodity Price Index for Use as a Deflator of Money Values in the Economy of the United States*, 2nd ed. (Worcester, MA, 2001), 18–19.

[77] Galbraith, *Money*, 57.

A chronic shortage of coin cannot explain every aspect of the history of money, but the implications of its scarcity extended in every direction within early modern society. As Craig Muldrew has observed, "money caused much economic dyspepsia in early modern England," aggravated by the makeshift means by which ordinary people responded to the shortage of coin.[78] Though credit sustained many exchanges, commerce between strangers and across long distances demanded greater flexibility and more immediate solutions. The variability exhibited by all of these social relations of exchange was a small indication of a larger fact: monetary systems rested on complex conceptual thinking, and the liberties of early modern usages sprang from particular assumptions about the nature of money itself. These early modern ideas about money will be the subject of the next chapter.

[78] Muldrew, "'Hard Food for Midas'," 118.

CHAPTER 2

The Phantasm of Money: The Animation of Exchange Media in England, ca. 1600–1770

Coins bear a special affinity to people, not least, because they usually display the image of a head or body, a characteristic that has passed into linguistic understandings of money as the "face" side of coins. "Heads" often represent the authority of the state through their identification with a monarch or political symbol, coupled with incontrovertible wisdom, such as ancient tags or political mottoes. These features lend coins their legitimacy, but more than that, in modern contexts, they aim to forge a connection between their bearer and governing institutions. In contemporary times, this is what makes money "real" and enables it to pass as money between strangers and over geographical distances.

But numerous examples across cultures and historical eras show that sometimes all that is needed for money to pass as money is a set of properties that makes its form countable and therefore useful in "tale" or tallying – hence, the opposite side of the coin. Its features might also include its handiness and portability. In the case of cowrie shells, for example, their uniform size and tiny almond shape endowed them with perfect countability, and their local status as precious commodities contributed to their acceptance as currency. Their history as a money form suggests that "tradition attaches a symbolic meaning to certain objects so that they are merely counted out in payment."[1] Particular articles of consumption also served as currency, such as eighteenth-century

---

[1] As Paul Einzig explains at considerable length, few objects were ever passed solely by tale. Distinctions between cowrie shells meant that they sometimes functioned as "popular media of barter" and sometimes as "limited currencies," but seldom as simply "a unit of account." Paul Einzig, *Primitive Money in Its Ethnological, Historical and Economic Aspects*, 2nd ed. (Oxford, 1966), 80, 315ff.

beaver pelts and tobacco in the American colonies.[2] The fact that objects like cattle and corn were weighed or measured instead of being counted technically disqualifies them as tale, but nevertheless, according to a more liberal theory of primitive money, an object may be regarded as such if it achieves a degree of sameness among units and if a community establishes a commonly agreed practice of using the units to both accept and pay out amounts.[3] In these cases, then, value is determined by popular consensus rather than the classical, generic measures determined by institutional dicta. As a result, such forms of money tend to draw on irregular styles of representation displaying peculiarly local qualities – hence, their stigmatization as primitive currencies by modernizing institutions.

The distinction between powerful "heads" and locally styled "tales" prompted anthropologist Keith Hart to point to a persistent oscillation between two powerful poles governing the life of money and representing the limits set by authority and the forces acting upon the process of exchange:

> One side reminds us that states underwrite currencies and that money is originally a relation between persons in society, a token perhaps. The other reveals the coin as a thing, capable of entering into definite relations with other things, as a quantitative ratio independent of the persons engaged in any particular transaction. In this latter respect money is like a commodity and its logic is that of anonymous markets. Heads and tails [*sic*] stand for social organisation from the *top* down and from the *bottom* up, epitomised in modern theory by the state and the market respectively.[4]

The dualism of state power and market forces, though unassailable from the vantage point of a modern coin, is in fact a relatively recent construction, dating from the eighteenth century with the growth of state bureaucracies designed to raise money for purposes of civic administration and warfare and enlightenment debate over the boundaries of economic life. Modern monetization struggled into existence in the

---

[2] Technically, these items did not function as money in the sense of counters but rather as commodities of value; therefore, they should be described as "commodity-money." Einzig, *Primitive Money*, 315–16.

[3] Einzig's definition of primitive money is as follows: "a unit or an object conforming to a reasonable degree to some standard of uniformity, which is employed for reckoning or for making a large proportion of the payments customary in the community concerned, and which is accepted in payment largely with the intention of employing it for making payments." *Primitive Money*, 317.

[4] Hart, "Heads or Tails? Two Sides of The Coin," *Man*, new ser., 21 (December 1986): 638.

wake of these developments, and not without difficulties. The insistence of states on a universalizing system of coinage ran contrary to economic life defined in its broadest sense. Eighteenth-century observers understood this fact: as Turgot aptly described it, economic activity comprised a "multitude of obscure facts" and a "mass of unknown causes," momentarily condensed into "prices of things bought and sold." The variability of coins in the past can help us to recognize that modern money imposes a selective order over a wide variety of interactions, many of which are inherent in exchange relations and evident in historical accounts drawn from the seventeenth and eighteenth centuries.[5]

The extraordinary variety of primitive money worldwide testifies to the determination and ingenuity applied to fashioning exchange media. This element of variability must be understood as an important aspect of the money form itself. As Paul Einzig's pioneering work argued, the search for simple monetary systems "should be conceived not as a mere study of the function of economic factors" working toward a definitive end, because money was not simply an expedient arrived at "when barter became too inconvenient." Over millennia, money was employed for purposes other than trade, depending on where and when it was devised. Einzig included in his study a consideration of the ceremonial and social aspects of monetary uses, arguing for its role as a standard of value and against the theory that money evolved first as a medium of exchange. Einzig's case ultimately rested on the connection between money and the dynamic human element involved in its use. Money, he argued, "is not a mere lifeless object, but a social institution. Without its background it has as little meaning as a verb divorced from its context."[6]

The late seventeenth and early eighteenth centuries offered a fertile breeding ground for the social life of money.[7] Animate thinking sprang up in the interstices of exchange using established money, such as it

---

[5] Eric Helleiner, *The Making of National Money: Territorial Currencies in Historical Perspective* (Ithaca, 2003), dates territorial currencies in Europe from the nineteenth century. Turgot quoted in Emma Rothschild, *Economic Sentiments: Adam Smith, Condorcet, and the Enlightenment* (Cambridge, MA, 2001), 236. Rothschild calls economic life "unpromising territory for the spirit of system" (236).

[6] *Primitive Money*, 15.

[7] For a related argument concerning the homologies between money, coins and character, see Deidre S. Lynch, "Person Effects and Sentimental Fictions," *Eighteenth-Century Fiction* 12 (January–April 2000): 345–68, as well as her discussion of money generally in *The Economy of Character: Novels, Market Culture, and the Business of Inner Meaning* (Chicago, 1998). See also Catherine Gallagher, *Nobody's Story: The Vanishing Acts of Women Writers in*

was, and provided a constant countervailing set of images in the face of universalizing trends in the diffusion of money. As the previous chapter demonstrated, contention mounted over the "heads" of coins as the English Crown strove to claim authority over methods used to determine monetary value. Such struggles occurred within an atmosphere of enthusiasm for experimentation in finance at home, which at times succeeded in turning a sense of heads and tales into complete disarray.[8] Joined to these developments was a sense of popular liberty in determining "tales" across a wide map of English and colonial places as commerce carved out new arenas for migration, trade, and occupation. Writers on the subject of money also contributed to the formation of a spirited sense of money by melding concepts of the natural world with those of exchange. Borrowing from seventeenth-century natural philosophy, which was engaged in the study of circulation of blood within organisms, early political economists formulated analogous organic theories about money. Through the confluence of three sources – formal theoretical discussion in texts of political economy, vernacular references in proverbial wisdom and everyday speech, and print culture – early modern people developed a cogent sense of the vitality of money.

METAPHORICAL LANGUAGE AND THE ATTRIBUTES OF MONEY

Discussion about the animate nature of money reaches back to Aristotle, who assigned money only one natural use, as a medium of exchange. To employ money through lending in order to accumulate more money suggested a regenerative power, which Aristotle and the medieval Scholastics condemned as illicit. "[U]sury," argued Aristotle, "means the birth of money from money, [and] is applied to the breeding of money, because the offspring resembles the parent. Wherefore of all modes of making money this is the most unnatural."[9] Money had only one truly

---

the *Marketplace, 1670–1820* (Berkeley, 1994); James Thompson, *Models of Value: Eighteenth-Century Political Economy and the Novel* (Durham, 1996).

[8] On the enthusiasm for experimentation, see Geoffrey Clark, *Betting on Lives: The Culture of Life Insurance in England, 1695–1775* (Manchester, 1999); Richard Dale, *The First Crash: Lessons from the South Sea Bubble* (Princeton, 2004).

[9] The translation is by Jowett, from *Politics*, I, iii, 1258b, as cited in Prof. E. Cannan, W. D. Ross, Dr. J. Bonar, and Dr. P. H. Wicksteed, "Who Said 'Barren Metal'? A Symposium," *Economica*, no. 5 (June 1922): 105–11. A pun was involved in this debate, which those who knew Greek tacitly understood: Aristotle used the word for "offspring," *tokos*, as the term for interest for money.

natural use, as a medium of exchange, which accorded with its inert substance. Thomas Aquinas seconded Aristotle's belief in the wrongfulness of lending for profit, arguing that "a kind of birth takes place when money grows from [other] money."[10] The association with wonton sexual regeneration underscored the prohibited nature of lending at interest.[11]

Pursuing the question of the sterility of money, medieval theologians distinguished an acceptable category of lending through the concept of *capitale*, which Peter Olivi described as having "a certain seminal quality of generating profit." While the saying *pecunia non parit* – money does not beget money – was a "cliché" and "an *idée fixe* among the Schoolmen," countercurrents of thought were established upon the notion that the ownership of money could claim rights to recompense, given the fact that money as capital, in the words of Olivi, could be "put to work for a certain probable gain."[12] Money produced wealth by laboring rather than giving birth, a shift in definition that achieved distance from the unnatural act of lending, tainted by suggestive association with female reproduction, by orienting its meaning toward more wholesome activity. Thus, the debate over usury spawned another way of infusing the notion of money with life, through the morally positive valence of work.[13]

In the late sixteenth century, Shakespeare crystallized for posterity a remnant of medieval debate in *The Merchant of Venice*. Antonio's quarrel with Shylock, the rapacious moneylender, soon became more commonly understood than the doctrine of usury itself:

> If thou wilt lend this money, lend it not
> As to thy *friends*, – for when did *friendship* take
> A breed for barren metal of his friend?[14]

---

[10] *Unde fit quidam partus cum denarius ex denario crescit.* Saint Thomas of Aquinas, *Sententia Libri Politicorum* in *Corpus Thomisticum Sancti Thomae de Aquino*, ed. Roberto Busa (Rome, 1971), lib. 1, Lectio 8, n. 13.

[11] Jacob Viner pointed out the parallels between this debate and Catholic controversy over birth control. "The Economic Doctrines of the Scholastics," reprinted in *History of Political Economy* 10, no. 1 (Spring 1978): 91–2n.

[12] Julius Kirshner, "Raymond de Roover on Scholastic Economic Thought," in *Business, Banking, and Economic Thought in Late Medieval and Early Modern Europe: Selected Studies of Raymond de Roover*, ed. Julius Kirshner (Chicago, 1974), 28–9; in this same volume, see also "Scholastic Economics: Survival and Lasting Influence from the Sixteenth Century to Adam Smith," 306–31.

[13] On usury and theories of money, see Joel Kaye, *Economy and Nature in the Fourteenth Century: Money, Market Exchange, and the Emergence of Scientific Thought* (Cambridge, 1998), esp. Chap. 4.

[14] 1.3, 128–30.

Scholarly commentary, alongside popular parlance, absorbed the phrase "barren metal" in discussions of interest on loans and the sterility of money. In fact, the advance of modernizing attitudes toward interest can be measured by tracking the rise of disdainful references to the concept implied by the phrase. A suspicion of linguistic manipulation fueled resistance to the idea of the power of money to reproduce. Jeremy Bentham finally expressed dismissiveness, noting that Aristotle "had never been able to discover, in any one piece of money, any organs for generating any other piece." His comment also indicated just how far an acceptance of interest had come.[15]

Given the obfuscation generated by this and similar semantic arguments in the early modern period, historians of economic thought have been slow to explore the common practice of assigning attributes of life to money in the language of political economy. Only recently (and often grudgingly), modern economists have recognized that animate attributes, imported through figures of speech, might play a formative role in their profession. Deirdre N. McCloskey's deft polemic, *The Rhetoric of Economics*, demystified the explanatory methods of economics by pointing up the ways in which economic arguments often rest on rhetorical and literary devices. Though the field of economics makes claims to strict factual bases and exacting methods, "economic speech" depended on figures of speech that are subjective and, some would say, deceptive, such as metaphor, metonymy, synecdoche, and irony. Because disciplinary boundaries over several centuries have worked to segregate the field in the area of "science," economic writings usually escape the kind of literary examination that might expose inconsistencies in its language. McCloskey demonstrated the usefulness of such an endeavor for breaking down resistances to a broader search for knowledge in the field of economics.[16]

Historians of economic thought have since taken McCloskey's call for textual analysis to the discourses of the past, where the use of natural metaphors in early economic tracts is strikingly evident.[17] The obstacles to recovering "the heritage of thought banished by the heirs of Schumpeter," however, are considerable. "Economics, née political economy,

---

[15] Bentham quoted in Cannan, "Who Said 'Barren Metal'?" 105–6.

[16] Deirdre N. McCloskey, *The Rhetoric of Economics*, 2nd ed. (Madison, 1998), Chap. 5, "Figures of Economic Speech," 69–86, esp. 83–6; for the social character of scientific knowledge, Chap. 8, esp. 150–3.

[17] See, for example, Andrea Finkelstein, *Harmony and the Balance: An Intellectual History of Seventeenth-Century English Economic Thought* (Ann Arbor, 2000).

née moral philosophy, has been a prime locus of the hashing out of definitions of both the Natural and the Social in Western culture," Philip Mirowski observed, but the insistence on "scientific method" by generations of economists has rendered "much of the interesting historical content" invisible.[18] Like any other discipline, economics is constructed by people whose interests and means of expression are bound by what they already know and believe. If economic language is, in fact, a composite of metaphors and other signs, rather than a transparent set of mathematical and scientific terms, then economics must recognize the "social character" of its knowledge base.[19]

Employing the insights of literary critics, Arjo Klamer and Thomas C. Leonard have contended that in economics, as in any branch of knowledge, metaphors do the work of cognition. "Metaphors are markers that orient the discovering wanderer," and while their place in economics "requires a developed theory of semantics and epistemology," it is nevertheless possible to construct basic insights into economic thinking from what we know about the general use of metaphor.[20] This feature constitutes the stuff of mental life in general: we can't get rid of metaphors even if we wanted to, because we simply cannot think without them.[21] This was Nietzsche's position in a famous passage from his notebooks. "Truth," he insisted, is a

> movable host of metaphors, metonymies, and anthropomorphisms: in short, a sum of human relations which have been poetically and rhetorically intensified, transferred, and embellished, and which, after long usage, seem to a people to be fixed, canonical and binding. Truths are illusions which we have forgotten are illusions; they are metaphors that have become worn out and have been drained of sensuous force, coins which have lost their embossing and are now considered as metal and no longer coins.[22]

Nietzsche's call for a kind of epistemological humility in the face of a fundamentally unknowable universe made metaphors a sign of our

---

[18] "Doing What Comes Naturally," in *Natural Images in Economic Thought: 'Markets Read in Tooth and Claw'*, ed. Philip Mirowski (Cambridge, 1994), 6.

[19] Ibid., 7–17."   [20] "So What's an Economic Metaphor?" in Mirowski, ibid., 27.

[21] Arjo Klamer and Thomas C. Leonard, "So What's an Economic Metaphor?" in Mirowski, ibid., 26.

[22] Friedrich Nietzsche, *Philosophy and Truth: Selections from Nietzsche's Notebooks of the Early 1870s*, ed. Daniel Breazeale (Atlantic Highlands, 1979), 84–9. The passage is also analyzed in Marc Shell, *Money, Language and Thought: Literary and Philosophical Economies from the Medieval to the Modern Era* (Berkeley, 1982), 50–5.

lack of comprehension. Not knowing what reality really *is*, we settle for what things are *like*. Is it mere coincidence that he resorted to coins in order to explain how metaphors worked? Evidence in the history of thought about money suggests that coins have presented an ideal instrument of cognition for the same reasons that they work as a money form – because of their handiness and ubiquity, their transferability, their power of association, and, not least, their abstract, symbolic character. With their "heads" and "tales" rubbed away, they become tools, vehicles, or better yet, blank slates for endless imaginative activity.[23]

Recent economic theory employing semiotics suggests that money indeed creates its own universe of knowledge. Reversing the argument that metaphor helps us understand the operations of money, semiotic theory argues that money as a medium of exchange operates as a semiotic system and thus determines how we understand the world: money itself creates meaning within a bounded system of signs and symbols circulating through language, social relationships, and other forms of communication. As Carl Wennerlind has pointed out, "There are profound similarities between linguistic discourse and monetary exchanges," with analogous potential and limitations for structuring thought and action.[24] In theoretical terms set out by Jean-Joseph Goux, money makes visible a "structural logic of . . . the general equivalent . . . where values are no longer economic, where the play of substitutions defines qualitative values."[25] Alan Dyer applied semiotic theory to an analysis of a broad "pecuniary culture," seeing money as "the key symbol of life" within a particular form of capitalist universe. Following Marx in identifying money as a mediating force in society, Dyer criticized economists for failing to pursue the complex transformation of reality into symbols wrought by money.[26]

Demystifying this process through semiotic analysis "may make us aware of the hidden codes in our representation of social life and reveal previously veiled or obfuscated power relations," Wennerlind

---

[23] Given this psychological element involved in monetary relations, Simmel argued that money served as a vehicle for freedom, particularly as it promised "unconditional interchangeability" that permitted the transformation of economic life into a "plurality of values." Georg Simmel, *The Philosophy of Money*, trans. Tom Bottomore and David Frisby (Boston, 1978), 427–8.

[24] Carl Wennerlind, "Money Talks, but What Is It Saying? Semiotics of Money and Social Control," *Journal of Economic Issues* 35, no. 3 (September 2001): 559.

[25] *Symbolic Economies: After Marx and Freud* (Ithaca, 1990), 3–4.

[26] Alan W. Dyer, "Making Semiotic Sense of Money as a Medium of Exchange," *Journal of Economic Issues* 23, no. 2 (June 1989): 503.

suggested, and his research on the death penalty in eighteenth-century England bears this out.[27] The power of money may extend as far as measuring and valuing human life, so much so that the commodification of people appears natural and unquestionable. According to Marx, the medium of money knows no bounds; driven by human desire, it extends its powers of measurement and persuasion to everything within its reach. Human life itself is pulled into the vortex of monetary signification because money possesses the capability of procuring all things.[28] Because we accept the conceptual framework and terms of the symbolic system of money, the commodification of people and nature proceeds from the constant "re-presenting of objects and experiences as comparable containers of exchange value."[29] In order to transcend such forceful influences, we must aim to produce "a radical rupture of the complete symbolic system in which money was initially given its meaning."[30]

It is no coincidence that the effort to pin down a precise, state-authorized meaning of money coincided with an increasing alertness to the contest among competing semantic distinctions of words in the late seventeenth century. John Locke was deeply involved in both epistemological enterprises, as Constantine George Caffentzis has demonstrated; and as both philosopher and statesman, Locke was opposed to handing over the power to determine the meaning of both money and words to a free play of social forces. Against Cambridge Platonists on the one hand and lawyers and polemicists on the other, Locke refused to see ideas and words as independent entities enjoying lives of their own; instead, he argued for making words authoritative and precise.[31] Like Hobbes, he decried the use of "figures" of rhetoric such as metaphor, preferring to "speak of Things as they are" rather than employing such language to "move the Passions, and thereby mislead the Judgement" of audiences. He compared the arts of eloquence to those of "the fair Sex," against which few argued, he lamented, because most men "find pleasure to be Deceived." Despite his efforts to circumscribe the power

---

[27] "Money Talks," 559; "The Death Penalty as Monetary Policy: The Practice and Punishment of Monetary Crime, 1690–1830," *History of Political Economy* 36, no. 1 (2004): 131–61.

[28] Karl Marx, "The Power of Money in Bourgeois Society," in *Economic and Philosophic Manuscripts of 1844*, reprinted in Robert C. Tucker, ed., *The Marx-Engels Reader*, 2nd ed. (New York, 1978), 101–2.

[29] Dyer, "Making Semiotic Sense," 505; Wennerlind, "Money Talks," 564.

[30] Wennerlind, "Money Talks," 565.

[31] Constantine George Caffentzis, *Clipped Coins, Abused Words and Civil Government: John Locke's Philosophy of Money* (New York, 1989), esp. 110–14.

of unauthorized words by tarring them with female coloration, the subtle democratic pressure of language triumphed over his exclusionary
efforts. The fact that Locke resorted to simile to denounce rhetoric was
proof that even the avowed empiricist found it difficult to free himself
from the metaphorical conventions of his era. As a later chapter will
argue, the gendered identities inserted into his argument also informed
much of the thought about money offered by Locke's contemporaries.[32]

Locke was similarly incapable of abstaining from figures of rhetoric
when discussing the workings of money. Maintaining a rigid stance in
matters of coinage, he advocated adherence to a strict standard of intrinsic value and insisted that the stamp on a coin give a clear indication of
its actual weight in silver. Clarity, in this case, was a sign of allegiance
to the new principles of government and the new science, a badge of
dominion over the known world. Yet money exercised another kind
of authority, which it derived from its possessor, leading Locke into a
problematic analogy. His explanation of the source of money's power
to yield interest through loans depended on a comparison between the
possessor of much money to a landowner with more property than he
can use. "[W]hy then," he asked, does the borrower "pay *Use*?"

> For the same Reason, and upon as good Consideration, as the Tenant pays
> Rent for your Land. For as the unequal Distribution of Land, (you having
> more than you can or will manure, and another less) brings you a Tenant for
> your Land; and the same unequal Distribution of Money, (I having more
> than I can or will employ, and another less) brings me a Tenant for my
> Money.[33]

Locke presented the case for money as counterintuitive, noting that
"Land produces naturally something new and profitable, and of Value
to Mankind," whereas "Money is a barren thing, and produces nothing."

---

[32] John Locke, "Of the Abuse of Words," in *An Essay Concerning Human Understanding*
(1689; London, 1997), 452; Klamer and Leonard, "So What's an Economic Metaphor?"
24–5. Klamer and Leonard note the "delicious irony" in Lock's condemnation of
metaphor (25). For discussion of Locke and semantics, see N. Kretzman, "The Main
Thesis of Locke's Semantic Theory," in *Locke on Human Understanding: Selected Essays*,
ed. I. C. Tipton (Oxford, 1977), 123–40. For Hobbes's views on metaphor, see Thomas
Hobbes, "Abuses of Speech," in *Leviathan*, ed. C. B. Macpherson (Harmondsworth,
1968), 102.

[33] "Some Considerations of the Consequences of the Lowering of Interest, and Raising
the Value of Money," 2nd ed. (corrected, 1696), in *Locke on Money*, 2 vols., ed. Patrick
Hyde Kelly (Oxford, 1991), 1:250.

He continued his analogy when he explained the reasoning behind rates of interest compared with rent:

> Because of the many, and sometimes long intervals of Barrenness, which happen to Money, more than Land. Money at *Use*, when return'd into the Hands of the Owner, usually lies dead there, till he gets a new Tenant for it, and can put it out again; and all this time it produces nothing.[34]

In order to remain consistent, Locke might have preferred to corroborate Aquinas's sense of money as a medium without life; in spite of that, he echoed Olivi by describing a notion of money as working capital, which earns payment because of the activity in which it engages. In another instance, Locke reached for a nutritional analogy similar to those used earlier by William Petty and Thomas Hobbes: "For Money being an universal Commodity, and as necessary to Trade, as Food is to Life, every body must have it, at what Rate they can get it." If money was not literally alive, it was nevertheless capable of imparting life in the way that soil or foodstuffs might feed human beings.[35]

Money inspired similar metaphorical language in works of political economy throughout our period, originating in the earliest writings from the seventeenth century. In explaining the relationship between the amount of money in circulation and the condition of trade, Rice Vaughan's *Discourse of Coin and Coinage*, written some forty years before its publication in 1675, suggested that "the good government of the course of money may breed plenty of money, and plenty of money doth help to increase manufactures."[36] Circulation itself inspired repeated attribution of "life" and "deadness" to money. In the later part of the century, Charles Davenant noted that "money in the chest is but a barren treasure" and therefore should be encouraged to circulate.[37] And in the 1730s, Berkeley was persistent in his use of the trope of money "lying dead" when not circulating – Vickers cites five examples from his *Querist* (1735–7), including the proposition "Whether money circulating be not

---

[34] Ibid., 283.

[35] Ibid., 214, 250. After an extended discussion of the analogy of interest and rent, Locke points out that "to receive Profit for the Loan of Money, is as equitable and lawful, as receiving Rent for Land, and more tolerable to the Borrower, notwithstanding the Opinion of some over-scrupulous Men" (251).

[36] Vaughan, *A Discourse of Coin and Coinage* (London, 1675), in *Old and Scarce Tracts on Money*, ed. J. R. McCulloch (London, 1933), 37.

[37] *Political and Commercial Works of . . . Charles D'avenant*, 5 vols., ed. Charles Whitworth (London, 1771), 1:448, 160, cited in Douglas Vickers, *Studies in the Theory of Money 1690–1776* (Philadelphia, 1959), 54n.

the life of industry; and whether the want thereof doth not render a state gouty and inactive?"[38] As the science of political economy defined itself during these years, it claimed the subject of money as a central problem in its own right, laden with attributes, many of which were imbued with life.[39]

Investigating economic metaphors in an early modern context means looking at prevailing themes in political economy as they relate to ideas about money in the larger context of contemporary print culture. When writers required frameworks and language for positing how production and exchange operated in the late seventeenth century, they reached for the triumphant models of their era, namely, those offered by natural philosophy.[40] As the formal discipline of economics came into being, theorists drew heavily from the science of physiology. Analogies between the natural world and the wonders of economic production and distribution made sense. "Nature, like the economy, was produced by the self-activity of living organisms," Paul Christensen argued, and both realms "depended on the extraction and transformation of nutritive and other materials from the earth, which were circulated and consumed."[41] Men with training in medicine wrote extensively on the subject of economic life during this period: Hobbes authored a work on optics, William Petty was a professor of anatomy (as well as music), John Locke and Nicholas Barbon trained as physicians, and, in a slightly later period, Francois Quesnay was a practicing physician to the court of Louis XV. Their use of metaphors of generation and circulation, as part of mechanistic philosophies, joined theories about the workings of the human body to understandings of economic activity.[42]

Writers on political economy engaged the available vocabularies of natural philosophy and medical science in order to convey the most important aspects of the economic life they observed: motion and circulation. William Harvey's discoveries concerning circulation of the blood

---

[38] Vickers, *Theory of Money*, 150.

[39] Ibid., 6. Vickers argued that the quest to understand money was aimed in particular at "considerations of functional efficacy" during this time.

[40] The literature on this subject is considerable: see R. G. Frank, *Harvey and the Oxford Physiologists* (Berkeley, 1980); Elizabeth Fox-Genovese, *The Origins of Physiocracy* (Ithaca, 1976); J. Lyon and P. R. Sloan, *From Natural History to the History of Nature* (Notre Dame, 1981); Finkelstein, *Harmony*.

[41] Paul P. Christensen, "Fire, Motion, and Productivity: The Proto-Energetics of Nature and Economy in Francois Quesnay," in *Natural Images in Economic Thought*, ed. Philip Mirowski (Cambridge, 1994), 249.

[42] Finkelstein, *Harmony*, 104–5.

exercised considerable influence on Hobbes, whose discussion of trade in Chapter 24 of *Leviathan* provides an often overlooked example of early ideas of political economy. In order to explain the workings of money, Hobbes constructed his theory from a creative synthesis of classical and cutting-edge theories of physiology, joining a "nutritional emphasis" to the more current ideas of Harvey.[43] As "a sufficient measure of the value of all things else," money was made to represent "all commodities, Moveable and Immoveable" in a society in which people regularly traveled from place to place:

> [A]nd the same passeth from Man to Man, within the Common-wealth; and goes round about, Nourishing (as it passeth) every part thereof; In so much as this Concoction, is as it were the Sanguification of the Common-wealth: For naturall Bloud is in like manner made of the fruits of the Earth; and circulating, nourisheth, by the way, every Member of the Body of Man.[44]

The twofold activity of money, flowing and feeding the Commonwealth, depended on the action of migrating individuals and goods moving across distances within a bounded universe.[45] Hobbes described each process in terms of physiology, beginning with the title of his chapter ("Nutrition, and Procreation") and including a digestive process that he called "Concoction." The latter was not precisely a change of substance, but more a condensation, because commodities were reduced to the value of gold and silver, the "commodious measure of the value of all things else between Nations." And so the process could continue, because money was "withall so portable, as not to hinder the motion of men from place to place; to the end a man may have in what place soever, such Nourishment as the place affordeth."[46] Given permission from a watchful sovereign protecting the interests of the nation, money made movement within an established colonial universe not only possible but resourceful.

Hobbes's blend of naturalism and Renaissance science, bearing a uniquely heterodox mix of social and gender hierarchies, demonstrated

---

[43] Paul P. Christensen, "Hobbes and the Physiological Origins of Economic Science," *History of Political Economy* 21, no. 4 (1989): 689–709. Christensen calls this a "'provisioning' approach to economics" (690).

[44] *Leviathan*, ed. C. B. Macpherson (Harmondsworth, 1972), 300.

[45] See also ibid., 295, 299 on trade. Hobbes's consideration of the role of human labor may have played a significant part in his incompletely explicated theory of value, because his analysis seems to "point towards the classical production approach to exchange values." Christensen, "Hobbes and Physiological Origins," 707.

[46] *Leviathan*, 300.

the epistemological confusion of the mid-seventeenth century.[47] As Timothy L. Alborn has explained in examining economic discourses over time, "Different appeals to circulatory images informed several competing economic discourses including physiocracy, mercantilism, Smith's logic of free trade, and Malthusian agrarianism."[48] For Hobbes, circulation existed within a confined circuitry overseen by a sovereign king, but the ideologies informing life within this realm coexisted in peculiar dissonance. Steering clear of the apparatus of theology, Hobbes combined descriptive elements of a patriarchal order with features drawn from naturalist and economic discourses. He referred to land and sea as "the two breasts of our common Mother," the source of commodities that God, alternating between beneficence and a rather mercenary good will, "usually either freely giveth, or for labour selleth to man-kind."[49] While nature was inscribed as female and thereby made productive, the Commonwealth was a fusion of both genders. The "Procreation" of his argument referred to "Children of a Commonwealth . . . those we call Plantations, or Colonies, which are numbers of men sent out from the Commonwealth, under a Conductor, or Governour, to inhabit a Forraign Country." These individuals departed from "their Metropolis, or Mother," who "requires no more of them, then [sic] Fathers require of the Children, whom they emancipate, and make free from their domestique government . . . or else they remain united."[50] Such vacillation between powerful mothers who procreate and equally powerful fathers who lay down laws characterized Hobbes's approach to the problem of gender and authority, which, like his theories concerning commercial life, distributed active roles to both women and men without resolving the apparent paradoxes.[51]

Other works on political economy likened money to animate bodily processes through a physiological model, modifying the nutritional function of circulation to suit different aspects of the function of money. William Petty acquired formal training in physiology and other branches

---

[47] Christensen, "Hobbes and Physiological Origins," 692–4. The heterodoxy apparent in Hobbes is also discussed from a social perspective by Keith Thomas in "The Social Origins of Hobbes's Political Thought," *Hobbes Studies*, ed. K. C. Brown (Cambridge, MA, 1965), 185–236.

[48] "Economic Man, Economic Machine: Images of Circulation in the Victorian Money Market," in *Natural Images*, 178.

[49] *Leviathan*, 295.   [50] Ibid., 301.

[51] On Hobbes and gender differences, see Susan Moller Okin, *Women in Western Political Thought* (Princeton, 1979), 197–99.

of medical study in Leyden before joining Hobbes in Paris, where the two men studied and worked together on several projects on medical subjects. Like Hobbes, he employed an organic model in his writings on political economy. Petty preferred to call money the

> Fat of the Body-politick, whereof too much doth as often hinder its Agility, as too little makes it sick. 'Tis true, that as Fat lubricates the motion of the Muscles, feeds in want of Victuals, fills up uneven Cavities, and beautifies the Body; so doth Money in the State quicken its Action, feeds from abroad in time of Dearth at home; evens accounts by reason of it's [sic] divisibility, and beautifies the whole, altho more especially the particular persons that have it in plenty.[52]

The implications of Petty's concept of money were the same: money was allied with motion, which proceeded throughout a network of localities; to stop it up would be tantamount to extinguishing the life of the body of the Commonwealth.

The argument likening money to blood achieved two objectives for writers on political economy: it naturalized the movement of money, rendering it inevitable, and, in the context of the larger framework of mercantile theory, it complemented a metaphorical discussion of a healthy body of the state. Contended the author of another pamphlet,

> You often hear of the Circulation of Money as that ought to circulate in a Nation, so ought Bullion to circulate in the World; and our Coin, as long as it keeps a Proportion of Value with it. You may as well expect to keep Life in the Body, by stopping up the Arteries, and leaving the Veins open, and so filling the Heart with Blood, as to keep the Life in Trade, by leaving those Ports open at which Bullion enters, and stopping up those at which it goes out. As the Blood by running preserves Life in the Body, and conveys a proper Increase to every Part, though it self be neither; so Bullion, by running about the World, preserves the Life of Trade, and brings Riches where-ever it comes, tho' in itself it be neither. [53]

Assuming that circulation was necessary for the full benefits of trade, writers could then argue that anything less than reciprocal movement compromised the proper functioning of the body of the state. Organic metaphors of circulation offered a flexible means of conceptualizing economic life, allowing for challenges to the excessive regulation posited by

---

[52] *Verbum Sapienti* (1691), 14–15.
[53] [J. Jocelyn], *An Essay on Money and Bullion* (London, 1718), 14.

mercantilist theorists while preserving a sense of the inexorable nature of commercial traffic across the globe.

Daniel Defoe's use of circulatory metaphor stands as a reliable indication of the way in which the concept had penetrated discourses of economic life and print culture at large by the early decades of the eighteenth century. [54] When describing the conveyance of commercial goods across space, Defoe mapped the center and peripheries of trade across a physical body of the English nation. "The circulation of trade within ourselves, where all the several manufactures move in a just rotation from the several countries where they are made, to the city of London, as the blood in the body to the Heart; and from thence are dispers'd again, as the nature of the demand directs, to all the several parts of the Kingdom." Such movement gave the nation its distinctive commercial framework that made it uniquely prosperous. Indicative of his keen awareness of contemporary means of financing trade, Defoe pointed to credit as another important feature of commercial circulation, which he nevertheless believed presented a major peril to small tradesmen. His views on money as specie were similarly conservative and led him to argue against its "being carried abroad." One of the virtues of the circulatory model was its suitability as a comprehensible vehicle for debate over the extent to which trade should flow freely or under the supervision of the state.[55]

Joining contemporary debate over the virtue of precious metals, Hume also utilized circulatory language in trying to explain the impact of an increase in gold and silver in Europe. "[I]n every kingdom, into which money begins to flow in greater abundance than formerly, every thing takes a new face: labour and industry gain life; the merchant becomes more enterprising, the manufacturer more diligent and skilful, and even the farmer follows his plough with greater alacrity and attention," he pointed out. The energizing effects of money, if not labeled as blood, implied the same restorative function. Hume also employed a nutritional metaphor linked to circulation when he argued that the even distribution of money mattered more than its precise quantity. What mattered was the extent to which a nation engaged in some form of activity, thus generating ways of employing money profitably. "[I]ndustry

---

[54] John Law used organic metaphors when describing both money and credit: "Money is the blood of the State and must circulate. Credit is to business what the brain is to the human body." Quoted in F. C. Green, *Eighteenth-Century France: Six Essays* (New York, 1931), 7.

[55] Daniel Defoe, *The Complete English Tradesman*, 2nd ed. (London, 1727), viii–ix, xiii–xiv.

and refinements of all kinds incorporate [money] with the whole state, however small its quantity may be; they digest it into every vein, so to speak, and make it enter into every transaction and contract." Such wide distribution offered advantages to a sovereign, who could thereby "draw money by his taxes from every part of the state."[56] The circulation of money supported Hume's larger vision of a vibrant commercial state, which throbbed with beneficial enjoyments made possible by the successful enterprises of the merchant and farmer.

References to living attributes and organic behavior insistently recurred in discussions of money in the late seventeenth and eighteenth centuries as early writers of political economic tracts limned methods with which they assessed economic life. Whether through metaphors of circulation or descriptions of functions within the body of the state, money flowed, moved, and nourished the societies that populated them. Competing arguments over the issue of regulating such circulation can be traced through the eighteenth century and beyond Adam Smith, until mechanistic metaphors challenged circulation as a way to explain optimal methods of producing wealth.[57] It is clear, too, that metaphors of gender were deployed in order to illustrate degrees of power and authority during a century of political turmoil, when such issues were hotly contested. The need to employ animated images as a way of explaining and understanding money suggested a broader context for making sense of theory in political economy. Conjoined with images of money derived from moral teachings and imaginative literature, the "life" of money received reaffirmation outside the jurisdiction of formal theorists. It is this popular vein of wisdom about money to which we now must turn.

MONEY RUNS: PROVERBIAL KNOWLEDGE IN EARLY MODERN PRINT CULTURE

"Money," wrote the French diplomat Scipion de Gramont in 1620, "is the blood and soul of men and he who has none wanders dead among the living." Like his English contemporaries, de Gramont harnessed the rhetorical device of metaphor in illustrating principles of governance. He was also paraphrasing a widely embraced proverb, "He that hath lost

---

[56] David Hume, "Of Money," *Essays Moral, Political and Literary* (London, 1963), 293, 301–2.
[57] Alborn, "Economic Man, Economic Machine," 180–1.

his credit is dead to the world."[58] Writers of seventeenth-century political and economic theory in fact drew many of their figures of speech
from the store of proverbs commonly known throughout the early modern world.[59] The sixteenth and seventeenth centuries "witnessed the
golden age of proverbial expression in European intellectual life," and
the English boasted the regular use of an estimated 12,000 proverbs and
proverbial phrases at this time.[60] Hybrid offspring of different cultures
and eras, proverbs offered contradictory perspectives on everything,
including matters of money and spending. More formal sayings were
derived from classical literature, the Bible, or Shakespeare, while many
more vulgar expressions appeared to be handed down from everyday
experience. An allied form of expression, the maxim, claimed elite status
within scholarly tracts; their definition lay somewhere between formal
doctrine and proverbial speech as they sought to claim the incontrovert-
ibility of one and the wide acceptance of the other. Proverbial expressions communicated a dynamic mixture of oral and written wisdom
that audiences at every social level would have understood. By offering
"rules for reasoning," they served as didactic tools in a wide range of
endeavors.[61]

The striking fact about proverbs related to money is their consistent
use of metaphors of animation. Though it is impossible to generalize for
all proverbs, certain common themes stand out among the many that
deal with money. Early modern Europeans grasped the most obvious
fact that money itself exercised authority, and proverbial wisdom helped
them conceptualize the forms that it took. "Money is a monarch" or

---

[58] *Le Denier Royal* (1620), 9, cited in Fernand Braudel, *The Structures of Everyday Life: The Limits of the Possible*, trans. Sian Reynolds (New York, 1981), 478; George Herbert, Outlandish Proverbs (London, 1651), 334. For the correspondence between legal knowledge and proverbial sayings, see Donald F. Bond, "English Legal Proverbs," *Publications of the Modern Language Association* 51 (December 1936): 921–35.

[59] J. A. W. Gunn, "'Interest will not lie': A Seventeenth-Century Political Maxim," *Journal of the History of Ideas* 29 (1968): 551.

[60] Adam Fox, *Oral and Literate Culture 1500–1700* (Oxford, 2000), 112–13. Fox argues that proverbs were "[o]f central importance to the modes of thought and expression which epitomize England in the sixteenth and seventeenth centuries" (112). For a definitive overview, see James Obelkevich, "Proverbs and Social History," in *The Social History of Language*, ed. by Peter Burke and Roy Porter (Cambridge, 1987), 43–72. I am grateful to him for his advice on this subject.

[61] Paul D. Goodwin and Joseph W. Wenzel, "Proverbs and Practical Reasoning: A Study in Socio-logic," in *The Wisdom of Many: Essays on the Proverb*, ed. Wolfgang Mieder and Alan Dundes (New York, 1981), 142; for an important treatment of gender in proverbs, see Mineke Schipper, *Never Marry a Woman with Big Feet: Women in Proverbs from Around the World* (New Haven, 2003).

(more cynically) "Money is the only Monarch" magnified the potential of money to dominate in human affairs. That proverbial wisdom conceived of money as preempting actual monarchs lent a machiavellian note to the otherwise familiar tone of advice resident in the saying. More often, proverbial speech chose the master/servant relationship as an accurate representation of the effect of money on social relations. Thus, what might have seemed like absolute dominion lodged in a political metaphor became recast in a way that made power more widely available. According to one early modern rendering, "Money makes masteries" promised wide accessibility. Other forms depicted a continuum of relationships: "Make mony thy friend, thy seruant, and companion, and not thy master," "Money does either serve as a slave or command as a master," and in its cautionary form, "If Money be not thy Servant, it will be thy Master."[62] Such observations captured the important dynamic within monetary relations: the dyadic relationship between subject and object, which Georg Simmel characterized as typical of monetary relations in general.[63]

Popular regard for the magic of money – what Karl Marx later called its "alchemy" – constituted a second theme played out in proverbial renderings. Everyone seemed to agree that money worked wonders regardless of obstacles and adversaries, and so it possessed agency in ways that implied an animate identity. "If money goes before, all ways lie open," or "Money makes all gates to fly open," suggested its helpfulness in a material sense. Yet more than this, a multiplicity of proverbs celebrated the definitive power of money, including "Money makes marriage," "Money makes the man," and "Money makes the merchant."[64] Contemporaries would have been quick to distinguish the peculiar nature of money's own alchemy from a sense of mastery that people derived from money. Though an individual could harness money to intentions in order to achieve specific objectives, money also worked its power independently of human agency. It was the apparent capacity to

---

[62] Morris Palmer Tilley, *A Dictionary of the Proverbs in England in the Sixteenth and Seventeenth Centuries* (Ann Arbor, 1950), 468. See also Henry G. Bohn, *A Hand-Book of Proverbs Comprising an Entire Republication of Ray's Collection of English Proverbs* (London, 1855); James Howell, *Paroimiographia: Proverbs* (London, 1659).

[63] See his discussion of the objectification of value through economic activity in *Philosophy of Money*, 65–73; see also William M. Reddy's discussion of dyadic relationships with regard to exchange asymmetries: *Money and Liberty in Modern Europe: A Critique of Historical Understanding* (Cambridge, 1987), 71.

[64] G. L. Apperson, *English Proverbs and Proverbial Phrases: An Historical Dictionary* (London and Toronto, 1929), 421–2.

counteract reason and reverse the forces of nature, and even fortune, that made money truly magical. "Money will make the Pot boil, tho' the Devil piss in the fire."[65] As Roger L'Estrange pointed out in his celebrated *Aesop* (3rd ed., 1692), "The old saying, that money does all things is not much wide of the truth."[66]

Proverbs concerning money relied, finally, on a third theme: a generalized sense of vitality invested in money. This was owing to the fact that many proverbs relied structurally on similes and metaphors, thus endowing all their subjects with life.[67] "Poverty is the mother of all arts" and "Money governs the World" embodied money in recognizable authority figures (parents, gods, kings and queens). But more than that, these proverbs capitalized on the fact that money wielded powers that were essential: money conferred life and, more to the point, human attributes. It imparted energy and potential. "Money is the sinews of war" – it had muscles and tendons. "Money is a great traveler in the world" – it was capable of movement.[68] "Money begets money" – it was regenerative. This latter feature underwent its own transformation from association with a notorious aspect of usury to a privileged place in the homely advice of Benjamin Franklin.[69]

Popular wisdom thus comprehended a truth that mercantilist policy strove to contain: configured as coin, "money is round" and therefore "it is to runne from every man."[70] Its capacity to part company with its possessor, to vanish all too quickly, suggested a kind of intentionality: "Ready money will away" or "Money is wise, it knows its way."[71] In a related vein, "running" into debt was allied with other phrases having to do with the debtor's need to escape creditors or bailiffs for lack of money: "He is run off his legs," "To run over shoes," and "To outrun the constable."[72] At the grassroots level, the very words for coins made the point about money's mobility: the Welsh *Keniog* derived its name from the verb *to run*, indicating its small denomination, and the

---

[65] Thomas Fuller, *Gnomologia: Adagies and Proverbs* (1732); see also [Ned Ward], *The Miracles Perform'd by Money: A Poem* (London, 1692).

[66] Cited in Apperson, *English Proverbs*, 421.

[67] On proverbs and metaphor, see Peter Seitel, "Proverbs: A Social Use of Metaphor," in Mieder and Dundes, *Wisdom of Many*, 122–39.

[68] Tilley, *Dictionary*, 468.   [69] Apperson, *English Proverbs.*, 421.

[70] This version is from 1619; Howell cited it as an Italian proverb in 1659. The *Oxford Dictionary of English Proverbs*, 2nd ed., comp. William George Smith (Oxford, 1948), gives it as "Money is round, and rolls away" (429).

[71] *Oxford Dictionary of English Proverbs*, 429.   [72] Bond, "English Legal Proverbs," 926.

Scavernog took its title from the word for hare.[73] (Not only coins have been characterized as mobile: in early years of its use, Cantonese called paper currency "flying money."[74]) Though many expressions conceived of this movement in interpersonal rather than geographical terms, some proverbs followed such reasoning to a logical conclusion. Put in anthropomorphic terms, "Money is a great traveller in the world." Or, in cases where it was in command, money caused people (and business affairs) to move: "Money makes the mare to go" and "Money makes the old woman trot." Howell's seventeenth-century version of the latter was "Need maketh the old wife trott" – perhaps an indication of changing expectations in a culture habituated to monetary exchange.[75]

Proverbial knowledge allowed money to assume the characteristics of living creatures and sometimes the human form itself. Cautionary tales involving money and avarice were common stock in popular literature, running from John Bunyan's "Mr. Money-love" to the characters of Aesop's fables, which enjoyed tremendous popularity in the late seventeenth and early eighteenth centuries.[76] The intimacy between users and their money suggested a relationship with the potential for seduction, as moralists were well aware. The personification of money appeared in ballad form, as in "The Worlds Sweet-heart," which presented money as a lady to be courted: "Whereby it is shewed that Mistris Money, Is the worlds Sweet-heart and Honey," showing "all mens affections are equally bent, to Money, which maketh them ful of mettle."[77] The characterization of money as female, owing to the malleable qualities it offered as the means of empowerment for men, was a common theme of literary representations throughout the period, one which receives treatment in a later chapter.

We know relatively little about the application of proverbs to life apart from anecdotal accounts that prove that people frequently did,

---

[73] *Worth of a Penny*, 19.

[74] James Engell, "Wealth and Words: Pope's *Epistle to Bathurst*," *Modern Philology* 85, no. 4 (1988), 437.

[75] Apperson, *English Proverbs*, 422; Howell, *Proverbs*, 9.

[76] The success of *The Pilgrim's Progress* (first published in 1678) testified to its skillful blend of contemporary styles of popular literature. *Aesop's Fables* constituted another contemporary example of such hybridity. See Annette Patterson, *Fables of Power: Aesopian Writing and Political History* (Durham, 1991); Jayne Elizabeth Lewis, *The English Fable: Aesop and Literary Culture, 1651–1740* (Cambridge, 1996); Peter Linebaugh, "Aesop and Abolition," pamphlet publication of History 499, "History of the Death Penalty," University of Toledo, March 1998.

[77] Roxburgh Ballad Collection, Rox. I. 462 [1640?].

in fact, quote them to each other privately and in public settings.[78] Isolated within collections, proverbs seem to maintain a kind of didactic ambivalence, their insights safely remote from context. But when they became incorporated within forms of popular literature, proverbs about money revealed a more direct, dialectical relationship with experience. The animate quality implied by proverbs suggested that money might exert its own power in many ordinary aspects of life, such as getting a living, spending money as a form of entertainment, changing masters, and simply hitting the road. The proverb functioned as both rationale and a beacon of truth in these instances, especially as many expressions were derived, literally, from articles of law. It is possible that on an individual basis, in private and in imaginative settings, proverbs claimed an authority that resembled law itself.[79]

A considerable number of literary works – advice books, satires, poetry, and humorous broadsides, as well as works of fiction – focused on the subject of money in the early modern period. Their content demonstrated a willingness, if not an eagerness, to absorb and deploy the teachings of proverbial knowledge.[80] In some cases, entire works of advice consisted of proverbs strung together, larded with random contemporary observations, such as *A Hue and Cry After Money* (1689) by "Poor Robin," or William Winstanley (1628?–1698). As an early biographer observed, Winstanley's first profession as a barber served him well: "[t]he scissors, he retained, for he borrowed without stint, and

---

[78] Fox, *Oral and Literate Culture*, gives many examples, some recorded by Sir Nicholas L'Estrange: 138–9, 140.

[79] The connection between proverbs and law was an intimate one because many English proverbs were drawn directly from the law. As Donald Bond has demonstrated, "These proverbs correspond, on a popular level, to the Latin legal maxims of the learned, which represent the concentrated experience of generations of lawyers." Many, as Bond argues, have to do with the sanctity of contract: "An honest man's word is his bond," "Promise is debt," and "You can't get blood out of a stone (*var.* turnip)" are just a few examples. "English Legal Proverbs," 921, 924, 926. See also Fox, *Oral and Literate Culture*, 128.

[80] Proverbs circulated among many different kinds of texts, perhaps intended as a way to lend credibility to otherwise specious undertakings. *Pecuniae Obediunt Omnia. Money Does Master All Things, A Poem Shewing the Power and Influence of Money over All Arts, Sciences, Trades, Professions, and Ways of Living, in This Sublunary World* (York, 1696) offered an elegant epic ridicule of social practices. *Put Money in Your Purse: or the Gold Rule* (1754) was actually "A Satire, with Notes" on the venality of contemporary political affairs. Francis Quarles's *Wisdom's Better Than Money: or, the Whole Art of Knowledge, and the Art to Know Men* (1698) extended advice in the form of "Four Hundred Sentencious Essays, Political and Moral." Many other examples survive.

without acknowledgment also, from his predecessors."[81] His works of popular literature illustrated with brazen clarity the thin line between the author's invention and the wisdom of the public domain. As James Obelkevich points out, "intertextuality was rampant" in the early modern age of literature and "the notion of plagiarism . . . did not yet exist."[82] Many of the views on money thus reproduced in print were in fact a curious amalgam of messages communicated at the "subliminal" level of popular lore – what one seventeenth-century compiler called "the Philosophy of the common Peeple" – and wisdom borrowed from more venerable and authoritative sources.[83]

As Walter Ong pointed out in his analysis of Tudor prose style, the technique of collecting "loose collections of material of all sorts" was a practice handed down from ancient bardic tradition. Practicing the Greek concept of rhapsody (*rhapsoidia*) – the art of "stitching together" various bits of lore and wisdom – the author of popular literature performed the same function of communicating from an accumulated store of plebeian knowledge about the world.[84] As the eccentric poetry and prose of John Taylor (1578–1653) indicates, newly evolved social attitudes might slip into print this way, rendering a "traditional" subject more timely. Taylor figures as perhaps the single most important influence on popular literature regarding money in the late seventeenth and early eighteenth centuries, functioning as a pathway between early modern and modern attitudes toward money.[85] His work is worth examining in detail for its indication of proverbial knowledge already in the public domain, as well as its fresh conviction that circulating coins were indeed alive.

---

[81] *Athenae Oxon.*, ed. Bliss, iv. 763, cited in the *Dictionary of National Biography*, 63 vols. (1885–1900), 62: 680; see also *Oxford Dictionary of National Biography*, 60 vols. (2004), 59: 774–5.

[82] "Proverbs and Social History," 56. Winstanley borrowed heavily from the works of John Taylor (see the discussion that follows).

[83] Howell, *Proverbs*, "To the Knowingest Kind of Philologers" [n.p.]; Fox, *Oral and Literate Culture*, 134–5, 172.

[84] Walter J. Ong, "Oral Residue in Tudor Prose Style," *Publications of the Modern Language Association* 53, no. 3 (1965): 149.

[85] The best full-length study of Taylor is Bernard Capp, *The World of John Taylor the Water-Poet, 1578–1653* (Oxford, 1994). Capp's view of Taylor is consonant with mine: he believes that Taylor's writings "can be seen as one of the most striking attempts of the age to build a cultural bridge" between elite and popular tastes (196).

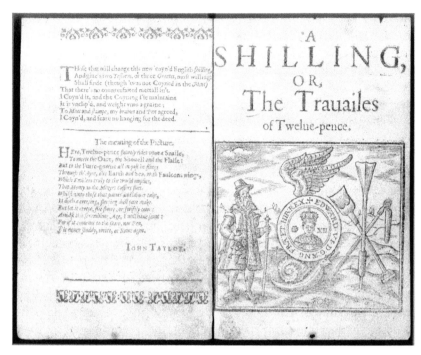

Figure 1. Frontispiece and title page of John Taylor, *A Shilling, or, The Trauailes of Twelue-pence*, 1621. Reproduced by permission of the Houghton Library, Harvard University.

The literary output of John Taylor made him "for half a century the most popular poetaster of his time."[86] A waterman by profession, Taylor enjoyed the hard life of a self-employed hauler of people and goods on the Thames. As a writer, he made witty *wanderlust* his trademark, exploring the theme of circulation and the condition of masterlessness. Some scholars have celebrated his early contributions to the literature of travel as he tapped into the burgeoning seventeenth-century hunger for accounts of voyages of discovery.[87] Yet there is more to be culled from the image-stocked verses of this colorful character. Taylor's world,

[86] P. G. Waldron, *The Biographical Mirrour*, 3 vols. (London, 1795–1802), 2:22; *Dictionary of National Biography* (1921–11), 29:431–8. The latter remarks, "As literature his books – many of them coarse and brutal – are contemptible; but his pieces accurately mirror his age, and are of great value to the historian and antiquary" (433).

[87] W. W. Wooden, "The Peculiar Peregrinations of John Taylor the Water-Poet: A Study in Seventeenth Century British Travel Literature," *Prose Studies* 6 (1983): 3–20; John Chandler, ed., *Travels Through Stuart Britain: The Adventures of John Taylor, the Water Poet* (Stroud, 1999), vi–ix.

according to Bernard Capp, was remarkable for its social flux and political revolution, which created optimal conditions for a maverick popular versifier and entrepreneur. Taylor's insight into the new market for popular publications was part of his prescient profile – what Capp calls "the first modern 'personality,' skilfully [*sic*] manipulating the media and 'famous for being famous'."[88] The fact that Taylor found success promoting his own free spirit is a reliable gauge of popular taste for the subject of self, coupled, as it happened to be in more than one of his works, with money.[89]

After publishing *Taylors Pennilesse Pilgrimage, or Iourney (Without Money) from London to Edenborough in Scotland, and Backe to London* (1618), Taylor hit upon a theme that reverberated in pirated form for the next century: *A Shilling, or, Trauailes of Twelue-pence* (1621). The trope of money on the run, pictured iconically on the frontispiece of the book, derived from no less a source than the Geneva Bible. According to Proverbs 23, verse 5, "For riches taketh her to her wings, as an eagle, and flieth into the heauen."[90] The forty-odd pages of doggerel verse came straight from the coin itself: "Imagine (to his griefe and glory,)/ Twelve-pence himselfe declares his wandring story:/ Relating how he first was borne and bred,/ And how about the world he Trauailed."[91] Chattering randomly of his relative powers in the contemporary world, Twelve-pence offered a seamless ragbag of observations over the course of a life that began in the silver mines of America:

> From vast *America's* rude barbarous bounds,
> From rocky, barren soyle, and sterill grounds,
> Where men did not their Creator know,
> And where the *Devil's* the *God* to whom they bow,
> There from my Heathen *Dam*, or *mother Earth*
> With Paines and trauaile, I at first had birth.

Taylor's lines repeatedly allude to proverbs or verses from the Bible, Shakespeare, and the classical poets, at times, adopting a didactic tone in order to draw value from a string of random observations of ordinary

---

[88] Capp, *World*, 196.
[89] Capp points out that Taylor may have styled himself after Thomas Coryate (d. 1617), who published an account of his walk to Venice in 1608 as *Coryats Crudites*. Taylor engaged in a pamphlet war with Coryate and thus "created a name for himself" in the publishing world (ibid., 18).
[90] *Oxford Dictionary of English Proverbs*, "Riches have wings," 541.
[91] *A Shilling or, The Trauailes of Twelue-pence* (n.p., 1621).

life. Many of Shilling's insights had to do with how money fared as it confronted the demands of contemporary life, and Taylor repeatedly illustrated the triumph of money over every situation. In the perennial competition between money and credit, Shilling confidently claimed precedence:

> I know, not why my reputation's such,
> But still my credit hath beene wondrous much,
> I am more willing taken, now and then
> Then a seal'd Bond of any Aldermen,
> For by long proofe, the Prouerbe true doth say,
> That *ready money euer will away.*

Referring to another common theme in proverbial sayings, the poem recognized the negative implications of money's tendency to depart so easily, echoing the wisdom of the Biblical verse "The destruction of the poor is their poverty":

> Yet let him but want *money*, and 'tis plaine,
> He's th'onely briefe and abstract of disdaine,
> Despised, scorn'd, detested, and contemn'd,
> And roundabout with miseries behem'd.

Taylor's point was not that the poor deserved charity, but rather that the triumph of money was simply a fact of life:

> Should all the Witches in the whole world sit
> In Counsell, and imploy their damned wit,
> To cast my Lady Argent in disgrace,
> And make some other thing supply her place:
> The fruits of all their labours they should finde,
> Would be like throwing feathers 'gainst the winde.

Echoing another proverb, Taylor reminded his readers of the magic of money to make reversals of fortune:

> I haue made Mariages in many a place,
> Where hath bin neither beauty, wit, or grace,
> All's one for that, I am of that high price,
> I can make vice seeme vertue, vertue vice.

This was no devilish pact advertising sin and corruption, but the assertion of worldly experience over rules of morality, plainspoken by an honest coin. Taylor was making a bid to separate money from its ancient association with vice.

This renovation of money rested on a gender-specific agent: the shilling was the tool of men, a means to their mastery of women and worldly enjoyment:

> Would'st haue a Whore, a coach, smoke, drinke, or dice?
> *Money* will bring thee all at any price.
> Woul'dst [*sic*] haue all pleasures in variety,
> *Money* will thy insatiate wants supply:
> Then seeing *money* can doe what it will,
> Haue not men reason to regard it still?

The issue of gender perturbed Taylor, who vacillated between making money male and dominating and female and subjugated. For "If Money were a woman," the poem speculated, "I doe see, / Her case most pittie pittifull would bee." A vanquished damsel, she would end her days imprisoned like a "Turkish Galley [Slave]" by a "miserable Knave." The confusion of voices in Taylor's verses enabled an authorial identity to reflect on his own treatment of money, which suggested that the best course of action was to place money in the servant position and pass it along a continuous circuit of expenditure:

> I know my selfe as able to abuse it,
> As any man that knowes well how to use it,
> But sure I neuer should my Master make it,
> But as my servuant take it, and forsake it.

In the interests of maintaining Shilling's freedom and physical independence, money was made male and constantly disruptive.

The revealing aspect of this lively performance lay in the utter randomness of the experience of Twelve-pence. Passing through the hands of many "masters" and visiting "all ages, Sexes, Trades, and Arts," Twelve-pence respected no distinctions or geographical boundaries. Moreover, by ventriloquizing through the coin, Taylor was able to place a "self" – not precisely Taylor's own – at the center of a narrative from which the coin devised a grandiose, over-the-top tale of triumph. Claiming to have trumped the voyages of Sir John Mandeville, Christopher Columbus, Magellan, and Cavendish, among others, Shilling announced his immortality, having "no end, untill the world come to a finall dissolution and period."

> I am made endlesse, round, which doth portend,
> Till the world end, my Iourney ne'r shall end.
> And men may plainely in my roundnesse see,
> An Emblem of the world's rotundity.

Thus, the poem delivered a message of worldliness and life in the world as money. In representing scene after scene of how the world carried on its business, Shilling showed how the fact was readily understood by everyone he encountered. The "toyling Plow-man," the "Gownes" at Westminster Hall, and the "folkes [who] throng to & fro" in the shops of the town were looking out for money's sake. Its power to work miracles, to exert mastery over others and to make possible movement and pleasure rendered money universally indispensable.

As a distant cousin of the literature of roguery, the genre of the talking coin was largely entertainment; yet it carried a message about money and culture as terse as that of Bernard Mandeville almost a century later. The desire for pleasures and comfort propelled human nature along a secular path, fostering a tolerance for blatant self-interest and even chicanery as part of the struggle for survival in the world. Judging from the many instances of plagiarism upon Taylor's frank gloss on life, as well as direct references to it, *Trauailes of a Twelue-Pence* was something of a plebeian classic, a contradictory epithet, yet one that is accurate, given its tone and what we know about its diverse audience. Taylor appears to have received little in the way of conventional recognition after his death,[92] but other genres of popular literature continued many of the practices and revivified some of the voices present in Taylor's works. Bernard Capp has argued that Taylor acted as a "cultural mediator" whose literary productions were "part of that interplay, bridging different cultural strata" of the early modern age.[93] Proverbs relating to money aided him in this project. An "inextricable reciprocity between the spoken and written realms" contributed to this shared milieu, along with "a degree of universality in the attitudes and values" enshrined by proverbs.[94] As literary critics have argued, a common store of images and concerns may have passed across different reading publics through the medium of print culture in the seventeenth century; it was only later, during the eighteenth century, that distinctions between elite and popular literary taste became clearly defined.

Later adaptations of the speaking and traveling coin provide clear examples of how elite and popular strands of literature covered similar themes, though in different ways. William Winstanley's unabashed

---

[92] Winstanley's heavy borrowings should be counted as tributes, particularly as he acknowledges his debt to the Water Poet in his *Hue and Cry After Money*. It is likely, too, that Addison and other eighteenth-century writers of traveling coin narratives had read Taylor; cf. the assessment by Capp, *World*, 189–90.

[93] Capp, *World*, 195, 193.   [94] Fox, *Oral and Literate Culture*, 170–2.

emulation of Taylor in the late seventeenth century is one such example. Poor Robin's *Hue and Cry After Money* pirated lines from *Twelue-pence* and paid honor to Taylor's epic by musing over the meaning of its cover illustration:

> I remember when I was a Boy, I read a Book Written by *John Taylor* the Water Poet called *The Travels of Twelue-pence*, which had for the Frontispiece the picture of a King *Edward* shilling, with wings on the top of it flying to a Usurer; and on the bottom a Snail carrying it with a slow pace backward to a Spade and Oares.[95]

Other readers of Taylor may have ingested the image as Poor Robin did, along with the written message, and come to think of money as a scurrying creature with wings. "The Hunting After Money" (1709) offers suggestive evidence of this: half illustration, half moralistic poetry, the broadsheet depicted personified vices and virtues (Prodigality, Frugality, Covetousness) in hot pursuit of a fowl with the body of a coin, similar to the figure pictured in the frontispiece of Taylor's *Twelue-pence*. This image might have received further inspiration from the inauguration of the machine-made guinea in 1668 as a trustworthy gold coin of the realm.[96] Poor Robin's *Hue and Cry After Money* went one step further, making money human and respectable: "Monsieur Money," unlike poor Shilling, claimed to be "a Pleasant, Amiable, Light-hearted Gentleman, one whose Company is desired of all Men, and who makes Gentlemen of all those where he comes to inhabit were they never before so Clownish or Simple."[97] The technique of personifying money enabled Winstanley to comment on class identities and the familiar power of money to disrupt social hierarchies.

Poor Robin played the part of a lesser man, one who lacked money and had a hard time acquiring it. "I think whensoever this Money walks abroad that I am always out of the way," he complained.

> And let Schollars say what part of speech they will that Money is of, I think it is no Noun Substantive, because by me it can neither be *seen*, *heard*, nor *understood*, and the mischief on't is, never a Usurer will lend me an hundred pounds of it upon a Mortgage of Land lying on *Pernassas Hill*.[98]

---

[95] *A Hue and Cry After Money* (1689), 5. The image, as Poor Robin understood it, had to do with a larger tableau depicting a peculiarly English aptitude for managing and generating wealth. Winstanley used this passage as a way of allying himself with those "prest with the yoke of wringing poverty," rather than with skilled investors."

[96] See Chapter 5 for further discussion of this broadside.

[97] [Winstanley], *Hue and Cry*, 6.   [98] Ibid., 2.

Through this lame, humorous attempt at crypticism, Winstanley pointed
to money's elusive, magical properties. His readers would have recognized, too, an allusion to the proverb "Prate is but prate; 'tis money
buys lands."[99] The true moral and ethical dilemma, however, lay in the
claim that money superseded land and everything it stood for, including
civic virtue: "But without Money how is a man unman'd?" he asked,
adding later on, "as the Greek Proverb will always be veryfied, *Cheremater*, *Cheremater*, *Aner*; Money, Money, is the Man; for as the World goes
now a man without it is in effect nothing." Little did Winstanley realize
that he would presage a characterization of his age that one day would
become enshrined in extensive academic debate.[100]

Poor Robin revealed a more troubled cynicism than Poor Richard, his
later American counterpart, engendered, perhaps, by the turbulence of
the later seventeenth century.[101] His observations vacillated between a
vague nostalgia for moral righteousness and admiration for the power
of money to effect personal transformations:

> [N]o it is only Silver and Gold that now bears all the sway, 'tis the onlyest
> Cordial to make the heart Merry: 'twill make *Jack* be a Gentleman, and *Joan*
> so fine you cannot know her from my Lady; 'twill make an old Toothless
> deformed, crooked Widdow, that hath neither beauty, wit, nor good condi-
> tions, to match with a spruce, fine, handsome young Gentleman, that wants
> not her but only her Wealth.... It is a mettal of such Soveraign power, that
> clap but two or three pieces of it into a Lawyers hand 'twill make his Tongue
> run as nimble as Quicksilver.[102]

Part of the excitement and terror bred by money was its power to violate the moral standards of a more stable, ordered world. At worst, it
desecrated honor and virtue, tempting every person to eschew moral
standards. "What is it but for Money which makes the Trades-man to
use false weights and measures," Poor Robin observed rhetorically, the

---

[99] Bohn, *Hand-Book of Proverbs*, 116.

[100] See J. G. A. Pocock, *The Machiavellian Moment: Florentine Political Thought and the Atlantic
Republican Tradition* (Princeton, 1975), Chaps. 13 and 14; Steven Pincus, "Neither
Machiavellian Moment nor Possessive Individualism: Commercial Society and the
Defenders of the English Commonwealth," *American Historical Review* (June 1998),
705–36.

[101] The literature on Poor Richard is legion: see Wolfgang Mieder, *Proverbs Are Never Out
of Season: Popular Wisdom in the Modern Age* (New York, 1993), esp. 100–21; Robert
Newcomb, "The Sources of Benjamin Franklin's Sayings of Poor Richard," PhD diss.,
University of Maryland, 1957; Stuart A. Gallacher, "Franklin's 'Way to Wealth': A
Florilegium of Proverbs and Wise Sayings," *Journal of English and Germanic Philology*
48 (1949), 229–251.

[102] [Winstanley], *Hue and Cry*, 4.

Usurer to sell his Soul to Hell by taking advantages of Bills, Bonds and Morgages [*sic*]; the Scrivener to forfeit his Ears to the Pillory for Forging and Counterfeiting Writings. Quoting "the Poet" (Taylor), Poor Robin used doggerel verse (most likely, his own) in the vein of Taylor to underscore his point:

> For Money Mens lives may be purchas'd and Sold,
> 'Tis Money breaks Laws, and that mends um again:
> Men venture their Quiet and Safety for Gold,
> When they won't stir a foot their Rights to maintain.[103]

Winstanley's perspective, more cynical than practical, was remindful of religious strife, civil war, a restoration, a bloodless revolution, and years of colonial expansion. Endorsing the profitability of rational observation, he marshaled copious evidence to show that money broke down barriers and altered conditions that were otherwise fixed in the timeless account of human affairs.

TRAVELLING COINS IN EIGHTEENTH-CENTURY PRINT CULTURE

Winstanley's brazen imitation of Taylor's shilling, though a popular piece of ephemera, never achieved the celebrity of Joseph Addison's tale of a "twelvepeny-piece," published as Number 249 of *The Tatler*.[104] Addison's coin led a procession of works based on the idea of a speaking object later in the century; these included a watch, a corkscrew, a lady's slipper, a pin, a "French Louse," and several forms of money, along with a miscellany of other portable items.[105] Addison's pretext for the literary conceit called attention to the parallels between men and money: a contentious friend challenged Addison to compare favorably the trivial and empty lives of "Busie men of the age, who only valued themselves

---

[103] Ibid., 2.

[104] All references are taken from Barett Wendell and Chester Noyes Greenough, eds., *Selections from the Writings of Joseph Addison* (Boston, 1905).

[105] See, for example, *The English Man's Two Wishes:.... History of the Travels, and Various Turns of Fortune of a Shilling* (London, [1728?]); [Charles Johnston] *Chrysal; or the Adventures of a Guinea* (London, 1760); [R. Ainslie W. S. Edinburgh] *The Life, Adventures, and Serious Remonstrances of a Scotch Guinea Note* (1826), which begins thus: "It has been a frequent custom among the members of our family to write their *Adventures*, as witness the very interesting ones of my elder brother, the Golden *Guinea*; and I am about to follow their example – being myself a paper one" (5). I owe thanks to Tim Hitchcock for bringing the first citation to my attention.

for being in motion" with the "Adventures that this Twelvepeny-piece has been engaged in, were it possible for him to give us an account of his Life." Shilling responded by speaking to Addison in a dream that night:

> Methoughts the Shilling that lay upon the table reared it self upon its edge, and turning the face towards me, opened its mouth, and in a soft silver sound gave me the following account of his Life and Adventures:
>
>   I was born, says he, on the side of a mountain, near a little village of *Peru*, and made a voyage to *England* in an Ingot, under the Convoy of Sir *Francis Drake*. I was, soon after my arrival, taken out of my *Indian* habit, refined, naturalized, and put into the *British* Mode, with the face of Queen *Elizabeth* on one side, and the Arms of the Country on the other. Being thus equipped, I found in me a wonderful inclination to ramble, and visit all the parts of the new world into which I was brought.[106]

Though following many of the strategies of Taylor, Addison created a far more amiable victim of circumstance than the earlier, earthier coin. Sent on errands, used to purchase food or "sometimes a Play-book," kept as a luck piece by "a superstitious old woman," and "employed in raising Soldiers against the King" (used "to inveigle Country Fellows") during the Civil War, Addison's Shilling now touted a tale full of urbane fascinations and imaginative intrigues. Shilling was also capable of changing identities, at one point "beaten flat, with an hammer," and in old age achieving the status of "a Medal" of "great credit and antiquity." Clipped, rubbed, "spoiled and pillaged" by "an Artist," the coin endured an ultimate transformation around the time of the Great Coinage. Unlike Taylor, who felt uncomfortable in making money a woman, Addison seized the opportunity to give Shilling a "change of Sex." The "beauty and lustre" created by the great melding and recoining of silver finally made Shilling a female object of desire, and thus the inspiration for "the finest Burlesque Poem in the *British* Language, . . . *The Splendid Shilling*."[107] Given this transformation, Shilling's sensitivity to the needs of others propelled her into a new network of circulation belonging to gift exchange: mixed by mistake with a "penyworth of Farthings," she became a vehicle of charity when her owner tossed the contents of his purse into the hat of a blind man. Not by accident, Addison restored the coin to free circulation and anonymity as an idealized woman.

---

[106] *Tatler*, 11 November 1710, 46–7.
[107] Ibid., 47–8. "The Splendid Shilling," by John Philips (1676–1709) appeared in 1701.

Literary critics have found much interest in the many novel-length narratives of coins and objects that followed Addison's playful squib. Such works based their imaginative performances on the parallels between a system of money and the exigencies of life, making circulation a central trope of human experience. Christopher Flint sees these works as "a measure of the dispersion . . . of persons and things" in the eighteenth century; through their exposure of human desire and amorality, speaking object novels accentuate "the dismantling effects of human commerce" in an era of luxury and excess. Because the monetary protagonist was distinct from the human characters he or she encountered, the novel could offer allegedly objective insights into an illicit, materialistic guise of human society, and in some cases an embattled aspect of the English state. The speaking object "gains access to subjectivity only through the impoverished subjectivities of others, gradually unfolding a vision of the national state in which identity itself is fungible." These novels offered shallow representations of characters and situations caught up in passionate drives toward bodily and material needs. The universality of this grasping behavior featured as a key aspect of the narrative.[108]

But were speaking coins able to offer a coherent ethical stance from their vantage point in the world of money? Liz Bellamy has argued that their checkered careers demonstrated only the demise of virtue. "The characters of the novel of circulation are almost invariably selfish and self-seeking," she pointed out, "the products of a fragmented society unrestrained by effective ethical codes." This fact represents a moving away "from the classical preoccupations to construct a tradition of economic thought which was based on the assessment of the economic consequences of individual actions."[109] The appearance of this literary genre signaled the dismissal of the familiar relations of the "harmonious country estate" and "obligations and dependence" to "the mythical realm." In the new world of finance, the "exchange process is portrayed as a lottery, devoid of rationale, principle, or justification, and whether individuals gain or lose, acquire great wealth or dissipate it, the outcome is perceived to be negative."[110] Charles Johnston's two-volume bestseller *Chrysal, or, The Adventures of a Guinea*, published

---

[108] Christopher Flint, "Speaking Objects: The Circulation of Stories in Eighteenth-Century Prose Fiction," *Publications of the Modern Language Association* 113 (March 1998): 219, 221.

[109] Bellamy, *Commerce*, 3. See also Thompson, *Models of Value*.

[110] Bellamy, *Commerce*, 3, 126, 128.

in 1760, offered a variation on these themes by urging the reader to heed enlightened advice: "let reason curb expectation; reduce imagination to common sense." But good Augustan counsel was not suited to all users of money, as speaking coins were well aware. The prospects for popular immunity to the galloping cupidity endemic to the world of trade were dim indeed.

Apart from the moral issues raised by these works, the reader cannot miss the deep confusion between money and persons, what Margot Finn calls the "constant slippage between the category of the person and the category of the thing."[111] As Goux's telling phrase has it, "the play of substitutions defines qualitative values" for both money and people in these stories.[112] In a subtle reading of monetary fictions, Deidre Lynch has offered a complex set of cultural processes at work. By enabling money to really talk, novels such as *The Adventures of a Bank-Note* and *Chrysal* engaged readers in recognizing "money's status as a marker of social agreement." The stories represent a gesture of "consent to a standard of value, their selection of the general equivalent . . . that draws persons into a community of mutual dependence." As such, the speaking coin also can be seen as "humaniz[ing] an economic system" known for its risks and perils.[113] Yet Lynch also showed that talking money was not univocal in its rendering of the social aspect of commercial culture. The "impersonality and facelessness" of currency enabled it to call attention to the disenfranchisement of certain persons in the established system of social representation. When speaking coins became associated with women, for example, they showed how such persons fell prey to becoming the objects, rather than the users, of money. Circulation resulted in their "sexual undoing," as they became the property of successive men. Coins thus acted as indicators pointing to priced people who were at the behest of those in possession of wealth and power. Money, then, could suggest imbeddedness in a social network and a complete severance from the ties that bound.[114]

Daniel Defoe's fictional female characters vividly demonstrate these points. Moll Flanders and Roxana understood sex as a means to money, whether through prostitution or conventional matrimony. In

---

[111] Margot C. Finn, *The Character of Credit: Personal Debt in English Culture, 1740–1914* (Cambridge, 2003), 34.

[112] Jean-Joseph Goux, *Symbolic Economies: After Marx and Freud* (Ithaca, 1990), 3, quoted in Thompson, 98.

[113] Lynch, *Economy of Character*, 96.

[114] Ibid., 98–100; Engell, "Wealth and Words," 439.

such market transactions carried out between the sexes, Moll recognized, whores, not wealthy women, required good looks in order to get along in life. The life of a prostitute like Roxana offered a prime example of the confusion of meanings of "worth," "value," and "virtue" in human terms, condensed in the financial transaction of purchasing sex. Moll spoke eloquently of the homology between her own widowed identity and money: she was like "a Bag of Money, or a Jewel dropt on the Highway, which is prey to the next comer."[115]

Contemporaries were acutely aware of the correspondence between coinage and their signification of social relations between people; these typefaces were the screens upon which they envisioned the dramatic personae of contemporary nations. John Evelyn's treatise on medals made clear the meaning of the stamp on money:

> Effigies and Image of the Prince...ought not to be look'd upon as merely stamp'd for Ornament or Honor, or to proclaim and set forth Titles only...but as publick Vouchers of the real and intrinsic Value of the Species and Matter according to the constant and general Estimation of the World.

The stamp stood as assurance of weight of precious metal, so that scales need not be used.[116] Conversely, Evelyn pointed out, "to put a King's Title or Effigies to unweighty Money, and not of authentic Value, is . . . to render the Prince himself a *Faux Monoyeur*." Thus, the coin was imbued with the king's presence and authority, rather like a political variety of transubstantiation. Evelyn's treatise also included a lengthy section on "Heads and Effigies of Illustrious, and Famous Persons" presented in "Sculps and Taille Douce" as well as "A Digression concerning Physiognomy." These tiny works of art aspired to reproduce nature, offering scope for the noblest representations of humankind.[117]

For elites, the direct association between coin and personhood was backed up by a strict sense of hierarchy. Evelyn's favored medals belonged to an upper echelon of coinage because they boasted of "workmanship, variety of subject and Erudition, not frequent or of any notable Use in common Money." The only kind of money that

---

[115] Thompson, *Models of Value*, 93 and Chap. 3, passim.
[116] It was the prerogative of the state "upon a Legal Account" to create this "publick Testimony, that such a piece was of such a Weight; and so might pass in Traffick without the trial of the Scales." John Evelyn, *Numismata. A Discourse of Medals, Antient and Modern* (London, 1697), 5, 224.
[117] Ibid., 228.

approached the interest value of medals, according to Evelyn, was that which featured "Head[s] and Effigies" – ideally, those of monarchs or great persons of antiquity.[118] Within this category, the vast spectrum of images was subject to even further discrimination according to the historical significance of the subject. In his *Dialogue Upon the Usefulness of Ancient Medals*, Joseph Addison also drew the reader into the life-like world of numismatics and medals, where civic and moral lessons came alive through molded images. Addison's interlocutors – Philander, Cynthio, and Eugenius – were notably more learned than the imaginary, plebeian voice of Taylor's Shilling: "They were all three very well versed in the politer parts of learning, and had travelled into the most refined nations of *Europe*." Extensive exposure to the wisdom of the ancients lent their conversation an improving tone that popular literature lacked. Their first lesson focused on subjects that would have been familiar to all social classes: the problem of "intrinsic value" and the question of how much life could be inferred from the face of a coin.[119]

The three characters tried to determine whether "it is better to have a pocket full of *Otho's* and *Gordians* [ancient coins] than of *Jacobus's* or *Louis d'ors* [contemporary money]" – a debate that recast the conflict between the ancients and moderns in terms of historical knowledge versus the usefulness of current money. Philander's defense of medals consisted of a lively encouragement to imbue coins with human qualities. "[Y]ou are not to look upon a cabinet of Medals as a treasure of mony, but of knowledge, nor must you fancy any charms in gold, but in the figures and inscriptions that adorn it. The intrinsic value of an old coin does not consist in its metal but its erudition," he insisted.[120] He continued with a list of "several uses of old coins," which included "the shewing us the Faces of all the great persons of antiquity," along with various "Wives" and "Children, that no authors have mentioned." Cynthio objected that learning about the great deeds of men was onerous enough without adding characters of such insignificance, but Philander continued undeterred, enthusing, "In devices of this nature one sees a pretty poetical invention, and may often find as much thought on the reverse of a Medal as in a Canto of *Spenser*."[121] At this, Cynthio and Eugenius showed signs of relenting from their previous position of

---

[118] Ibid., 3.
[119] Joseph Addison, *Dialogues upon the Usefulness of Ancient Medals* (1726) in *The Miscellaneous Works of Joseph Addison*, ed. A. C. Guthkelch (London, 1914), 281–3.
[120] Ibid., 283.   [121] Ibid., 284–5.

skepticism. Literary vehicles promised to impart liveliness to characters more effectively than ancient history. Cynthio admitted,

> [Y]ou have drawn up all your medallic people, and indeed they make a much more formidable body than I could have imagined. You have shewn us all conditions, sexes and ages, emperors and empresses, men and children, gods and wrestlers. Nay you have conjured up persons that exist no where else but on old Coins, and have made our Passions and Virtues and Vices visible. I could never have thought that a cabinet of Medals had been so well peopled.[122]

The lesson concluded with Philander's attempt to make clear "a great affinity between Coins and Poetry." This vital link to the imagination rendered coins greater than simply a medium of exchange. As Cynthio put it, "I could never fancy before this evening, that a Coin could have any nobler use in it than to pay a reckoning."[123]

The sophisticated texts of Addison embraced the life lodged in coins with as much intensity as proverbs, though with less literalism and more detachment. From different perspectives, popular and refined literary discussions of the animated aspects of money showed how readily contemporaries engaged in identifying with money as a part of civic and commercial life. As Catherine Ingrassia points out, the very character of the "self" in eighteenth-century novels depended on money for its development. "Reading a novel, like investing in a speculative financial venture, demanded readers' imaginative participation in a narrative that could potentially be a vehicle with which early modern subjects could reinvent themselves and envisage their lives differently."[124] Addison's *Spectator* offered a related observation, placing money at the center of human motivations: "I am apt to think," he confided, "that could we look in to our own Hearts, we should see Money ingraved in them in more lively and moving Characters than Self-Preservation."[125]

At every social level, money became a vehicle through which eighteenth-century people understood negotiations of the self within social dynamics embedded in contemporary political and economic life. The tension between the dual capacities of money – its stability as

---

[122] Ibid., 286.
[123] Ibid., 293–4. In the case of "imaginary persons" on old coins, Philander remarks, "Their proper country . . . is the breast of a good man" (300).
[124] Catherine Ingrassia, *Authorship, Commerce, and Gender in Early Eighteenth-Century England: A Culture of Paper Credit* (Cambridge, 1998), 2.
[125] *Spectator*, 6 August 1712.

authority and its fungibility as a mutable medium – were everywhere in evidence. As Goux explains, money and exchange "far exceeded the sphere of economic value for which it was initially produced."[126] The most basic proverbial teachings communicated the metaphorical lability of money: its movement across geographical space, its power to alter circumstances, and its insistent descriptive power as a "process of symbolization." This chapter has sketched in brief form the ways in which money laid claim to life in theories of early political economy, proverbial wisdom, and literary culture. Yet we miss much of the significance of this triumphant sweep if we fail to appreciate the conflict-ridden history of the acceptance of money as a cultural marker. Before exploring how the power of money was brought to bear on particular aspects of eighteenth-century social relations, we must turn to the moral attributes associated with money in the early modern era.

[126] Goux, *Symbolic Economies*, 3.

PART II

MUTABLE MEANINGS OF MONEY, ca. 1640–1730

CHAPTER 3

Circulating Mammon: Attributes of Money in Early Modern English Culture

"And having food and raiment let us be therewith content," the Bible instructed, "For the love of money is the root of all evil."[1] The familiar injunction, with its attendant suspicion of tokens of exchange, cast its net over a wide ambit of European economic and social life from medieval times. During the eleventh century, as the use of money penetrated more activities in European life, avarice surmounted pride as the most loathsome vice.[2] Theologians did not spare the church in their attacks on covetous behavior. The pope functioned as an archetype of greed, and as one wit noted, "Roma" was an acronym for *radix omnium malorum avaritia* (the root of all evils is avarice).[3] The protestant reaction against papal corruption gave new life to this sentiment. Drawing from the Sermon on the Mount, preachers personified the entreaties of money against the commands of faith as the competition between two masters. Martin Luther adequately measured the reach of reformed thinking when he reckoned that "Mammon has two properties: it makes us secure, first, when it goes well with us, and then we live without fear of God at all; secondly, when it goes ill with us, then we tempt God, fly from him, and seek after another God."[4] The sacramental nature of wealth prevalent in Old Testament teachings came under attack as emphasis on Christ's rejection of dealings with money invited a broad

---

[1] 1 Timothy 6:7–10.
[2] Lester K. Little, *Religious Poverty and the Profit Economy in Medieval Europe* (Ithaca, 1978), 36.
[3] Richard Newhauser, *The Early History of Greed: The Sin of Avarice in Early Medieval Thought and Literature* (Cambridge, 2000), 127.
[4] *Table-Talk*, 1566, trans. William Hazlitt, from *Oxford Book of Money*, ed. Kevin Jackson (Oxford, 1995), 257.

theological foundation for seeing coins as symbols of the menace of materialism.[5]

As a metonym for avarice, money in the shape of coins circulated as moralistic religious and literary messages writ small, functioning as potent signs with multiple meanings. Their onerous didactic function derived, in part, from linguistic slippage, which elided the distinction between money as a medium of exchange and its rhetorical function as a referent of wealth. Yet their precious metal substance, along with their graven images, rendered coins nearly equivalent to idols that exercised power of their own.[6] Franciscans forbade followers to touch coins because their mere presence prompted sensations of corruption by worldly excess, and medieval marginalia featured images of apes defecating coins as a reminder of their true nature to readers of gothic texts.[7] But in other instances, coins could represent a form of contract – an "earnest penny" or "god's penny" – between believers and saints. Bending a coin, thus rendering it unfit for exchange, marked it as a future donation to Henry VI in fifteenth-century England. This gesture was sometimes thought to endow the piece with miraculous powers, as a form of telecommunication to the venerated king. Coins were bent hurriedly over corpses after sudden death and hung around the neck of a victim of accidental strangling in order to obtain the saintly monarch's aid in salvation. In this way, customary use might neutralize the potential for evil harbored within a coin.[8] In later centuries, protestants and Catholics alike employed the suggestive images of coins in moralistic teachings, ubiquitous in oral and print culture in the form of sermons, writings, and statuary, which illustrated right conduct in exchange, self-control, and charity. The diary entries of Philip Henry, a minister of the late seventeenth century, reveal a continuing alertness to the intrinsic

---

[5] As Jacques Ellul has described the contrast, wealth was severed from a notion of abundance indicating the intervention of divine will and became "reduced to money": it became "a sign with no referent." *Money and Power*, trans. LaVonne Neff (Downers Grove, 1979), 70.

[6] By the late tenth century and after, moralists employ images that show *filargiria* and *avarus* as a failing that renders the individual "a servant not of God, but of coins." Earlier texts by Cassian also indicate that an external impulse could "[serve] as a catalyst leading to evil action," and coins were often responsible. Newhauser, *Early History of Greed*, 63, 127.

[7] Marion A. Habig, ed., *St. Francis of Assisi: Writings and Early Biographies* (Chicago, 1983), 682–3, 686; Little, *Religious Poverty*, 34.

[8] On this topic, see Eamon Duffy, *The Stripping of the Altars: Traditional Religion in England 1400–1580* (New Haven, 1992), 183–6.

power of coins: among the many strange deaths he recorded was the demise of a man who was felled by "an Apoplexy in his shop counting money."[9]

A popular celebration of money warred against an underlying fear of its gravitational pull toward greed, a tension manifested in popular antipathy to the miser. Early modern iconography inherited a host of medieval emblems relating to avarice, which depicted figures, usually female, grasping at or scooping up coins, sometimes with devils sitting on their shoulders or peering over their heads.[10] Their monitory presence on church facades, in carvings within church interiors, as well as in paintings and popular woodcuts was meant to ward off the ubiquitous temptations of greed, symbolized by bags of money or chests of coin. Desire, like fortune, often took the shape of a woman, alongside images like "Lady World," a symbolic concatenation of profane elements, who represented avarice or simply "all existing vices and lusts."[11] Richard Newhauser lists 116 different images of avarice in the literature of Late Antiquity and the early Middle Ages, a diversity which suggests that imaginative life employed every possible vehicle, from bird lime to ravenous wolves, to depict the passion, with an abundance of material ripe for misogynistic depictions if the message of unbridled female passion suited the occasion.[12] The most commonly used representation in Newhauser's sample, however, was Judas, the apostle who betrayed Christ for "blood money," a parable that communicated a powerful sense of the destructive delusions bred by avarice. Also popular was the trope of slavery because it demonstrated how avarice ruled the will of its victims. The miser was said to be governed by desire without knowing it, "fettered by a thousand chains." In the words of St. Chromatius, a fifth-century theologian, "Avarice is slavery to Mammon."[13]

In the popular bureau scenes found in Netherlandish paintings of the sixteenth century, depictions of the act of counting coins depended on

---

[9] Quoted in Michael Mascuch, "Social Mobility and Middling Self-Identity: The Ethos of British Autobiographers, 1600–1750," *Social History* 20, no. 1 (1995): 52.

[10] German iconography before and after the Reformation yields many examples of images of avarice; see also the carved bench ends of St. Mary, Wilby, in Suffolk (available at www.suffolkchurches.com).

[11] E. de Jongh, "Vermommingen van Vrouw Wereld in de 17de Eeuw," quoted in Basil S. Yamey, *Art and Accounting* (New Haven, 1989), 145n.

[12] Newhauser mentions the use of "daughter of devil," "Delilah," "enchantress," "five foolish virgins," "inhuman mistress," and "woman hiding money," among others. *Early History of Greed*, 132–42.

[13] Ibid., 137, 140. The image of fetters comes from Prudentius.

supporting characters to assure the viewer that the scene was other than a negative portrayal of dealing with money. In Quentin Massys's "The Banker (or Money-Changer) and his Wife," dated 1514, the banker's meticulous labor of "telling" or counting money is counterpoised by an image of wifely virtue sitting at his elbow. As the banker weighs and examines each coin, his partner leafs through an illuminated Book of Hours; her beatific countenance, along with that of the virgin depicted in her book, spreads a detoxifying aura over the heap of coins in front of her husband. In later adaptations, particularly those by Marinus van Reymerswaele, her Book of Hours has been changed to an account book, suggesting either a more realistic portrayal of the wife as her husband's bookkeeper or a more pointed critique of the triumph of material interests over spiritual life. In scenes that depict a pair of men involved in business transactions, the atmosphere mutates into a more profane and ambiguous activity. These mannered depictions appear to be tax gatherers or accountants (art historians over the years have also speculated that they were "Two Jewes Usurers"), and given the hunched posture and exaggerated facial expression of one of the male subjects, the satirical nature of these paintings seems fairly certain.[14] At least one version acquired the moralistic title of "The Misers." Situated far from the redeeming presence of moral forces, the transaction was thrust into a moral vacuum, where money could inject a poisonous influence.[15]

The negative attributes of money manifested themselves in ways that were not always scripted by divines. An important example of syncretism of popular and religious belief can be traced through the evolving figure of Mammon, made familiar to English culture through the Bible and major works of literature such as *Piers Plowman*, Spenser's *Fairie Queene* and Milton's *Paradise Lost*. Ancient Aramaic and Hebrew meanings of the word, which meant "riches" or "wealth," were eclipsed by a specific personification drawn from the New Testament, but with an accretion of idiosyncratic features. The Mammon of the Sermon on the Mount originated simply as a master representing covetousness who threatened to compete with God for the souls of humankind.

---

[14] Facial gestures, such as grimaces, were meant to accompany certain business transactions in early modern exchange practices, though no art historian has commented on this fact. For debates surrounding bureau paintings, see Yamey, *Art and Accounting*, 45–56.

[15] Yamey, *Art and Accounting*, 45–56. See also Keith Moxey, "The Criticism of Avarice in Sixteenth-Century Netherlandish Painting," in *Northern Mannerism*, ed. G. Cavalli-Bjorkman (Stockholm, 1985), 21–34.

Embroidering upon this image, religious teachings of the Middle Ages imagined Mammon as a devil endowed with power and dominion, and regarded him as a primary character in demonology. His association with the underworld converged neatly with his link with the earthly origins of precious metal and added further invidious detail to his identity. This transfiguration from metaphor to dramatic persona was later absorbed by more formal works of theology. Though St. Jerome had resisted elevating Mammon to a deity, emphasizing instead the ancient meaning of the word as wealth, Peter Lombard appears to have sided with the personifiers, arguing, "Riches are by the name of a devil, namely Mammon, for Mammon is the name of a devil, by which name riches are called according to the Syrian tongue."[16]

These images were constantly informed by popular belief, for as Robert Scribner has shown, the "dialogue between the church and the magical arts in the early middle ages was as much a matter of creative assimilation and acculturation as . . . rejection" of unorthodox teachings, and "boundaries between sacred and secular remained highly porous." During the upheaval of the Reformation, demonology received a significant boost into the panoply of spiritual forces by a curious convergence of developments. According to Scribner, "[t]he Protestant elaboration of the moralized universe had the effect of increasing anxiety" while removing "the protective means inherent in the Catholic sacramental system." The intervention of the Devil, affirmed by passages of scripture, thus became a greater likelihood.[17] The Faustian legend provided a popular framework for demonic intrusions into daily life, and as bargains were struck and souls were sold, the presence of money only underscored its involvement with a sinful underworld.

English literary accounts depicted Mammon mired in earthly concerns. Spenser's late sixteenth-century Mammon hid within a "gloomy glade, Cover'd with boughes and shrubs from heavens light," where the repulsive creature sat watch over "Great heapes of gold." Coated with soot, his features of "griesly hew, and fowle," the monster nevertheless valiantly identified himself as the "God of the world and worldlings," in charge of "Riches, renowme, and principality, / Honour, estate, and

---

[16] *Magister Sentarium* II, dist. 6.

[17] Historians of the European Reformation have argued that "the Devil and demonic spirits had become wilder and more incalculable" by the sixteenth century as Protestant demonology absorbed magical aspects of secular culture. See Robert W. Scribner, "The Reformation, Popular Magic, and the 'Disenchantment of the World'," *Journal of Interdisciplinary History*, 23, no. 3 (Winter, 1993), 481, 486–7.

all this worldes good, / For which men swinck and sweat incessantly."
Mammon's obsessive drive to possess coins called attention to the per-
versity of accumulation.[18]

Similarly, the first book of *Paradise Lost* made an association between
heaps of money, stigmatized activity, and obscure interiors, with
Mammon directing men to plunder the globe in search of riches. Goaded
on by this fallen "Spirit," avaricious mortal agents

> ...with impious hands
> Rifled the bowels of their mother Earth
> For treasures better hid. Soon had his crew
> Opened into the hill a spacious wound,
> And digged out ribs of gold. Let none admire
> That riches grow in Hell: that soil may best
> Deserve the precious bane!

Milton's contemporaries might have seen a connection between this
allusion to gold-mining and the pillaging of precious metals from Africa
and South America.[19]

John Bunyan registered his own sentiments about the gravitational
pull of money in *The Pilgrim's Progress*, in which characters like Christian
and Mr. Money-love embodied the tension between ethereal abstraction
of heavenly ideals and the profane nature of material reality.[20] While
Mr. Money-love and Mr. By-ends discuss whether or not one should
become religious in order to "get a rich wife or more and far better customers to his shop," Christian recoils in disgust, identifying
these views with "heathens, hypocrites, devils, and witches." "For if it
be unlawful to follow Christ for loaves, as it is, how much more abom-
inable is it to make of him and religion a stalking horse to get and enjoy
the world," he points out to readers.[21] Further along the way, when the
pilgrims encounter a silver mine, Christian recognizes precious metal
as "a snare to those that seek it." In lines implying the enslaving power
of money, Christian underscores the justice of their fate when they are

[18] Edmund Spenser, *The Faerie Queene*, ed. Thomas P. Roche Jr. (New Haven and London, 1981), Book II, Canto VII, 3–8.

[19] John Milton, *Paradise Lost*, ed. Gordon Teskey (New York, 2005), Book 1, lines 678–92; Pierre Vilar, *A History of Gold and Money, 1450–1920*, trans. Judith White (London, 1976); Peter Spufford, *Money and Its Use in Medieval Europe* (Cambridge, 1988).

[20] Michael McKeon, *The Origins of the English Novel, 1600–1740* (Baltimore, 1987), 295–7, 300–301.

[21] *The Pilgrim's Progress*, ed. Roger Sharrock (Harmondsworth, 1965), 141–2.

swallowed up, along with Demas, the son of Judas, by the earth:

> One calls, the other runs, that he may be
> A sharer in his lucre: so these two
> Take up in this world, and no further go.[22]

Christian and Hopeful are made to understand the significance of their brush with lucre. The earthly aspect of money, ever present and poisonous, threatened to anchor its victim in the world forever.

Just as paradigms of providence and evidence of divine disfavor were in flux in the seventeenth century, so too were the formal boundaries of money under negotiation. Institutions of church and state realigned their respective roles in the case of usury. Conflicts diminished after legislation passed in 1571 and particularly after 1624, when the practice of lending with interest was no longer seen as a matter within religious jurisdiction. As early thinkers on the subject of money and credit argued, lending at interest benefited commerce and society at large.[23] With its economic benefits laid out clearly, the practice of lending was thus defined in technical terms, so that abuses became a matter of individual conscience outside the jurisdiction of the state. In a study of early modern business practices, Richard Grassby succinctly summed it up: "The logic of the market confounded all theology," and as the records of many devout businessmen reveal, money came with a price, which few people were reluctant to pay or to charge.[24]

But discomfort with the accumulation of money persisted. Countervailing sentiment against self-enrichment came from several directions: political and social theories relating to the doctrine of stewardship, for example, argued that worldly wealth was not a personal possession but the common property of humanity, borrowed from divine sources for the duration of a lifetime. New lines of political thinking promoted the idea that too much money in one place was undesirable for the polity.[25] As

---

[22] *Pilgrim's Progress*, 144–6.

[23] Norman Jones, *God and the Moneylenders: Usury and Law in Early Modern England* (Oxford, 1989), 160–3; see also Thomas Wilson, *A Discourse Upon Usury*, intro. R. H. Tawney (London, 1925); Benjamin N. Nelson, *The Idea of Usury: From Tribal Brotherhood to Universal Otherhood* (Princeton, 1949).

[24] Richard Grassby, *The Business Community of Seventeenth-Century England* (Cambridge, 1995), 86–8, 295.

[25] During the Commonwealth era, the Hartlib Circle endorsed several charitable projects that indicated an emerging sense of "the public good," among which were plans for workhouses, schools, and hospitals. Paul Slack, *From Reformation to Improvement: Public Welfare in Early Modern England* (Oxford, 1999), 77–101.

a revised concept of philanthropy evolved, considerable debate ensued over when and how private fortunes should be distributed throughout society, rather than hoarded up as personal treasure. "[E]ver a state flourisheth when wealth is more equally spread," Francis Bacon had pointed out earlier in the century.[26] The learned statesman, probably knowingly, was paraphrasing a proverb, "Money, like manure, does no good till it is spread."[27] Such popular wisdom did not shrink from the association between money and filth, which would persist and even thrive alongside money's claim to an ever-expanding store of redeeming virtues.

THE ANIMATION OF MONEY IN THE DIARIES OF
NEHEMIAH WALLINGTON AND RALPH JOSSELIN

It is easy to overlook the signal importance of money in the personal records of seventeenth-century people, largely because the subject was so continuously a part of daily rumination. Yet a brief examination of the diaries of Nehemiah Wallington and Ralph Josselin sheds considerable light on contemporary understandings of the attributes of money, along with the social ethos within which such characteristics flourished. Paul Seaver, Wallington's biographer, has remarked upon the Puritan's odd indifference to his "own domestic economy," which Seaver believed stemmed from his "apparent lack of interest in money matters, or rather – since money was a source of constant worry – from his vagueness about the nature of his difficulties."[28] In fact, Wallington exhibited typical apprehension about coins and aversion to material wealth, and these dual sentiments acted as lightning rods for imaginative reflections on the subject of money. In this respect, his writings have more in common with those of Josselin, the propertied rural clergyman, than first meets the eye.

Wallington and Josselin were active participants in a consensus that located money within a vital mental universe of enchantment. In their

---

[26] This statement is drawn from Bacon's writings on usury. See James Spedding, R. L. Ellis, and D. D. Heath, eds., *Works of Francis Bacon*, 14 vols. (1874; Stuttgart-Bad Cannstatt, repr. 1963), 14:416, quoted in Jones, *God and the Moneylenders*, 183.

[27] Henry G. Bohn, *Handbook of Proverbs* (1855), 453. The point was also made by Aristotle.

[28] Paul S. Seaver, *Wallington's World: A Puritan Artisan in Seventeenth-Century London* (Stanford, 1985), 118. Seaver also noted that Wallington failed to record the existence of an account book though he assiduously cataloged 50 volumes of notebooks that he had written over the course of his life.

struggles against desire for money, their fears of its allurements and mastery, and their willingness to attribute power to ordinary coin, they affirmed a belief that wealth in all its earthly forms circulated according to a grand scheme of providential design. Money was infused with social life; it confronted its users with repeated tests of moral probity and charitable awareness as it reminded them of choices involving their own desires and the needs of others. The ethic that Craig Muldrew described as the "serial sociability of the culture of credit"[29] also involved money and sustained a sense of the embodiment of life through financial activities. Under the management of divinity, money accreted positive meaning. As Wallington and Josselin demonstrated in their watchful attitudes, early modern people grappled with an overwhelming sense that ordinary tokens of exchange were subject to powers outside their own authority.

Money represented much more than simply income for London artisan Nehemiah Wallington (1598–1658), whose shop of humble wooden wares and an assortment of small goods barely kept his household solvent during the civil war era. For the devout Puritan, money belonged to a bounded, problematic universe crowded with circulating signs of providence, which, like the coins in his cash box, continuously ebbed and flowed. Though an obvious necessity in sustaining a trade, money was never a neutral commodity: as specie, it presented a changeable identity that alternated unpredictably between positive and negative poles. For Wallington, money announced its stigmatized presence early in life. In his brief autobiographical narration, it featured in one of his earliest recollections, allied with temptation and sin: at the age of ten, having stolen nine pence from his father, he suffered from the terrors of retribution and "could not be in peace till I had restored it againe where I had itt." In a second instance, when nearly twenty, he stole a shilling "of[f] the tabel where lay an heape of mony," and he and his brother spent the coin on a drinking spree.[30] He summed up his attitude toward the enticements of money for the duration of his life in a list of "Remedyes against Discontent." "I did consider that worldly welth is called unrighteous mamon," he wrote, "and they be snairs and pulbacks from heaven."[31]

---

[29] Craig Muldrew, *The Economy of Obligation: The Culture of Credit and Social Relations in Early Modern England* (Basingstoke, 1998), 63.
[30] FSL, Writing Book, 1654, 3, 6.   [31] Ibid., 158.

Numerical accounting provided but a superficial measure of money, as early modern users vigilantly scrutinized the circumstances surrounding its activity in order to typecast its qualities and determine whether it was good or bad. Wallington recorded his trade in terms that went beyond rhetorical appearance and ascribed divine agency to the flux of his income: "[T]he Lord did send me such trading that I took above nine pounds," he wrote on August 21, 1641; in January of the following year, a period marked by the threat of civil conflict in London, "so good was my God that he sent in customers that I took in almost forty shillings." Yet he also understood fluctuations in money as evidence of another manner of divine intervention. When a day's business amounted to only two shillings during a quiet interval amid local unrest, he noted, "God hath given me better than money, which is peace of conscience."[32] Providence thus constructed overlapping transactional spheres, subtracting from Wallington's personal material gain in the form of coin while adding to the store of good that belonged to the city of London in the form of quietude. And how could it be otherwise for the devout and rather disconsolate turner, who filled thousands of pages of journals and historical notices with ruminations that included lists of fires, executions, accidental deaths, and "Gods Judgments" upon violations of religious and civil law? In the midst of war and religious upheaval, Wallington reasonably concluded that "the portion of Gods people is not to have abundance of this worldly welth."[33]

To see Wallington's chartings of the flow of coin simply as a function of sectarian belief would cause us to miss the way in which particular social relations contributed as much to his thoughts about money. As an artisan of modest means, Wallington seldom possessed much ready cash and he seems to have avoided keeping careful account of its comings and goings. "[T]he very nature of the artisan's household economy defied precise accounting," Paul Seaver has argued from this evidence, given the changing cast of assistants often left unsupervised in Wallington's shop and the flux of social life in the neighborhood. Such tenuous financial circumstances worked to keep money firmly embedded in a web

---

[32] Ibid., 122. On Wallington's departure from the contemporary belief in a "divine clockmaker," see *Wallington's World*, pp. 45–8. See also Thomas, *Religion and the Decline of Magic*, 125–32, on the irregularities of belief related to the doctrine of providence in the seventeenth century.

[33] FSL, Writing Book, 36–7, 158; for an example of many recorded incidents, see Nehemiah Wallington, "Remarkable Judgments of God," in *Historical Notices of Events Occurring Chiefly in The Reign of Charles I.*, 2 vols., ed. R. Webb (London, 1869), 1:43ff.

of relationality built through the custom transacted in his shop. Caught up in "a network of small creditors who sustained him," Wallington depended on day-to-day repayments of loans in order to maintain solvency. Seaver noted how the money Wallington possessed on any given day might abruptly shift hands as loans were called in or unexpected payments of credit suddenly enabled him to pay his own bills.[34] Such relations left a salutary imprint on coins, which otherwise proved resistant in their more transparent function as a means to self-enrichment.

In Wallington's private reflections, little distinction was made between financial means and money itself. He devoted many pages in his journals to close examination of his receptivity to the downward pull of earthbound pleasures associated with wealth. Renunciation might inspire copious discussion of the objects of his avoidance: "The World our enemie in tempting us" consumed several pages of chastisements directed at himself, while "The benifeet of pouvertie" offered a collection of meditations on Biblical passages having to do with the superior virtues devolving upon those lacking money. "[T]his world (which is pleasures and profets of this world) is a fawning false and flattering enemie: and oh how many are overcome with a false opinion and conceit of worldly things thinking that good store of silver and gold, fine aparell, stately fine dwellings, rich furniture, feasting and good cheare, mirth iollitie" provide security, "but it is nothing so for they are all base borne things," he recorded. Citing Proverbs 235, he added, "But riches makes themselves winges and flie a way as an Eagle."[35] Such commonplace wisdom repeatedly punctuated his thoughts. Lack of money was a sign of God's goodness: "A Child thinkes a Knife is a brave thing to playe withall: but the Father takes it a way from him: for hee knowes it will hurt him or kill himself." And finally, he added, "For the desire of mony is the roote of all evill which while some lusted after they erred from the faith: and pearced themselves through with many sorrows."[36]

The power of money, in Wallington's view, could be measured in various magnitudes; it exerted physical force in the form of comforts purchased by money, which in turn desensitized the believer against salutary pricks of conscience. His asceticism echoed the stringent denials

---

[34] *Wallington's World*, 120, 123.

[35] GL, Notebook 204, December 1630 (260). This proverb also appeared in Philip Henry's reflections upon the Great Fire of London: Matthew Henry Lee, ed., *Diaries and Letters of Philip Henry* (London, 1882), 192.

[36] GL, Notebook 204 (441).

of a Saint Francis or a sectarian leveler. "I thanke thee O Lord that I have no more for if I had thou seest how my heart would bee more drawen from thee unto voluptuous plasurs and the nearer to earth the furder [sic] from heaven," he recorded.[37] In his correspondence with acquaintances, Wallington revealed his sternest self on this topic. To a merchant who had expressed sorrow for his "worldly Losses," he railed, "[Y]ou have lost your heart together with your wealth. How can I feare, Least this Mammon was your God, Hence was Gods ielousie in removing it and hence your immoderate teares for losing it." Wallington was convinced that the poor were to inherit the kingdom above. "Now heaven is open to you which was shut before," he added, "and could never have given you entrance, with a load of iniquity."[38] Like Bunyan's pilgrims, the believer was obligated to take the right path, measured literally in distance from temptation. "The wife of Lot turned into a pillar of Salt," Wallington reminded himself, citing an image also featured in *The Pilgrim's Progress*, "doth as yet preach unto us, that wee Looke not back to those things that are in the world: but that we goe the straight way to our heavenly country."[39]

While such aversion to money may have fostered a rather hapless oversight of shop finances, Wallington's engagement in what Seaver has called "a continuous round of petty debt" supported another aspect of his thinking about money, his evident belief in the incessant circulation of monetary wealth.[40] His most active demonstrations of faith in such a universe occurred when things went well: in one instance, having just borrowed thirty shillings from his father and momentarily encouraged by fresh business, Wallington paid out money to a chapman for his wares and loaned him half of the shillings he had obtained from his father.[41] Reassurance sometimes came in the form of gifting as well as repayment. In the autumn of 1643, when an elderly widow settled her accounts before departing for New England, she repaid two pounds she owed Wallington and then gave him a further five pounds as a loan that she most likely never would collect. This must have constituted a minor windfall for the perpetually stretched accounts of the shop.[42]

Though clearly Wallington possessed little of it, the comings and goings of money prompted him to contemplate the place of riches and charity in a larger sense; as quotidian synecdoche, money often

---

[37] Ibid. (441).   [38] BL, Sloane MS 922 (79).   [39] GL, Notebook 204 (334).
[40] *Wallington's World*, 123   [41] GL, Notebook 204 [June 11, 1637] (437).
[42] *Wallington's World*, 124.

represented the part for the whole in his vigilant assessment of the society around him. An aspect of the routine maintenance of conscience among Puritans, and certainly a main theme in sectarian literature, Wallington's assertion of doctrine relating to charity is nevertheless striking for its clarity and precision. He inscribed himself within a godly commonwealth, where "we are stewards and have nothing but that we have received; we came naked into the world, and we must so again return shortly, [when] we must give account of our stewardship." According to these teachings, the wealth of the faithful (and with it, the money one earned through diligent work) was part of a common stock, devolving upon the individual in much the same way as a long-term loan, with strings attached, might be handed down by a generous parent. Thus, management of money should strive to affect justice in a larger social sphere. "If we were poor, we would think it the rich man's duty to relieve us; the royal law is to do as we would be done by; this is the law of God, the law of Nature, the law of Nations; it is equity to do it; it is iniquity to omit it," Wallington averred.[43] Beneath these judicious espousals lay intense Puritan convictions underpinning economic and political norms, which condemned covetousness and pride, the overweaning desire for riches, and the love of money for its own sake.

Despite disclaimers to the contrary, Wallington struggled against the desire for more money and wondered at its ultimate influence on his soul, repeatedly comparing the merits of wealth and poverty. His sense of self-worth wobbled accordingly: "All you godly people, that are in any trouble or adversity: remember this and perswad your selves here of, that Gods Love, and Gods favour is not withdrawen from you." He added, "[F]or, as it is no argument that the Lord loves a wicked man because he is rich, so it is no argument that God rejects the godly because they are poor."[44] He recorded with pain the distress he felt at "dwelling betwixt two Naighbours which did take much money with grate gaine & some days taking as much mony in a day as I did take in a weeke and with dobel or trebel gaine."[45] His criticisms of the newly rich under the Commonwealth, who are "proud" and "seek themselves" in their expenditures on "brave houses, fine apparel, or belly cheer," helped to convince him of his true inclinations. Wallington seemed to recoil from what he saw as the requisites of making more money, identifying wealth as part of a distinctly different social order. Despite the fact that

---

[43] Ibid., 128.   [44] GL, Notebook 204 (333, 334).   [45] FSL, Writing Book, 61.

many of those he criticized were Puritan, he shunned them, regarding their lives as given over to "misgetting, miskeeping, misspending."[46] And so he reconciled himself to the vicissitudes of a rough middle road between riches and poverty, perhaps relishing just a little the "punishments upon the breakers of the tenth commandement," which included "A covetous Worldly man Burned" and "A Covetous Theefe Cutt his own Throat."[47] Attitudes toward money, in this instance, were dependent on not only Wallington's religious belief but also his marginal perspective.[48]

Holding fast to the letter of the law, Wallington's temperament easily led him to plumb the very depths of his principles over the routine determination of a just price for his wares. A customer's stray comment might hurl him headlong into a process of prescriptive purging of angst, word by word. He was not alone in his uncertain search for the right road in business behavior; he lived in an age of intense debate over marketing practices, buoyed by boisterous sectarian ethical avowals and public religious conflict that characterized the midcentury. Quakers were perhaps the boldest opponents of the customary haggling over prices, believing that too many words inevitably led to deceit.[49] As a devout Puritan, Wallington agreed with this stricture, as he noted on a day when he uncharacteristically engaged in sharp practice, charging more than he thought he should for an item. "I did not take God with me in my selling," he wrote, "but multiplied more words than I need with some lying words. For what words can a man use after he is bid the price he can afford and take for his ware, but they must be sinful and lying words, and therefore just with God that I should lose my customer."[50] Yet success reaped from overcharging was precisely what he witnessed in the businesses of his more gainfully minded contemporaries, because they "will rather break the rule of justice than lose sixpence or a shilling" in carrying on their businesses, he noted ruefully.[51] One can imagine the satisfaction Wallington took from an apologetic letter he received from a like-minded business associate, who expressed "Thankfullnesse" for

---

[46] Ibid., 129.   [47] Ibid., 151.

[48] The only commodity Wallington seemed to desire beyond control was books, a weakness for which he chastised himself. Ibid., 461–2.

[49] Richard Bauman, *Let Your Words Be Few: Symbolism of Speaking and Silence among Seventeenth-Century Quakers* (Cambridge, 1983); David Harris Sacks, *The Widening Gate: Bristol and the Atlantic Economy, 1450–1700* (Berkeley, 1991), 313.

[50] *Wallington's World*, 131.   [51] Ibid., 128.

Wallington's gift of two books after having inadvertently imposed "hard bargains" upon the humble turner "through the dishonestie of the chapman." It was clear to this friend that Wallington was a stringent scrutinizer of trade practices and acquaintances alike and separated them into distinct categories of saved and damned according to their attitudes toward wealth.[52]

Money, the medium representing the desire for riches at large in the world, exerted a corrupting influence on shopkeepers, leading them down a path of scurrilous practices, proven by what Wallington saw as the "lying, deceit, oppression, bribery, usury, false weights, false measures, . . . or like iniquity" of those who made their fortunes in business.[53] For Wallington, the realms of market and morals were inseparable, such that dishonesty in one led inexorably to retribution in the other. "God is set upon justice in another manner than you think of," he seemed to be warning himself as he contemplated emulating more successful businesses.[54] Fearing the judgments of others, who, like him, knew exactly how much money each neighboring shop took in and would detect any attempts at "sharp practice," Wallington shunned the profiteering methods of his more competitive contemporaries.

Wallington was not alone in his apprehensions about the physical presence of money: contemporaries made careful note of strange occurrences related to counting or coveting coin, which suggested a strange mixture of alertness to providential judgments and magical thinking. Oliver Heywood recorded how, after collecting his wages, he experienced "an itching much to see what was brought" and so counted his money on the Sabbath; later, he recorded being overcome by remorse and vowed "to doe so no more." In another instance, he wrote of the fierce local disputes that ensued when neighbors accidentally unearthed Roman coins while plowing a field. "*Am. sacra famos*," he added, taking some comfort from the ancient wisdom.[55] Heywood also recounted a vivid case in which a boy struck a pact with the devil in order to get "mony enough to spend" and, after receiving instructions from the devil in a "back-lane," he thus acquired the power to multiply shilling pieces. Only after various magical occurrences, including the appearance of a

---

[52] BL, Sloane MS 922 [January 14, 1638](219).   [53] Ibid., 129–30.   [54] Ibid., 127.

[55] Oliver Heywood, *Autobiography, Diaries, Anecdote and Event Books*, 4 vols., ed. J. Horsfall Turner (Brighouse and Bingley, 1882–5), 12 May 1678, 1:343; 14 May 1679, 2:262. The tag is from Virgil's *Aeneas* 3:57: *Auri sacra fames*, "the accursed hunger for gold." See also Philip Henry's recording of a similar instance, cited earlier.

"devils shilling" that passed for "good mony" and the levitation of the boy's bed by the devil's hand, did the power of prayer expel the alien presence from the boy's life.[56] The search for hidden hordes of precious metal drew many people down the path of dealing with cunning folk and magic manuals. As Keith Thomas has pointed out, "The battle with Satan and his hierarchy of demons was thus a literal reality for most devout Englishmen," necessitating "perpetual combat" and ceaseless watchfulness, confirmed repeatedly by contemporaries' reports of brushes with embodied signs of diabolic power.[57]

For Wallington, money represented temptation to such an extent that it was capable of personifying evil, thus, taking on a life of its own. In the course of doing business, he encountered a brass shilling that had made its way into his money box, which he inadvertently paid out as change to a customer. When the customer pointed out the coin, Wallington retracted it and gave him another. Returning it to the box, Wallington soon fell victim to an inner storm of voices, which fought over what to do with it:

> Constience did begin to chide and sayd I had a Thife in my boxe a brass shilling which will canker all the rest. And now the battel begins and the flesh begines to baffel me saying that being I tooke it I may paye it a way againe – And a shilling losse to thee is a grate matter it is more than thou wilt gaine a good while[.] And there is many honest men that holds it lawfull to put away brasse mony if they take itt, and many such like Cavils the flesh did say to me.[58]

Plagued by a Bunyanlike dialogue between his conscience and "the flesh," Wallington seemed to see the coin caught between the two sides, its identity up for grabs. Was it a "thife" who destroyed the value of all the coins in the cash box through its creeping contagion?[59] Signs of life in money thus sprang up like so many seedlings in the fertile soil of Wallington's imagination, embodied in more than just metaphor as he wrestled with feelings of guilt that bothered him through the night.

---

[56] Ibid., 1:344–5.

[57] Owen Davies, *Cunning-Folk: Popular Magic in English History* (London, 2003), 93–5; Keith Thomas, *Religion and the Decline of Magic* (Harmondsworth, 1971), 562, 564.

[58] FSL, Writing Book, 426–7.

[59] For a similar rendering of Biblical teachings, See [Francis Quarles], *Wisdom's Better than Money* (1698), Maxim 15: "What thou givest to the poor, thou securest from the Thief; but what thou witholdest from his Necessity, a Thief possesses. God's Exchequer is the poor man's Box; when thou strikest a Tally, he becomes thy Debtor." (156) Maxim 70 also points out, "The poor man's Peny is a Plague in the rich man's Purse." (193)

Biblical imagery and popular religious metaphors produced a potent mixture, leading him to rise at five in the morning to find a solution through prayer. "[M]y Resolutions bent," he vowed, "as soone as it was light to take this brasse shilling with two brace halfe crowns & a six pence and call my servents to witness that I hate deceite & so chope them to peeces."[60]

The hectoring of the brass shilling was arrested before this planned slaughter took place by the timely intervention of a worldly wise (and far less conflicted) chapman. When paid with the coin (which Wallington was at pains to point out to him), along with pieces of silver, the peddler pronounced them "all very good" and willingly took the troublemaker away. Wallington by now had exhausted his tolerance for counterfeit money. He sought out the two brass half crowns and sixpence mingling among his shop change and did what he could to destroy their circulatory existence: he cut the half crowns in two and nailed the sixpence to a post. The Christian symbolism of the latter act may have eluded him, but he no doubt drew satisfaction from such a dramatic show of revenge. Only through desecration of the heinous simulacrum could the conscience-bound turner find true peace of mind.[61]

Though dangerous as tempters, coins could function positively as token offerings of penance, and Wallington devised a system of fines for his daily infractions, measured in seriousness by the increments of small change. He made a practice of keeping his own personal poor box, and throughout his notebooks, Wallington indicated the many instances generating a need to pay into the fund stored there. Among his New Year's resolutions (maintained as a running list for several years), he vowed "that I take not the least pin nor anything else from anyone and that if I do, then I restore it fourfold and [give] one farthing to the poor." Each resolution came with its attendant fine for violation. To look "after a woman to lust after her in my heart" resulted in a levy of one penny, whereas "negligence in his calling seemed worthy only of a one-farthing fine."[62] A roster of fines, of course, was perfectly in keeping with Puritan and church law generally, as Oliver Heywood confirmed in his account of suffering to pay for absence from church during the early years of the Restoration.[63] It is impossible to know just how often Wallington lived up to his resolutions, though we are given one indication: when his house was robbed one Sunday morning, he noted that "the poor's

---

[60] FSL, Writing Book, 427.   [61] Ibid., 428.   [62] *Wallington's World*, 124–5.
[63] Heywood, *Autobiography*, 1: 190.

box" was taken "with, as I think, about twenty shillings in it."[64] This was no mean accumulation of petty fines but a mother lode of sacrifice that must have brought Wallington a fair amount of psychological relief.

It is not without irony that we can view a zealous English protestant, over a century after Luther, measuring his adherence to religious precepts according to monetary increments. Yet Wallington was exceptional in his assiduous attention to the attributes of money, judging from the abundant evidence of shopkeepers and businessmen who transcended such fears in order to succeed in trade.[65] Future research into the moral meanings of money in the sixteenth century may reveal more about the relationship between coins and religious belief during the age of reform. What is clear is the fact that in seventeenth-century England, money was firmly situated at the intersection of conflicts between self and other and good and evil, a cognitive reality readily apparent in midcentury constructions of personal histories. While journal keeping was somewhat biased in combining "the more methodical and introspective sides of life," as Alan Macfarlane has pointed out,[66] it nevertheless affords a view of a fascinating practice of interweaving the arithmetical and psychological and the monetary and moral, which Wallington displayed with so little inhibition.

The diary of Essex minister Ralph Josselin (1617–1683), recorded between 1641 to 1683, overlaps with the notebooks of Wallington and affords an interesting, if limited, basis for comparison, aided by Macfarlane's classic analysis of Josselin's family life. As Vicar of Earls Colne during the Civil War, Josselin distanced himself from sectarian extremes, though he became a "moderate Cromwellian" whose "unique 'worm's eye' view of contemporary events" of the war constituted the original reason for transcribing and publishing parts of his diary a century ago.[67] He was a full generation younger than Wallington, boasted degrees from Cambridge, and enjoyed useful family connections that aided him in securing a good living in Essex. As a landowner with several sources of income, Josselin certainly enjoyed more financial security than Wallington; yet he nevertheless displayed many similar views on money, leading us to hypothesize that the cultural fabric of the times, and not so much personal and financial particularities, contributed

[64] *Wallington's World*, 120. The story is also told in the introduction to *Historical Notices*.
[65] Grassby, *Business Community*, 287–8.
[66] *The Family Life of Ralph Josselin* (Cambridge, 1970), 8.
[67] Ibid., 18; see also E. Hocklifee, ed., *The Diary of the Rev. Ralph Josselin, 1616–1683*, vol. 15 (1908).

to a belief in an animated notion of money circulating in a bounded universe.

As the history of early modern hospitality has shown, customary assumptions about obligations to the community ensured that at least a portion of the wealth belonging to a prosperous individual would be laid out for others.[68] Like Wallington, Josselin expressed uneasiness about the accumulation of money under his roof, and like the humble London artisan, the comfortable village clergyman believed in the necessity of putting wealth back into circulation by giving to the poor. As Macfarlane observed, copious evidence in the diary indicated "that Josselin did not look on such charity as a one-way process; he regarded it as investment which would bring returns of a spiritual and social kind." A paraphrase of Scripture in the diary, "He that gives to the poore lends to the Lord," and Josselin's keen sense of divine reciprocity support this view. As Josselin noted, "I observe no kindness of mine at any time to any poore distressed ones but god quickly makes it up." Gaining money and giving it away represented opposite sides of a balance sheet of spiritual accounting.[69]

Whether in the form of random acts of providence or through enhanced favor in his village, Josselin believed that every act of generosity belonged to a larger scheme of intentions and providence. Numerous instances of lending and giving money punctuate his account of his affairs, and not all gestures are limited to the local poor.[70] He regularly doled out sums to his sisters, even though at one point he recorded that he himself was in "great straites for mony."[71] His sense of acting as custodian of his sisters after the death of both parents seems to have converged with his sense of stewardship with regard to the poor. These daily reminders of responsibility to others must have given him at least partial relief from the "vaine thoughts" that were often linked to providing for his immediate family.[72]

---

[68] The definitive study of this is Felicity Heal, *Hospitality in Early Modern England* (Oxford, 1990), but see also the important discussion of gifting and credit relations in Margot C. Finn, *The Character of Credit: Personal Debt in English Culture, 1740–1914* (Cambridge, 2003).

[69] *Family Life of Ralph Josselin*, 51. Macfarlane points out that George Herbert voiced a similar belief that "money thus lent to the Lord" was a good investment for one's children (51–2n.).

[70] Alan Macfarlane, ed., *The Diary of Ralph Josselin, 1616–1683* (Oxford, 1976); see, for example, entries for 10 January 1645/6, 27 December 1651, and 10 June 1652 (53, 266, 280).

[71] Ibid., 23 December 1646; *Family Life*, 129–31.

[72] See the extensive entry for 12 September 1648, *Diary*, 135–8, analyzed by Macfarlane, *Family Life*, 178–9.

But frequent acts of charity did not protect Josselin from true distress over money matters. According to Macfarlane, his most intense bouts of anxiety coincided with the period when his personal wealth increased most rapidly.[73] These years also coincided with considerable political unrest, which, along with Josselin's continuing study of the Book of Revelations, provided additional fodder for both his dreams and his general state of unease.[74] Theological discourse on the subject of self-enrichment abounded, and we might simply view the evidence as the workings of conscience in the mind of an observant clergyman. Yet it is worth probing the confusion of images in these anxieties, because they seem to have granted as much animation to money as the mental habits of Wallington. Most notable is the dream he recorded in August of 1653, which fell within this period of personal gain. As he remembered it, the dream began with a gift:

> . . . one sent mee a bushel of wheate, and in the mouth of the sacke was a bundle of mony, which I conceived was 10s. it proved 13. at first telling, thinking I was mistaken I told it over againe and still it increased more halfe crownes and more 1 s. so that I could not reckon it, but thinking it was not so much I told it againe, and yett it proved more: awaking I thought presently of gods providing for us unexpectedly and by way of wonder, and that his should not want though the young lyons famish.[75]

Macfarlane called attention to the "acquisitive symbolism" indicating "either worldly or spiritual harvests," a reasonable interpretation, especially given the coincidence of the calendar date of mid-August. Just as important, perhaps, is the juxtaposition of cash and wheat, a vivid combination of two fundamental sources of wealth, one of them timeless and organic and the other of base metal. Perhaps this was Josselin's personal rendition of the miracle of loaves and fishes (echoing wheat and silver), given that his own interpretation transformed a suspect cache of coin into a God-given gift. It is also possible that Josselin's dabbling in stocks in hops may have had something to do with his vision of coins emerging from a bushel of grain.[76] What was so disturbing for Josselin and,

---

[73] Macfarlane links the frequency of "personal dreams" during the years 1653–59 with the "greatest period of anxiety over his rapidly increasing estate," (187) though elsewhere he points to 1648–51, when Josselin was in his mid thirties, as "the period of real crisis" related to a sense of personal sin (178).

[74] On Revelations, see Josselin, *Diary*, 9 December 1650 and 2 November 1651, and continuing references to imagery; for dreams, see 18 May 1653, 10 July 1653, 30 June 1654, and 3 February 1654/5.

[75] Ibid., 13 July 1653.   [76] His stock investments are discussed later.

in the end, generated his immediate sense of "wonder" was the way in which the organic nature of the wheat seemed to spread to the coins in the bundle, which grew in number with inexorable force, destroying the minister's ability to tell how much was there. Numerology might have helped Josselin deem this bounty as sacred, as the shillings advanced past the unlucky number of thirteen. With the permission of providence, Josselin thus witnessed the magic of money, and in an uncharacteristic instant, it appeared to be endowed with holy, not profane, power.

In fact, Josselin appears to allude to a constant wrestling with the desire to have or accumulate money, which he cryptically refers to as "the evill of some former temptacions" in an entry of July, 1650. In the context of citing the high prices of corn at Colchester, he expressed relief in being preserved from the entreaties of some hidden desire, one that apparently appealed less to him now, as "I have some experience of the sorrowes, and trials in the world."[77] Earlier struggles against "minde vanities" and "sinfull evills" suggest that he associated his easy access to food and firing in times of want with a selfish desire for wealth and comfort.[78] It is also possible that "the power and rage of Satan" that he felt shortly after the death of the father of the local lord of the manor had something to do with his anxieties about the ensuing legacy left to him, which amounted to a rather paltry sum of twenty shillings.[79] Macfarlane's contention that Josselin later became preoccupied with business concerns during the years 1653–4 certainly seems true, because Josselin provided repeated proof, in one characteristic entry noting that "I finde my heart in a very dead and unspirituall frame."[80] But this did not foreclose the occasional moment of denial, such as his determined equanimity toward an "indifferent" harvest in August 1654. "[D]esired of god he would provide for mee from the hearts of other," he recorded, "seing [sic] I was by him taken of, from scrambling in the world, and all my mony gone."[81]

For the most part, Josselin's conscience operated quite reliably: he often made a point of giving away at least a bit of money soon after he received pay or rent from others.[82] In one instance, three days after receiving a legacy of forty shillings from a parishioner, he made a gift

---

[77] Ibid., 21 July 1650.
[78] Ibid., 14 January 1648/9, 21 January 1648/9, and 4 February 1648/9.
[79] Ibid., 26 March 1648 and 27 March 1648.   [80] Ibid., 9 April 1654.
[81] Ibid., 26 August 1654.
[82] Ibid., 10 January 1645/6, when he received "6 weekes pay" and promptly gave "two of [God's] servants 10s."

to an Essex physician (one of his patrons) of "a piece of plate cost 5s. 6d. per ounce it cost mee 5 li. 19s. 6d. as a token of my love to him in giving mee the schoole."[83] Though at times the rapid turnaround of receiving and paying out had to do with a persistent shortage of coin, which forced debtors to wait until their own loans were repaid in order to pay others, several instances seem to illustrate a different impulse: a wish to balance the accounts of conscience by reacting to the receipt of a gift by passing on an offering of one's own, thus contributing money to a channel of wealth that circulated rather than accumulated in one place. As Margot Finn has pointed out, gift-giving "worked at once to mark social distinctions and maintain social solidarity" and "undercut the primacy of contractual and monetary transactions." Similarly, these donations worked alongside monetary activity to neutralize its power of self-aggrandizement.[84] The round of giving was clearly understood as a circuitry that demanded a vigilant style of maintenance. When Goodwife Potter gave Josselin "an 11s. piece," he recorded, "this love is from thee oh god, requite it fully into her bosome againe," by way of return. And to test his family in their attention to charity, he impersonated a beggar at his own doorstep one winter night and was rewarded for his success with a penny.[85]

Josselin was, in fact, a determined manager of money, demonstrating skills that operated alongside his religious orientation. Like the godly merchants of Bristol examined by David Harris Sacks, this country clergyman farmer absorbed himself in the business of building up his capital with the assurance that such activity did not contradict the strictures of his religion. In relation to other clerical livings in his county, Josselin's £28 per annum in the 1640s fell below average, but his acumen in acquiring other forms of income brought his annual receipts to around £200 in the 1650s. Even so, as Macfarlane pointed out, this made him "very prosperous, but by no means exceptional" as a wealthy yeoman.[86] For this reason, it is worthwhile outlining the several concerns of a man

---

[83] Ibid., 7 June 1652 and 10 June 1652. The plate was given to Dr. Laurence Wright, who was responsible for obtaining Josselin's position as master of Earls Colne School. *Diary*, 126n.

[84] Josselin's expressed views on gifting conform perfectly with Margot Finn's arguments about the importance of circulating credit and obligation: see *Character of Credit*, 8–11 and Chap. 2, passim.

[85] Josselin, *Diary*, 29 January 1646/7 and 4 February 1646/7.

[86] Macfarlane, *Family Life*, 59, 76–77; cf. Kent, where incomes could range from £1,000 to £1,500 per annum.

of modest prosperity at midcentury, because such financial activities represent the standard monetary goals of a significant middle band of society.

Josselin's financial aims focused to a large degree in providing for his family; this fact generated a certain amount of moral conflict because it seemed to represent a self-interested objective, but the minister appears to have quelled his discomfort in the face of expectations placed upon a man of his station. With a household of this rank and size (six living children, in addition to his wife) dependent on him for much of his career, considerable expenses loomed before Josselin. For his sons, he faced the need to purchase apprenticeships, and for his daughters, he would be expected to accumulate dowries. His older son was settled as a draper's apprentice for £100, and Josselin gave him an additional £50 in order to set up his own shop. A younger son's apprenticeship cost £45, duly noted in Josselin's accounts, though the boy's later exploits probably cost his father much more in frequent small increments. One daughter was taken on as some form of servant at the cost of £50 and two other girls were sent to school, which Macfarlane estimates at roughly £6 per annum for several years.[87] The cost of the four girls' dowries was considerable: the eldest received £200, in addition to valuable goods; two of the other daughters received a combination of dwelling, land, and cash to the tune of more than £1000, with £600 of it in cash. These amounts constituted a fair achievement in terms of asset building over Josselin's lifetime, full proof of his assiduous efforts to make the most of the opportunities that came his way.[88] Josselin did not shrink from such occasions, which included the purchase of lands, made possible through friendships with the local lord of the manor and his steward and investment in the hop trade. "I have bought a part in a shippe: it cost me £14. 10s.," he recorded in 1644. "God send mee good speed with the same."[89]

As Michael Mascuch has argued, the individualistic self was born in the chrysalis of deeply traditional structures such as the family, and worries about the welfare of one's family qualified the meaning of "self" in these instances, because concern for others might take precedence over purely selfish motives that worked toward aims such as personal

---

[87] Ibid., 48–9.
[88] Ibid., 93–4. It is worth noting that Josselin was criticized by neighbors for using his connections to the local lord of the manor and his steward, which enabled him to purchase copyhold tenures as they came due (63).
[89] Josselin, *Diary*, 8 August 1644.

advancement.[90] Josselin's play with money and risk occupied a middle ground of interest, denoted as virtuous effort on behalf of offspring, yet nevertheless dangerously near to the polluting powers of Mammon. He evidently wrestled with his conscience over this matter, too, as he recognized that concerns for his household were draining a good deal of energy and attention in the direction of a sinful objective. On several occasions, he attempted to right the balance, at least mentally, by tallying up the money and goods passing out of his hands and into the community. The exercise was technically his duty: by law, as a clergyman, he was required to devote a tenth of his income to charitable uses. Nevertheless, compared with his methodical diary keeping, Josselin's efforts to track his giving were irregular, and this fact seems noteworthy.[91] Macfarlane reckoned that Josselin probably gave away about ten pounds per annum, which was slightly less than a tenth of his income during his prosperous years, though perhaps more than what was required at other times in his career. The figures were close enough to warrant a continuing pinch of conscience for a clergyman whose dreams featured animated images of money.[92]

In Josselin's defense, it must be said that an attempt to quantify the clergyman's giving reveals the difficulties of such an exercise: it remains impossible to ascertain the worth of his spontaneous small gifts, meals shared, loans never recovered, and the costs of ritual entertaining. All of these, by definition, were donations to the spiritual welfare of the community. Josselin also took into consideration the intangible benefit he derived from study and attempted to put a number on it:

> I sett apart the tenth of all my incomes in money as minister, the 10 of my rents in money, & the 10th of my profitt by any bargains. the 20th part of the money I take for all corn I sell. to pay my tenths & to serve in gods worship and free charitable bounty to gods peace as neare as I can, allowing out 20s. yearly for books.

This last allowance, a prescient form of tax deduction, revealed how Josselin construed his giving as not only literal donations ("giving many

---

[90] Michael Mascuch, "Social Mobility and Middling Self-Identity: The Ethos of British Autobiographers, 1600–1750," *Social History* 20, no. 1 (1995): 45–61.

[91] Three instances occur on 30 January 1645/6, 29 March 1652, and 19 November 1666, respectively.

[92] Macfarlane, *Family Life*, 52. The breadth of giving must also include the rounds of gifting and lending to neighbors and friends, which Macfarlane calculated had amounted to over £1,000 during Josselin's lifetime. Macfarlane includes a helpful discussion of the distinctions between "kin," "neighbors" and "friends" (148–50).

things in kinde at the doore") but also the cultivation of his own spirituality, which he regarded as part of his donated tenth in more than one entry.[93] He made an honorable attempt to disperse money across great distances, noting in one instance that he was sending the proceeds of a church collection to the "Indians," presumably in America.[94] Even such hasty stabs at determining his own income proved to Josselin that a prosperous living introduced baffling complexities into the "accounts" of the wealthy. It is no wonder that less sophisticated people like Wallington simply concluded that an abundance of riches led the wealthy into the valley of deceit.[95]

Despite obvious differences in means, Josselin and Wallington shared similar anxieties about the encroachment of money upon a sense of social ethics and moral rectitude. Though Josselin began his professional life with much less wealth than he claimed at his death, his belief in a grand system of reciprocity seems to have remained intact. He took pains to record the death of a local butcher's wife, whose tight-fisted behavior during her final days seemed to have fit the stereotype of a miser, especially because she was discovered to have had "hid . . . in the ground a vast sum of mony."

> [W]ho was so miserable shee grutcht [grudged] any thing to her selfe, and . . . shee would have no fire in her house in her ilnes, shee sent for a poore woman . . . to goe for her to the phisician, . . . being shee could not worke shee would goe the cheaper and so shee gave her 2d. and 2d. more for the phisitian, whose judgment of her shee was willing to have, but not to receive any thing from him – and thus said shee mony runs away and spred her hands.[96]

Her resort to proverbial wisdom ("Money is round, and rolls away") rather than scriptural teachings must have confirmed Josselin's view

---

[93] Ibid., 52. Josselin discussed his habit of book buying at several points in the diary. In one instance, he stopped himself from further purchases until he dutifully paid up all his debts. In another entry, he created what Viviana Zelizer would call "special monies" by designating a fund "that providence doth by guift or otherwise unexpectedly and freely supply mee withall" for the purchase of books. Josselin, *Diary*, 1 May 1653 and 30 January 1645/6.

[94] *Diary*, 26 December 1652.

[95] Josselin later repented his neglectfulness with regard to "good uses as I once engaged" of his income. He resolved to do better in his entry on 19 November 1667 given that "the nature of my estate is very much altered."

[96] *Diary*, 2 March 1656/7.

of the woman as lacking in good sense and moral probity, proven by the fact that the woman had lied about her true financial means.

A great many factors, some of them intellectual and supernatural in nature, contributed to Josselin's abiding sense of the needfulness of reciprocity that involved the circulation of money. Like Wallington, he actively subscribed to the doctrine of stewardship, which contemporary writings on the poor repeatedly affirmed. Ensuring this circulation was an array of forces working through providential acts, rendered visible through Josselin's daily recording of his deeds and the occurrences that coincided with them. Macfarlane called attention to the role of overlapping realms of "the social, spiritual, and physical," which made Josselin expect retribution or reward in one area of his life to be played out in another: "[R]eciprocation might return along a different plane from that on which it departed."[97] Life experience was thus caught up in a peculiar form of double-entry bookkeeping, with an omniscient creator in charge of the balance sheet. Personal illness, weather, and varying returns on stock, through this indirect method, worked to imbricate money within the intersection of sacred and natural planes. One such example occurred during Josselin's active attempts to build his capital, and his entry for January 23, 1651/2, gives a vivid sense of the extent of Josselin's involvement in monetary transactions:

> I was quite out of moneys, and went where some was owing mee, received it not, I knew god would provide for mee against my needs, and therefore I desire not to care for these things, when I came home I found a tenant there with rent, and presently two more paid me some mony so I paid my sister. 40s. I now have paid her all, and I paid goodwife Mathew 3 li. I have also paid her all, and my wife had about 40s. for her stocke. I procured 10 li. for goodman Sparrow. my roll of debts is now brought downe to 8 li, blessed bee my god, and I owe not 40s. more in all the world.

Providential deliverance from a lack of money conformed to the larger universe of noteworthy signs from divine power noted throughout Josselin's diary.[98] Providence saved him and his family from plague and smallpox and sent him dreams about his chapel and his children, leading him to place a pointing finger in the margins of entries that he believed

---

[97] Macfarlane, *Family Life*, 195.

[98] Josselin's entry for 29 November 1651 offers one such example: it intersperses discussions of his credit transactions with his musings regarding recent prophesies, followed by his gratitude for the improvement of his daughter's health and his "perswasion" that the lord "will preserve us from that noisome arrow [smallpox] that is going abroad."

to be prophetic. If money was involved in miracles, they were ones that were initiated from above. What Craig Muldrew identified as a network of trust included this critical component of divine intervention. In times of trouble, the metaphors of belief, laden with the language of debt and payment, became literal truths. As Wallington noted in his account of a person completely bereft of money, "God will make you able to pay" and "God is a good pay master."[99] Such timely intervention, situated within a seventeenth-century social context of friends and near relations, helped both Josselin and Wallington to steer clear of the "evill" and "divels" surrounding money.

The enchantment of money through the metaphors and doctrines of religion served as a powerful means of hedging in the passion of avarice in the early modern world. By providing a vehicle for fears of worldly pollution and divine retribution, life-infused money reminded ordinary users that the evils of excess posed a constant threat to their well-being and thus created a bridge between the material satisfaction of their private selves with loss to the larger community. But an ethically informed variety of the living coin would not survive the cultural and material changes of the late seventeenth and early eighteenth centuries. The end of an age of miracles with regard to religion helped to sever the relationship between money and providence, particularly as intellectual movements of the Restoration and after 1688 emphasized the rewards of a rational and scientific approach to the natural world. On a more practical level, a "strong hostility to magic" made it a violation of church law to employ popular methods of sorcery to locate lost money. This technique and other profane activities with coins became associated with vulgar superstitions and improper conduct.[100]

Accompanying these intellectual shifts were more profoundly significant material changes in the economic culture of early modern England, which fostered a view of money as beneficial. The detoxification of money was never complete, and fresh avowals of the divisive impact of riches would surface in the eighteenth century.[101] But arguments for the

---

[99] FSL, Writing Book, 138.

[100] Thomas, *Religion and the Decline of Magic*, 253, 256, 309. On the passion of avarice, see Albert O. Hirschman, *The Passions and the Interests: Political Arguments for Capitalism before Its Triumph* (Princeton, 1997).

[101] John Wesley's position on stewardship represented one such critical response to the materialism of his age. See John Walsh, "John Wesley and the Community of Goods," in *Protestant Evangelicalism: Britain, Ireland, Germany, and America, c. 1750 – c. 1950: Essays in Honour of W. R. Ward*, ed. Keith Robbins (Oxford, 1990), 25–50.

virtue of money, as a source of individual satisfaction as well as a vehicle of philanthropy, became more widely accepted. Asceticism might even pose hazards to the man of business, which even Calvin had recognized, and religious manuals advised avoidance of extreme behavior, including excessive attention to the dangers of money.[102] Popular religious literature in Restoration England downplayed the evils of wealth, preferring to emphasize the necessity of charity instead. By the beginning of the eighteenth century, "religion had achieved a certain independence from the rest of the culture," allowing for a broader acceptance of worldly pursuits and their material consequences.[103] Proponents of a domesticated form of avarice spoke through popular fables of the early enlightenment, which provided "a psychologically compelling account of the positive social function" of the desire for money.[104] Material abundance did not spell peril after all. Though pilloried as "Man-Devil" by his critics, Bernard Mandeville stated an obvious truth in his *Fable of the Bees*: hypocritical behavior in the face of money and luxury was a feeble distraction from the real business of English culture, which was wed to market imperatives.

Yet the anxieties of Wallington and Josselin prove that the "disenchantment of the world" and money did not proceed in linear fashion, despite the banishment of popery, the rise of reason and scientific truth, and the production of a great deal of wealth. Robert Scribner has reminded us that "the processes of secularization and desacralization may not be as closely tied to the development of Protestantism as has been assumed" and the "decline of magic" is an equally ambiguous process not yet fully illuminated.[105] The animation of money may provide the means to extend such an investigation into the ideologies informing early political economy, where its survival as a means of measurement and metaphor provided a continuing dialogue with the forces of material change.

---

[102] Grassby, *Business Community*, 288.
[103] C. John Sommerville, *Popular Religion in Restoration England* (Gainesville, 1977), 116–17; *The Secularization of Early Modern England: From Religious Culture to Religious Faith* (Oxford, 1992), 16.
[104] E. G. Hundert, *The Enlightenment's Fable: Bernard Mandeville and the Discovery of Society* (Cambridge, 1994), 22.
[105] Scribner, "The Reformation," 493–4.

CHAPTER 4

Refuge from Money's Mischief: John Bellers and the Clerkenwell Workhouse

The patterns of thought evident in the diaries of Wallington and Josselin reveal personal ethical conflicts over wealth and virtue generated by the insistent circulation of money throughout seventeenth-century English society. Such private rumination, at times dramatized by speaking coins, gave voice to arguments against avarice and worldly values. But these well-weathered assertions competed against powerful materialist arguments in favor of commercial ventures and pleasures afforded by greater personal wealth. From the Restoration to the end of the century, developments in trade and finance generated intense public interest in money. Discussions of currency and wealth came to occupy considerable space in the flourishing public forum of print culture, especially following the lapse of the Licensing Act in 1695. Building on theories that had circulated since the 1620s, the nascent science of political economy posed basic questions about the nature and purpose of money in the new nation state. Shifting views of money must be considered against this background, particularly with regard to the embattled moral strictures that informed the ruminations of Wallington and Josselin.

The writings of Quaker reformer John Bellers (1654–1725), seen in relation to his project to employ the poor in London, offer a means of tracing the development of ideas about money during these formative years. A merchant with little formal education, Bellers nevertheless stands as a worthy contributor to the emerging science of political economy, recognized by Karl Marx as "a veritable phenomenon" in its history.[1] His *Essays About the Poor, Manufactures, Trade, Plantations, and*

---

[1] Karl Marx, *Capital: A Critique of Political Economy*, Vol. I, trans. Ben Fowkes (New York, 1976), 619n.

Immorality (1699) included a terse but important subsection on "Mony" and his more practical treatise, *Proposals for A Colledge of Industry* (first published in 1695 and reprinted by Robert Owen in *New View of Society* in 1818), laid out principles relating to the moral questions of distribution and justice in matters of economic life. Historians of economic thought have overlooked the richness of Bellers's thought because of the limited ways in which they have approached economic theory predating Adam Smith.[2] In fact, the issues touched upon in these little books – especially the relationship between trade, employment, and money – were central subjects in the major works of political economy of the following century as theorists built on the foundations provided by William Petty, Josiah Child, Nicholas Barbon, and other early writers. While seventeenth-century writers had focused primarily on the "want of money" as "the first cause of the decay of trade," Bellers focused on its destabilizing properties. Studying the social relations rippling through society from sites of exchange, he anticipated the eighteenth-century discussion of the inequality of modern commercial society featured in the works of Adam Smith and the Scottish Enlightenment, and later, in the theories of Marx. Proof that Bellers was an astute observer of economic life, his attention to the subject of money exposed important and enduring tensions beneath ordinary market behavior.[3]

---

[2] Bellers is not mentioned in Terence Hutchison, *Before Adam Smith: The Emergence of Political Economy, 1662–1776* (Oxford, 1988), though he receives notice for his proposals for training the poor in Joyce Oldham Appleby, *Economic Thought and Ideology in Seventeenth-Century England* (Princeton, 1978), 143–4. Douglas Vickers, *Studies in the Theory of Money, 1690–1776* (Philadelphia, 1959), gives him considerable credit for identifying the need for greater employment of the laboring classes and the connection between that and the demand for goods (18, 22, 147).

[3] The quotation is from Gerard de Malynes, cited in Hutchison, *Before Adam Smith*, 21. No extensive treatment of the life of Bellers exists in English apart from an entry by Timothy V. Hitchcock in the new *Dictionary of National Biography* and brief coverage provided within introductions to volumes of his writings: A. Ruth Fry, *John Bellers, 1654–1725: Quaker, Economist and Social Reformer* (London, 1935); George Clarke, ed., *John Bellers: His Life, Times and Writings* (London, 1987). Brief treatment appeared in a denominational tract for a general audience: Charles Kohler, *A Quartet of Quakers* (London, 1978). There is one book-length biography in Russian, Tatiana Aleksandrovna Pavlova, *Dzhon Bellers i angliiskai a sotsialno-ekonomicheskai a myslvtoroi polov* (Moscow, 1979), and a redaction of Bellers's ideas in Eduard Bernstein, "John Bellers, Champion of the Poor and Advocate of a League of Nations," in *Cromwell and Communism: Socialism and Democracy in the Great English Revolution*, trans. H. J. Stenning (1919; Nottingham, 1980). See also Timothy V. Hitchcock, ed., *Richard Hutton's Complaints Book: The Notebook of the Steward of the Quaker Workhouse at Clerkenwell, 1711–1737*, Vol. 24 (London, 1987), viii–xiv; William C. Braithwaite, *The Second Period of Quakerism* (London, 1919), 571–94. I am grateful to Tim Hitchcock for bringing Bellers

At the heart of Bellers's thought was the problem of distribution: what was to be done about the fact that leisured elites were the beneficiaries of a vast cornucopia of goods and resources, while the labor of producing such wealth fell in inverse proportion upon those at the bottom of society? Long before prominent writers constructed more formal theories for such a stance, Bellers argued that wealth was as much a moral as a material issue, and labor lay at the root of an analysis of its creation.[4] The growth of private wealth and public luxury in this era was matched in conspicuousness by swelling ranks of the nation's poor. While his contemporaries adhered to a notion of the utility of poverty, advocating a large, independent population of laborers toiling for minimal wages, Bellers pressed for direct involvement in improving the material lives of the indigent. Though some aspects of his thought are in keeping with the more benevolent aspects of paternalism of the period, Bellers's notion of a polity conceived of propertied citizens united as one with the bottom rungs of society – what Tawney called "a profound consciousness of social solidarity" – was extraordinary for his day.[5]

Bellers's perspective was informed, in part, by his religious and social marginalization as a second-generation Quaker in Restoration England. The paradox of excluded persons existing at the periphery of a restored monarchy and nation was not lost on the Society of Friends, who, as a group, viewed the reconstituted government askance, given their subjection to civil and religious persecution by the Quaker Act of 1662. This law coincided with the Act of Settlement of the same year, which imposed contradictory forms of regulation upon the poorest sector of English society, what Keith Wrightson has called a "penumbra of casual labour."[6] Initially inspired by unrest of the civil war period, the law required local authorities to return migrant laborers to their parishes of origin if they could not provide proof of rightful residence in new places of abode. Ejections from localities and badging of paupers (required by

---

to my attention and for his own work on Bellers and the Clerkenwell Workhouse. I would also like to thank the Mellon Consortia Conference at the University of California, Berkeley, and especially Blair Hoxby, for comments on an earlier version of this chapter.

[4] Before Adam Smith, George Berkeley, Bishop of Cloyne, took a position similar to that of Bellers on the problem of employment, which he combined with monetary analysis in his *Querist* in 1735–7. Hutchison, *Before Adam Smith*, 141–8; Vickers, *Theory of Money*, 141–69; 170–1.

[5] R. H. Tawney, *Religion and the Rise of Capitalism* (1926; Harmondsworth, 1984), 269.

[6] Keith Wrightson, *Earthly Necessities: Economic Lives in Early Modern Britain* (New Haven, 2000), 313, 324.

law in 1697) were humiliations by anyone's standards. Bellers was aware of the fact that some Quaker Meetings forbade their poor from seeking parish relief or begging from the general public and acted instead to extend relief efforts to their own members. In defiance of the Act of Settlement, Quakers also provided security for wandering Friends who appeared in their localities in search of employment.[7] While enhancing the public view that the sect fostered levelling principles, actions like these set an example for the second generation of Quakers who, like Bellers, sought to design alternative solutions to the problem of poverty at the turn of the century.[8]

Moving within circles of influential Quakers from the start, Bellers seemed destined to assume an important role in the affairs of the Society of Friends. His parents had counted George Fox among their friends, and his marriage documents display the signature of William Penn. At the age of twenty-six, Bellers took financial charge of a plan "for buying flax to employ poor Friends in spinning," an undertaking suggested by Fox in 1669 and now, in 1679, in need of the expertise of the young cloth merchant. He also provided the Women's Meeting with cloth, which members then fashioned into clothing for the poor. He would have known of similar projects in Reading, Norwich, and York from his many visits and consultations with Friends across the country. His marriage to Francis Fettiplace, the daughter of a substantial Gloucestershire Friend and Lord of the Manor in Coln St. Aldwyn, in 1686, assured him of the status and financial means to underwrite experiments of his own making. As a reputable member of a sect founded on spiritual equality, Bellers emerged as an active philanthropist and publicist for the rudimentary principle of economic justice.[9]

Bellers's formal tracts appeared at the height of his career, when his personal means had increased and the plight of the London poor had worsened. The "seven lean years" of 1693–9 were marked by notably low wages and wartime shortages, while rising poor rates provoked complaints and calls for workhouses from landed interests. Riots by Spitalfields weavers publicized the fact that the importation of foreign luxuries (in this case, silks, by the East India Company) were hurting the industries of London artisans.[10] Harvest failures and a coinage crisis

---

[7] Braithwaite, *Second Period*, 566, 576.   [8] Ibid., 556.

[9] Clarke, *John Bellers*, 3–4; Fry, *John Bellers*, 6–7, 13–16; Hitchcock, "Introduction," *Complaints Book*, x–xi.

[10] Braithwaite, *Second Period*, 576, 582.

added further to the miseries of the laboring population. This was the context for one of the first waves of pamphlet protest against the burden of poor rates, an issue that contributed to a burgeoning arena of public debate throughout the eighteenth century. Antipathy to directing revenue to unemployed laborers was on the rise, bolstered by statistics of political arithmetic, which argued that the poor dissipated more of the nation's wealth than they produced.[11] Cutting against the grain, Bellers proposed that more, not less, expenditure should be directed to the poor, channeled through projects for their employment. In these arguments, we can trace the survival of principles of reciprocity and stewardship as they fared in the new cultural environment of the capital, as well as within the intellectual context of newer points of political economy.

John Bellers was hardly unique in publicizing a scheme for directing the labor of the poor. Like his more renowned contemporaries, Thomas Firmin and John Cary, Bellers acted within a forum galvanized by overlapping circles of debate concerning wealth, luxury, and virtue.[12] While the Board of Trade investigated the problems of poverty, and as "social mercantilism" evolved from the discussions of seventeenth-century political economy, a movement for a national reformation of manners at the turn of the century participated in what one historian has called the "moral panic" of post-Revolution England.[13] At the time of his writings, highly publicized debates were focusing public attention on the more immediate problems of how to improve the laboring population through a program of workhouse employment and education. "[P]articularly in the 1690s," Paul Slack has argued, "the prospects for a national reformation again seemed to its advocates very real."[14] The campaign moved forward under various local initiatives by newly established Corporations of the Poor across England and in London. While forceful reform ideas emanated from Cary in Bristol,

---

[11] This was the argument of Gregory King; though his writings were not published in his lifetime, Charles Davenant circulated many of his theories at the turn of the century. See Braithwaite, *Second Period*, 576; Hutchison, *Before Adam Smith*, 49.

[12] Cary's famous proposals eventually led to the establishment of thirteen workhouses in Bristol. Hitchcock, "Introduction," xi–xii.

[13] Stephen Macfarlane, "Social Policy and the Poor in the Later Seventeenth Century," in *London, 1500–1700*, ed. A. L. Beier and Roger Finlay (London, 1986), 252–77; Charles Wilson, *England's Apprenticeship, 1603–1763*, 2nd ed. (London, 1984), 355; David Hayton, "Moral Reform and Country Politics in the Late Seventeenth-Century House of Commons," *Past and Present*, no. 128 (1990): 51.

[14] Paul Slack, *From Reformation to Improvement: Public Welfare in Early Modern England* (Oxford, 1999), 102.

the Board of Trade sketched plans for workhouse education. A more comprehensive national plan for "improving" the poor proved to be ill fated, however, when an ambitious bill failed in Parliament in 1705. Its demise signaled a growing resistance to committing public revenue to welfare measures for the laboring population.[15] The polemics of this debate indicated a paradigmatic shift in how human motivation and economic prosperity would be discussed and formulated, with its most radical position cast in trenchant terms by Bernard Mandeville.[16]

Mandeville's unsparing delineation of human nature in a commercial society helps us to place the ideas of Bellers in the context of this period of transition. Along with Daniel Defoe's splenetic attacks on charity at the beginning of the century, successive versions of Mandeville's *Fable of the Bees* contributed to public skepticism with regard to efforts at reform. Published in 1714, but significantly revised to include highly controversial material on charity schools and moral choices in 1723, the *Fable* provoked extended debate in print on the subject of social ethics.[17] It is not clear whether Mandeville ever read Bellers, and it must be added that Mandeville composed his revisions in the very different atmosphere of a later decade, with an eye toward cultivating a different audience. But a comparison of the two nevertheless highlights the dramatic debates occupying the public sphere of print culture as Mandeville's works tested the limits of public tolerance for irony directed at troublesome moral issues. Against Bellers's belief in a sensibly social, if not wholly altruistic, humanity, Mandeville posed a self-centered "economic man" constructed from a mixture of Hobbesian theory and mercantilist wisdom and informed by an enduring sense of original sin.[18] Mandeville's thesis that the public owed its thriving state to the private vices of a falsely virtuous elite contradicted the very premise of

[15] Ibid., 118.

[16] Bernard Mandeville, *The Fable of the Bees: or, Private Vices, Publick Benefits*, 2 vols., ed. F. B. Kaye (Oxford, 1924). On Mandeville, see M. M. Goldsmith, *Private Vices, Public Benefits: Bernard Mandeville's Social and Political Thought* (Cambridge, 1985); E. G. Hundert, *The Enlightenment's Fable: Bernard Mandeville and the Discovery of Society* (Cambridge, 1994); and for related discussions of social context, see Lee Davison, ed., *Stilling the Grumbling Hive: The Response to Social and Economic Problems in England, 1689–1750* (New York, 1992).

[17] A helpful collection of responses can be found in J. Martin Stafford, ed., *Private Vices, Publick Benefits? The Contemporary Reception of Bernard Mandeville* (Solihull, 1997).

[18] Jacob Viner, "Introduction to Bernard Mandeville, *A Letter to Dion* (1732)," in *The Long View and the Short: Studies in Economic Theory and Policy* (Glencoe, IL, 1958), 332–42; Hutchison, *Before Adam Smith*, 117–18.

Bellers's epistemological framework: the motives and actions of members of human society, in contrast to the animal world, must be perfectly transparent and harmonious, and, more importantly, in accordance with a social pact based on virtue founded on principles of the Bible. Bellers saw vice as a spoiler, not an incentive, of a prosperous society, predicting that "Vicious Distempers will shorten the Days of some, and Extravagancies will expel others out of their Ancestors Estates."[19] Yet Mandeville based his contentions on the obvious fact that certain segments of English society were flourishing amid the push and shove of commercial life. He had little truck with projects for the poor: "Charity, where it is too extensive, seldom fails of promoting Sloth and Idleness, and is good for little in the Common Wealth but to breed Drones and destroy Industry," he argued. "The more Colleges and Alms-houses you build[,] the more you may [continue to build]."[20] As for contemporary "poetic lamentations" complaining of popular vices, these, he thought, were inspired more by nostalgia than a true knowledge of human nature as it really was.[21]

Bellers's earnest tracts aimed at shaping a general moral consensus based on the need for what Alasdair MacIntyre has called "other-regarding virtue."[22] Viewing the public as a small community writ large, Bellers insisted on a link between happiness and virtue: all members of his audience would seek to promote the well-being of others, inspired by a common divinity and through an identification with fellow citizens. These assumptions operated successfully at the local level in seventeenth-century England, particularly among Quakers, and so Bellers presumed that a larger sphere of action was within reason. But Mandeville and his continental contemporaries jettisoned the view that human beings thrived on mutual acts of charitableness and followed Hobbes in viewing their nature as wholly self-regarding. Mandeville's reconciliation of self-seeking behavior to the larger purposes of society, defined narrowly as commercial prosperity, obviated the need for

---

[19] John Bellers, *Essays About the Poor, Manufactures, Trade, Plantations, and Immorality, and of the Exellency and Divinity of Inward Light* (London, 1699), 17.

[20] "An Essay on Charity Schools," *Fable*, 1:267. See also Viner, "Introduction," 40.

[21] Hundert, *Enlightenment's Fable*, 20. Mandeville nevertheless advocated the need for a knowing statesman who could "constantly regulat[e] the circulation of private interest." Istvan Hont and Michael Ignatieff, "Needs and Justice in the 'Wealth of Nations'," in *Wealth and Virtue: The Shaping of Political Economy in the Scottish Enlightenment*, ed. Istvan Hont and Michael Ignatieff (Cambridge, 1983), 11.

[22] Alasdair MacIntyre, *A Short History of Ethics* (New York, 1996), 115–16, 136.

Bellers's brand of commonality among citizens. Moreover, Mandeville viewed acts of other-regarding virtue as hypocritical. Fashionable urban philanthropy was inspired by vanity, not virtue, at least as far as the public displays in London seemed to suggest.[23] Pierre Nicole, a Jansenist contemporary, underscored the point by describing the social relations flowing from material desire and cupidity as positively social and good enough; these supplied "no less peace, security, and comfort, than if one were in a Republic of Saints." The bond between virtue and happiness thus could be severed, without detriment to industry and material progress.[24]

By examining competing attitudes toward money in Bellers and his contemporaries, we can see the social life of money at an important juncture in its history. As Bellers participated in honing the premises of early political economy, he made a case for the crucial significance of labor in relation to prosperity – a position that emerged logically from the context of current debate, though prescient in many respects. But going beyond this, he vigorously resisted new theories of money, which his contemporaries were keen to explore and celebrate. Bellers's aversion was fascinating in its creative synthesis of old and new: while he echoed the moral indignation of medieval Schoolmen, he brought forth ideas based on seventeenth-century sectarianism, which he substantiated with naturalistic discourse of the new science of political economy. "Money in a Body Politck, is what a Crutch is to the Natural Body, cripled; but when the Body is sound, the Crutch is but troublesome," he wrote in his *Proposals for a Colledge of Industry*. His intention was to figure out how to channel the individually oriented capacity of laborers toward a common goal. "So, when the particular interest is made a public interest, in such a college money will be of little use there."[25]

For Bellers, money was an essential instrument of artifice and corruption, more the acid than the glue of civil society. "[T]ho' money hath its Conveniences, in the common way of living," he argued, it was

---

[23] Slack, *From Reformation to Improvement*, 120–1; Sarah Lloyd, "Pleasing Spectacles and Elegant Dinners: Conviviality, Benevolence, and Charity Anniversaries in Eighteenth-Century London," *Journal of British Studies* 41 (January, 2002): 23–57.

[24] Pierre Nicole's *Moral Essays* were translated into English in 1691. Quoted in Hundert, *Enlightenment's Fable*, 31.

[25] John Bellers, *Proposals for Raising A Colledge of Industry of All Useful Trades and Husbandry, with Profit for the Rich, A Plentiful Living for the Poor, and A Good Education for Youth* (London, 1696), 9.

not without its Mischiefs; and call'd by our Saviour, *The Mammon of Unrigh-teousness*; most Cheats and Robberies would go but slowly on, if it were not for Money: And when People have their whole Dependance of Trading by Money, if that fails, or is corrupted, they are next door to ruine; and the Poor stand still, because the Rich have no Money to employ them, tho' they have the same Land and Hands to provide Victuals and Cloaths, as ever they had; which is the true Riches of a Nation, and not the Money in it; except we may reckon Beads and Pin-dust so, because we may have Gold at *Guiney* for them.[26]

In an age of commercial adventure across Africa and the Americas, Bellers distinguished himself from mercantile theorists who would have celebrated the enrichment of English traders through the acquisition of precious metals in the last half-century. His reference to Guinea was not an incidental one: since 1662, an eponymous gold piece had become a favored coin of the realm among those well off enough to trade in amounts worth as much as 18 to 22 shillings. Bearing the jaunty image of a colonial elephant as its "head," it originated as private currency produced by and for the use of the Merchant Adventurers Company but soon enjoyed a wider popularity.[27] The value of the guinea shifted according to the price of gold and the fortunes of that corporation, which probably inspired the sarcasm of Bellers's remark, until it was stabilized at 21 shillings in 1717.[28] The "Mischiefs" of money, then, occurred at multiple levels, from that of shop transactions to more arcane financial activity, and sometimes at a very base level of chicanery in Africa. Invoking "Midas's Golden Curse," Bellers warned of misplaced priorities that could lead a nation to "Starve for want of Bread, tho' had our Hands filled with Gold."[29]

Bernard Mandeville bluntly articulated the opposing view, which would prevail in the advanced political economy that belonged to a consumer revolution of the next century. "To procure all the comforts of life, and what is called temporal happiness, in a large polite nation, would be every whit as practicable without speech as it would be without money," he contended. Paying lip service to moral concerns, he

---

[26] Ibid., 3–4.

[27] Samuel Pepys found "Ginnys...very convenient – and of easy disposal," not to mention profitable as an investment for those who could buy them in lots. *Diary*, 29 (October 1666) 7:346.

[28] A. E. Feaveryear, *The Pound Sterling: A History of English Money* (London, 1931), 89–90; *Oxford English Dictionary*, s.v. "guinea." The coin later bore a stamp of an elephant and castle.

[29] Bellers, *Essays About the Poor*, 8.

admitted that money is "deservedly call'd the Root of all Evil," but on this point, he had more to say:

> [I]t has done more Mischief in the World than any one thing besides: Yet it is impossible to name another, that is so absolutely necessary to the Order, Oeconomy, and the very Existence of the Civil Society; for as this is entirely built upon the Variety of our Wants, so the whole Superstructure is made up of the reciprocal Services, which Men do to each other.[30]

Mandeville advocated the "due Care" of the government to support the standard value of money, "which the Worth of every Thing will be weigh'd by." Yet a second function of money lay at the heart of human motivation. "The Poor have nothing to stir them up to be serviceable but their Wants, which it is Prudence to relieve, but Folly to cure," he observed sententiously. He followed up this famous statement with an observation of the role of money in this all-important calibration:

> The only thing then that can render the labouring Man industrious, is a moderate quantity of Money; for as too little will, according as his Temper is, either dispirit or make him Desperate, so too much will make him Insolent and Lazy.[31]

Mandeville took for granted that the marketplace would serve as the level playing field for the scramble for subsistence, adding, "There are great Blessings that arise from Necessity; and that every Body is obliged to eat and drink, is the Cement of civil Society."[32]

In truth, Bellers understood the necessity of money as a medium of exchange, but he showed a remarkable determination to subvert the way in which contemporary society assigned it importance. He mocked the theory of precious metal as a store of value, asserting that "the Labour of the Poor" constituted "the Mines of the Rich, and beyond all that Spain is Master of."[33] Insisting that money was a mere, empty sign of exchange value between people – "it's the Measure and Scales by which we Measure and Value all other things, it being portable and durable" – he reversed the proper order of things, defining it as "a Pledge for what it is given for" and, in another instance, "a Pledge among Men for want of Credit."[34] Substantive wealth existed in the commodities for which

---

[30] Mandeville, *Fable*, 2:349.   [31] Ibid., 1:194; "due Care" from 2:350.
[32] Ibid., 2:350.
[33] This quotation is from the preface to the 1695 edition of the *Proposals* and reappears in part in the 1696 edition (cited here), 2.
[34] Bellers, *Essays About the Poor*, 13; *Proposals*, 3.

money was offered, and exchange generated credit in the first instance, placing it one step closer to the intrinsic value of commodities. Credit signified more in the world of exchange than money. This was because Bellers, like most early modern people, believed that credit relations carried the weight of ethical obligation and also preserved the human element within market transactions. Only through circulation – in this case, through all of society – could money renounce its inherently problematic identity.

> Land, Stock upon it, Buildings, Manufactures, and Mony, are the Body of our Riches; and of all these, Mony is of least use, until it's parted with; Land and Live Stock increase by keeping, Buildings and Manufactures are useful whilst kept, but Mony neither increaseth, nor is useful, but when it's parted with, and as Mony is unprofitable to a private Person but as he disposeth of it, for something more valuable, so what Mony is more than of absolute necessity for a home Trade, is dead Stock to a Kingdom or Nation.[35]

Bellers also expressed a common late seventeenth-century belief, argued by Charles Davenant, and later by John Locke, that hoarding money rendered it "barren,"[36] while releasing money into circulation worked "for the improvement of the general stock and wealth of the nation." As Locke put it, resorting ineluctably to vivid metaphor, "Money in its circulation [drives] the several wheels of trade, whilst it keeps in that channel (for some of it will unavoidably be drained into standing pools)."[37]

The problem with money and the larger realm of exchange, Bellers believed, was the fact that the marketplace was no respecter of human need. Exchange relations were rife with "dear Bargains, bad Debts, or Law-Suits." "As the World now lives," he explained in one passage of his *Proposals*, "every Man is under a double Care, besides his Bodily Labour; First, To provide for himself and Family: Secondly, To guard against the Intrigues of his Neighbour's over-reaching him, both in buying of, and selling to him." Tradesmen could not be trusted; "they are all straining the Necessity of the Mechanick, not regarding how little he gets, but

---

[35] Bellers, *Essays About the Poor*, 12–13.

[36] "[M]oney in the chest is but a barren treasure," according to Davenant. Vickers, *Studies in the Theory of Money*, 54n.

[37] John Locke, *Considerations of the Consequences of the Lowering of Interest, and Raising the Value of Money*, as cited in Vickers, *Studies in the Theory of Money*, 54. Locke also referred to money left out of circulation as that which "may lie dead, and thereby prejudice Trade." *Locke on Money*, 221.

to get as much as they can for themselves." "[I]t's not who wants [the Mechanicks'] Commodity, but who can give him Money for it," Bellers protested.[38] The rules of the market thus disrupted the proper order of distribution. This aspect of Bellers's contribution to political economy, along with his theory of labor, was radical in its implications. By the time that Robert Owen and Karl Marx rediscovered his writings in the nineteenth century, such dynamics of market society had been naturalized through strenuous theoretical debate. Bellers was hailed as a prophetic critic of industrial capitalism, when in fact he was simply commenting on the transparent dynamics of early modern commerce.[39]

Embedded in these discussions was an assertion about money that ran counter to contemporary thinking: money was dead, not alive. "Land, Cattel, Houses, Goods and Money are but the Carcase of Riches," he argued. "They are dead without People; men being the Life and Soul of them."[40] Having drained life from money, Bellers was assured of locating it where it really belonged: in human beings. Underpinning all of his writings lay an argument about the true wealth of the nation resting in its laborers, whose bodies and hands produced food and manufactures for everybody else. Like Petty and Locke before him, Bellers spelled out an approximation of a labor theory of value (more accurately termed a "labor cost theory of value"[41]), but for Bellers, this principle served as the basis for a wholesale critique of contemporary social thought. The poor provided the "Conveniencies of Life" for the more fortunate, a fact that he savored for its ultimate irony: "Without them, [the Rich] cannot be Rich; for if one had a hundred thousand Acres of Land, and as many Pounds in Money, and as many Cattle, without a Labourer, what would the Rich-Man be, but a Labourer?"[42] He wondered at the effort applied

---

[38] Bellers, *Proposals*, 13.

[39] The story of how Francis Place offered his own copy of Bellers's *Proposals*, rediscovered while sorting through his library, to Robert Owen has been told many times. Owen enthusiastically reprinted the work and distributed a thousand copies in 1818. See Braithwaite, *Second Period*, 586–7; Robert Owen, *Life of Robert Owen, Written by Himself*, 2 vols. (1857–8), 1:240. Marx mentions Bellers in many instances, often citing his work at length in footnotes. See, e.g., *Capital*, 228n, 443n, 467n, 553n, 609n, 619n, 764.

[40] Bellers, *Essays About the Poor*, 7.

[41] Vickers, *Studies in the Theory of Money*, 63–4; Hutchison, *Before Adam Smith*, 34–5; 69–70. David Hume and Adam Smith would make a related assertion about labor as "the real measure of the exchangeable value of all commodities." Adam Smith, *An Inquiry into the Nature and Causes of the Wealth of Nations*, ed. Edwin Cannan (Chicago, 1976), 1:34. Hume's words were "Everything in the world is purchased by labour" "Of Commerce," *Political Discourses* (1752), 12, cited ibid., 34n.

[42] Bellers, *Proposals*, [ii], 2.

to tending and multiplying the nation's corn and cattle when compared with the negligence with regard to the reproductive life and standard of living of laborers. "[T]he world is out of frame," he argued, when laborers are discouraged from marrying and establishing families.[43] Turning King's arithmetic on its head, Bellers presented copious calculations as proof of his contention that a fraction of England's laboring inhabitants could support a large and prosperous population. In fact, he argued, the proportion of ordinary laborers to the stock of the kingdom determined the very value of money, which, without this plentiful labor force, would be negligible.[44]

Blending a religiously imbued altruism with common sense bred in the counting house, Bellers relied upon a notion of reciprocity as a basis for social relations. "[T]hey that provide Food for the Poor, lend to the Lord, who is the best Pay-Master," he claimed.[45] Reminding readers of their debt owed to the laboring poor, Bellers directed his argument to the rich "to stir them and others, to a consideration of the great Stewardship they are in and must give an account of, whilst they possess manifold more, than there is in Proportion for the Body of the Nation." Images of credit and debt replaced a dependence on contractual relations based on money, as he reminded his readers that "a comfortable living in the Colledge to the Industrious Labourer, [is] the Rich Man's Debt, and not their Charity to them." Invoking the Bible in his *Essays About the Poor*, he cited Prov. 22. v. 7, "The Rich ruleth over the Poor, and the Borrower is Servant to the Lender." Through arithmetical calculations, he reckoned that each person should enjoy the use of no more than £40 of the wealth of the nation; especially so for those who "are excused from Labour to earn their Bread." Though the exercise was rhetorical, Bellers sought to convince his audience that their enjoyment of wealth vastly exceeded the bounds of necessity, made possible, in part, by the machinations performed by money.[46]

Thus, Bellers arrived at a proposal to arrest the errant life of money and even dispense with it altogether in his plan for a self-sufficient labor collective for the poor. His aims were nothing less than a total redesign of economic life, writ small. "[I]n such a Colledge Money will be of little Use there," he declared. Addressing Parliament in his dedication, Bellers set out his own labor theory of value, which at first glance sounded as much like common mercantile parlance. "Embodying the

---

[43] Ibid., 2.   [44] Bellers, *Essays About the Poor*, 5–8.   [45] Bellers, *Proposals*, 2–3.
[46] Ibid., 23; *Essays About the Poor*, 15.

Poor so together" will make them "of equal Value to Money (by raising a plentiful Supply of all Conveniencies of Life)," he explained. He clarified the theory in another rendering of the definition of money: "This Colledge-Fellowship will make Labour, and not Money, the Standard to value all Necessaries by." Even though he recognized the value of its circulation, Bellers would insulate the inhabitants of his college from the imperial reach of money.[47]

Where would such a collective netherworld belong on the spectrum of associations familiar to the age? Historians have characterized institutions for the poor during this "age of confinement" as repressive, as most indeed were.[48] Ironically, several of Bellers's ideas were first tested on Quaker prisoners confined under the Restoration on religious grounds; Bellers supplied them with materials for hand manufactures that were later distributed to Friends.[49] (A more incidental irony may be noted in that when Bellers's ideas were finally put into practice at Clerkenwell, the institution shared a wall with a building that had been used as a prison in the 1670s.[50]) Bellers was nevertheless sensitive to popular antipathy to institutional confinement and coercion. His proposal offered an answer to "Why the Name Colledge [sic], and not a Community, or Work-house?" that directly addressed the question of freedom on the one hand, and religious adherence on the other, in the context of late seventeenth-century expectations:

> *Answ.* A Work-house bespeaks too much of Servitude, for People of Estates to send their Children for Education; and too much of *Bridwel*, for honest Tradesmen to like it; and the Name *Community* implies a greater Unity in Spirit, than Colledge doth; and therefore not so proper to be used to such a mixt multitude of Men and Boys; the word *Colledge* more relates to an outward Fellowship than an inward Communion, and therefore better suits the Subject.[51]

Voluntary association, self-improvement (through education), and respect across a spectrum of social differences were imperative. Bellers lent insight into contemporary opinion by anticipating objections (more than likely, those he had already heard from his friends) to his plan.

---

[47] Bellers, *Proposals*, [ii], 3, 4.
[48] Michel Foucault, *Madness and Civilization*, trans. Richard Howard (New York, 1973), 38–64; Robert Jütte, *Poverty and Deviance in Early Modern Europe* (Cambridge, 1994), 169–70.
[49] Braithwaite, *Second Period*, 571.   [50] Hitchcock, "Introduction," xivn.
[51] Bellers, *Proposals*, 26.

Too much "confinement" and coercion figured among the most likely problems. In his own defense, he cited the widely held notion of human nature and the leisure preference of labor, which he accepted only up to a point: "neither would the Poor work, if there were not greater Inconveniencies." Then he added a more specific point of comparison: "The Confinement will not be more, if so much, as the Best Governed Prentices are under in *London*, and many other places."[52] Total liberty could not provide what good parents sought after for their children: food and shelter, moral guidance, and some form of occupational training. Bellers's plan offered an institutional alternative to the close, household context of traditional apprenticeship, as well as to the punitive confinement of the contemporary workhouse.

Bellers's proposals constituted a practical blueprint rather than a utopian tract, and he set about tirelessly lobbying on its behalf, proving himself to be "insistent," "indefatigable," and even (in the words of his principal biographer) "a little boring."[53] Considered by the Quaker Yearly Meeting in London in 1697, Bellers's *Proposals* circulated among Quaker civic leaders throughout England until circumstances led to the adoption of a drastically revised version in London in 1698. Opening in 1702, the Clerkenwell Workhouse (so called by contemporaries) first admitted elderly residents and eventually added children, adolescents, and a collection of fee-paying adults, including "scholars," until it numbered nearly one hundred residents at its peak.[54] In its economic structure, the project was far from Bellers's ideal plan. Instead of housing the fantastic sum of 200 inhabitants, incorporating many trades and farm labor, the house was designed to employ the able-bodied in spinning on a part-time basis in an urban setting. But the spirit of the venture reflected Bellers's ideal of communal living by requiring all residents to assist each other in earning a living and educating the young. With additional help from the contributions of Friends, the house began its career as a modified workhouse.[55]

One signally enlightened principle, born out of the amalgam of its spiritual and contractual origins, informed the administration of the project: that the inmates were entitled to openness and fairness in all their dealings with the administrators of the house. The Friends worked

---

[52] Ibid., 25.   [53] Fry, *John Bellers*, 7, 20.
[54] Hitchcock, "Introduction," xiv–xvi.
[55] For the larger social and political context of Bellers's activities and this project, see Macfarlane, "Social Policy and the Poor," 252–77; Hitchcock, "Introduction," x–xv.

to avoid any semblance of coercion in admitting people into the house, and so residents entered the establishment in a contractual manner (at least from around 1719) despite the fact that most candidates had been identified as eligible owing to their need. Each was asked whether he or she were willing to adhere to a list of rules and accept the "bill of fare," read aloud at an induction interview. Candidates assumed their place in the group in the same contractual spirit. Everyone was thus equipped to call attention to departures from the promises made by the institution, a privilege invoked frequently at the house. Thanks to the assiduousness of its fourth steward, Richard Hutton, we have a detailed record of the many conflicts generated by such an undertaking.[56]

Hutton's "Complaints Book" offers a bird's-eye perspective into daily proceedings, which ranged from logging miscellaneous bills for an inmate's health care to sober reflections on the beleaguered goals of the project. To Hutton's credit, he managed to correct the initial financial problems of the house by increasing its yearly income, but this was done at the price, perhaps, of raising suspicions that the house was exploiting the resident children for their labor or failing to distribute provisions that were the inmates' rightful due. Whenever an inmate suspected (or heard rumored) that rightful shares of food or freedom were not forthcoming, he or she usually complained to, or worse, made considerable trouble for, the steward. Money and accounting for value dominated many debates within the house despite Bellers's theoretical attempt to minimize its importance in the project. It seems clear that the subjectivity of the inmates, already constructed by an economic culture of monetary desire, led them to measure their experiences and compare themselves with others using the touchstone of money.

Most striking about Hutton's Complaints Book is the simple fact of the profusion of objections of all kinds issuing from the workhouse inmates and their families. Two potentially ungovernable groups, similar in their insistence upon getting their own way, dominated the population of the house: the young and the elderly.[57] "To keep in good order a family made up partially of men and women who are aged and too liable to be discontent, also boys and girls whose parents or other relations has [*sic*] and yet may give much uneasiness, seems to

---

[56] The notebooks have been transcribed, edited, and introduced by Timothy V. Hitchcock in *Complaints Book*.

[57] Hitchcock also emphasizes the antagonism arising between "the poor and the fee-paying inmates" *Complaints Book*, xvii. On this issue, see the discussion that follows.

be very difficult," recorded Hutton, with characteristic understatement. Both groups labored under keen expectations of entitlements, whether through seniority or dependency. Food seemed to bulk large in the concerns of everyone; next to that, the allocation of tasks and the disciplining of children presented nettlesome difficulties. Rumors of mistreatment (a concept variously interpreted) ran rampant. Often communicated to people outside the workhouse, such stories prompted visits from suspicious parents and inquiring Friends. Angry confrontations were not unusual, and Hutton felt compelled to hand over several conflicts to Friends' Meetings for resolution.

Hutton and his assistants were inclined to blame such perpetual fractiousness on the inadequate upbringing or uncivil habits of the disadvantaged. But given the nature of residents' complaints, which ranged from demands for common articles of consumption to issues concerning personal freedoms and opportunity, one can only conclude that this sampling of poor and needy Londoners expressed commonplace, and therefore irrepressible, desires. It seems significant that many conflicts intersected with the use of money and the attitudes arising from access to it. Bellers's prediction that the project would make money unnecessary seems to have been wrong, or perhaps his misgivings were set aside initially because of the financial constraints of the modified plan. In any case, residents obviously had access to personal funds on the premises, and even children possessed pocket money. The link between money and mischief nevertheless proved correct: nearly all significant conflicts implicated Mammon in tortuous resolutions played out in the pages of Hutton's records.

The vanity of human wishes was ever present in the schoolmaster's account of "the ancient people," who grumbled about food and other matters "in very railing and unsavoury expressions, even in the presence of the children, servants & c." The elderly residents, less inhibited owing to the status accorded to their age, chafed at the rules and order of the house. They balked at the need for punctuality and seating assignments, household chores, and dietary regimen. They often laid out their demands with little apology. "And because they [are] living in plenty their desires begin to wander and their humours crave for such things as are not according to the bill of fare, nor could be prepared without a considerable addition of servants. For who can suit everyone's humours in respect of diet, unless each at every meal have according to their own appointment," the schoolmaster recorded. Though keenly aware of the need to impose as much uniformity as possible on the conditions of the workhouse, the steward repeatedly accommodated the special needs of the elderly, especially in the area of diet. This did not stop some from suspecting unfair skimping. "And thou made dumplings one day instead of figgy puddings," a particularly unsatisfied resident complained. "What did they cost? I suppose thou did it for cheapness, they were not worth above a farthing a piece."[58]

Everybody needed to eat, a fact that made food an important fulcrum on which to balance issues of fairness, economy, and taste. The "constrained humility" with which most people entered the community soon gave way to an unconstrained attitude of self-interest, particularly when their minds turned to food.[59] Dietary allowances of the house seem generous by contemporary standards: 8 ounces of butter per week, 13 ounces of bread per day, and an average of 6 ounces of meat per meal.[60] The quality of bread was described as "special" by a visiting Friend who had been skeptical about rations to inmates.[61] Other memoranda in the Complaints Book indicate that the sick and weak might receive extra allowances of sugar, chocolate, claret, oysters, and fish, though other residents were known to complain about the unfairness of this practice.[62] "But the heart burning and contention that such work as this made in the family would scarcely be believed were it related," Hutton sadly recorded when he first arrived at the house and discovered many differing arrangements and the resentments that followed, "which consequently would not have happened had all been received on the same foot."[63] One of Hutton's assistants tried to mollify the dissatisfied complainer: "[B]ut if thou should have a different diet from the rest it would breed contention in the family." But the man had paid "more than the rest" and expected "different from the rest" for his larger pecuniary outlay, and so his complaints continued.[64]

Money provided a means of escaping the regimen of sameness, and inmates took the liberty of using it to solve their personal difficulties with arrangements they did not like. Individuals were known to seek out additional food outside the premises; in one case, a boy picked

---

[58] Hitchcock, *Complaints Book*, 44, 68.   [59] Ibid., 68; see also 36, 59, 60, 70.
[60] Ibid., 3.   [61] Ibid., 50.   [62] Ibid., 60, 73.
[63] Ibid., 60. In the particular instance Hutton was describing, an elderly resident was accustomed to eating his meal on his lap by the fire. Another resident finally "seized the friend's chair hauling him and his dinner altogether into the middle of the kitchen and then took a chair and sat down in the same corner himself." (59–60)
[64] Ibid., 47.

the pockets of two other boys, obtaining ninepence, "and ran away and spent it," probably on food, as he was later discovered to have sought "buns" on credit at a neighborhood shop.[65] Some members were allowed to pay into the house in order to secure services and privileges; significantly, the practice came to the fore in numerous conflicts sparked by those who had such privileges, not by those excluded from them. Members were reminded that they were not allowed to sell leftovers from their allotted portions of food, which the house wished to reclaim as a means of saving expense. The particularly fractious elderly resident mentioned above disputed the rule and also purchased additional food from outside the house to the cost of between 18 pence to 2 shillings a week.[66] Hutton recorded numerous quarrels between his wife and the man, whose personal maid added to the fray with her own accusations. "[P]ray God send us out of this house or else we shall be starved to death," the servant reportedly complained to Hutton's wife, "and we had been starved before now had it not been for my master's pocket and my own."[67] The personal servant also threatened the Huttons' maid, leading the weary steward to reflect on the "consequences of having persons in the house who rule as masters in the family by having servants to themselves." Financial means provided the complaining threesome with access to money, goods, and services, all of which created an imbalance of power within the community.

For these reasons, money was a commodity under suspicion, and Hutton and his wife were known to inquire into the personal activities of residents who appeared to have some involvement with it. In the case of a "poor craving man in the family" who was known to "complain and thereby get money of several friends who come to see him," Hutton's wife pressed the man to reveal how much he had at the time. Though her primary goal seemed to be related to settling the man's debts, her actions provoked further dispute with the persistently troublesome elderly resident, who witnessed the inquiry and told Mrs. Hutton that she had no business asking residents about their reserves of money.[68] Suspicions were just as often reversed as residents wondered what the Huttons did with the income of the house – the troublemaker reported that they were rumored to have "money out at interest," which was in fact true: the Quakers owned shares of stock in the East India and South Sea Companies, which had generated an unspecified amount of income

---

[65] Ibid., 3. [66] Ibid., 41–2. [67] Ibid., 47. [68] Ibid., 49–50.

over the past year.[69] Accusations of hoarding money at the expense of the poor residents surfaced repeatedly, and the steward did his best to dispel any aura of foul play. Hoarding was a violation of fundamental standards of spiritually based philanthropy, and so Hutton was at pains to make his accounting practices completely transparent.[70]

Despite antipathy to the presence of money among the inmates, the steward gave some members of the house allowances, usually as "encouragement" to perform extra tasks, the cost of which amounted to 7 pounds 8 shillings for the fiscal year ending in September 1717.[71] But this strategy led to further dispute over the real worth of such paid services. When a woman named Elizabeth Rand had failed "to clean two pairs of boys' breeches," as she had been asked, a dispute broke out that quickly proceeded into the murky realm of measuring personal worth and dignity. She had been given an extra 4 shillings allowance (possibly because she was particularly able-bodied compared with other adult residents), but when pressed, Rand resisted taking orders from the steward, who recorded the ensuing exchange:

> To which she lightingly answered, ah, four shillings for a whole year, and [she] bid me do my worst and turn her out as soon as I would, for she would not stay if she begged her bread from door to door, but she [added that she] would not go till the cold weather was gone.... And upon signifying to her the end of friends' charity to poor friends, ... she told me, she received no charity but worked hard for her maintenance and at many times saith she has not so much as she deserves considering her service in the house.

Though Rand's four shillings per year seems like a negligible sum, the figure represents considerable potential for disruption if viewed as one of possibly twenty such allowances within the community. The Mammon of Unrighteousness drained more from Hutton's store of authority than from the treasury of the workhouse, as he must have realized in his conflict with Rand. He soon discovered that his very judgment in managing money was under attack. As Rand dramatically announced in her diatribe "in the public workroom at breakfast," "[M]y heart

---

[69] Ibid., 27.

[70] Ibid., 42, 46, 64, 90; David H. Solkin, "Samaritan or Scrooge? The Contested Image of Thomas Guy in Eighteenth-Century England," *Art Bulletin* 78, no. 3 (September, 1996): 467–84.

[71] Hitchcock, *Complaints Book*, 23, 24, 26.

pities those poor creatures that are under thy care, for thou wilt pinch them."[72]

Special allowances of money clearly worked against the aims of the community because they enabled a certain degree of physical freedom, another intensely coveted commodity in the workhouse. Hutton created a memorandum that listed the drawbacks of giving residents the "liberty" of "work[ing] for themselves": such an arrangement drew individuals out of the house "to go ... about the town more than may be convenient," suggesting that freedom of movement must have interfered with the scheduled tasks and activities of the day. Such activity prevented members from "assisting each other in times of weakness," Hutton noted, and besides the obvious importance of this for maintaining a sense of collective identity, every act of assistance provided by residents saved the expense of hiring services for the inmates.[73] Money also undermined a sense of humility and subordination to the group, a perspective intended to supercede self-interest. In Rand's case,

> she spent a great part of her time in walking abroad, and would frequently go out and come in in a resolute frame of mind contrary to the orders of the house, which introduced a liberty & disorder in the same which with her undue and frequent provocations and bad behaviour was a great disadvantage in the family, especially amongst the children (who ought not to hear and see they who have the care over them lessened in their authority) who we find by experience should have better examples.

Exposure to the world outside the workhouse stoked the desire for independence of mind. If this was a typical side effect of using money, Hutton concluded, then he was ready to militate against private employment.[74]

Pressure from parents of children, as well as the elderly inmates, also gradually undermined the connection between an ethos of reciprocity and physical labor within the institution. Coercion of any sort was seen as intolerable, and the more so with regard to spinning yarn and thread in order to generate income for the maintenance of the house. There seemed to be universal disapproval of making the children work, so that Hutton assumed an apologetic tone when explaining to those who objected that the children's "tasks" took up only the morning hours. An argument with the local authorities over the question of the exemption of the house from paying poor rates forced more discussion of the

[72] Ibid., 23.   [73] Ibid., 30.   [74] Ibid., 30.

contradiction being lived out within its walls. The work performed by the children did not make the institution a "workhouse" but rather a charitable "house of industry" invested in teaching the children profitable habits, as well as reading, writing, and ciphering. To contend that "it was no charity to maintain children and keep them at work" was understood as the harshest accusation against the good intentions of the project.[75] Likewise, Hutton struggled to defend the house policy of having the elderly residents lend a hand in household tasks or, when that was not acceptable, to help each other whenever possible. At every turn, residents felt the indignity of their position, which they often connected to coercive work policies or economy-saving measures.[76]

Particularly defiant critics threw the ultimate term of opprobrium at the steward: inmates were subjected to "Egyptian servitude," and Hutton resembled "an Egyptian task master" who commanded "the children every day as Pharoah did the children of Israel and rule[d] over them with rods and whips and rigour just as the Egyptians did."[77] These charges came from unusually disruptive people (one, an inmate who generated continuous tumult until his ejection from the house; another, a father of a young resident), but they caused the administrators considerable discomfort. Hutton also experienced anguish over the fact of employing the children in spinning mop yarn. His accounts showed that the income from their work provided necessary ready money, but he was forced to justify the policy on the occasion of a visit from a committee of Friends. The larger concern of the visitors seemed to be the treatment of the young. Bellers had supposed that the rule of an institution would be perceived as comparable to that of a domestic-based master, but he had failed to take into account the enlightened sensibility of wealthier female Friends, who apparently disapproved of disciplinary measures in an institutional setting. "[H]ere is a parcel of little creatures, poor little creatures indeed," one of the visitors lamented, according to Hutton's account. Hutton was a careful recorder of gestural detail, too, and one wonders if this was partly intended as satire. "Oh, how they work and in their shirts too. Some of the friends held up their hands saying, oh, poor little creatures." The steward was at pains to defend all aspects of their employment, which, he noted to himself,

[75] Ibid., 71–2; 77.

[76] Ibid., 100, for changing rules regarding the duties of the "ancient friends"; on their quarrelsome nature, see 67–8 and 70, the latter document being a list of rules and warnings read aloud to the older residents.

[77] Ibid., 44, 77.

were no worse than those imposed on young people by contemporary conditions of apprenticeship. Though the children were never beaten, the teacher in the workroom was said to carry a cane, and this policy served as a lightning rod for further disagreement.[78]

A sense of dignity was abundantly apparent among residents and families associated with the house. Physical abuse constituted an intolerable act, and, added to that, speaking sharply to the children appeared to be equally forbidden. The staff seemed to despair of keeping order given the way in which parents' disputes undermined the authority of Hutton and his associates. Parents were so meddlesome that, at one point, the schoolmaster recommended that "all communication of parents with children at the house be entirely cut off (except in case of sickness or the like)."[79] Parental complaints ranged from concern about rumors of beatings and inadequate food to dissatisfaction with placements of daughters as apprentices in housewifery. "[M]others especially, have not been easy therewith," Hutton recorded, "esteeming their children qualified for better business (as shop maids, seamstry &c) by reason of the education" provided by the workhouse. Hutton alerted the Friends to the urgent need for a superlative schoolmistress who might negotiate this difficult impasse.[80]

If Hutton and his aides had expected financial need to have eroded parental involvement in the upbringing of their children, events soon proved the contrary. The attachment of kin stretched across the void created by the surrender of children to the house. Several families insisted on their rights as consumers of services for their children, leaving the schoolmaster to ruminate over the belligerence of their interference:

> Nay this I know, that many children and young men of much better fashion than this house generally affords have, do and doubtless will, live at such a distance from their parents as not to see them some years together during which abdication they have approved themselves more manly and studious than whilst under the caresses of an unweaned and frivolous affection. And should these maintained on your charity claim greater indulgence than they?[81]

Perhaps the prospect of gaining an education for their children prompted high hopes and keyed-up emotions. Perhaps some parents harbored shame and resentment over their having turned over their

---

[78] Ibid., 78–9; 36–7 on "indulgent parents" unwilling to place children there because the cost was too low.
[79] Ibid., 94.   [80] Ibid., 71.   [81] Ibid., 93.

offspring to an institution of an ambiguous nature that bestowed neither outright charity nor privileged distinction. In any case, the tenacity
of argumentative parents suggests that they sensed that lack of means
had undercut parental authority in some fundamental way.

One particularly vivid confrontation lends some insight into these
issues. A father of children in the house, Thomas Smith, appeared for
an unexpected visit and quickly provoked arguments with the steward
and his wife and then the schoolmaster and the stewardess. Demanding
that he see his children every day, "if he had a mind for it, for it was
a public house," he accused the steward of being "a saucy impudent
fellow" and called his wife "a saucy impudent hussy and he would
come every day and see them too, if they were alive, and said, he would
take them, he could maintain them himself, he valued none of us." His
grievances became clearer when the schoolmaster, who also recorded
the incident in the Complaint Book, later came downstairs for his own
confrontation:

> When I appeared he immediately broached a whole flood of complaints
> about his sons being cruelly beaten, pretending that if they wanted an ounce
> or $\frac{1}{2}$ of finishing their tasks were beat for it unmercifully. And exclaimed
> against the house by making it parallel to Egyptian servitude, saying, why
> should they be limited to such a time for their tasks, and not take their own
> time. The boy being asked if he was beat for such a thing confessed the
> contrary, whereupon I took occasion to observe that his vulgar and very
> abusive deportment before his own children was the readiest expedient to
> lessen our authority, by preserving in them that disposition which had all
> along and still would procure them more of the same. To palliate which, he
> pleaded affection.

The scene must have been quite dramatic: both Hutton and the schoolmaster recorded that Smith delivered all his thoughts in so loud a voice
that he drew the attention of servants and "the whole neighbourhood."
As a coup de grace, Smith turned on the servant, Hannah Newton, calling her a "saucy slut":

> Upon which the stewardess bid him take [the children] just then & withal
> reminded him how capable [he was] of maintaining them. To which he
> replied, he had as much money as she before she came thither.

In accusing the father of being too poor to take care of his own children,
Hannah Newton had identified the root of the conflict more accurately
than Hutton or the schoolmaster of the house. Smith was there to prove

his own worth not just as a parent but, more to the point, as an independent, respectworthy person. Newton, by her own account, proved to be an articulate and psychologically acute observer. She described the rage that Smith displayed: "Vaunting about in a very unbecoming manner he seemed to lay a pretty great stress upon the authority he had for what he did." The dispute was really a contest between the lack of monetary means of a London laborer and his fundamental rights to having a say in the treatment of his offspring.[82]

Measuring personal worth in terms of money served as a figure of speech in the eighteenth century, famously demonstrated in literary works, among other evidence. Yet the meaning of money to residents of the Quaker Workhouse at Clerkenwell depended on particular standards not directly comparable to those touted by fictional characters who were measured by the value of their inherited estates. In most instances, money functioned as a means of their escaping the regimen of the collective pact, underscoring its role as a vehicle of physical freedom, autonomy, and the sense of dignity that residents craved. Probably more important, though, was the view of money as a bulwark of defense against the demeaning and controlling influence of charity. In his celebrated *Dictionary*, Samuel Johnson defined the poor as "those who receive alms," placing them in a gift relationship (in anthropological terms, also an exchange relationship) rather than in a state of measurable deprivation. Workhouse residents, perhaps too heavily armed by way of their spiritual independence, rebelled against the role of receivership even while disabled by poverty.

The question remains whether the Clerkenwell Workhouse invalidated Bellers's theories of social life and political economy. Its history was hampered by the prerogatives demanded by families, the tedium imposed by the institution, and the desires enhanced by a burgeoning consumer society. The latter aspect seemed to be tied to the imaginative power of money, and despite the wishes of the Quaker reformer to exclude the medium at the door, he could not keep it from intruding into his enterprise. Hutton's account provides copious evidence of the vital place of money in the minds of ordinary laborers. The competing claims of the virtue of collective identity stood little chance of overriding the allurements of money, particularly for denizens of one of Europe's great commercial cities. At the same time, the project itself required a flow of money for survival, and by 1737, owing to Hutton's efforts to

---

[82] Ibid., 76–8.

make a financial success of the institution, the Workhouse, by necessity, had transformed into a school for Quaker children based partly on income from a large foundation. Labor as the "standard to value all necessaries by" failed to match up to the more fungible standard of money in eighteenth-century London.[83] Not until socialist thinkers of the nineteenth century raised its flag once more would the principle of the fundamental value of labor be translated into future experiments of social justice.

[83] Hitchcock, "Introduction," *Complaints Book*, xix.

CHAPTER 5

Quarrels over Money: The Determination of an Acquisitive Self in the Early Eighteenth Century

Over the course of the seventeenth century, the dominant connection between money and moral danger was in decline. R. H. Tawney presented this historical conundrum at the end of his classic study, *Religion and the Rise of Capitalism.*[1] What happened to inhibitions regarding money that had preoccupied thoughtful people in the seventeenth century? Tawney's treatment of the subject centered on the role of religious ethics in policing worldly interests – including self-interest – before the emergence of a modern economic outlook associated with the late seventeenth century. At this juncture, he believed, the institution of the church failed to recognize the potency of the power of self-interest to overwhelm commitments to a larger community. Our examination of John Bellers and the Clerkenwell Workhouse suggested that an orientation toward money and its complex associations with the self shaped a popular mentality evident throughout the early-eighteenth-century Quaker institution. Yet the ways in which money became detoxified as it became deeply embedded in the lives of individuals remains unclear. Why had apprehensions of the menace of avarice, so discomfiting to Nehemiah Wallington and his seventeenth-century contemporaries, become largely irrelevant by the eighteenth century?

At least part of an explanation can be located in the development of a new notion of the self, which hastened the disenchantment of money during the first half of the eighteenth century. While earlier ethical principles had drawn careful boundaries around the regime of money, cautioning against too much attention to the self, or not enough consideration of the other, eighteenth-century pursuits unapologetically altered the equilibrium of an earlier century. Money moved into the center of the

---

[1] R. H. Tawney, *Religion and the Rise of Capitalism: A Historical Study* (London, 1926).

social realm as part of a more explicit, this-worldly orientation. More-over, the aggressive pursuit of wealth in the eighteenth century was reconfigured as an activity for the population at large. One of the princi-pal insights of Bernard Mandeville, according to E. J. Hundert, was his insistence that such behavior was to be "understood not as an activity confined to marginalized minorities, but as central to the self-definition of large urban and commercial populations," enabling an "historically domesticated form of self-aggrandizement" to come into being.[2] In this and other ways, money lost its direct line of communication with the supernatural.

At the same time, the construction of character no longer derived its fundamental strengths from the type of private virtue associated with seventeenth-century religion. Self-control was not simply the victory of an individual will, struggling in isolation from the temptations of the world, but rather, the product of character shaped in congress with society. Lockean psychological theories joined the self to the body and its physical senses, rendering passions not only natural, but beneficial. Pleasure became intrinsic to what it meant to be human, and the principle of self-love introduced conciliating changes to the boundaries of the European self. As Albert O. Hirschman explained the process, "the wedging of interest in between the two traditional categories of human motivation," reason and passion, brought "a message of hope" to European society. Europeans were thus enabled to defend impulses and actions formerly condemned as reprehensible. Samuel Johnson's witticism, "There are few ways in which a man can be more innocently employed than in getting money," spoke to the general acceptance of a universe of worldly pursuits and the need to get on with making them possible.[3]

It is in this context of changing attitudes toward human motiva-tion that the social life of money must now be placed. Though the link between money and the emergence of a modern self may seem to reiterate a familiar story, the argument that follows introduces a dif-ferent thread of development: the connection between money and the self relied upon a lengthy historical reconciliation with profane, pop-ular understandings of money that stretched back many years before the enlightenment. It was a process taking place in popular culture and

[2] E. J. Hundert, "The European Enlightenment and the History of the Self," in *Rewriting the Self: Histories from the Renaissance to the Present*, ed. Roy Porter (London, 1997), 74–5.

[3] Albert O. Hirschman, *The Passions and the Interests: Political Arguments for Capitalism Before Its Triumph* (1997; Princeton, 1977), 43; Boswell's *Life of Johnson* (New York, 1933), 1:567; also quoted in Hirschman, *Passions*, 58.

reflected in the realm of print in the seventeenth century, in the form of broadside ballads, advice books, and proverbial literature. Money became accepted as it "really was" through its power to gratify and fortify the self in a struggle to master worldly circumstances. The popular printed works that disseminated narratives of urban experience and travel bolstered this tide of thinking. Ultimately, the celebration of money as an aid to solving material dilemmas silenced seventeenth-century strictures against bodily pleasures and the aggrandizement of personal fortune. The extension of the regime of money, long restrained by a nexus of religious and social prohibitions, moved forward into a century identified with the pursuit of happiness.

MONEY AND GEOGRAPHICAL MOBILITY

The detoxification of money was born of demographic imperatives. Migration to London and abroad made money transactions an inevitability. More likely to employ coin than credit relations, commerce between strangers remained relatively free of the kind of social content and moral meaning that might have ensued from personal debt. While travelers were nonetheless aware of the fortuitous offering of aid along the way, narratives of transit were ever more conscious of transactions based on ready money. A distinctively secular regard for money, with its trademark celebration of good fortune, understood money as having the power to detach the individual from immediate encumbrances. Such considerations rose on a wave of geographical movement that affected a great many people, including the well educated and industrious.

The diary of John Harrower testified to the daily expense required of a single man "in search of business" away from home in the eighteenth century. Over more than five weeks in transit from his native Shetland, Harrower managed to spend pennies on frugal meals and lodging places until he arrived in London in mid-January. He recorded finding a room at a tavern near the London Docks, where, he assiduously noted, the landlord was currently in prison for debt. Breakfast cost him sixpence (four times as much as it had cost in Newcastle) and his expenses soon extended to commodities like "3ds. worth of punch" at a coffeehouse, though he found himself "obliged to make it serve me for Dinner."[4]

---

[4] "Diary of John Harrower, 1773–1776," *American Historical Review* 6, no. 1 (October 1900): 67–8, 70.

A tour through London enabled him to view Saint Paul's Church and also "the Bank of England where I seed the gold lying in heaps." But his own supply of money was dwindling; after eight days, "reduced to the last shilling," he "was obliged to engage to go to Virginia for four years as a schoolmaster for Bed, Board, washing and five pound during the whole time." Harrower had sold himself as an indentured servant.[5]

Pinning down popular sentiments regarding money, especially those encountered through travel, is difficult to do, apart from the fragmented evidence revealed in journals like that of Harrower. Yet it is clear that migratory experience, real and imagined, fostered a particular set of monetary relations that championed mastery of the world through money. The challenges faced by an individual on the move, so different from those of the artisanal world of Wallington or the propertied existence of Josselin, necessitated a frank acceptance of the benefits of ready money. This urbane realism is immediately apparent in popular oral and print culture of the early modern period, where money was celebrated as an object of desire and love. Popular ballads offer abundant evidence of these sentiments, potently planted in a genre recognized as worldly, practical, and outside the conventional system of patronage. Their structure and delivery depended on a certain degree of listener response and affirmation of the ideas on offer.[6] Those with insistent messages of survival by coin may well have opened up spaces for "a broad spectrum of interpretive positions" on the perennially relevant topic of economic life.[7]

Though it is difficult to know exactly how such a medium was received, we can theorize that the ballad, like other genres, constituted a "political as well as aesthetic" category and thus functioned as a coherent system of values in its own right.[8] Listeners and readers understood meanings encoded in street ballads as belonging to a particular, profane outlook on life; in some categories of ballads, such as the travelogue, this perspective was constructed as the inevitable flip side of an idealized

---

[5] Ibid., 70–2.

[6] Natascha Würzbach, *The Rise of the English Street Ballad, 1550–1650*, trans. Gayna Walls (Cambridge, 1990), 21 and Chap. 3, *passim*.

[7] Würzbach, *Rise*, 18–21; Kevin Sharpe, *Reading Revolutions: The Politics of Reading in Early Modern England* (Yale, 2000), 328; Paul Griffiths, Adam Fox and Steve Hindle, eds., *The Experience of Authority in Early Modern England* (Basingstoke, 1996), 6.

[8] Sharpe, *Reading Revolutions*, 57–9; Rosalie Colie, *The Resources of Kind: Genre Theory in the Renaissance* (Berkeley, 1973). As Adam Fox has shown, they also could be effectively harnessed to subversion, carrying libels or seditious messages: *Oral and Literate Culture in England, 1500–1700* (Oxford, 2000), 299–334; Würzbach, *Rise*, 248–9.

universe. Ballads, like proverbial wisdom, often delivered contradictory messages. Those verses focusing on survival in the world fell into a nebulous "advice" category, unrecognized by compilers of later centuries, as the subject matter lacked historical and romantic themes. According to Natascha Würzbach, ballads generally became more secular in content and more individualistic in theme between 1550 and 1650, while at the same time, they gradually came into competition and dialogue with printed works offering similar kinds of entertainment and advice. Yet as inexpensive and ubiquitous printed "wares" available for purchase and perusal, ballads seem to have held their own in a brisk marketplace of oral and printed information.

Ballads often coupled the use of money with movement across space; coins were props for the forward motion of heroic action, no matter how mundane. "There's Nothing to be had without Money" opened with a standard moral, to save a penny, in its tale of navigating a contemporary monetary world:

> Hee that brings mony in his hand
> Is sure to speed by sea or land;
> But he that hath no coyne in's purse,
> His fortune is a great deal worse:
> Then happy are they that always have
> A penny in purse their credit to save.

The structure of the narrative that followed, however, worked against such a simple truism. The protagonist, prompted by his sojourn through London, experienced a personal epiphany of sorts. Rejecting his father's miserliness, he embraced a hearty enjoyment of spending – "But I, his sonne, will let it fly" – and established a "gallant name." Henceforth, he perambulated the city as an early modern *flaneur*, advertising urban delights, all the while enjoining the listener in a communal affirmation of hanging onto a penny for come what may:

> All parts of London I have tride
> Where merchants wares were plenty –
> The Royall Exchange, and faire Cheapside
> With speaches fine and dainty –
> They bring me in for to behold
> Their shops of silver and of gold;
> There might I chuse what wares I would –
> *But god a' mercy, penny.*

A great deal of ambiguity hung on the singer's final line. Were listeners reminded of the standard meaning of "godspenny," a coin reserved for the poor? Was the ballad deliberately teasing the category of customary charity, suggesting that, but for the young man's obvious self-restraint, the penny might have run away from him? Remarkably, the balladeer avoids debt, aided in part by his godspenny. His incessant encounters with "fashions rare and strange," his visit to the courts at Westminster Hall, and his stop at the Globe on the Bankside might well have demanded a good bit of expenditure. His only brush with danger involved "painted drabs," whose seductions prompted him to change his chorus to *"To gull me of my penny."* The need for alertness to moral conflict, identified with feminine evil, was otherwise set aside; all the rest of Mammon's apparatus had fallen away. Promising to confine himself to "honest women," apparently on offer with all the other delights of the city, the singer closed by vowing to use money to enjoy life, fairly and generously. The sociability of spending – not credit – featured as the model of a successful world:

> Yet will I never niggard be
> While I remaine on earth,
> But spend my money frolickely
> In friendship, love, and mirth:
> I'le drinke my beere, I'le pay my score,
> And eke dispense some of my store,
> And to the needy and the poore
> *I'le freely give my penny.*[9]

This final assertion, set against independent spending, was a gesture of popular liberty, not deference. "There's Nothing to be had without Money" was not simply the vulgar wisdom of the people, mobilized in ballad verse, but a formula for balancing multiple demands upon conscience and personal desires.

An attachment to metaphors of gender enhanced the volatile aspect of money in ballad imagery, and so temptation in the shape of a woman could easily transform into a more appealing courtly image. The traveler in this case was "Mistris Money, The Worlds Sweet-heart," who demonstrated her universal power to open doors and satisfy needs on the road. Sung perhaps with intentional irony to the tune of "The Begger Boy,"

---

[9] *Roxburghe Ballad Collection*, 1:400–1.

the verses declared the acknowledged "beauty" and "sweet" nature of the elusive lady, wooed by men of every profession and rank in town and country, from "The Citty of London" to "The Shepheard that lyeth abroad in the field." In the shape of coin, not credit, money promised immediate satisfactions in a mobile life in which ready cash was a necessity:

> In every country where ever you ride,
> the savour of coyne is sweet as the hony,
> And all the Inns on the roade doe provide,
> to entertaine sweet mistris Money.[10]

Once again, migratory existence revealed a basic truth: commerce with strangers unmasked the true mercenary tendencies of human nature:

> Hark where you doe come & you shall still find,
> that for your money you shall be attended,
> Thy Host and my Hostesse will be very kind,
> but when that your silver and coin is spended
> Saith then you may goe with much grief & woe
> because you have parted from your deare hony;
> For that respect which to you they did show,
> was for the love of mistris Money.

Such worldly cynicism about the social relations of commerce was mitigated by a repeated emphasis on the positive effect of money: "Thus all mens affections are equally bent,/to Money, which maketh them ful of mettle." Money was to play a positive role in constituting the self, as a foil for motivation and a means of fortifying the character and determination of a good man.

The ballad primer of economic principles, situated outside an immediate reality, was freed from the ordinary cultural inhibitions of propriety. Thus, the ballad could take up ethical positions that were generally scorned as profane.[11] This was the case in "A Dialogue betweene Master Guesright and poore neighbour Needy," which likewise spoke of the issue of human motivation, this time, by setting the idealistic principles

---

[10] *Roxburghe Ballad Collection*, 1:462 [1640?]. The dates of the printed broadsides in the collection run from roughly 1560 to 1700, though the ballads themselves may originate before Elizabethan times. William Chappell, "Introduction," *Roxburghe Ballads* (London, 1871), ii. "[I]t is a fact that the ballad-proper gradually ceased to be composed after Tudor times." Robert Graves, *The English Ballad: A Short Critical Survey* (London, 1927), 22.

[11] Graves, *English Ballad*, 21.

of a prosperous gentleman against economic life comprehended more realistically by a commoner. Poore neighbour contended that the love of money was the motor beneath all exchange, while Master Guesright defended an implicit gift economy. Their debate brought forth a stream of Smithian explanations – uttered from below – of how daily services were performed: namely, for money and not simply on the basis of good will:

> Inprimis, your Tailor, is loving and kind,
> Nor doe I with him any fault find,
> But rest you assured and take it from mee,
> That most he doth, he doth for his fee.
> Your Barber most nimbly will trimme your fine patte,
> And if that you please turne up your mouchtatto,
> But marke you what followes my kind loving neighbour,
> He lookes to be gratified well for his labour.

Covering more than a dozen occupations, "poore neighbour" silenced his acquaintance with ubiquitous evidence of self-interest. In parting, the two agreed that "what we intend to none we will tell, / But keepe to our selves and to fare you well." Listeners might well have been uncomfortable with such an unequivocal assertion about the social bonds of commerce in the early modern world.

The seventeenth-century forcing bed of the money-minded self was hardly a simple progression of empowerment. Wallington's world would most likely see the coupling of self-interest and money as grounds for accusation and slander, part of the general negative environment shared by the moneylender and other stock figures of mercenary tendencies. Ballads might just as easily exploit this sentiment, as evident in "The Mercenary Soldier," published as a broadsheet in 1646, which aimed to expose what it believed to be the true motivations of Parliamentary soldiers during the Civil War. Its picture of the common English soldier as guileless mercenary discredited commitment to any cause other than the typical motives of money:

> No money yet, why then let's pawn our swords,
> And drinke our health to their confusion,
> Who doe instead of money send us words?
> Let's not be subject to the vain delusion
> Of those would have us fight without our pay,
> While money chinks my captain 'Ile [sic] obey.

Mocking the unlikely future of regular pay for Parliamentarians, the ballad made the most of the stereotypical soldier's revelry in bodily enjoyments, including plentiful drink, smoke, and "a Female of an easie rate":

> 'Ile not be slave to any servile Groom,
> Let's to the Sutlers and there drink and sing,
> My Captain for a while shall have my room,
> Come hither *Tom*, of Ale two douzen bring,
> Plac'd Ranke and File, Tobacco bring us store,
> And as the pots doe empty, fill us more.

Dismissing the political issues at stake, the ballad relied on the stock convention that connected money and soldiers with insincerity, self-interest, and rough hedonism.[12]

MONEY IN THE PUBLIC SPHERE OF POPULAR PRINT

Money was perforce discussed with caution and even ambivalence in the seventeenth century, and any celebration of its virtues required considerable diplomacy. Such finesse was, as it happens, in abundant supply in the hands of a variety of authors aiming to satisfy the seventeenth-century appetite for advice literature. The aim of cultivating civility and propriety in current times provided the ideal opportunity for ventures into the contested territory of money. A premier example was Henry Peacham's *The Worth of a Peny, or, A Caution to Keep Money*, first published in 1641, and still in print in various pirated editions in the mid-eighteenth century.[13] The little book advertised itself as an aid in determining "how to save it, in our Diet, Apparell, Recreations," echoing in its title the need to lay money by and avoid spending one's last penny. In truth, however, its contents rhapsodized more on worldly delights than moral strictures, and could be seen as a handbook for navigating urban space. As Peacham put it in his other successful publication, *The Art of Living in London*, arrival in a city was like entering "into a wood where there is as many briers as people, everyone as ready to catch hold of your fleece as yourself." He added, "For the city is like a quicksand: the

---

[12] "The Mercenary Souldier" (London, [1646]).
[13] *With the Causes of the Scarcity and Misery and the Want Hereof in These Hard and Mercilesse Times* (London, 1641).

longer you stand upon it the deeper you sink, if here money or means to get it be wanting."[14]

Peacham knew too well the calculus inspired by money, as he fit the description of the writer fallen on hard times: son of a well-known sixteenth-century rhetorician and educated at Trinity College, Cambridge, the younger Peacham authored and illustrated several accomplished books of emblems and epigrams before turning his hand to advice books. He also worked intermittently as a schoolmaster, and possibly as the tutor to the son of the Earl of Arundel, but he found the teaching profession the "dullest imaginable." Henceforth, Peacham divided his efforts between a search for sustained patronage and reliance on the marketplace of letters. His considerable knowledge of music and art were on display in his best-known work, *The Compleat Gentleman* (first published in 1622), reprinted at least twice during his lifetime and several times after his death. Inspired by his travels on the Continent, where he became convinced of the need to enhance the standard education offered to young English gentlemen, Peacham argued for a greater cultivation of arms, history, and the arts in the style of a Renaissance courtier.[15] But his later productions revealed a familiarity with a more hard-bitten existence, when, perhaps because he was reportedly "addicted to melancholy," he fell into poverty.[16]

His *Worth of a Peny* straddled the genres of chapbook and ephemera for the educated or partly educated (a later edition boasted "the Greek and Latin Sentences Englished"), an indication of how publishers understood such publications to cross class lines.[17] Its later editions must have competed for attention alongside Poor Robin's *Hue and Cry After Money* (1689) in a mixed bag of recycled works on money. As a window upon the material world of mid-seventeenth century England, Peacham afforded a view of countless transactions. Despite its rather righteous

---

[14] *The Art of Living in London* [1642], Folger Documents of Tudor and Stuart Civilization (Ithaca, 1962), 244–5.

[15] Said to be held "in high estimation with the gentry of that age," the little book represented "a record of the manners, education, and way of thinking of the better sort of Cavalier gentry before the Civil wars." G. S. Gordon, "Introduction," *Peacham's Compleat Gentleman, 1634* (Oxford, 1906), v.

[16] Alexander Chalmers, *General Biographical Dictionary*, 32 vols. (London, 1812–17) 24: 215–17.

[17] Fox, *Oral and Literate Culture*, 6–9. Fox mentions Peacham as an author and collaborator with engraver Wenceslaus Hollar; see also John Horden, "Peacham, Henry (*b.* 1578, *d.* in or after 1644)," *Oxford Dictionary of National Biography* (Oxford University Press, 2004) [http://www.oxforddnb.com/view/article/21667, accessed 5 February 2005].

title, the booklet urged keeping up with the times rather than hiding from the hurly-burly, and praised sensible spending on common enjoyments. Several pages listed various commodities and entertainments available for "the simple worth of a single pennie," ranging from "a faire Cucumber" and "all the Newes in England, of Murders, Flouds, Witches, Fires, Tempests, and what not, in one of *Martin Parkers* Ballads" to "the hardest book in the world . . . an Horn-book" and "as much Red-Oker as will serve [a Chamber-maid] seven years for the painting of her cheeks." Not all possible purchases were aimed at improvement – "For a peny, you may see any Monster, Jackanapes, or those roaring boyes, the Lions" – and many were simply services demanded by those with business in town – "For a peny you may have your horse rubbed and walked after a long journey." Later editions layered on more contemporary commodities, such as "Lozenges for a could or cough" and "a dish of Coffee, to quicken your Stomach, and refresh our [sic] Spirits." Sprinkled with satirical humor, Peacham's booklet was both entertainment and advertisement culled from the latest offerings of the early modern metropolis.[18]

Peacham demonstrated a competent sense of a few principles of early political economy, which he explained by drawing from a melange of mercantile doctrine, mixed with Classical, Biblical, and proverbial truths. He railed against the present "generall scarcity" of money, which he attributed to coveting and hoarding coin. "[L]ike the Griffons of *Bactria*," some people "brood over" their wealth, or literally bury it in "walls, thatch, or tiles of their houses, tree-roots, and such places," he complained, and then never retrieve their treasure, to the detriment of their nation. Miserliness was bad, particularly as the fund of silver and gold appeared to be in short supply. "[I]t is impossible for Charity to be regarded, Vertue rewarded, or Necessitie relieved" when individuals or "whole estates and kingdomes" clung to their stores of gold. Prefiguring Mandeville, he pointed out that even reckless spending was better for society than saving. Deploying the proverbial association of money with manure, he set his point alongside wisdom from the Ancients:

> And most true it is, that money so heaped up in chests, and odde corners, is like (as one saith) unto dung, which while it lies upon an heape doth no good, but dispersed and cast abroad, maketh fields fruitful. Hence *Aristotle* concludeth, that the prodigall man is more beneficial to, and deserveth

---

[18] *Worth of a Peny*, 20–2; for a later edition, see *The Worth of a Penny* (London, 1669), 20–1.

better of his countrey then [sic] the covetous miser; every trade and vocation
fareth the better for him, as the Tailor, Haberdasher, Vintner, Shoemakers,
Sempsters, Hostlers, and the like.[19]

Holding up the "covetous person" for mockery, the book called attention
to stinginess demonstrated through pinched habits of consumption: "in
stead of Satten, he suits himself with Sacken" and "trembles as he passes
by a Taverne door, to hear a reckoning of eight shillings sent up into the
halfe Moone, for Wine, Oysters, and Faggots." This behavior was not
to be confused with asceticism or puritanism; the covetous person was
mean and foolish:

> [H]is owne naturall drink (you must know) is between that the Frogs drink,
> and a kind of pitifull small Beere. . . . too bad to be drunk, and somewhat too
> good to drive a Water-mill: the Haberdasher gets as little by him, as he did
> by an old acquaintance of mine . . . who when he had worne an hat eight and
> thirty years, would have petitioned the Parliament against Haberdashers,
> for abusing the Countrey in making their ware so slight. . . . [F]or Playes, if
> he read but their titles upon a Post, he hath enough. . . . For Tapsters and
> Hostlers, they hate him as Hell, as not seeing a mote in his cup once in seven
> yeares.[20]

In an economy in which artisans, tradesmen, and servants depended
upon the employment and vails emanating from the material wants of
gentlemen, letting go of one's money constituted a social virtue, a form
of largesse in a commercial society. One solution to the current shortage
of money, then, was more widespread spending by gentlemen, though
Peacham's advice to that class also included avoidance of a lengthy
list of these same "occasions . . . ready every hour to pick your purse":
"necessitous persons ever upon borrowing hand with you; clothes in
the fashion; this or that new play; play at ordinaries, tavern feasts, and
meetings; horse and coach hire . . . [and] boat hire."[21] For the better off,
managing one's money in such a setting required a politic mixture of
customary generosity and vigilant wariness.

　　Alongside this anecdotal defense of a consumer society, Peacham
argued that money ultimately reinforced hierarchy in a society offering traditional means of opportunity. He complained that the circulation of money was often limited to those who already had a great deal,
which confounded the striving of lesser types. "One very well compared

---

[19] *Worth of a Peny*, 1–3.　　[20] Ibid., 3.　　[21] *The Art of Living in London*, 245.

worldly wealth, or money, unto a football," he quipped: "some few nimble-heeled and headed run quite away with it, when the most are onely lookers on, and cannot get a kick at it in all their lives."[22] Getting ahead came at a price, literally: placing a son at university or in the City required money, which trumped considerations of "wit and capacity." Finding a "good match" for a daughter also had its price: she may be "by birth well descended, vertuous, chaste, faire and comely," but "if you have not been in your life time thriftie to provide her a portion, she may live till she be as old as *Creusa*, or the Nurse of *Aeneas*, ere you shall get her a good match, *Num Genus & Formam Regina Pecunia Donat*." A later edition gave a contemporary lilt to this Latin tag: "Money's a Queen, that doth bestow, Beauty and Birth, to High and Low."[23] Rounding out his proof from more proverbial (in this case, Dutch) wisdom, he added: *"Gentility and fair Looks lay nothing in the Market."*[24] Money and marriages warranted their own, separable category of worldly wisdom.

Peacham spared no criticism of credit relations, as much an obstacle to personal freedom as poverty itself, and offered two proverbs on the point: "That miserie is ever the companion of borrowed money" and "A miserable thing it is, to owe mony to him, to whom thou wouldest not." Cataloguing the social and psychological drawbacks, he argued that a person in debt was "undervalued, despised, deferred, mistrusted, and oftentimes flatly denied." Stark was the contrast with those free from debt, who were more likely to be "bold, confident, merry, lively, and ever in humour." Peacham reveled in the details of their liberty, mimicking Biblical imagery of the Holy Spirit in his syntax: "they go where they list, they weare what they list, they eat and drink what they list, and as their mindes, so their bodies are free[.]" Such worldly free spirits were never "dog'd home" by "City-shopkeepers," instead, enjoying warm welcome at places of business, entertainment at Court, and special entry to every grand event.[25]

And what about those without money? Revealing a modern sensibility, Peacham regarded providence as only remotely involved in the welfare of "the body of a Common-wealth." With a Hobbesian flourish before Hobbes, Peacham described a social body of natural design, which "cannot subsist without hands and feet to labour." His view of social distinctions, which he understood to be inevitable, depended on

---

[22] *Worth of a Peny*, 5.   [23] Ibid., 6.   [24] Ibid., 6–7.   [25] Ibid., 8; *Worth of a Peny*, 7.

a nutritional metaphor: the ranks of laborers were consigned to toil for life, while "the rich being the belly, . . . devoure all, yet do no part of the work." Divine favor (which sounded more like the wheel of fortune) enabled some individuals to escape the condition of poverty ("God raiseth up, as by Miracle"), while others fell into it by their prodigality. At the bottom of the heap were those who "live in perpetuall want, as being naturally wholly given to idlenesse."[26] The stigma of poverty was as powerful an obstacle as anything inherent in the character of the poor. "Whosoever wanteth money is ever subject to contempt and scorne in the world, let him be furnished with never so good gifts, either of body or minde," Peacham intoned, first echoing both classical and Biblical wisdom ("The Destruction of the Poor is their Poverty," *Prov.* x. 15.) But venturing more, Peacham offered some historical reflection on attitudes toward the poor:

> If we do but look back into better and wiser Ages, we shall find Poverty, simply in it self, never to have been (as now adayes, in this last and worst act of Time) esteemed a Vice, and so loathsome as many would have it; it having been the badge of Religion and piety in the primitive times since Christ; and of wisdome and contempte of the world, among the wisest Philosophers, long before. But, *Tempor a mutantur*, The times are chang'd. And in these times we may say with the wise man, *My sonne*, better it is to die then be poore, for now money is the worlds God, and the card which the Divell turnes up trumpe to win the Sett withall, for it gives birth, beauty, honour and credit, and the most think it conferreth wisdome to every possessor, *Pecuniae omnia obedient*, hence it is so admired, that millions venture both soule and bodies for the possession of it.[27]

Poverty invited contempt. all things obey money. Was this timeless wisdom or an accurate account of contemporary London? Certainly an allusion to Christ-like poverty would be greeted with mixed sentiments amidst the bustle of seventeenth-century London, where an other-worldly ascetic would more likely be associated with sectarian extremism, reprobate idleness, or simple vagrancy. It is significant that eighteenth-century editions of Peacham's *Worth of a Peny* were re-titled *Pecuniae Omnia Obedient* (All Things Obey Money), for this was the final, salient thrust of its argument.

Peacham's teachings on the subject of money, like those of early modern street ballads, circulated within a broad universe of readers and texts

---

[26] *Worth of a Peny*, 9–10.   [27] Ibid., 15.

characterized by ill-defined boundaries. As Kevin Sharpe has demonstrated, solitary study in such an environment enabled each reader to make up his or her own mind on many important matters. The consumer "read authority and constructed his or her own worldview differently," picking and choosing among truths offered up by the ancients and contemporaries in turns.[28] Satire and ironies abounded in popular literature and ballads pertaining to money, inviting a skepticism and irreverence that only enhanced a reader's sense of authority. *Worth of a Peny* might well have amused the reader familiar with Aristotle, who would have appreciated the juxtaposition of his argument about spending alongside the proverb about dung; a less well educated reader might have taken away a different impression, seeing venerable support for a commonplace truth – money, like manure, was best when spread widely. The objective of self-regulation, predicated on an advanced state of interiority, was reconfigured in a liberal cosmos of spending and keeping money. With their "selves" in charge, late-seventeenth-century readers might well be prepared to view multiple truths about money as engaged in a heated contest for precedence. It was by no means clear, however, that the power of money might be attached directly to an unfettered, unapologetic self.

QUARRELS OVER MONEY BEFORE MANDEVILLE

> *If Love of Mony be the Root of Evil,*
> *The want of it is certainly the Devil:*
> A truth whichever was and ever will
> Be known to all the *Brethren of the Quill*[.]
> > *The Miracles Perform'd by Money;*
> > *A Poem* (1692).

Quarrels over money accelerated in the decades straddling the turn of the century, as the public sphere of print became the locus of multiple discussions of its power and desirability. Ned Ward's anonymously published *The Miracles Perform'd by Money; A Poem* spoke from a literary perspective, complaining that flattery and hypocrisy governed a contemporary marketplace of authors and patrons. His theme was old, but the context was new. In a changed political scene and a formative decade of fiscal innovations, money became the topic *de jour*. Writers

---

[28] Sharpe, *Reading Revolutions*, 297, 331.

engaged the subject from the perspective of political economy and the state, as developments in public credit, stock investments, and the appearance of the Bank of England in 1694 required debate. Running up to the Great Recoinage, the years between 1694 and 1696 saw "a flood of pamphlets" on issues of intrinsic value, the power of commerce, and the national interest.[29] The formal lapse of censorship laws in 1695 quickened the production of print, all to the good of monetary pronouncements. The appetite for works on money was apparently boundless, or at least imagined so by aspiring authors: one enterprising booklet offered "the true value of the Coyns and Money mentioned in the Bible" translated into current values of English sterling and gold.[30] Other entries became legendary for their redefinition of convention, such as the witty contributions to *The Spectator* on the subject of money, which strove to prove "that the Love of Money prevents all Immorality and Vice" through its power to occupy all a person's time and energy. The periodical also demonstrated the intertextuality of discussions of money by employing cant words, proverbs, and allusions to contemporary literary works on the subject.[31] Overlapping discourses and subject matter combined in a groundswell of interest, engaging discourses on politics, patronage, religion, and economics, in a general contest over ethics and the self.

The problematic nature of money continued to haunt these discussions, muting the full triumph of a masterful self allied with money. Writers who identified with the margins of society, such as Ned Ward, were eager to expose money as a symbol of mutability and commodification. In his *Miracles Perform'd by Money*, he portrayed the match between publisher and author as promiscuous as the many contemporary marriages based on money: talentless, well-connected "scribblers" won favor in the marketplace of print, just as old and "unperforming" partners triumphed in the marketplace of marriage. Ward's comparisons also meant to suggest that people, like objects, were fungible as saleable

---

[29] Joyce Oldham Appleby, *Economic Thought and Ideology in Seventeenth-Century England* (Princeton, 1978), 220.

[30] John Axford, *Hidden Things Brought to Light for the Increase of Knowledge in Reading the Bible* (2nd ed., London, 1709), 3. The author supplied such useful information as a conversion of Hosea 3:2 : "*So I bought her unto me for fifteen pieces of silver*, is thirty seven shillings six pence," 16.

[31] See no. 450, August 6, 1712 and no. 509, October 10, 1712 in Donald F. Bond, ed., *The Spectator* (Oxford, 1965), 4:81–6, 306–19.

commodities:

> Women like Books and Pictures now a Days,
> Are put to Sale, and who the Price can raise,
> Not he whose Merits decently can Crave 'em,
> No, no the Lucky He bids most shall have 'em[.][32]

The ethos of the marketplace pervaded social relations in general:

> A thousand Accidents tempt Flesh and Blood,
> *But powerful Guinea cannot be withstood,*
> For 'tis a Truth which Mankind will confess,
> That ready *Mony* speaks all Languages.[33]

The anonymous author of "A Hymn to Money" (1704) made a similar connection. "[T]he whole Fraternity of Scribblers in and about the Cities of London and Westminster, and Parts adjacent, as well as elsewhere, have consecrated and vow'd all their Labours to [MONEY]," contended the dedication. The satire begged "Thou Great Diana, whom all Men adore" to descend "unto the humble Swain," presumably so that all-out warfare might eliminate the less fit. The mockery continued through a lengthy list of professions that labored for money, from "Ladies of Delight" who "Do amble round the Streets at Night," to "Law Politicians" and even "the whistling Ploughman." Though Ward had dedicated his poem to "Sir Martin Monyless," the author of "A Hymn to Money" more boldly addressed his ode to the "Treasurer to the Mighty and Renowned Prince, MAMMON, Sovereign of the Universe" in a sidelong attack on the current ministry, using the moral language of protestant virtue.[34]

Battles over money mimicked the battle between ancients and moderns, this time, in the realm of economic life, rather than natural philosophy. The venality of the times prompted a "Person of Quality" to plea for a return to moral certainties by publishing *Wisdom's Better Than Money* (1698), a new edition of old maxims drawn from the seventeenth-century works of Francis Quarles. His *Emblemes and Hieroglyphikes*, first appearing in the 1630s, had once charmed Puritans and Churchmen alike; this new volume offered the wisdom of the ancients and the Bible in "Four Hundred Sentencious Essays, Political and Moral." Such advice would

---

[32] [Edward Ward], *The Miracles Perform'd by Money; A Poem* (London, 1692), 15–6.
[33] Ibid., 12.   [34] *A Hymn to Money. A Satyr* (London, 1704), 1.

have been suitable repast for Nehemiah Wallington: "The poor man's Peny is a Plague in the rich man's Purse" and "What thou givest to the poor, thou securest from the Thief; but what thou witholdest from his Necessity, a Thief possesses. God's Exchequer is the poor man's Box." In another instance, the reader was warned against covetousness, employing the familiar Biblical (and nutritional) metaphor: "Wouldst thou multiply thy Riches, diminish them wisely; or wouldst thou make thy Estate entire, divide it charitably; Seeds that are scattered encrease, but hoarded up they Perish."[35] Quarles's text, even when read alongside other genres, offset the wave of worldly satire on money and offered a classic morality for the new era.[36]

One of the most complex contributions came in the form of a broadside called *The Hunting after Money*. Probably published in the first decade of the eighteenth century, the polished verses and lavish engraving were the work of a studied hand. Its message, at first glance, appeared traditional: money, the invention of Satan, was brought into existence "to corrupt the Mind" and bring strife between neighbors. But through a hybrid mixture of images and symbols, a more contemporary message came through its presentation, starting with the debate over precious metal in the new coinage:

> Strange Charms that Men shou'd such a Value place,
> To be in Love with *Casar*'s Royal Face;
> Else where's the Intrinsick Value to be seen,
> Unless to purchase ev'ry kind of Sin.

Such references to the recent concerns of political economy did not preclude social elements ("Lords, Lacqueys" and "Punks, Players, Pimps, and Bawds"), along with older, more popular references, such as the following nod to John Taylor, the Water Poet:

> The Poet's Fancy gave it Wings to fly,
> And ev'ry one is Hunting it full cry:
> Whether 'thas Legs or no, I cannot say.
> But this I'm sure 'twill run like Dirt away.

Fans of Shilling might have taken umbrage at the slander: demoting money to the status of filthy lucre, the broadside pictured Taylor's

---

[35] [Francis Quarles], *Wisdom's Better Than Money: or, the Whole Art of Knowledge, and the Art to Know Men* (London, 1698), 156, 179, 193.

[36] Sharpe, *Reading Revolutions*, 323–4.

Figure 2. *The Hunting after Money*, [1709?]. Reproduced by permission of the Houghton Library, Harvard University.

wayward shilling, the winged coin, pursued by a determined pack of hounds. A closer examination of the allegorical characters pictured in the chase, however, reveal that Frugality, far from receiving just reward by winning over others, was trudging behind the quicker figure of Flattery. Bearded and wigless, Frugality appeared archaic and ill-equipped for the chase: he made his way barefoot, with his boots tossed over his shoulder, along with what appeared to be an oar, perhaps another allusion to Taylor's pilgrimages. His dogs, labeled "Dilligence," "Industry," and "Labour," were clearly behind the quicker hounds belonging to Flattery, fittingly labeled "Hazard" and "Rapin." The older virtues were hardly in command in the new age of money-hunting.

The misdirection of money took centerstage in the broadsheet. Prodigality, dressed as a fop, showered coins over his head in a caricature of largesse, as his foot trod on the scales of justice.

> But here comes one that contradicts 'em all,
> That Golden Ass, that Spen[d]thrift Prodigal!
> Preposterous fop! That thinks it an abuse
> To put his Money to its proper Use[.]

Covetousness was equally guilty of misdirecting the circulation of money, as his hound named "Deceit" indicated. Costumed as a Puritan, his behavior indicated selfishness and hypocrisy:

> All Worldly Int'rests does to Heav'n prefer,
> And to his crowded Bags makes all his Prayer;
> As tho' his *Money* would his Crimes defray,
> Or bribe his Jury on the Judgment Day[.]

In its condemnation of squandering wealth on luxuries and entertainment, the broadside lamented the loss of a morality of fellowship and probity, now poisoned by monetary transactions:

> With use of *Money*, use of Friend began,
> And then 'twas first that Man did ruin Man:
> Whilst Poverties, the only Blessing sent
> From Heaven, if attended with Content,
> An Honest Mind is to be valued more
> Than the Rich Miser with his glittering Store.[37]

The broadside suggested an epilogue to Bunyan's allegory, with little to recommend as recourse to worldly profanation, apart from a complete severance from money. The viewer was encouraged to take a final cue from Prodigality, who cried *"Money* is Dirt," though "he never stands on't." The polite reader would have no difficulty in recognizing the word as a decorous euphemism.

---

[37] *The Hunting After Money*, [1709?], Goldsmiths Collection.

Among the outpouring of popular didactic works at the turn of the century, proverbs and morality tales also contributed to the debate over money and discussion of its proper use, helping to champion the mastery of self over other. Though proverbs were gradually receding from elite discourse and the literature of high culture, this did not mean that they declined in popularity within other domains. In particular, the stellar success of new editions of *Aesop's Fables* offered a second life to the wise saying. From the mid-seventeenth century, "the Aesop craze" offered proof of the contemporary taste for didactic moralism and universal truths offered by proverbs and parables. Aesop's tales aimed to advise on "how to negotiate a ravenous and capricious world," a perennial theme in popular literature, though one that no doubt had more relevance to the age of the financial revolution than their originator could have foreseen. In form, they generally combined "a stable set of symbolic conventions" with "concrete examples [intended to] instill socially relevant precepts." But the personal stamp applied through these appended interpretations also opened the door to surreptitious arts of persuasion that could end by subverting established principle.[38]

Sir Roger L'Estrange, the somewhat notorious Tory polemicist and perhaps the most successful compiler of Aesop in the late seventeenth century, appended highly partisan "Reflexions" to the end of each tale, rendering the fables an overt demonstration of authoritarian didacticism. The "Change of Times and Humours," L'Estrange observed, alluding both to the world of print and the current resistance to accepting advice not asked for, "calls for New Measures and Manners; and what cannot be done by the Dint of Authority, or Perswasion, in the Chappel, or the Closet, must be brought about by the Side-Wind of a Lecture from the Fields, and the Forests."[39] L'Estrange's appended lessons reinforced a sense of rightness in the world as it was given, as demonstrated in "An Asse, an Ape, and a Mole:" "There's No contending with the Orders and Decrees of Providence," ran its moral, "and Every man's Own Lot (well Understood and Manag'd) is Undoubtedly the Best." The beasts of L'Estrange's universe of archetypes discovered that risk-taking repeatedly ended in misfortune, such as when two travellers discovered an abandoned bag of money, only to be caught with the

---

[38] Jayne Elizabeth Lewis, *The English Fable: Aesop and Literary Culture, 1651–1740* (Cambridge, 1996), 4, 9; Annabel Patterson, *Fables of Power: Aesopian Writing and Political History* (Durham, 1991); Sharpe, *Reading Revolutions*, 199–200.

[39] Sir Roger L'Estrange, *Fables of Aesop* (1692), [v].

booty by a "Hue and Cry" posse searching for "a Gang of Thieves."[40]
The irony of the wily aristocrat co-opting Aesop, the inarticulate slave
rewarded with subversive wit and profound words, was not lost on a
sophisticated readership or on hack writers searching for the latest literary enthusiasm. In the wake of L'Estrange, legions of "Grub Street
Aesops" attempted to best him in a "pamphlet war" over moral authority that lasted into the eighteenth century.[41]

Directly mirroring this competition was a related skirmish between
competing "moral reflexions" on proverbs appearing at the beginning of
the eighteenth century. One of the protagonists, a gentleman of letters
named Oswald Dykes, happened to be the amanuensis of Sir Roger
L'Estrange. His *English Proverbs, with Moral Reflexions* (1709) openly
acknowledged the "Imitation" of his patron, adding to his title page a
tag from Virgil: *"Invenies alium, si te hic fastidit,"* translated by Dykes as "If
one will not, *another* will; or, why was the *Market* made?" Dykes proved
the public sphere of print culture to be a democratic forum, and the
market metaphor signaled more than simply the competition between
authors. In the form of proverbial wisdom, Dykes presented an ideology
of individualism situated in market culture shorn of paternalist ideals.

In stark contrast to the stance of his mentor, Dykes advertised a fla-
grantly liberal position as guide rather than master: his principles were
those of the marketplace, not the pulpit. His tales aimed "to please both
the Palate and the Pocket, without being too sawcy, nice, or imperti-
nent on the one Hand, and too dull, heavy, or insipid on the other." The
buyer was the final arbiter, "for every Man will be his own Carver at
such a Treat as this is[.]" Regarding proverbs themselves as "dry," Dykes
adjusted them "as exactly as I could to the present Times," ensuring that
audiences would recognize their own lives in the material at hand.[42]
Contemporary taste and individual choice also informed Dykes's revi-
sion of the very *raison d'etre* of the proverb. Its "Use and End" was
not, as the Greeks might have intended, "an Expression directing the

---

[40] Ibid., 26, 137.
[41] Patterson, *Fables*, 146 and Chap. 5, *passim*. See also Mark Kishlansky, "Turning Frogs
     into Princes: Aesop's Fables and the Political Culture of Early Modern England," in
     Political Culture and Cultural Politics in Early Modern England, ed. S. Amussen and
     M. Kishlansky (Manchester, 1995), 338–60; Peter Linebaugh, "Aesop and Abolition,"
     pamphlet publication of "History 499," "History of the Death Penalty," University of
     Toledo, March, 1998.
[42] All quotations are taken from the second edition: *English Proverbs with Moral Reflexions;
     [In Imitation of Sir Roger L'Estrange's Aesop.]* (1709), ii–iii.

CONDUCT of human Life, couch'd under a DARK COVER" meant to "conduce to the leading of a good Life." Instead, the path to a moral self depended on the inner determination of the individual, who should resist the "Power" of those who tried "to regulate our MANNERS." The "Constitution" of a moral society, Dykes explained, "must wait for the favourable Concurrence of our WILLS; which have the sole Liberty of practising, or not, according to its Dictates, at our own Choice and Discretion."[43]

Strict conscience, the mentality of the compulsory "ought," Dykes explained, was neither common nor fashionable: "*Conscience*! (said a certain *bad Pay-master* to his *Creditor*, that demanded a *Debt* justly due to him, for *Conscience-sake*) WHAT'S THAT? THE ITCH?" He strove to offer a thoroughly representative sampling of current maxims, gathering them from "common Conversation, from the Court to the Cottage; and the GENERAL LANGUAGE of Rich and Poor, Great and Small, Old and Young." He even claimed "to oblige all Parties, and hit all Humours in a new UNITED KINGDOM."[44] Not surprisingly, Dykes omitted religious sayings from his roster of proverbs. He alleged that proverbs of "a heavenly Nature" were "above the Reach of Heathen Morality," and besides, an author nowadays was obliged to avoid sectarian differences and heavy points of principle. "One Man's Meat is another Man's Poison, and Minds differ as much as Faces or Features in a medly-mix'd English Constitution," his preface explained. Dykes was probably inspired more by the prospect of a wide public audience for his publication than by the points of principle he espoused. But whatever the motivation, his moral offerings were spared any glint of high-minded ethical debate.[45]

More to the point, Dykes presented life not as it strove to be, but as it more often was, namely, unmitigated striving on behalf of passion-driven individuals. "I thought I could not set forth the Manners of the Age better, than by giving the truest Characters of Things and Persons, in the daily Practices of Vanity and Vice, of Licentiousness, Immorality, and Prophaneness," he explained. Echoing Hobbes and Mandeville, but without any of their apprehensions or cynicism, he explained ordinary moral failures as "generally spring[ing] from the Source of our own extravagant Crotchets, or our own selfish Humours, as well as the common FASHION of the World: And this is the sole Reason, why I have so often us'd the Terms of OWN and SELF throughout the whole

---

[43] Ibid., vii–ix.   [44] Ibid., xxxv.   [45] Ibid., iv.

Work."[46] In fact, Dykes was presenting a variation of the well-known maxim, "Interest will not lie," a principle that relied on the assumption of self-interest as the truest, most reliable guide to navigating the currents of life.[47]

With a stated interest in tracing the peregrinations of the self, Dykes devoted considerable attention to reflections on money in contemporary times. Familiar proverbs introduced his musings: "Money makes the Mare to go," "Sue a Beggar, and catch a Lowse," "Set a Beggar on Horse-back, and he'll Ride," "Near is my Shirt, but nearer is my Skin," "Need makes the old Wife trot," "Cut your Cloak according to your Cloth," and "Fast bind, fast find" explicitly addressed issues relating to money. Other topics, such as luxury and debt, eventually led back to the same subject. Though always cognizant of moral strictures, Dykes's faithfulness to accurate reportage led him to adjust convention to fit a pragmatic assessment of current times. Much of the value of his book rested on its sensitive measure of the strength of monetary priorities in governing moral practice, rather than the other way round. In "Money Makes the Mare to go," Dykes railed against the "Market of Marriage," and cited the "Ancients" when he argued that money was "the Root of all Evil, the Mother of Mischief, and the general Idol of the whole World."[48] Yet he acknowledged that "MONEY, be it never so bad, is yet a most necessary Evil at this Time of Day; and it wonderfully supplies all our Wants, both Publick and Private, almost to a Miracle[.]"

Much of what followed was obvious (money "cloaths the Naked, and feeds the Hungry" and "sets the Poor at Work in City, Town and Country"), but more subtly, Dykes described a constantly circulating cosmos that depended upon nothing more than "ready Money":

> An indigent Person can purchase neither House nor Land; neither Lodging, Attendance, nor common Civility or Respect, without ready Money. People will not budge, even to the going of an Errand, without it: And, perhaps, the Mare in the Proverb was resty too, for want of her Oats. . . . 'Tis the READY [money] only, that makes all Things easy. A Gentleman without a Penny in his Pocket, is neither fit for a Coffee-House, nor the common Conversation of the Town.

[46] Ibid., v.
[47] J. A. W. Gunn, "'Interest Will Not Lie': A Seventeenth-Century Political Maxim," *Journal of the History of Ideas* 29 (October–December 1968): 551–64; Hirschman, *Passions*, 42–3.
[48] "Money Makes the Mare to Go," 63–5.

Though credit was common, Dykes indicated that such a strategy led to "Duns and Disappointments, Inconveniences, Troubles, and Vexations."[49] Spending was dangerously seductive, and he warned his reader not to go to the market without "Cut your Cloak according to your Cloth" in mind. His advice against going into debt was couched in a rather self-defeating catalogue of inducements to spending, which ran on for four dense pages. Debt and, the loss of freedom it entailed became the primary object of fear, and, like Peacham and the ballad of "Mistris Money," Dykes made a point of advising his reader to take caution to hang onto a reserve of ready money.[50]

Dykes's model of the self, honed by market individualism, had little truck with the ethics of custom and common law. Though his reflections on "Need makes the old Wife trot" admitted that it was sometimes hard "to keep Body and Soul Together," Dykes condemned the practice of breaking the law in order to supply material want.[51] Though once an arguable legal proverb, Dykes's assessment of "Necessity has no Law" proved how a new culture of individual probity and counting-house commerce was placed to counteract such customary law. "Now, this is a gross Mistake, as they interpret it, on Behalf of their unjustifiable Practices; for the Law it self has sufficiently provided Relief for the Poor, the Oppress'd, the Necessitous."[52] He followed this up with a more contemporary rendition, "Necessity must be govern'd by the Law." It was time to contradict the ancients, he argued. "They thought that the Gods themselves were not able to resist this Force, or grapple with this Necessity; and that they were all Slaves to the invincible Decrees of Fate." Nowadays, necessity could be overcome by "the Will, which ought to be as free as the Air is, for Action." Dykes meant that each individual was responsible for his own welfare. "There's no Fatality in the Case of being needy, or of living in Necessity," he argued. "But every Man has the Freedom of getting his daily Bread, if he will but take Pains for 't." His Hobbesian universe was to operate according to a morality of work: "Labour overcomes all Things in the common Vogue of the whole World."[53] This premise, rather than community-bound principles, maintained Dykes's society of market relations.

The proverbial wisdom of Dykes presented a new political economy of the people, celebrating money, freedom, individualism, and liberal spending. His ideal "self" exchanged community obligations for autonomy and appeared to relish, or at least focus on, the gamble of

---

[49] Ibid., 65–7.   [50] Ibid., 15–19.   [51] Ibid., 192.   [52] Ibid., 193–4.   [53] Ibid., 195–6.

staking individual effort against the risks of the unknown. None of this would be possible without hard cash (or ready money), a revealing detail that situated Dykes's standpoint among the people rather than gentlemen of property. The moral ambiguity of the world he described came under fire when Samuel Palmer (d. 1724), a disputatious Dissenter recently ordained as a minister of the Church of England, pilloried him as a vulgar popularizer.[54] Palmer's *Moral Essays on Some of the Most Curious and Significant English, Scotch and Foreign Proverbs* (1710) aimed to restore the proverb to its elite status as venerable wisdom of the ancients and secondarily, to aim a blow at the "Light, Wanton and Ludicrous" attempt at *"Moral* Discourse" offered by the hack writer.

Palmer accused Dykes of putting entertainment before moral probity, stooping low to snatch dialogue from "Two Fish-Women" and scolds at Billingsgate in order to illustrate his points. The collected proverbs, Palmer found, were "so Lean, Trite, and Insignificant" that "[o]ne wou'd think they had been take from the *Laundrey*, at best from the Common *Vocabularies*." If this was moral wisdom, then Dykes had got the world upside down: the public sphere of print had induced him to play to the common audience with suggestive allusion – he was "Writing Booty," according to Palmer – and this was tantamount to "opening a Sink, and spreading the Infection."[55] Inscribed as low, common, and female, the standards of the streets ought not to be countenanced, especially as it revealed the rumblings of a revolution in moral thought.

Palmer expressed discomfort in finding himself hostage to the public sphere of print, which, after all, had forced even the aristocrat (L'Estrange) into a position of compromise when it came to literary style. Palmer averred that his goal was to restore public "Regard" to "Virtue," but he candidly acknowledged that this was not an idea that would succeed in the literary marketplace. "Morality won't admit the Liberties of Jest," he worried, yet "very few will be drawn in to Read without an expectation of being Diverted as well as Taught." Hoping to steer a middle course, he apologized for his omission of religious matter, which, he protested disingenuously, would have taken far more

---

[54] As a London Dissenter of some renown, Palmer had emerged triumphant from a pamphlet war with Samuel Wesley, father of John Wesley, in defense of dissenting academies in 1705. *Dictionary of National Biography*, ed. Sir Leslie Stephen and Sir Sidney Lee (Oxford, 1921–22) 15: 154–55.

[55] *Moral Essays on Some of the Most Curious and Significant English, Scotch and Foreign Proverbs* (1710), xii–xiv.

time and care. "Moral Virtue is so near Ally'd to Religion, that I can't but esteem it a Noble Service to promote It," he claimed; but in truth, his wish to reach more readers induced him to avoid creating "a Work fully agreeable to the Character and Office I bear in the Church."[56] Though Palmer was obviously ambivalent about the world he was entering via his collection of wholly secular, homespun proverbs, he believed that the times called for such a contribution; like L'Estrange, he hoped he could counter what looked like a revolt from below with classic moral wisdom, couched in contemporary terms.

Palmer's pick of proverbs concerning money was hardly new, but if read in the context of contemporary debate over the subject, their advice signaled a rear-guard action against winning forces. "Out of Debt, Out of Danger" and "None but Fools and Knaves lay Wagers" advocated not just a vigilantly regulated self, but what amounted to a retreat from contemporary life.[57] He devoted energy to adversaries who had long since folded their tents and fled. In "No Alchymy like to Thrift," he satirized "Vain and Extravagant" alchemists, whose discourses were full of "the most Mysterious and Unintelligible Jargon in the World!"[58] Riches, Palmer argued, people "may find in their own Bosom. Every Man carries the Philosopher's Stone about him; and if we have Wisdom and frugality in our Management, a good Estate may be got out of a very little One prudently sav'd." He appended rules for "a good Oeconomist": "That nothing be Lost" by negligence or extravagance, and expenditure on pleasures of "the Eye, the Ear, [and] the Taste" be curbed. This was bitter medicine indeed, and not a brand that would sell for long in the new century.[59]

When Palmer turned to the subject of everyday spending, his reading of the times became apparent. In "'Tis good to take Care for a Wet-Day," he censured the current tendency to spend unwisely on "Extravagancies," including the ones "that don't make so much Noise, nor bear so Ill a Name" as the commonly condemned vices of drinking, womanizing, or gaming: namely, "The Table and Dress" and "a Gay Humour of appearing Genteel." Such indulgence and "Prodigal Expence" brought on only dangerous consequences, though the violators evidently felt

---

[56] Ibid., xiv–xvi.   [57] Ibid., 132–4, 175–6, 288–90.

[58] On alchemists in England, see Carl Wennerlind, "Credit-Money as the Philosopher's Stone: Alchemy and the Coinage Problem in Seventeenth-Century England," *History of Political Economy* (2003), Supplement to Vol. 35: 235–62.

[59] *Moral Essays*, 162–4.

justified in their actions. Alas, "an unlucky Proverb . . . is often cited on such Occasions," Palmer noted: "Spend and God will Send." Profligates were trusting to Fortune, not Providence. "And this is a very significant Distinction," Palmer insisted, though the point was lost, wedged between rules for modest living. His closing advice, to live within "a Groat a Day" and to regulate "Table Dress and Diversions," was aimed at "People whose subsistence depends upon the Shop and their Hands." The proud spending of "the Middle sort" seemed particularly galling to Palmer, perhaps because their pretensions to gentility were so completely obvious.[60]

In fact, the whole dilemma of regulating the self through money seems to have gone awry, if we can take Palmer's complaints as inadvertent evidence of the times. As contemporary philosophers of the passions knew, Palmer's spenders were in fact talented accountants of the conscience, capable of curbing one appetite to satisfy another.[61] In "Save at the Spigot, and Let Out at the Bung," he lamented that a "Mixture of contrary Vices produces the Oddest and most Unaccountable Turns in People's Conduct." Good behavior in some persons "is not because their Virtue is stronger and more Perfect than Others, but One Vice is over-ballanc'd by Another!" The true target, according to Palmer, was a new brand of avarice. "[A]n Old Miser shall turn Libertine, and waste more on a Strumpet in one Hour, than ever He had Soul enough to distribute in Charities in his Life." Covering their inconsistency with "a very Grave Proverb, *Let's Save what can be Sav'd*," such people will "be as Peevish as a Sick Monkey for the Expence of a Trifle at Home, but Confound a Child's Fortune at *Ombre*, *Picket*, and *Hazard* Abroad."[62] It was clear that the determination of when and how to spend money did not necessarily adhere to a grand scheme of morals wrought by Biblical precepts. Instead, a new ruling arbiter, the self endowed with money, appeared in charge of picking and choosing pleasures at will. Appalled by the picture which he himself had drawn, Palmer ended this lesson in the same way he concluded so many others, by predicting that people engaged in such exercises will "find themselves Ruin'd by the Ridiculous Experiment."[63]

---

[60] Ibid., 280–3; Peter Earle, "The Middling Sort in London," in *The Middling Sort of People: Culture, Society and Politics in England, 1550–1800*, ed. Jonathan Barry and Christopher Brooks (Basingstoke, 1994), 156–8.

[61] Hirschman, *Passions*, 16 and *passim*.

[62] These were popular card games of the eighteenth century.

[63] *Moral Essays*, 288–90.

THE ECLIPSE OF AVARICE IN THE EIGHTEENTH CENTURY

Attacks on avarice would continue into the eighteenth century, though in the midst of altered circumstances. Vast contemporary fortunes now made such criticisms appear academic against the colossal weight of accumulated money. A signal demonstration occurred in 1728, when John Dunton produced *An Essay on Deathbed Charity*, castigating the miserliness of Thomas Guy, bookseller and Bible merchant, and benefactor of the hospital that bears his name.[64] Later biographers fully revealed the extent of Guy's charitable contributions during his lifetime: along with founding the hospital to the tune of £18,793 16s (and afterward leaving £219,499), he also built several wards at St. Thomas's Hospital, endowing them with £100 per annum, and an almshouse with a library at Tamworth in Staffordshire, his mother's birthplace. He was also known to support many relations with annual allowances. It is true that his major giving occurred when he was in his seventies, but biographers for a century after his death seemed to take particular relish in repeating the fact of the postponement of such generosity until his later years, along with colorful anecdotes of his ill-tempered miserliness and ungracious solitude. Ending his betrothal in a quarrel over a few shillings, dining on his shop-counter, "with no other table-cloth than an old newspaper," entertaining by the light of a farthing candle, and acquiring at least some of his money through ill-gotten gains (success with South Sea stock and by dealing in "seamen's tickets during Queen Anne's wars," through which he advanced pay at interest to naval men) proved Guy to be an unappealing character in hindsight.[65] Nevertheless, the paradox remains that the greatest benefactor in eighteenth-century Britain was remembered for his parsimony.

Guy's misdirection of money elicited not just Dunton's pamphlet, but two remarkable genre paintings by a Dutch artist, John Theodore

---

[64] Dunton's essay was fully titled *An Essay on Death-bed-charity, exemplify'd in the life of Mr. Thomas Guy, late bookseller in Lombard-Street, Madam Jane Nicholas, of St. Albans. And Mr. Francis Bancroft, late of London draper* (1728). The tract was fueled by personal animus as well as principle, as Jane Nicholas was the mother-in-law of the author and, as he pointed out in his diatribe, "dyed a Cheat to her two Sons-in-Law," 7. Dunton was also reputed to have been friends with Guy at an early point in Guy's life, but later rejected him.

[65] Alexander Chalmers, *The General Biographical Dictionary*, 32 vols. (1812–1817), 16:480–2; James Caulfield, *Portraits, Memoirs, and Characters, of Remarkable Persons*, 4 vols. (1819), 2:78–84; *Eccentric Biography* (1803), 131–2.

Heins, Sr. (1697–1756), in 1737. "Thomas Guy the Usurer" and "Thomas Guy on His Deathbed" owe a good deal to the genre of avarice painting on the Continent, as well as satirical works by Hogarth. Set against the latter artist's lavish portrait of Thomas Coram, as well as the many popular prints of venality and corruption produced during those decades, these depictions seem peculiarly vicious in character. David Solkin has pointed out that Heins's pictures were created shortly after the passage of the Mortmain Act, which forbade the bequest of land to charitable institutions, thus protecting heirs from losing patrimony to the machinations of charities and their lawyers who exerted pressure on aging wealthy men. Backers of the Act would have agreed with Dunton: last-ditch efforts at salvation were unlikely to save the soul of the donor; besides this, they robbed posterity of their rightful due.[66] One image depicts Guy in his shop, interrupted in the surreptitious act of counting of coins by the arrival of a clergyman and two other visitors. The trio has arrived to request that Guy subscribe to a charity to relieve victims of a fire, a fact indicated by a document unfurled by the hopeful men. Other documents in the room link Guy to lending at interest and designs for a hospital, and Guy's surly expression suggests that the men will be refused. The second painting of the pair, a deathbed scene, shows a lawyer, possibly one of the men in the first painting, examining Guy's will at the scene of his death, recoiling in shock, as it becomes clear what is contained in the documents before him. Guy's hand can be seen nearby on the bedclothes, the key to his money box just out of reach. High in the corner of the painting, a devil flies away with the soul of the miser. Heins later engraved and published the first painting as a print, which Solkin suggests had a "considerable impact," shown through its ability to galvanize the governors of Guy's Hospital into action to defend their benefactor.[67]

As for Dunton's earlier pamphlet, similar reasons may explain its vitriol: Dunton's objections may have arisen from the timing of Guy's bequests, or because of a general discomfort with the scale of his charitable act.[68] Like the conventional paintings of Heins, parts of Dunton's work were not even original; as David Solkin points out, much of what Dunton had to say about "death-bed philanthropy was lifted straight out

[66] David H. Solkin, "Samaritan or Scrooge? The Contested Image of Thomas Guy in Eighteenth-Century England," *Art Bulletin* 78, no. 3 (September 1996): 474–5.

[67] Ibid, 476–8.   [68] Ibid., 467–84.

Figure 3. John Theodore Heins. "Thomas Guy, Counting his Money," 1737. (Scene from the life of Thomas Guy). Reproduced by permission of the Norwich Castle Museum and Art Gallery.

of recent publications by other writers, and principally from the 'Essay on Charity and Charity-Schools'" included in Bernard Mandeville's 1723 edition of *Fable of the Bees*.[69] Nevertheless, it is worth resurrecting

[69] Solkin, "Samaritan or Scrooge?," 469.

Dunton's denunciation of Guy as a belated contribution to the long-standing quarrel over money and the self. Significantly, the pamphlet expressed genuine criticism of the age and eschewed all suggestions of satire, thus distancing itself from arguments made by Mandeville. In its thirty-eight pages, the work addressed the entire panoply of issues identified with the careful regulation of monetary behavior in relation to others, illustrating points through familiar imagery and even a fable about money and travel.[70] Likening Guy to "a Cut Purse, that being espy'd or pursued, will drop a Purse of Gold because he can keep it no longer," Dunton accused him of keeping to himself what rightfully belonged to others. Alluding to Guy's attempt at securing salvation after death, he contended that such benefactors were "like Men in a Ship-wreck, that fling all away but one *Plank*... on which they may swim to Shore," revealing more concern for themselves than for anyone else.[71]

The demand for disinterest in charitable giving marked Dunton as a man of the past. As Donna Andrew has pointed out for this period, "[c]harity was interested, indeed supremely interested" and "embodied the conjunction ... of all interests simultaneously – private, public, and spiritual."[72] But for Dunton, who had spent his first forty years in the atmosphere of the seventeenth century, the attention to self evidenced in Guy's behavior clashed with a different frame of reference. The miser was a "foolish Mammonist" who would no doubt meet his match in the afterlife. His Faustian bargain with money revealed an over-reaching egoism. "[Y]ou are resolved ... to keep the Staff in your own Hand," a voice pronounced in a mock dialogue between the miser and divine will. The accumulation of riches is wrong, "for Justice is Presupposed to Charity," according to Isaiah. Where there was money and the self, there must be steady attention to keeping it in circulation by giving it away.[73]

By thrusting Guy's philanthropy into the public court of print, Dunton rendered the great man's behavior a parable on the misuse of money. The campaign in fact had some impact on the course of giving in the eighteenth century, despite its obsolete nature: according to Andrew,

---

[70] Dunton appears to draw a story from Melancthon, which he likens to a fable with a "Moral" to teach. Dunton, *Essay on Death-bed-charity*, 19–20.

[71] Ibid., 5, 15.

[72] Donna Andrew, *Philanthropy and Police: London Charity in the Eighteenth Century* (Princeton, 1989), 40.

[73] Ibid., 10, 13, 18.

Figure 4. John Theodore Heins. "The Death of Thomas Guy," (Scene from the life of Thomas Guy). Reproduced by permission of the Norwich Castle Museum and Art Gallery.

"Guy's Hospital, built in 1727, was the last major philanthropic venture to be erected by bequest in eighteenth-century London."[74] The debate over money in the popular literature of the times was thus capable

[74] Ibid., 40.

of strengthening residual, long-standing beliefs: that the circulation of wealth must be continual, not deferred, and that the principle of stewardship must endure in a world of money and finance.[75] On the other side of the case, however, was the persistent claim, championed by Dykes and a longstanding ballad tradition, that money dissolved the ties that bound and made for free movement, free spending, and even a subversion of hierarchy. These themes hardly constituted the triumph of individualism over older social values, but they were released into a century that would foster their continuance.

What seemed less apparent to writers of the early eighteenth century was the way in which money was implanted within the very structure of governance and economic life, through measurements applied not just to financial instruments, but to people themselves. It remains to be shown how the use of rewards in the regulation of the poor, as well as the management of the migration of labor, reaffirmed the paradoxical nature of money's nature. While extending its virtual orbit through popular life, heightening its image as a democratic enabler, the medium of money continued to exert its trademark power to create hierarchies, especially as a marker of gender and class.

[75] John Walsh, "John Wesley and the Community of Goods," in *Protestant Evangelicalism: Britain, Ireland, Germany, and America, ca. 1750 – ca. 1950: Essays in Honour of W. R. Ward*, ed. Keith Robbins (Oxford, 1990), 25–50.

PART III

REGULATING PEOPLE THROUGH MONEY

CHAPTER 6

The Measure of Money: Equivalents of Personal Value in English Law

According to theorists of money, political institutions may exert a powerful influence over qualities of money taken for granted by society, as well as the relationships in which money engages.[1] States play a determinative role in authorizing a universally recognized abstract unit of account, and through their administration of taxes, fines, and other payments, they establish a superstructure of governance over the multiple ways in which money is employed. At the turn of the twentieth century, this line of thinking was pursued by German scholars interested in the nature of money, including Georg Friedrich Knapp in his *State Theory of Money*. "The soul of currency is not in the material of the pieces, but in the legal ordinances which regulate their use," Knapp argued.[2] John Maynard Keynes based some of his investigations on this theory[3] and its ramifications are being explored currently in the field of ancient history.[4]

---

[1] The following discussion is indebted to Geoffrey Ingham, "On the Underdevelopment of the 'Sociology of Money'," *Acta Sociologica: Journal of the Scandinavian Sociological Association* 41 (1998): 9–13; Philip Grierson, "The Origins of Money," *Research in Economic Anthropology* 1 (1978): 1–35.

[2] *The State Theory of Money*, 4th ed., abridged and trans. by H. M. Lucas and J. Bonar (1905; London, 1924), 2. He also acknowledged the work of his contemporary Georg Simmel, whose *Philosophy of Money* had appeared in 1900, but indicated that "it treats only the sociological side of currency" (vii).

[3] Ingham, "On the Underdevelopment of the 'Sociology of Money'," 9 and 16n.

[4] Recent literature includes Andrew Meadows and Kirsty Shipton, eds., *Money and Its Uses in the Ancient Greek World* (Oxford, 2001), and David M. Schaps, *The Invention of Coinage and the Monetization of Ancient Greece* (Ann Arbor, 2004); see also Eric Helleiner, *The Making of National Money: Territorial Currencies in Historical Perspective* (Ithaca, 2003); M.-T. Boyer-Xambeu, G. Deleplace, and L. Gillard, *Private Money and Public Currencies: The Sixteenth Century Challenge*, trans. Azizeh Azodi (London, 1994).

This "authoritative foundations" theory, depending on the directive power of the state, may allow for an extension of the social life of money into realms of experience outside economic matters. Rejecting the functional theories of money centered on economic transactions, this model assumes that the social relations of money are highly variable and even external to political jurisdiction. That is, if the actual functions and qualities attributed to money operate outside the conventional categories of "medium of exchange," "store of value," and so on, then a theory of money must account for alternative meanings imposed upon currency.[5] This is particularly pertinent to our purposes because it helps to explain how money becomes intertwined with the identities and values attached to persons in a system of rewards in the eighteenth century.

Though the early modern state marshaled only a relatively rudimentary set of institutions in governing the use of money,[6] contemporaries saw such power as superseding the claims of individuals. Mercantile thought underscored the need to control the flow of money into channels restricted for public use. "Money is of a publick, or political, not a natural use," argued one pamphlet; it was intended for restricted uses aimed at maintaining exchange, such as setting values on commodities for exchange and supporting the aims of the state in times of war. "Idle and exorbitant expenses" (i.e., luxuries), counterfeiting, and "transporting it against our laws" constituted abuses of money because they misdirected wealth down pathways deemed disadvantageous to the community.[7]

The need to engage the help of citizens in maintaining public order made necessary an intensified employment of money by the state in the early modern period. Monetary rewards and fines were meant to generate public incentive when officers of the government were few and their responsibilities irregular. Royal proclamation and statute law entreated ordinary citizens to fill the gap. Hobbes had seen rewards in the seventeenth century as related to salary, wages, and gifts, all of which aimed "to encourage, or enable men to do ... service." As the need for enforcement of the law was fundamental, punishments and rewards acted as "the Nerves and Tendons, that move the limbes and joynts of

---

[5] Ingham, "On the Underdevelopment of the 'Sociology of Money'," 13; Grierson, "Origins of Money," 6–12.

[6] John Brewer, *Sinews of Power: War, Money and the English State, 1688–1783* (Cambridge, MA, 1988), 15, comments on the relatively "small size of England's institutional apparatus."

[7] Anon., *Use and Abuse of Money* (1671).

a Common-wealth."[8] With the expansion of claims by the state on constables and beadles, such payments aided in the growth of bureaucracy and the professionalization of police.[9]

Yet the relationship of money to the public order had roots in ancient English customary law, or what appeared to be so from the late medieval period. The bridge between this complex set of origins and the seventeenth century is obscure; English law absorbed much from "immemorial custom," while popular practices of English culture, over centuries, absorbed much from common knowledge of English law.[10] The problematic connections between rewards and persons – what we would identify today as "blood money" – deserves brief examination in relation to its historical origins. It is the "experience of tradition" of the law that provides the foundation for social thought, as Donald R. Kelley has argued, and helps us to reconstruct the set of assumptions underpinning this particular use of money in the past.[11]

MEASUREMENTS OF HUMAN WORTH IN ENGLISH LAW

Few accounts of the history of money fail to mention the archaic notion of *wergeld*, or "worth payment," a system of assigning monetary amounts to persons in medieval Europe. Widespread in the legal codes of Germanic peoples inhabiting the borderlands of the former Roman Empire, and elaborated from the fifth to twelfth centuries in Ireland, Wales, Norway, and Russia, this putative system of fines attached to persons in fact may be at the heart of the origins of money. The idea may have existed across cultures in the ancient world, and later resonances can be detected in unexpected places in the early modern era.[12] According to

---

[8] *Leviathan* (1651; Penguin ed., 1968), Part II, Chap. 28, 362.

[9] J. M. Beattie, *Policing and Punishment in London, 1660–1750* (Oxford, 2001), esp. 146–7, 228–56. I owe thanks to John Beattie for advice on an early draft of this chapter.

[10] Donald R. Kelley, *The Human Measure: Social Thought in the Western Legal Tradition* (Cambridge, 1990), 101, 102–3. See also Martin Ingram, "Juridical Folklore in England Illustrated by Rough Music," in *Communities and Courts in Britain, 1150–1900*, ed. Christopher Brooks and Michael Lobban (London, 1997), 63–82; Donald F. Bond, "English Legal Proverbs," *Publications of the Modern Language Association* 51 (December 1936), 921–35.

[11] Ibid., 5.

[12] In seventeenth-century China, for example, a list of rewards was appended to an edict prohibiting Christianity (dated 1682), which offered differing amounts of silver for

custom and law, victims of insult or injury could demand compensation in a monetary amount according to a scale of values, set in some cases by communal agreement. *Wergeld* amounts differed according to social rank, with the highest values assigned to king and clergy. Though studies have argued that the basis for such numerical determinations rested in the economic value or the "private utility" of a person within a household, this reasoning does not hold true for every case. Certain *wergeld* amounts appear to have been set mainly in relation to other amounts as a way of signaling status and honor; as such, *wergeld* was more about social relations than the operation of "market mechanism[s]." At the same time, the system demanded a leap into a realm of abstract thinking. This might have been one of the earliest opportunities to relate money to a more general notion of personal "worth."[13]

While some historians have voiced skepticism about actual applications of *wergeld*, it is this realm of abstraction that has made the concept of *wergeld* so laden with meaning for theorists.[14] Georg Simmel identified the notion of *wergeld* as a significant link between money and "a quantitative concept of the value of human beings" divorced from utilitarian objectives; it introduced "an objective supra-individual element" into the determination of personal worth. Simmel viewed this step as an advancement over supposing "a person's value as a whole to consist of what other individuals enjoy and lose by them," shifting the basis to one "embodied in themselves as an objective quality expressible in money."[15] His historical account of concepts of money sketched an evolution into a later era, when monetary payments would seem inappropriate and even intolerable in the case of matters pertaining to the human soul or the absolute individuality of the person. Such was the case with the condemnation of money substitutions for penance

information on Christian missionaries, priests, and entertainers of Christians, according to the rank of the Christian. Display case, "Encounters: The Meeting of Asia and Europe, 1500–1800," Victoria and Albert Museum, London, 23 September–5 December 2004.

[13] Grierson also points out that *worth*, drawn from the Old English word for *price*, is derived from the Germanic and Latin roots for *man*. Grierson, "The Origins of Money," 13–14; Ingham, "On the Underdevelopment of the 'Sociology of Money'," 10.

[14] Nira Pancer suggests that the law was not put into practice in this way in France, where the use of violence substituted for such compensatory payments of honor. *Sans peur et sans vergogne: de l'honneur et des femmes aux premier temps mérovingiens (VIe–VIIe siecles)* (Paris, 2001), 116–17.

[15] Georg Simmel, *The Philosophy of Money*, trans. Tom Bottomore and David Frisby (Boston, 1978), 355, 358, 359.

during the Protestant Reformation.[16] The move away from economic origins, which Simmel associated with primitive societies prior to "social development," signaled a turn to public institutions as central powers responsible for setting values and establishing "supra-individual" grids of value.[17]

As part of a system of Anglo-Saxon governance, *wergeld* offered a monetary means of resolving feuds and staving off vengeance. In the earliest document written in the English language and what may be considered one of the earliest pieces of English legislation, King Ethelbert published a list of compensatory payments sometime between 601 and 605 A.D. Anticipating the occasions when conflict might require mediation, the list supplied specificity in almost comical detail: "If the nail of the big toe is knocked off, 30 sceattas [silver pennies] shall be paid as compensation," according to one stipulation; "If a thumb is struck off, 20 shillings," followed by four different payments for the loss of each finger, ranging from 11 shillings for a little finger to 9 shillings for a forefinger. In slaying another man, the accused was to pay 100 shillings as compensation: "20 shillings before the grave is closed, and the whole of the *wergeld* within 40 days." In the case of the murder of a "dependant of a commoner," only a 6-shilling compensation was due. However, the destruction of "the generative organ" was worth "three times the *wergeld*," while the sum of only 6 shillings was due if the attacker "pierces it partially" or "right through." Other amounts acted as a warning against violations of a more moral or civil nature, such as robbing a slave on the highway, lying with another person's serving maid, or breaking a fence.[18] "These early medieval dooms spoke with one voice from the perspective of debt and duty," Delloyd J. Guth has pointed out. Monetary sums thus became entwined with "that traditional duality of legal and moral imperative."[19]

As wealth equivalent to the "worth" of a human being, the *wergeld* employed fluctuating combinations of units of value. In Scotland in the twelfth and thirteenth centuries, the *wergeld* was figured in both shillings and cows, ranging from 16 to 1,000 cows, according to the social rank

---

[16] Ibid., 366–7.   [17] Ibid., 364.

[18] F. L. Attenborough, ed. and trans., *The Laws of the Earliest English Kings* (Cambridge, 1922), 1–2, 7–17. Technically, prices fixed on objects were fines rather than *wergeld* amounts, though the system of enforcement relied on a single index of value.

[19] Delloyd J. Guth, "The Age of Debt, the Reformation and English Law," in *Tudor Rule and Revolution: Essays for G. R. Elton from His American Friends*, ed. Delloyd J. Guth and John W. McKenna (Cambridge, 1982), 81.

of the victim. A legal treatise of the thirteenth century fixed the rate of exchange at one cow to 6 shillings for such purposes.[20] By no accident, the English word for fee is derived from the Old English *feoh*, or "cow," and the Latin root for pay derives from *pacare*, "to pacify" or "to make peace with."[21] What mattered was the recognition of relative units of value and the transfer of some form of wealth in place of physical punishment. Ethelbert's catalogue of values, in the words of one assessment, offered "a new and merciful alternative to the tradition of retaliation." As a set of recommendations, it introduced "into society a new idea – that it was not wrong to take money instead of blood."[22]

The parallels with transubstantiation and other aspects of religious practice and belief would have been evident to English contemporaries. This was no mere coincidence: the Christian Penitentials exerted an influence on Ethelbert's laws, particularly as his list followed on the heels of the introduction of Christianity to England. Originating during the fifth century, the Penitentials selectively assigned monetary amounts, along with prayer, fasting, and imprisonment, to violations of ecclesiastical law. The custom of commuting penance into monetary amounts may have derived from Irish and English secular laws;[23] but regardless of origins, in actual practice, church and secular law worked together to impose punishments and fines. This was particularly true with regard to feuds. In the case of homicide for revenge, for example, one particular penitential law stipulated that money payment to kindred could cut penance in half.[24] The reasoning behind both systems was similar: in order to arrive at a definitive standard of values, both *wergeld* and the Penitentials relied on the assumptions that equivalencies might be established between categories of injury and levels of monetary

---

[20] Paul Einzig, *Primitive Money in Its Ethnological, Historical, and Economic Aspects*, 2nd ed. (Oxford, 1966), 252.

[21] Grierson, "The Origins of Money," 13–14. Cows also functioned as currency in primitive societies owing to the universality of the recognition of their value to society.

[22] A. W. B. Simpson, "The Laws of Ethelbert," in *On the Laws and Customs of England: Essays in Honor of Samuel E. Thorne*, ed. Morris S. Arnold et al. (Chapel Hill, 1981), 15.

[23] Thomas P. Oakley, *English Penitential Discipline and Anglo-Saxon Law in Their Joint Influence*, Columbia University Studies in History, Economics and Public Law, vol. 107 (New York, 1923), 53. In the case of the church, commutation to money payment originated in order to exempt those who were physically incapable of doing any other form of penance.

[24] Oakley, *English Penitential Discipline*, 168; John S. Beckerman, "Adding Insult to *Iniuria*: Affronts to Honor and the Origins of Trespass," in *Laws and Customs*, 159–181; Patrick Wormald, *Legal Culture in the Early Medieval West: Law as Text, Image and Experience* (London, 1999), 89, 195.

compensation and that through such compulsory gift-giving, peace and honor might be restored.[25]

The concepts attached to *wergeld* thus offered a real-world framework for a mental process that transformed representations of embodiment into symbols carrying abstraction. Historians of England have placed emphasis on this early grid of value as a foundation for later developments in monetary history. Though such methods of punishment were seldom, if ever, applied in France, *wergeld* law in England contributed to several conceptual schemes involving law and the social order. Despite its disappearance "with marvellous suddenness" in the twelfth century, this "elaborate system," according to Maitland, initiated a "legal process of giving credit" because some damages were paid in installments. Maitland also noted that proverbs relating to inheritance could not be understood without reference to *wergeld*.[26] Others more recently have suggested that the move to separating detinue (chattels that had to be replaced in kind) from monetary debt developed out of such earlier concepts of monetary substitution.[27]

But did this type of payment constitute a "price" placed on human life, in the sense of commodity exchange? Anthropologists long ago debated a related issue stemming from their dissatisfaction with the term "bride-price" used to describe part of marriage customs in South Africa and elsewhere: the term was inaccurate because it suggested purchase and sale where no such activities took place. "Bridewealth" has thus replaced the misleading language of an earlier generation of scholarship. The parallels with *wergeld* were evident to A. R. Radcliffe-Brown, who argued that the payment of cattle and other forms of wealth for wives addressed a "loss to the clan" and constituted an "indemnity" for the "infringement of the rights that a group of relatives or clansmen have over the members of the group." *Wergeld* values thus belonged to juridical rather than economic activity. Along with *bot* (a form of compensation for the destruction of property) and *wite* (a fine for the violation of rights),

---

[25] Through the intervention of Penitentials, certain violations, such as the rape of women and the murder of slaves, eventually received more severe punishments. Some offenses were punished by forcing the violator to emancipate one or more slaves (and later, serfs). Thus, in this instance, the law also indirectly established an equivalence between money payment and personal freedom. Oakley, *English Penitential Discipline*, 195–6.

[26] Sir Frederick Pollock and Frederic William Maitland, *The History of English Law Before the Time of Edward I*, 2nd ed., 2 vols. (Cambridge, 1968), 2:187, 271.

[27] Guth, "Age of Debt," 82; C. H. S. Fifoot, *History and Sources of the Common Law: Tort and Contract* (London, 1949), 227–8.

such monetary amounts established degrees of compensation for losses incurred in conflicts (or, in the case of marriage, contracts). In the words of Radcliffe-Brown, money appeased the group for "this invasion, this disruption of its solidarity."[28] More recent interpretations of bridewealth stress variety among marriage payments, including their role in negotiating power relations between groups of elders and chiefs and lateral relationships among kin. What seems clear is that economic elements were fully embedded within social and juristic interests, intertwined rather than dominant in the way that we might imagine material interests to be.[29]

Simmel expressed similar caveats regarding the concept of *wergeld* because it illustrated "the tendency to reduce the value of man to a monetary expression ... so powerful that it is realized even at the expense of objective accuracy."[30] The amount exacted for killing the king in early Anglo-Saxon England – 2,700 shillings – exceeded the total wealth anyone might accumulate in a lifetime. Money functioned here not as an economic entity but rather as a hypothetical unit of ceremonial payment. Its value rested more in its measure of the relationship between the king and everyone else than in any notion of just compensation; in other words, *wergeld* made the king incomparable. The roster of *wergeld* values was intended to operate as a political tool of deterrence; payment, when it occurred, constituted a ceremonial gesture, which contained within it a recognition of the authority and honor of the king. Equally important is the way in which the king, acting as an arbitrator of social tensions, can be seen as employing monetary units as an instrument of subordination. The establishment of *wite*, paid directly to the king, not only publicized a similar authorized version of the social hierarchy but also depended on the power of the state to collect revenue through a system of judicial profits. Growing out of the precedents of Ethelbert, laws concerning theft and fistfights indicated "the presence of a government that sees itself as responsible for many aspects of good order."[31]

---

28 A. R. Radcliffe-Brown, "Bride-Price, Earnest or Indemnity," *Man* 29 (July 1929), 131.
29 Grierson, "Origins of Money," 15–17; Jane I. Guyer, "The Value of Beti Bridewealth," in *Money Matters: Instability, Values and Social Payments in the Modern History of West African Communities*, ed. Jane I. Guyer (Portsmouth, NH, 1995), 113–32; Jack Goody and S. J. Tambiah, *Bridewealth and Dowry* (Cambridge, 1973); Adam Kuper, *Wives for Cattle: Bridewealth and Marriage in Southern Africa* (Boston, 1982).
30 Simmel, *Philosophy of Money*, 355–6.
31 Wormald, *Legal Culture in the Early Medieval West*, 194–5; Sir William Holdsworth, *A History of English Law*, 16 vols. (1938–52; London, 1982), 2:47–8.

In this way, ancient law established an intimate connection between monetary amounts and a comparative scale of human worth independent of exchange value. Over time, certain acts were exempt from such equivalence: treason, "secret homicide, robbery, coining, theft of property over the value of twelve pence, rape, arson, aggravated assault, [and] forcible entry" were deemed "unemendable," different in quality from other types of offenses. An extension of the concept of "the King's Peace" and the growth of governing apparatus, along with the influence of Christianity, encouraged a move away from this older method of adjudication of feuding kinship groups. According to legal historians, monetary settlements as a means of maintaining peace were a mark of a decentralized system of governance with a weak sense of both the authority of the king and the responsibility of the individual. Yet the fact remains that money and monetary measurements were integrated within the political and legal institutions of early medieval times, legitimated through a belief in their customary claim to royal sanction.[32]

MONETARY AMOUNTS IN SYSTEMS OF REWARDS

The example of *wergeld*, though defunct by the seventeenth century, assists us in identifying the state as a means of promoting linkages between monetary values and human beings. As early modern English law evolved out of medieval practices, courts retained a respect for the spirit of "unwritten law and custom," according to Bracton and Blackstone.[33] In his classic treatment of the history of English law, Holdsworth called attention to the survival of ancient practices, arguing that "criminal law will retain some traces of its origin in a very primitive society, and many traces of the processes by which ... distinctions have been evolved."[34] The system of rewards attached to English law was one of these relics, and here the intertwining of prices and people was abundantly evident in the seventeenth and eighteenth centuries. Though rewards reversed the direction of payment involved in fines for damages, they nevertheless maintained a sociological connection to

---

[32] Holdsworth, *History of English Law*, 2:48–9; cf. Wormald, *Legal Culture*, 194–5.

[33] "It was the boast of common lawyers from Bracton to Blackstone that English law alone escaped the rigidity of the *ius scriptum* and derived entirely from popular custom as expressed by the judiciary." Kelley, *Human Measure*, 103.

[34] Holdsworth, *History of English Law*, 2:43.

the authority of the state by imposing its imprimatur on disbursements connected to infractions of the law.

As long established legal expedients, rewards and bounties functioned as pleas for assistance during the Civil War era, when the king issued proclamations offering rewards for the capture of political and religious enemies of the Crown. The same method was used to capture the king himself, and eventually, those who executed him. Prize money of as much as £300 pounds was offered for the apprehension of one regicide after his escape in 1660.[35] The Rump Parliament had also passed legislation in 1652 offering rewards for aid in convicting highwaymen, burglars, and housebreakers.[36] During the 1670s, the "discovery of any 'Papists or Suspected Papists' in the Royal Houses" brought a mere £10, while rewards for Jesuits and other priests rose to £100. Service to the realm, perceived as both a duty and an honor, made such a payment a true reward for loyal citizenship.[37]

The call to action against offenders of the laws of person and property relied on a similar though somewhat more ambiguous sense of loyalty and obligation. In such cases, the security of the political order was one step removed, to that of the person representing the Crown or, still further, to ordinary citizens. Yet, as Radzinowicz pointed out, the "growing tendency" to employ the incentive of monetary reward suggests that seventeenth-century lawmakers believed this to be an effective means of dealing with crime. The government offered a reward of £1,000, for example, for the capture of any of six men involved in the attempted murder of the Duke of Ormonde in 1670.[38] This was much more than the £500 offered in 1678 for the apprehension of murderers of a justice of the peace of Middlesex. The murder of a London merchant during that same year resulted in a proclamation advertising a reward of £200.[39] It is impossible to determine exactly why some instances of crime commanded the figures they did, though the rank of the victims and their relationship to public authority obviously counted for something. It is also likely that private, ad hoc rewards pressed prices upward by offering larger sums for other instances of crime. In the absence of a

---

[35] Leon Radzinowicz, *A History of English Criminal Law and Its Administration from 1750, Vol. 2: The Clash Between Private Initiative and Public Interest in the Enforcement of the Law* (London, 1956), 84–5.

[36] Beattie, *Policing*, 230.   [37] Radzinowicz, *History*, 2:86.   [38] Ibid., 86.

[39] "A Proclamation for the Discovery of the Murtherers of Sir Edmund-Bury Godfrey," 20 October 1678; "A Proclamation for the Discovery of the Death of John Powell, Late of London, Merchant," 22 November 1678.

single administrative center of power in the police of the land, rewards mimicked a market model of competition.

Rewards according to statute followed a related yet distinct path: while rewards under proclamation arose on an ad hoc basis, rewards by statute aimed to enforce a constant surveillance against offenses against property. Though they "lacked the stirring value of a direct appeal," they covered general classes of crime of particular urgency.[40] Following the legislation of the Rump Parliament, a statute enacted in 1692 picked up where proclamations left off, offering £40 for the apprehension and conviction of highwaymen. The statute gained notoriety for its invitation to thief-catching. Over the next quarter century, additional statutes rewarded assistance against "burglary, housebreaking, private larceny of goods to the value of five shillings or more, horse-stealing, and coining," offenses punishable by death. An act passed in 1719 extended the definition of "highways" to include the streets of London and other urban centers.[41]

According to time-honored custom, citizens were expected to lend their support to the law through a sense of moral and civic duty. This was the assumption informing the practice of the "hue and cry," which enjoined ordinary citizens to pursue criminals at the call of the constable and often simply in response to the entreaties of victims and bystanders alike. With the passage of time, the system appeared to be weakening or at least failing to address the extent of crime across the nation. In seventeenth-century London, proclamations complained of "carelessness and negligence" of the Watch and Ward, along with that of ordinary citizens, who ought to be aiding the law.[42] According to Cynthia Herrup, the custom mostly survived only in name across Sussex because responsibility for apprehending criminals lay in the hands of legal officers and not the general public.[43] A fear of general disorder aroused the suspicion

---

[40] Radzinowicz, *History*, 2:35.

[41] Ibid., 2:57–8; Beattie, *Policing*, 230; *Crime and the Courts in England, 1660–1800* (Princeton, 1986), 52; Peter Linebaugh, *The London Hanged: Crime and Civil Society in the Eighteenth Century* (Cambridge, 1992), 59 and Chap. 6.

[42] For complaints, see "A Proclamation for the Apprehension of certain Notorious Robbers," 23 December 1668; "A Proclamation for Apprehending of Robbers on the High-way, & c. And for a Reward to the Discoverers, & c," 30 October 1690.

[43] Cynthia Herrup, *The Common Peace: Participation and the Criminal Law in Seventeenth-Century England* (Cambridge, 1987), 70–1. John Beattie's examination of court records showed the custom was "still working if only in an attenuated form" in the eighteenth century as commoners occasionally apprehended petty thieves and highwaymen. *Crime*, 36–7.

that networks of sympathizers were offering assistance to lawbreakers. The number of statutes adding the incentive of reward to the apprehension of felons suggests that many violators of the law were escaping punishment, and perhaps officers needed more assistance. An act of 1735 threatened constables with a fine of £5 if they failed to raise the hue and cry or join in the pursuit of criminals; at the same time, the statute promised £40 to anyone who caught the offender within forty days. Across the country, where constables were expected to circulate hue and cry warrants among townships, monetary incentives came to operate in different ways; in the West Riding, for example, a constable could receive a payment of two pence for each time he activated a warrant for the hue and cry. Though a paltry sum, the practice constituted an ancillary payment system functioning alongside the pursuit of criminals.[44]

The rewards system found one of its staunchest defenders in Henry Fielding, who complained of general ignorance of the law with regard to hue and cry and the duties of private persons to make arrests. His *Enquiry into the Causes of the Late Increase of Robbers* (1751) cataloged from legal history the many statutes and situations that called for the assistance of citizens, noting that response to the hue and cry and the arrest of criminals by private citizens were public duties bringing various, sometimes sizable, rewards. Officers also faced fines and imprisonment for neglect.[45] Fielding pointed out the tangible reward for catching felons for stealing goods out of shops and warehouses (10 & 11 Wil. III, c. 23, sec. 2): a non-transferable "Certificate" discharging the good citizen from parochial office.[46] But, he complained, this inducement was either not known or not respected among the people, who were likely to mete out "worse Treatment" to the thief catcher than the thief.[47] In defense of the unpopular practice, he added:

> [A]nd yet I will venture to say that if to do Good to Society be laudable, so is the Office of a Thief-catcher; and if to do this Good at the extreme Hazard of your Life be honourable, then is this Office honourable. True, it may be said; but he doth this with a View to a Reward. And doth not the Soldier

---

[44] Radzinowicz, *History*, 2:27; John Styles, "Print and Policing: Crime Advertising in Eighteenth-Century Provincial England," in *Policing and Prosecution in Britain, 1750–1850*, ed. Douglas Hay and Francis Snyder (Oxford, 1989), 83.

[45] *An Enquiry into the Late Increase of Robbers* (1751), repr. by the Wesleyan Edition of the Works of Henry Fielding (Middletown, 1988), 147–51.

[46] Ibid., 150.   [47] Ibid., 151.

and the Sailor venture his Life with the same View? For who, as a Great Man lately said, serves the public for Nothing?[48]

It was this view toward paying for police that informed Fielding's employment of the Bow Street Runners.[49]

The rewards system received an added boost by the proliferation of newspaper advertisements and handbills after 1700. An obvious resemblance was struck between printed crime advertisements and hue and cry warrants. As John Styles has shown for the provinces, the popularity of advertising fugitives from justice or stolen property resulted in the "virtual eclipse of the hue and cry between 1700 and 1730." Voluntary associations and acquaintances of victims piled rewards on top of rewards. Styles pointed out the contrast between the English style of policing and that of the Continent, arguing that advertising created an environment of "intensified surveillance" by "public rather than . . . official action." Yet this may be a meretricious distinction given that the government invested some energy in advertising rewards for apprehending coin clippers.[50] In such instances, the wellspring of concern may have been more individualistic than civic, reminiscent of Mandeville's maxim about private interest inspiring actions that only secondarily worked toward public benefit.[51] A more accurate assessment is that "a new device with private interest as its motive power" had replaced the simple expectation of the hue and cry's "hot and instantaneous pursuit."[52]

The extent to which the promise of rewards spread throughout laws passed in the eighteenth century is striking from any point of view. In John Beattie's estimation, "rewards emerged as a fundamental aspect of public policy and an established element in the system of criminal

---

[48] Ibid., 153. The "Great Man" may have been Walpole (153n).

[49] Ruth Paley, "Thief-takers in London in the Age of the McDaniel Gang, ca. 1745–1754," in Hay and Snyder, *Policing*, 313–14.

[50] Malcolm Gaskill indicates that by concentrating on horse theft, Styles missed the point about counterfeiting and the state. *Crime and Mentalities in Early Modern England* (Cambridge, 2000), 168.

[51] Styles, "Print and Policing," 85.

[52] Radzinowicz, *History*, 2:37. Radzinowicz cites a pamphlet of 1738, which complained that "large *publick Rewards*" only "prompt Men to do *publick Service*, not thro' Sentiments of *Duty*, and the Dictates of *virtuous publick Spirit*, but from the infinitely more sordid Principle of *private Interest*, and therefore shew the great Decay of *publick Virtue* among us." [Thomas Andrews], *An Enquiry into the Causes of the Encrease and Miseries of the Poor of England* (1738), 49, quoted in Radzinowicz, *History* 2:88.

administration" after 1689.[53] The direct connection between the capture of persons and payment for what amounted to their lives fixed the
epithet of "blood money" in the public domain.[54] Procedural protocol
often spawned new categories of currency. The Act of 1692, for example, required a set of specific procedures in order for citizens to collect
a promised reward. Individuals were required to obtain a "certificate
signed by the judge or the justices who had tried the offender" with
the sheriff of the county where the offense occurred. The use of certificates, a commonplace in communicating between legal officers, further
objectified the persons involved through a rather labyrinthine system
of transactions. Usually the reward was paid out in four to six weeks,
though not without interference from the clerk and under-sheriff, who
extracted poundage money, fraudulent gratuities, and fees for their services. Typical of eighteenth-century legal machinery, these procedures
helped to advance the equation between persons and prices down a
path of bureaucratic expertise and, often, corruption.[55]

Thief-catching became a notorious part of eighteenth-century legal
prosecution, rendered immortal by portraits, whether accurate or satirical, of gang leader Jonathan Wild.[56] Such thief-takers were powerful,
unscrupulous, and defiant of the law, yet, at the same time, often in
collusion with authorities. They constituted "a sort of entrepreneurial
police force dependent on fees and rewards."[57] Ruth Paley's exemplary
study of covert activities in London shows their considerable impact on
the administration of justice. Sir John Fielding, who took over as chief of
operations at Bow Street at midcentury, like his half-brother, defended
such assistance in prosecuting criminals, but his estimation of their reli-
ability was miscalculated. The extent of trickery taking place in more
ordinary settings (Paley mentions servant/master, tenant/landlord, and
debtor/creditor relationships) suggests that many people, not just hard-
ened gang members, initiated "vexatious or malicious actions" that

[53] Beattie, *Crime*, 51; *Policing*, 146–7, 231.
[54] Radzinowicz, *History*, 2:57.
[55] Radzinowicz, *History*, 2:72–3, on poundage money; on procedures, see 57–8; and on the
need for reform, see 88–91. By the time these practices were exposed in the first decades
of the nineteenth century, the connection between rewards and corruption had already
cast the system into disrepute.
[56] The most famous is, of course, Henry Fielding's satirical *Jonathan Wild* (1743), but Daniel
Defoe had already provided a more accurate picture in *The True and Genuine Account of
the Life and Action of the Late Jonathan Wild* (1725).
[57] Ruth Paley, "Thief-takers," 302.

would bring them monetary reward. The English system of private prosecution, entwined as it was in this age of rewards, did not necessarily safeguard individual liberties. Rather, it may have resulted in many "miscarriages of justice" brought about "sometimes by accident and sometimes at the instigation of individuals intent on securing their own ends."[58]

Informing was, of course, a centuries-old tradition in English legal prosecution, and so it is important to ascertain whether the frequency of such policing methods warrants calling this an eighteenth-century predilection.[59] Given the convergence of developments in the regulation of coinage, as well as property protection and vagrant apprehension (discussed later), evidence suggests that this was exactly the case. Particularly attractive were the rewards offered for the detection of coin clippers, which multiplied as the condition of coin plummeted toward the end of the seventeenth century. Isaac Newton's tenure as head of the Mint coincided with an intensification of prosecutions of clippers and coiners, detected and turned in by full-time agents employed by the government.[60] Disbursed regularly across the country, monetary enticements were used to the hilt during the 1690s. In the year following the Act of 1692, which applied to coiners as well as highwaymen, the Exchequer paid out more than £9,790 in rewards.[61] In 1694, another act stipulated reward payments specifically for coining offenses.[62] Authorities were sensible to the rise in apprehensions that followed on the heels of these laws, and though some individuals expressed distaste, further legislation against forgers and cattle thieves adopted the use of rewards to underscore a growing determination among lawmakers to reform society.[63] The fact that the nation desperately needed to insure its supply of

---

[58] Beattie, *Policing*, 421–22; Paley, "Thief-takers in London," 338–9.

[59] G. R. Elton, "Informing for Profit," *Cambridge Historical Journal* 11, no. 1 (1953): 149–67; Gaskill, *Crime and Mentalities*, 165–8.

[60] Gaskill, *Crime and Mentalities*, 169–70.

[61] Gaskill cites the figure of £49,000, but this figure is the sum of rewards and pensions. See *The Manuscripts of the House of Lords, 1692–1693* (London, 1894), 141; cf. Gaskill, *Crime and Mentalities*, 167.

[62] 6&7 W. III c. 17 (1694). Gaskill also points out that additional gain could be had through bounties added to the rewards promised by statute. *Crime and Mentalities*, 167.

[63] This was particularly true for the vagrancy statutes passed in the 1730s and 1740s. J. M. Beattie, "London Crime and the Making of the 'Bloody Code'," in *Stilling the Grumbling Hive: The Response to Social and Economic Problems in England, 1689–1750*, ed. Lee Davison, Tim Hitchcock, Tim Keirn and Robert B. Shoemaker (Stroud, 1992), 49–76.

good coin for purposes of revenue during a period of warfare made these strategies all the more necessary from the point of view of the state.[64]

Parliamentary rewards generated a subcategory of blood money called "Tyburn Tickets," certificates that exempted the holder from all parish and ward offices for life. Introduced as part of an act against shoplifting in 1699 (10 & 11 Wm III, c. 23, s. 2), these tickets were rewards for apprehending anyone guilty of housebreaking, horse stealing, or shoplifting goods to the value of 5 shillings or more.[65] The vernacular-style name for the exemptions derived from the connection between the offenses and the death penalty carried out at Tyburn. They amounted to a powerful incentive to women as well as men of the parish, who might be called up for duty as constables or overseers of the poor; such offices made increasingly heavy demands on citizens in the eighteenth century.[66] The reward of a Tyburn Ticket was also added to other statutory rewards later in the century, and a revised law against horse stealing offered a Tyburn Ticket as "the only recompense" for capturing the felon. Over time, peculiarities attached to the Tyburn Ticket suggest that it acquired a status and character all its own. While rewards were offered for apprehending anyone who stole a sheep or cow, for example, horse stealing remained linked only to the reward of a ticket. And as holders pressed for making the certificate widely applicable, seeking exemption from offices outside the specific parish in which the ticket was obtained, eminent eighteenth-century judges were called upon to rule on its geographical reach.[67] Once established, the practice of disbursing such rewards generated a growing metasystem of circulation and redemption.

With their grisly allusion to the public place of execution, Tyburn Tickets established an equation between "heads" and a publicly recognized certificate of value. The special aspect of the Tyburn Ticket was that it could be sold to another person and thus it could circulate as a form of money – or, more specifically, as a coupon or license. In effect,

---

[64] The single-mindedness of Newton in seeking out counterfeiters is well known. See Sir John Craig, *Newton at the Mint* (Cambridge, 1946), and "Isaac Newton and the counterfeiters," *Notes and Records of the Royal Society of London* 18 (1963), 136–45; Peter Linebaugh, *The London Hanged*; Gaskill, *Crime and Mentalities*, 171–3.

[65] On this act, see Beattie, *Policing*, 328–31. The practice was abolished in 1827 (7 & 8 Geo. IV c. 27). See GLRO, MR/CF, Index 47.

[66] Beattie, *Policing*, 325ff. On women's duties to serve, see Holdsworth, *A History of English Law*, 10:153n; Radzinowicz, 2:155–6.

[67] Radzinowicz, *History*, 2:156–7; Beattie, *Crime*, 52–55, and *Policing*, 147.

then, the tickets contributed to a larger flow of currency validating particular public policies. According to Mary Douglas, this type of currency is more like licensing than rationing coupons. "Both are instruments of social policy, but whereas rationing is egalitarian in intent, licensing is not. The object of licensing is protective, and to promote responsible administration."[68] When Tyburn Tickets came under scrutiny in the early nineteenth century, prices were then ranging from £12 to £40, though one ticket in Manchester sold for as much as £300.[69] Records for eighteenth-century Middlesex reveal irregular methods of accounting, with a few cases of apprehension by women.[70] By the end of the century, the trade in Tyburn Tickets was practically proverbial. According to one source, the office of parish constable in Covent Garden was sufficiently taxing as to warrant the sum of £25: "whoever is hit upon as a parochial constable says, 'This is a hard thing, and therefore I will buy myself off'."[71]

It is not coincidental that Tyburn Tickets, so similar to transferable coupons in an increasingly commercialized society, were born in the midst of public concern about shoplifting and other forms of property theft. Public concern over crime and immorality in London, perceived to be a growing menace, exploded in print at the turn of the seventeenth century. Highlighted by the activities of the Societies for the Reformation of Manners, attacks on property, counterfeiting of coin, prostitution, and illicit sexual behavior became subjects of much public debate. The Societies offered rewards of their own for the apprehension of Sabbath breakers and the like, thus engaging in the general enthusiasm for payment for police services. John Beattie has documented the extent of "the heightened alarm about crime in 1699," when the act against shoplifting

---

[68] "Primitive Rationing," in *Themes in Economic Anthropology*, ed. Raymond Firth (London, 1967), 131.

[69] Radzinowicz, *History*, 2:159; Paley, "London Thief-takers," 317. Paley reckons that a "more realistic figure would be in the region of £5 or less."

[70] GLRO, MR/CF/2, 1732, Widow Elizabeth Dodd; MR/CF/3, 1776, Sarah Mostyn and Mary Poultnoy. During most years between 1718 and 1776, the issue of tickets varied from one or two to as many as nine in Middlesex. An increase occurred in 1783–6. GRLO, MR/CF/5.

[71] Evidence of John Townsend, "Report of the Committee on the State of the Police of the Metropolis," 1816, quoted in Radzinowicz, *History*, 2:159. Radzinowicz devotes the bulk of his discussion to the internecine dealings over transfer of the tickets within parishes, which were reported to Parliamentary committees at the beginning of the nineteenth century. Joshua Gee also noted that "Tradesmen commonly fine off" in order to escape the duties of constable. *The Trade and Navigation of Great-Britain Considered* (London, 1729), 41–2.

extended the punishment of death to the crime of stealing more than
the value of 5 shillings from shops and, like a magnet, attracted additional clauses assigning capital punishment to other property offences.[72]
Thus, Tyburn Tickets were born in an era of increasing sensitivity to
exchange practices and the rules constructed around them.

Such responses to the threat to the public order generated their own
peculiar form of monetary circulation. Rewards by proclamation and
statute, "blood money," and Tyburn Tickets reveal a complex intertwining of civic and monetary thinking. Public opinion divided over the
practice of thief-taking, the inevitable result of the rewards system: while
some complained of the undermining of public virtue, others argued
for its effective delivery of public service. At a time when constituted
authority offered only the beginnings of administrative sophistication,
monetary payments created an infrastructure of regulatory scaffolding;
with prods and allurements, awards generated their own form of mutual
indebtedness, helping to cement popular loyalty to authority and the
public order. Tyburn Tickets were indicators of rank within a peculiar
social universe; those in possession understood their status according to
the newly designed legal system, calibrated by monetary increments.[73]
This was not so much a free market of commerce in criminals as a system
reliant upon carefully restricted flows of currency and people. Its success
depended on what Mary Douglas has called the "shrewd manipulation
of esoteric knowledge of genealogy, ritual and law."[74]

Enthusiasm for monetary rewards generated yet another opportunity
for collecting "blood money": beginning in 1713, rewards were attached
to a law requiring the apprehension of vagrants, enabling constables to
collect 2 shillings for every person turned in to the justice of the peace
of the district. The reward increased to 5 shillings under the extended
vagrancy statute of 1744, with an even higher reward of 10 shillings
for rounding up "Rogues and Vagabonds." By this law, anyone, not

---

[72] Beattie, *Policing*, 328–9; Beattie, "London Crime and the Making of the 'Bloody Code',"
53–4, 64–5.

[73] Paley also points out that parochial office could be avoided through systems of payment
independent of Tyburn tickets, and some parishes even instituted graded amounts
for those who wished to exempt themselves after receiving notice of their selection.
"London Thief-takers," 317. Tyburn tickets were not abolished until 1826 (7 Geo. 4,
c. 64, s. 32) through the reforming efforts of Sir Robert Peel. However, *Notes and Queries*
reported later transactions and exemptions, one as late as 1856. Radzinowicz, *History*,
2:161, 161n.

[74] Douglas, "Primitive Rationing, 137.

just a constable, was entreated to apprehend offenders.[75] Punishment for vagrancy resulted in "correction" rather than death; technically, then, vagrant rewards were not "blood money." Vagrants were deprived of their liberty, however, and either returned to their parishes of legal settlement or sentenced to confinement in a bridewell. Seen within the context of settlement law dating from 1662 and 1691, these statutes were part of a larger effort to clarify responsibility for the laboring poor and regulate the movement of labor. But by attaching rewards to the apprehension of vagrants, the state had blurred the boundary between civil and criminal regulation.

Parliament and local parishes may have had low expectations of widespread public response; yet the issuance of these statutes indicated a wish to call attention to the need for action against people deemed out of place. The significance of these calls for the apprehension of vagrants rested on the way in which monetary values interacted with a method of social classification. The jurisdiction of monetary measurements and incentives, extended into the realm of vagrant and criminal apprehension, gradually took on a life of its own, generating its own raft of terminology and a veritable subculture of eighteenth-century urban life. In the following section, the problem of vagrancy apprehension will be examined in closer detail in order to analyze the connection between prices and people in the first half of the eighteenth century.

MONEY, IDENTITY, AND THE POOR

As Thomas Turner indicated later in the century, tending to the personal predicaments of vagrants constituted part of the daily duties of a justice of the peace. "This morn relieved two women with a pass with *12d*," he recorded in May of 1756. "They were passed from Dorchester to Canterbury, having one child each, and one big with child." His insertion of charity into the more cold-hearted task of "passing" vagrants imbued his official role with the salutary aura of gift exchange, reminding us that such transactions were never purely juridical in nature. In the context of Turner's diary, we find their occurrence also mingled with commercial accounting. In December of the next year, he noted briefly, "Paid 4*d*. for 2 lb. tripe. Gave a man and a woman with a pass 6 d. on the

---

[75] Radzinowicz, *History*, 2:62.

parish account. At home all day."[76] Market-oriented and gifting behaviors sometimes overlapped, such as when a local landowner in Turner's parish got up a scheme to bring in poor laborers, "some with certificates and some without," to work on the land for low wages.[77] In this century of adventurous projecting and improvement, monetary transactions incorporated human beings as well as commodities; both applications were perfectly in keeping with the assumptions of parochial law and its attendant social order.

This is a different point from that made by Mary Poovey in her discussion of William Petty and "economic matters of fact" in *A History of the Modern Fact: Problems of Knowledge in the Sciences of Wealth and Society*, in which she emphasizes the importance of using numbers and monetary amounts to erect a legitimate and politically impartial methodology of political arithmetic.[78] The freedom to apply monetary measurements to certain classes of people was founded on an understanding of law and the social order repeatedly asserted in vagrancy law and parochial poor law management. Mingling in the public mind with notions of customary charity, such concepts belonged to a separable universe marked by transactions and circulation, with its own metagrammatic rules. As proposals for solving the problems of poverty multiplied alongside statutory amendments and policies, monetary amounts became attached in special ways to the migrant poor. The course of this development extended over the first half of the eighteenth century, when issues of social policy moved the problems of vagrancy and poverty to the forefront of public debate.[79]

During a period of urban migration and population growth, English people anxiously generated descriptive classifications for the unemployed and masterless at the beginning of the century. In 1715, the House of Commons reported an "increase of strange beggars, cripples, lusty idle men and women, vagabonds, blind people, pretended and real mad folks," concluding with the blanket gesture "and such like."[80] "These may be looked on as the Outcasts of Mankind," William Hay lamented

---

[76] David Vaisey, ed., *The Diary of Thomas Turner, 1754–1765* (Oxford, 1985), 42, 125.
[77] Ibid., 67.   [78] (Chicago, 1998), 120–43.
[79] Joanna Innes, "Prisons for the Poor: English Bridewells, 1555–1800," in *Labour, Law, and Crime: An Historical Perspective*, ed. Francis Snyder and Douglas Hay (London, 1987), 42–122.
[80] House of Commons Journals, 8 March 1715, quoted in Sidney and Beatrice Webb, *English Local Government: English Poor Law History: Part I. The Old Poor Law*, 3 vols. (London, 1927), 1:357.

in 1735, "who, as the Law now stands, are doomed to Beggary, both they and their Posterity."[81] Migrants of the lowest order, those who had no apparent place in the neighborhood, became the focus of increased public concern and, as Tim Hitchcock has underscored, alarmed "publicity" in London by midcentury.[82] Having abandoned a project to confine them in prisons, magistrates developed "a more scrupulous system of detection and transportation" to deal with vagrants: local authorities were ordered to reinvigorate an older statutory system of monetary rewards in a plan for apprehending a broad class of the wandering poor, who would then be carried to their parishes of origin.[83] Such efforts can be seen as an attempt to control the circulation of people within an established hierarchy of status, even while the tide of historical developments was working against a restriction of movement and, to a lesser extent, the erasure of prescriptive social distinctions.

The success of this strategy was limited and, according to some historians, of relatively little significance in the larger picture of poor law reform. A significant delay occurred in the actual application of the law in most parts of London, finally prompted by a "dramatic increase in county rates" in the 1740s. Local response to the prospect of public apprehension of vagrants was mixed at best, and one must read the historical record with a certain measure of skepticism as to the representative nature of the individuals who pressed local authorities for monetary reward.[84] The policy nevertheless deserves analysis because it figured in debates about poor law policy throughout the century and served to highlight a host of infractions against the liberties of laborers who had moved from their parishes of origin. The compromised nature of the legal rights of laborers in the eighteenth century must be seen in relation to the myriad proposals and diatribes condemning their freedom of movement.

The paradoxical social life of money may offer a key to analyzing changing fashions of poor relief in the eighteenth century, particularly

---

[81] William Hay, *Remarks on the Laws Relating to the Poor* (London, 1735), 5.

[82] Tim Hitchcock, "Beggar-man, Thief: The Publicity of Poverty in Early Eighteenth-Century London," unpublished paper, 16 July 1998; for a definitive work on this subject, see his *Down and Out in Eighteenth-Century London* (London, 2005).

[83] Nicholas Rogers, "Policing the Poor in Eighteenth-Century London: The Vagrancy Laws and Their Administration," *Histoire Sociale – Social History* 24 (May 1991), 137. I am intentionally conflating vagrancy with vagabondage here to avoid cumbersome terminology throughout this chapter. Though the terms referred to distinct groups of the poor, the legislation of the 1740s tended to conflate them, too, as will be shown later.

[84] Ibid., 137; Tim Hitchcock, personal communication.

if seen in a *long durée* of policy-making, with Speenhamland as its end-point. It is not far-fetched to point out that the functions of rewards and certificates operated in tandem with the circulation of notes and bills during the long eighteenth century. Thus, rewards for vagrant apprehension can be seen as monetary measures that functioned as "coupons" in a makeshift system of social regulation that mirrored the use of money. By engaging citizens and commercially minded contractors, parishes in London helped to construct a view of the vagrant poor that was influenced in a deep sense by the metaphorical world of money. Vagrants became commensurate with monetary signs, or (the term used by contemporaries) "heads," as they figured into attempts to circumscribe their movement and their labor.[85] As part of a financial calculus of rewards payments and the cost of relocation per head, their identities became subject to the will of others. Masterless people were caught in a tide of transition as new forms of individualism emerged from early modern assumptions. In an age of possessive individualism, they became "possessed" individuals.

This fact gained greater significance in the context of transatlantic labor migration in the first half of the eighteenth century. The characteristics of the vagrant poor overlapped with those of many transatlantic migrants, and as one segment of a larger pool of labor, they figured into plans to harness the vast resources of the colonial world. As men of property and standing embraced freedom and power in eighteenth-century Britain, they recognized profound differences in the vagrant poor. Without permanent residence, employment, or property, vagrants lacked the most basic claim to identity and autonomy. Because they were on the move, their condition was particularly exposed. Their vulnerability was thrown into relief whenever citizens (or mercenary contractors) chose to apprehend them for cash payment. As C. B. Macpherson once described the form of individualism emerging from the era of Locke, "[T]he man without property in things loses that full proprietorship of his own person which was the basis of his equal natural rights."[86] It was this deficiency of identity and power that led to the equation between people and monetary sums against the backdrop of migration. The following section, then, attempts to connect theories about money to more than just a particular chapter of eighteenth-century vagrancy law. The involvement of money as a means of categorizing and objectifying people indicates

---

[85] Sandra Sherman, *Imagining Poverty: Quantification and the Decline of Paternalism* (Columbus, 2001).

[86] C. B. Macpherson, *The Political Theory of Possessive Individualism* (New York, 1962), 231.

the manifest presence of monetary measures of human worth at the beginning of the modern age.

PUTTING PRICES ON THE VAGRANT POOR

"Beggar" is the most persistent and indisputable category of poverty in the past, and it appeared as a prominent aspect of early modern discussion of money and vagrancy.[87] As a supplicant pleading for monetary handouts, the beggar participated in an ancillary world of exchange, what Natalie Zemon Davis has called a "relational mode" of gift exchange.[88] Acceptability usually turned on whether the person was known to the neighborhood; throughout history, complete strangers met with varying degrees of pity, suspicion, and hostility. But unlike the medieval beggar, who stood a chance of being viewed as a sanctified imitation of Christ, the early modern beggar often aroused contentious sentiments related to poor law policies and their reform.[89]

The fundamental division between the alien and known poor helped to solve at least part of the problem of categorical confusion posed by the continual circulation of laborers in the seventeenth and eighteenth centuries. In the late seventeenth century, the punitive solution lay in confinement in a workhouse, but contemporaries made much of the distinction between the needy who wandered into the parish and those who were familiar inhabitants fallen on hard times. In *Some Proposals For the [I]mployment of the Poor, and For the Prevention of Idleness and the*

---

[87] Hitchcock, *Down and Out;* beggars are also discussed throughout general works on poverty for this period: see Bronislaw Geremek, *Poverty: A History* (Oxford, 1994); Paul Slack, *From Reformation to Improvement: Public Welfare in Early Modern England* (Oxford, 1999); see also his "Vagrants and Vagrancy in England," in *Migration and Society in Early Modern England*, ed. Peter Clark and David Souden (London, 1987), 49–76; Lynn Hollen Lees, *The Solidarities of Strangers: The English Poor Laws and the People, 1700–1948* (Cambridge, 1998); Charles J. Ribton-Turner, *A History of Vagrants and Vagrancy, Beggars and Begging* (London, 1887); Hitchcock categorized London beggars according to three modes: "stationary public beggar," "itinerant domestic beggar," and "beggarly self-employed." "Beggar-man, Thief," 1–2.

[88] *The Gift in Sixteenth-Century France* (Madison, 2000), 9.

[89] On the apprehension and ambivalence felt toward beggars during this period, see Paul Slack, *Poverty and Policy in Tudor and Stuart England* (London, 1987), 127–8, 167; Jeremy Boulton, "Going on the Parish: The Parish Pension and Its Meaning in the London Suburbs, 1640–1724," in *Chronicling Poverty: The Voices and Strategies of the English Poor, 1640–1840*, ed. Tim Hitchcock, Peter King and Pamela Sharpe (Basingstoke, 1997), 32–33; for the general dimension of growing antipathy towards begging and vagrants in Europe, see Robert Jütte, *Poverty and Deviance in Early Modern Europe* (Cambridge, 1994), 163–9, 169–77, passim.

Consequence thereof, Begging (1681), Thomas Firmin opposed the idea of herding such unfortunates into workhouses, partly on the grounds of inconvenience ("for suppose a Woman hath a sick Child, or Husband, or some Infirmity upon her self") and partly owing to common aversion to coerced labor.[90] That humiliation, he indicated, was designed for the refractory wanderer, who had fallen into anonymity and homelessness:

> True indeed, for Vagrants and sturdy Beggars that have no Habitation, and that will not work unless they are held to it as Galley-slaves are tied to their Oars; such Work-houses are very necessary, and I wish we had more of them, and that those we have were employed to that purpose; but for such poor People as have Habitations of their own, and are known in the places where they live, and that would take Pains at home, it is altogether unreasonable and unprofitable in my poor Judgment to bring them to a publick Work-house.[91]

To mark the "worthy poor," Firmin urged the use of badges, and he also pressed the virtues of hospitality upon recalcitrant contemporaries, importuning them to share occasional meals with the local poor. For those beggars he did not know, he reserved his severest judgments. Though his reference to galley slaves was a figure of speech, discussion of this style of punishment surfaced in the more complete accounts of earlier laws relating to "incorrigible rogues."[92] Firmin also may have been aware of the brief period in the sixteenth century when a statute condemning vagabonds to slavery had been revived from the reign of Edward VI.[93]

A fixed domicile provided the beggar with what the law referred to as "a good account of himself" or a "testimonial" – a personal biography attached to a place, which provided a legitimate claim to material

---

[90] Many, he implied, were female, an impression confirmed by historical research, and within that large category, he identified a considerable diversity: well-to-do widows who had lost their estates through the machinations of scheming investors, "persons of good Education and well related" who "hide as much as they can," alongside widows of no means at all who had "outlived all their Friends and near Relations," and those who "wrought hard when they were able" but through "Sickness, or some sad Accident, have come to Poverty in their Old Age." *Some Proposals*, 29.

[91] Ibid., 11.

[92] See *The Laws Concerning the Poor* (1705), 161, which refers to I Jac. c. 7. Rogues were to "be Branded in the left Shoulder with a burning Iron, having a great Roman R upon it as broad as a Shilling, and from thence shall be sent to the place of his last dwelling."

[93] The revival of 1 Edward VI. chap. iii, occurred in 1559. See R. H. Tawney and E. Power, eds., *Tudor Economic Documents*, 3 vols. (London, 1965), 1:325ff; Slack, *Poverty and Policy*, 122.

relief and respect.[94] The principle served as the very foundation of the Elizabethan poor laws, and it also developed as a part of the culture of poverty and philanthropy during the Restoration period. This was clear throughout John Locke's memorandum on the Poor Law, composed when he was a commissioner of the Board of Trade in 1697, in which he complained that "the streets everywhere swarm with beggars, to the increase of idleness, poverty, and villainy, and to the shame of Christianity." He contrasted "these visible trespassers" to the known poor, who were at "liberty to declare their wants, and receive broken bread and meat, or other charity, from well-disposed people." Among his proposals, which echoed the punitive measures of an earlier era, were requirements that "idle vagabonds" be "sent to the next seaport town" and put on board "his majesty's ships"; that careful issuance of passes and badges maintain a separation between authorized migrants, needy poor, and dissimulating vagabonds; and that beadles "seize upon any stranger begging in the streets" and bring them before guardians for punishment.[95]

From the point of view of the last half of the seventeenth century, such draconian projects can be understood as strategic attempts to pin down a mobile population at a time of demographic contraction. Though contemporaries were dimly aware of such changes, a decline in population after 1650 fostered an increasingly pervasive conviction that the domestic labor force ought to be more fully engaged; diminishing numbers also influenced emigration rates to the English Atlantic world and contributed to a shift to slave labor in the colonies.[96] The Settlement Acts

[94] Tawney and Power, *Tudor Economic Documents*, 341; Slack, *Poverty and Policy*, 63, 92–3, 123.

[95] The "Draft of a Representation, Containing [a] Scheme of Methods for the Employment of the Poor" appeared in *An Account of the Origin, Proceedings, and Intentions of the Society for the Promotion of Industry* (Louth, Lincestershire, 1789) and is reprinted in Mark Goldie, ed., *John Locke, Political Essays*, Cambridge Texts in the History of Political Thought (Cambridge, 1997), 182–98; quotations are from 190 and 197. Locke recommended the resuscitation of Elizabethan punishments that included whipping, hard labor, impressment, ear clipping, transportation, and, more generally, widespread internment in workhouses. As C. B. Macpherson pointed out, "When Locke looked at his own society, he saw two classes with different rights and different rationality" (*Theory of Possessive Individualism*, 228–9.) Locke was against the use of rewards for apprehension of vagrants, however.

[96] David Eltis, "Labour and Coercion in the English Atlantic World from the Seventeenth to the Early Twentieth Century," in *The Wages of Slavery: From Chattel Slavery to Wage Labour in Africa, the Caribbean, and England*, ed. Michael Twaddle (London, 1993), 218–219; see also A. W. Coats, "The Relief of Poverty, Attitudes to Labour, and Economic Change in England, 1660–1782," *International Review of Social History* 21 (1976): 98–115.

aimed to fix labor to localities by attaching people without property to the households of their employers. Official settlement required constant employment over the course of one year, apprenticeship, the paying of rates, or the renting of property. Handbooks on how to deal with settlement questions during the eighteenth century multiplied, providing necessary advice for justices, constables, and beadles.[97] While many hundreds, possibly thousands, of English people migrated without ever coming under the scrutiny of the law, officers were repeatedly entreated to be on the watch for violations. The surplus of advice on how to address the problem of circulating laborers provides evidence of how persons of property were mindful of the problems of migration and vagrancy and poised to act when circumstances called for "removal."[98]

The "myth of the static, rural past" has never suited the restless dynamism informing the social history of England. In fact, Britain was a complex island nation both vitalized and, at times, alarmed by people on the move.[99] Its own population demonstrated a persistent mobility suited to market agriculture, commerce, and colonialism. The primary reason for this was obvious: given the limited extent of land ownership among the vast majority of the rural population, some form of mobility was a fact of life.[100] Besides those who, by definition, lived a migratory life, such as tramping artisans and military men, many others moved out of necessity. Keith Wrightson has described the "bulk of the labouring population" as forming "a penumbra of casual labour"; "most people," he adds, "lacked a stable occupational identity" in the early modern period.[101] This condition contributed to the constant immigration into

[97] Norma Landau, *The Justices of the Peace, 1769–1760* (Berkeley, 1984), 339–42. The Reverend Richard Burn's *Justice of the Peace and Parish Officer*, first appearing in 1755 and in its 30th edition by 1869, was one of these.
[98] James Stephen Taylor, *Poverty, Migration and Settlement in the Industrial Revolution: Sojourners' Narratives* (Palo Alto, CA, 1989), 8–25; K. D. M. Snell, *Annals of the Labouring Poor: Social Change and Agrarian England, 1660–1900* (Cambridge, 1985), 71–80.
[99] Peter Clark, "Migration in England during the Late Seventeenth and Early Eighteenth Centuries," in *Migration and Society in Early Modern England*, Peter Clark and David Souden (Totowa, NJ, 1987), 220–1, 242; David Souden, "'Rogues, Whores and Vagabonds'? Indentured Servant Emigration to North America and the case of mid-Seventeenth-Century Bristol," ibid., 167.
[100] Historians have referred to the kind of mobility in search of places as servants in husbandry as "circular mobility." Roughly 40 percent of the population in 1688 engaged in this form of migration. Clark, "Migration in England," 215, 250–1; David Eltis, "Seventeenth Century Migration and the Slave Trade: The English Case in Comparative Perspective," in *Migration, Migration History, History: Old Paradigms and New Perspectives*, ed. Jan Lucassen and Leo Lucassen (Bern, 1997), 208
[101] *Earthly Necessities: Economic Lives in Early Modern Britain* (New Haven, 2000), 313.

London in the early modern period. According to Gregory King's estimates dating from the 1690s, close to one fifth of the population was pre-
cariously positioned with regard to residence. He described fully 1.3 million people as "cottagers and paupers," just the sort to find themselves
displaced by the major reorganization of landholding going on around
them; added at the bottom of the social pyramid were "vagrants," a
broad category including "Hawkers, Pedlars, Crate Carriers, Gipsies,
Thieves & Beggars," "[r]eckond [at] 30,000."[102]

Revisionist historians of migration stress the fact that geographical
movement of populations is part of ordinary happenstance; in the words
of Charles Tilly, "The history of European migration is the history of
social life."[103] Yet migration as a subject of historical discussion has been
distorted by an effort to explain personal choices and character traits
of the people who migrated. Too often, studies see migrants as either
victims of crisis or free agents seeking betterment. These identities are
seldom exclusive of one another, depending on the ages and life cycle of
the migrants, which are not always discernable from data. The division
erected between short-distance travelers, who seemed to be in search
of "betterment," and long-distance migrants in pursuit of "survival"
has distorted a more complex picture of migration as responding to
pressures of employment patterns and policies, or kinship networks.
This line of analysis also implicitly stigmatizes those who appear on
record when they fall into the purview of the law.[104]

Similarly, the dichotomy of vagrants and migrants creates an unhelp-
ful distinction because it depends on categories that were fluctuating
and of dubious validity even according to contemporaries. Sidney and
Beatrice Webb emphasized the characteristic anxieties that each age

---

[102] Gregory King, "Natural and Political Observations and Conclusions upon the State and
Condition of England," reprinted in George E. Barnett, ed., *Two Tracts by Gregory King*
(Baltimore, 1936), 18, 31; see also A. Roger Ekirch, *Bound for America: The Transportation
of British Convicts to the Colonies, 1718–1775* (Oxford, 1987), 61–7. Ekirch points out that
"a quarter of the population could be regarded as permanently in a state of poverty
and underemployment, if not total unemployment."

[103] Quoted in Jan Lucassen and Leo Lucassen, "Migration, Migration History, History:
Old Paradigms and New Perspectives," in *Migration, Migration History, History*, 9.

[104] These are the criticisms offered by Lucassen and Lucassen, "Migration, Migration
History," 18–19, of Paul Slack's definitive essay, "Vagrants and Vagrancy in England,
1598–1664," first published in 1971. See also Michael P. Hanagan, "Labor History and
the New Migration History: A Review Essay," *International Labor and Working-Class
History* 54 (Fall 1998): 57–79; Peter Clark and David Souden, "Introduction," *Migration
and Society*, 11–48; Peter Clark, "Migration in England during the Late Seventeenth
and Early Eighteenth Centuries," ibid., 213–252.

projected onto the notion of vagrancy. "[E]ach century, and often each decade, saw particular sections of persons added to or omitted from the list" of targets of vagrancy law: while the seventeenth century was on the watch for idleness and chicanery, eighteenth-century concerns focused on the potential for attacks on property and suspected dependency on local poor rates.[105] The term was a "catch-all category," as Nicholas Rogers argued, as the laws "adapted to address new crises in social relations" throughout the long eighteenth century. A succession of statutes (twenty-eight between 1700 and 1824, including twelve before 1760) can be seen as attempts to "plug loopholes in the existing laws" aiming at embezzlers of textile remnants ("endgatherers"), idle migrant workers, those suspected of committing a felony, female nonresidents suspected of pregnancy, and generally anyone who might qualify as "idle and disorderly." Depending on the year, the statute, and the neighborhood, vagrancy might act as a rallying cry for administrative belt-tightening, street-cleaning, or moral reform.[106] It is no wonder, then, that historians have treated the subject as a subset of other problems, such as the operation of the poor laws and the Acts of Settlement.

In Rogers's estimation, the laws belong to a larger "regulatory regime" of labor in the eighteenth century. The use of rewards for the apprehension of vagrants represented a routine step in dealing with a wage-earning population that lacked permanent residence and ties to employment.[107] One might add that it came with unintended consequences: the series of statutes relating to vagrancy in the mid-eighteenth century trained public attention on a mobile population of indigent laborers, inviting ordinary citizens to engage in a civil process of identifying and redefining a wide spectrum of the poor. The law itself maintained a current taxonomy of the wanderer, with descriptive categories changing repeatedly according to contemporary antipathy. Each recodification (occurring in 1714, 1740, and 1744) revised the terms by which offenders might be classified. What Rogers succinctly referred to as "catch-all category for social undesirables"[108] included

---

[105] *English Poor Law History*, 352n; Craig Dionne and Steve Mentz, eds., *Rogues and Early Modern English Culture* (Ann Arbor, 2004); A. L. Beier, *Masterless Men: The Vagrancy Problem in England, 1560–1640* (London, 1985); Slack, "Vagrants and Vagrancy," 49–76.

[106] Nicholas Rogers, "Vagrancy, Impressment and the Regulation of Labour in Eighteenth-Century Britain," in *Unfree Labour in the Development of the Atlantic World*, ed. Paul E. Lovejoy and Nicholas Rogers (London, 1994), 103–105; "Policing the Poor," 131.

[107] Rogers, "Vagrancy," 104.   [108] Rogers, "Policing the Poor," 131.

the three standard headings cited in early laws: "idle and disorderly persons," "rogues and vagabonds," and "incorrigible rogues." These classes aimed to comprise a wide spectrum of persons whose identities could alternate between categories: beggars, tricksters, actors, fortune-tellers, fencers, ballad singers, minstrels, pedlars and chapmen without licenses, and many others. Complaints of obstructions on the streets and roads of the kingdom revealed the same polymorphic confusion. Nevertheless, the direction of change was apparent to Richard Burn, a cleric and magistrate of considerable repute. "In the former acts, the descriptions were more general; and consequently, more latitude was given to the discretion of the justices," he observed. Of late, legislation provided numerous classifications with correspondingly specific procedures and remedies. While local authorities did not necessarily follow the rules, the dominant temper of the times urged greater administrative vigilance.[109]

With renewed interest in resuscitating earlier vagrancy statutes, the 1740s witnessed the posting of offers of rewards of 2 shillings, and later 4, 5, and 10 shillings to any person who apprehended and brought before a justice of the peace "any Rogues, Vagabonds or sturdy Beggars."[110] Not all apprehensions of vagrants resulted in monetary payment to a third party. Though the laws expressly offered payment of reward for turning in vagrants, procedures for collecting were lengthy, and many more apprehensions than disbursements occurred. Rogers estimated that "the proportion of rewards to apprehensions was rarely more than 20 percent," suggesting that their significance ought not to be exaggerated.[111] The Webbs themselves admitted that the arrangement was not as systematic as statutory exhortations suggest. They noted that the laws "operated in ways quite unexpected by the legislators" owing to the "frugal minds" of the justices of the peace and the deterrence of the crowd in checking the "zeal" of constables.[112] Nevertheless, the 1750s

---

[109] Richard Burn, *The History of the Poor Laws* (London, 1764), 125. On changes taking place in poor law administration at midcentury, see Joanna Innes, "The 'Mixed Economy of Welfare' in Early Modern England: Assessments of the Options from Hale to Malthus (ca. 1683–1803)," in *Charity, Self-Interest and Welfare in the English Past*, ed. Martin Daunton (London, 1996), 160–1.

[110] Burn, *History*, emphasizes 17 G.2.c.5. The legal precedents for rewards were numerous (22–52).

[111] Rogers argued that the Webbs were guilty of exaggerating the importance of rewards. "Policing the Poor," 129–30.

[112] *English Poor Law History*, 370–71.

witnessed a run on claims that resulted in a recommendation to reduce the offering to its original 2 shillings.[113]

Records at the local level are instructive because of the drama they reenact between pursuers and the pursued. Beadles seemed particularly eager to cash in on the opportunities afforded by the dozens of vagrants who populated the streets of London. Middlesex and Westminster Sessions Papers recount the relentless efforts of beadles who collected steady sums for turning in vagrants, many of whom were women who probably offered little resistance and, in some cases, were pregnant, decrepit, or sickly.[114] Constables and beadles alike set out on assignments to clear their parishes of undesirables, sometimes with obvious alacrity. In one case, a high constable for Middlesex hoisted himself over iron spikes bordering a theater stage in pursuit of "disorderly Persons," retiring only after being pelted with "a Bottle, Several Glasses, Pipes, Oranges, & Other Things," accompanied by "loud Hissings and Hollowings."[115] Such zeal could be expensive. In a single year at midcentury, the Middlesex Sessions paid out the unwieldy sum of £924 11s 9d for apprehending and conveying a total of 498 persons.[116] This was money spent on simply ridding places of unwanted vagrants; parishes were still responsible for the worthy resident poor, who, from an administrative perspective, represented a greater proportion of the poor at large.[117]

With parish policing administration still in a relatively primitive stage, parishes established contracts with middlemen to convey vagrants out of parishes in much the same way that criminals were handled. The years between 1718 and 1775 have been called "the age of the contractors" with regard to the business of transporting criminals

---

[113] GLRO, Middlesex Sessions Papers, MJ/SP/1757/July/7, "Report of the Committee Appointed to Examine What Benefit has arisen to this County from an Order of Sessions, dated the 14th July 1757," 13.

[114] Entries for 1752 and 1753, for example, are particularly numerous in Westminster, which may reflect extra effort by justices in publicizing the statutes pertaining to the apprehension of rogues and vagabonds. See GLRO, Westminster Parish Exams, Vol. F5043 (1752–1753); Middlesex Sessions Papers 1751/May: Minutes of a Committee Regarding Vagrants, 4 June 1751.

[115] GLRO, MSP/JAN/1751, Report dated 27 December 1750.

[116] Payment was for orders dated between July 1756 and July 1757. GLRO, MJ/SP/1757/July/7.

[117] Hitchcock, "Beggar-Man, Thief," 8–9. Hitchcock's calculations for the City of London between 1738 and 1742 show that of 153 persons apprehended for begging and loitering, "almost half, 75, had a legal settlement in the metropolitan London area" (8).

to the colonies,[118] and the epithet could well be applied to Londoners' methods of conveying vagrants back to their home parishes. According to Nicholas Rogers's estimates for the eighteenth century, between 8,000 and 10,000 migrants entered London each year, and roughly ten percent "were shipped out again in the wagons of hired contractors."[119] Sessions papers for Middlesex and Westminster indicate that local justices resorted to the use of contractors from the middle of the century. The notoriety of some contractors, particularly those who dealt with criminals, became legendary even to contemporaries in high places. But in the case of the transportation of vagrants, hardly a far-flung operation, reputations and fortunes were harder won. Personalities emerge from Quarterly Sessions records, disclosing the diligence of men who collected small fortunes from local authorities. In 1757, James Sturgis Adams appears to have conveyed 1,159 persons from 622 orders in a single year, receiving over £367 for his efforts.[120] The calculations per head enable us to draw a direct line between techniques of labor management applied to slaves and convicts and the laboring population.

MONEY, VAGRANCY, AND SOCIAL IDENTITY
IN THE MID-EIGHTEENTH CENTURY

The best means of examining the social dynamics beneath the reinvigorated vagrancy laws of the 1740s is through case studies. Perhaps the most vivid account comes from contemporaries' reports of "the Roundhouse Incident," which historian Tim Hitchcock has analyzed through painstaking archival research.[121] In his correspondence, Horace Walpole originally drew attention to the "shocking scene of murder" on the night of July 15, 1742. The events followed from an order by Westminster

---

[118] Peter Wilson Coldham, *Immigrants in Chains: A Social History of Forced Emigration to the Americas, 1606–1776* (Stroud, 1992), 59–70.

[119] Rogers, "Vagrancy, " 106.

[120] This figure combines his annual salary of £120 and the costs of maintenance of the conveyed vagrants. GLRO, MJ/SP/1757/July/7,8. These figures come from the assessment of a single parish in London, suggesting that Rogers's estimates of those hauled out of London are too conservative for this period.

[121] The following pages are greatly indebted to Tim Hitchcock's essay, "'You Bitches ... Die and Be Damned': Gender, Authority and the Mob in St. Martin's Roundhouse Disaster of 1742," in *The Streets of London: From the Great Fire to the Great Stink*, ed. Tim Hitchcock and Heather Shore (London, 2003), 69–81.

authorities for a general "privy search," a strategy originating in the late fifteenth century as a check upon vagrancy and adapted over the years to address problems of public order. Empowering constables, beadles, and watchmen to clear the streets of anyone who was deemed disorderly, the privy search could aim at particular categories of people, such as prostitutes, or entire neighborhoods suspected of harboring an excess of alien itinerants. In the case recounted by Walpole, the parish of Westminster appears to have employed the warrant in order to cash in on fines and bail fees. Parish officers

> took up every woman they met, till they had collected five or six and twenty, all whom they thrust into St. Martin's Roundhouse, where they kept them all night with doors and windows closed. The poor creatures who could not stir or breathe, screamed as long as they had any breath left, begging at least for water; one poor wretch said she was worth eighteen pence, and would gladly give it for a draught of water – but in vain! So well did they keep them there, that in the morning four were found stifled to death, two died soon after, and a dozen more are in a shocking way...several of them were beggars, who from having no lodging were necessarily found in the street, and others honest labouring women: one of the dead was a poor washerwoman, big with child, who was returning home late from washing.[122]

Hitchcock's reconstitution showed the contradictions of such a method of enforcing order: nearly fifty men were involved in seeking to clear the streets; they followed the routine procedure of using their authority to enter homes, shops, and other establishments after eleven o'clock at night. The apprehended women were thrust into the ground floor cell designated for females, which Hitchcock appropriately called a "hole," measuring slightly more than six feet square. Its one window was eventually shuttered for the night. Meanwhile, the wife of watchhouse keeper sold drinks to the men arriving with their captives as a small crowd gathered outdoors in response to the cries of the women already imprisoned. The suffocation of four women, discovered the next morning, provoked a public outcry, and by the following night, a full-scale riot had demolished the facade of the Roundhouse. The

---

[122] Letter to Sir Horace Mann, ca. 21 July 1742, in W. S. Lewis, Warren Hunting Smith, and George L. Lam, eds., *Horace Walpole's Correspondence with Sir Horace Mann* (New Haven, 1954), I:503–4. A century and a half later, W. E. H. Lecky sensationalized the incident in his classic *A History of England in the Eighteenth Century*, 3rd ed., 4 vols. (London, 1883), 1:483–4.

watch-house keeper, William Bird, was tried and convicted of willful murder and sentenced to hang. Though his sentence was commuted to transportation, Bird died before serving his term in Maryland, having been denied food and water on board the ship. Hitchcock's findings revealed a lengthy process of parochial malfeasance, venality, and scapegoating, widely reported in contemporary periodicals.[123]

The Roundhouse incident confirms a familiar image of eighteenth-century local corruption; yet it is even more informative if placed in the wider context of the involvement of money in local vagrancy regulation. The Watch Act of 1736 gave rise to what was thought to be a more effectively administered vigilance at the parish level, managed by the select vestry manned by wealthy merchants.[124] Like the Shoplifting Act of 1699, which was also sponsored by merchants and shopkeepers, this expansion of police aimed to stimulate more prosecutions and deter offenders through punishment. Perhaps Parliament also believed that parish policing might obviate the need for middlemen, the stock characters of the London underworld who preyed on the affluence of one part of the population and the subordinate status of another. The customary system of payments and fines lubricating each legal procedure, which topped up the negligible salaries paid to minor parish officers, invited corruption. Not so readily perceived, however, was the pattern emerging from the repeated classification of the vagrant population as lacking a subject identity that exposed them to the mastery of monetary relations.

Apprehension initiated an administrative ritual, a process that brought to light the full, public acknowledgment of the subject status of wanderers. The formal procedures of vagrancy law called for considerable paperwork from justices of the peace, constables, and even watch-house keepers as they carried out their duties. For the duration of the Roundhouse apprehensions, for example, William Bird was said to have sat at a long table, entering the names of the watchmen and their respective prisoners in his watchbook while drinking and discussion continued around him.[125] Surviving volumes of Sessions papers provide ample testimony of such activities. Record-keeping, made tiresome by repetition, resulted in the production of printed forms, with blanks inserted where specific information was required. Several such certificates, measuring roughly three inches by six inches, some printed and others in handwriting, appear in the Middlesex Sessions records for

---

[123] Hitchcock, "Gender, Authority and the Mob," 73–9.   [124] Ibid.,75.   [125] Ibid., 70.

1758. These tickets enabled the holder to collect a reward of 10 shillings for turning in a "Rogue and Vagabond":

> Whereas it duly appeareth unto me＿＿＿＿one of his Majesty's Justices of the Peace in and for the said＿＿＿that＿＿＿a Rogue and Vagabond, was found wandring [sic] and begging, in the Parish of＿＿＿＿in the said＿＿＿Which said＿＿＿was this Day brought before me by＿＿＿of＿＿＿in the said＿＿＿in Order to be dealt withal according to Law: I do hereby order you to pay unto the said＿＿＿as a Reward for apprehending and bringing before me the said Rogue and Vagabond, the Sum of ten Shillings, within one Week after Demand thereof made, upon his producing and delivering to you this Order, and giving unto you a Receipt for the said Sum. Given under my Hand and Seal the＿＿＿Day of＿＿＿in the Year of our Lord＿＿＿＿ [signature][126]

The drawback of the generic form, of course, lay in the likelihood of the subject not fitting a standard description. Because the designation "rogue" usually applied to idle people (and "incorrigible" was added to denote repeat offenders), at least one record displayed a hand-written alteration, with a line drawn through the words "Rogue and."[127] A later form read more like a promissory note, ordering the parish "to pay the Bearer . . . the Sum of Five Shillings in full for bringing before Me the Body of . . ." and on the overleaf, "Recd the full by me Nat[i] Storey."[128] Such certificates varied from parish to parish according to revisions of statutory law. A snapshot of activity in Westminster in the autumn of 1767 confirms Rogers's findings showing able-bodied women as the commonest victims of such trawling for vagrancy. A few of those found "wandering and begging" in the autumn of 1767 were older men, but most of the apprehended were single women in their twenties or younger; a fair number were Irish. In most cases, beadles and constables received payments roughly three weeks after turning in the offenders.[129]

In one sense, the intrusion of money into these activities represented an ordinary aspect of the administration of poor relief, as payment for services to the parish. It is clear that in the earlier years of the century, fees for passing vagrants occupied a considerable amount of administrative time and effort. Sessions records were filled with settlement removal orders, petitions for appeal of such orders, and deliberations

---

[126] GLRO, MSP/March 1758.   [127] GLRO, MJ/SPV/1740/10.

[128] GLRO, WSP, October 1767, 451.

[129] GLRO, WSP, October 1767; cf. Misc. MS. 241.5, listing hundreds of passes for the years 1747–55, using a variety of accounting and disbursement methods.

over what to do when vagrants fell ill, gave birth, or were unsure of the settlement of parents or spouses. Constables and others were often forced to petition for payment for transporting vagrants back to their home parishes, pleading, as Richard Speed, the Constable of Hackney, did in 1711, that he had "a Family to maintayne." In requesting the one pound, two shillings, sixpence owed him by the Middlesex Sessions, he acknowledged that "there being noe rate allowed to Constables in the said Parish for this purpose." Another, John Howitt, complained of the slow rate at which administrative wheels seemed to turn, noting that he was "lyable to be troubled if not soon paid."[130]

But more than simply a routine distribution of fees was taking place in the larger scheme of social regulation: money was involved in specific dynamics of power, demonstrated by distinct forms of social interaction. The practice of identifying and capturing vagrants for money contributed to the construction of a category of outcast status: such wanderers, identified as outsiders, might be seen as internal aliens who had experienced a kind of social death.[131] In his analysis of the condition of social death, Orlando Patterson pointed out that internal exiling of community members was typical of certain kinds of slavery in the past: the nullification of identity was forced on "an insider who had fallen, one who ceased to belong and had been expelled from normal participation in the community because of a failure to meet certain minimal legal or socioeconomic norms of behavior."[132] The confusion between vagrancy and criminal law made this "fallen" identity of the captured vagrant all the more pronounced. Sometimes humiliation was added to the mix: whipping vagrants, still on the books as a lawful punishment, was occasionally practiced in the eighteenth century; and at midcentury, the parish of Westminster advised carrying out flogging orders within the confines of the bridewells rather than in public – an acknowledgment of anxieties about the spectacle of such blatant abasement of common people.[133]

---

[130] GLRO, MSP, May 1711/9; MSP, July 1711/9.

[131] I have borrowed this term from Orlando Patterson, *Slavery and Social Death* (Cambridge, MA, 1982), 39–41. On this subject, my analysis has benefited from the insights of Anne Janowitz; see her "'Wild Outcasts of Society'": The Transit of the Gypsies in Romantic Poetry," unpublished paper, April 1996.

[132] Patterson, *Slavery*, 42.

[133] Beattie, *Crime*, 463. On the decline of whipping in the eighteenth century, see Beattie, *Policing*, 307–8, 444–6. The whipping of females was forbidden in 1792 in a further law regarding vagrancy (32 Geo III, c. 45).

Rewards, then, cannot be seen as wages for labor (though as money, they were just as useful) but rather as payments that solidified an alliance between state and citizen. Like Patterson's condition of social death, the process enforced the marginalization of vagrants by highlighting their liminal state in relation to others. In many cases, the victims of this conjunction of forces were women. Vagrancy became a subject identity and thus "a highly symbolized domain" in which authority exercised its power to impose social rules and categories upon every member of society.[134]

Contemporaries viewed the laboring poor from different perspectives during the first half of the eighteenth century: those with entrepreneurial interest in the greater transatlantic world wished to tap this vast reservoir of labor as it appeared to founder at home in England. A "coercive element" was apparent in the migration across the Atlantic world, evident, for example, in the Transportation Act of 1718.[135] Convicts and indentured servants were making up a greater proportion of emigrant labor after 1700 as free English labor, perhaps responding to the incentives of a real rise in wages, chose not to leave in the same high numbers of the previous century.[136] At the same time, unemployed labor at home was confined to bridewell prisons, resuscitated by an act of Parliament in 1706. Aimed at petty criminals and vagrants, these detention houses demonstrated a determination to tie down an undisciplined, often migratory, part of the population. Eventually deemed a failure, such solutions were largely abandoned in 1740 and 1742.[137]

Proposals for moving the same categories of people abroad combined the calculus of political economy with a determination to combat the problems of poverty and unemployment.[138] Joshua Gee expressed impatience with the reluctance to use workhouses to greatest advantage and offered an alternative that might offend fewer sensibilities: a plan for transporting idle servants, condemned persons, and beggars, as well as

---

[134] Patterson, *Slavery*, 38. "Institutionalized marginality, the liminal state of social death, was the ultimate cultural outcome of the loss of natality as well as honor and power" (46; see also 36–7).

[135] Eltis, "Labour and Coercion in the English Atlantic World," 207, 212.

[136] As Keith Wrightson points out, shifts in wages and prices after 1650 altered the picture of migration. By the early eighteenth century, "the real incomes of wage-earners rose substantially for the first time in more than a century" and changing demographic factors removed pressure that might have driven laborers to migrate to America. *Earthly Necessities*, 230–1.

[137] Innes, "Prisons for the Poor," 42–122.

[138] Charles Wilson, *England's Apprenticeship, 1603–1763*, 2nd ed. (London, 1984), 355.

"poor industrious Families" to the colonies in order to set them to work on plantations. Gee's proposals were hardly original, but the candor with which he discussed categories of "Convicts, Vagrants, and useless People" in relation to monetary concerns is noteworthy and instructive.[139] He spared no criticism of the failures of the current laws for regulating vagrancy, revealing the system to be hobbled by petty monetary transactions. Constables apparently could not be bothered to serve as officers of the poor law; "if they can find Money, [they] rather buy off than serve in their own Persons," while "our Tradesmen commonly Fine off, if they can, from serving Constable." Monetary payments, in his view, had undermined the notion of public duty, a sentiment echoed by Henry Fielding in the 1750s. Gee believed that the system for the apprehension of vagrants could work only if it were carried out systematically. The problem lay partly in the hierarchy of bureaucracy that the apprehender had to face and also in the reluctance that authorities showed in confining the unemployed:

> By the present Laws, every Person that takes up a Vagrant is intitled to the Sum of Two Shillings, to be paid by the Constable: Now if the Beadle was directed to pay the said Two Shillings, instead of the Constable, and the Church-Warden to repay him, and charge it in his Parish Account, and the said Beadle to carry such Beggar or other Vagrant to the Work-house, there to be set to Work, it would undoubtedly clear the Street of such Vagrants; and the Beadle should be subjected to a Penalty if he did not exert his utmost Endeavour to take up such strolling Beggars.[140]

The fact that so many laborers were on the move made such a plan not only conceivable but financially desirable. Monetary considerations helped Gee map out his intentions with convincing accuracy.[141]

James Oglethorpe employed a similar line of reasoning in his better-known thoughts on settling Georgia and South Carolina. Yet it is seldom recognized that the calculus of monetary thinking led him to cast his net more widely to include all "Persons reduc'd to Poverty" who were "not Wealth to the Nation," including those of "reputable Families, and of liberal, or at least, easy Education." These individuals qualified for membership in the category of movable persons owing to the fickleness of monetary business: "Some undone by Guardians, some by Law-Suits, some by Accidents in Commerce, some by Stocks, and Bubbles, and some by Suretyship." Money acted as an acid upon the

---

[139] Gee, *Trade and Navigation*, 47, 62.   [140] Ibid., 41–2.   [141] Ibid., 41–2.

reputation and security of such persons, rendering them in need of a haven such as Georgia. Oglethorpe's technique was that of the accountant balancing both sides of a ledger sheet. Ready to address the peculiar form of social disorder brought on by financial misfortune, he concluded, "These are the People that may relieve themselves and strengthen *Georgia*, by resorting thither, and Great Britain by their Departure."[142]

Oglethorpe meted out more summary treatment to common laborers, relying upon monetary metaphor as well as numerical calculation to offer them an escape from their plight. Social categories collapsed in the face of his overwhelming determination to arrive at the best possible fiscal plan, set out in a chapter entitled "England will grow Rich by sending her Poor Abroad. Of Refugees, Conversion of Indians, small Offenders, Roman Colonies":

> [T]here are others whom it may be proper to send Abroad for the Reasons hereafter given.... I think it may be laid down for a Rule, that *we may well spare all those, who having neither Income, nor Industry, equal to their Necessities, are forced to live upon the Fortunes, or Labours of others*; and that they who now are an heavy *Rent-Charge* upon the Publick, may be made an immense *Revenue* to it, and this by an happy Exchange of their Poverty for an Affluence.[143]

The dependency of so many individuals of the lower classes simply depleted national wealth. "If I work hard all Day and at Night give my Wages to the next Cripple I see, it may be profitable to my Soul, but my worldly Fortune is in the same Condition as if I had stood idle," he observed. Even those who worked for wages, according to his assessments, landed in the debit column:

> A Man who is equal in Ability, or to the Fourth Part of a Labourer (and many such there are,) we will suppose to earn Four Pence *Per Diem*, or Five Pounds *per Annum*, in *London*; his Wife and a Child of above Seven Years Old Four Pence *per Diem* more: Upon a fair Supposition (because 'tis the common Case) he has another Child too Young to earn any Thing. These live but wretchedly at an Expence of Twenty Pounds *per Ann.* to defray which they earn Ten Pounds; so that they are a Loss to the Rich and Industrious Part of the Nation of Ten Pounds *per Ann.*[144]

---

[142] [James Oglethorpe], *A New and Accurate Account of the Provinces of South-Carolina and Georgia* (London, 1733), 30–31.

[143] Ibid., 35. Emphasis in the original.   [144] Ibid., 37, 40.

All of these persons would be better off "on a Footing of their own" in the colonies, where the same family could produce "in the gross Value, the Sum of Sixty Pounds *per Ann.*"[145]

Oglethorpe's extensive comparisons between penury at home and productivity abroad were, of course, an attempt to persuade Parliament, as well as the public, of the benefits of his colonial project. But the competitive tenor of his enthusiasm carried him into ever more ambitious numerical estimations, in which numbers displayed a power that superseded other considerations. These calculations included a consideration of whether or not "700 poor Salzburghers" should join others in Georgia. Oglethorpe continued,

> Subjects thus acquir'd by the impolitick Persecutions, by the superstitious Barbarities of neighbouring Princes, are a noble Addition to the capital Stock of the *British* Empire. If our People be Ten Millions and we were to have an Access of Ten Thousand *useful* Refugees, every Stock-jobber in *Exchange-Alley* must allow that this would encrease our Wealth and Figure in the World, as one Added to a Thousand, or, as $\frac{1}{10}$ *per Cent*. This would be the Proportion of our Growth compar'd with our Neighbours, who have not been the Persecutors; but as against the Persecutor, the Increase of our Strength would be in a double Ratio, compounded as well of negative as of positive Quantity.[146]

The language of finance rendered the human quantities in Oglethorpe's plan perfectly calculable, demonstrating how monetary activity could lend a natural aura to the categorization of human beings.[147]

The coercive element was present in Oglethorpe's plan, too. Just as social categories collapsed, so too did definitions of free and unfree. The whole edifice rested on a foundation of the lowest categories of a social hierarchy, identified by historians as "unfree labor."[148] These individuals, differing in age, geographical origins, and gender, would have had little chance of being identified by such distinctions. Only with the hindsight of historical knowledge do we now know that their particular circumstances could explain why they were swept into this kind of project. Contemporaries instead became trained in thinking according to generic categories so ably demonstrated by Oglethorpe. Without their

---

[145] Ibid., 38, 41. See especially Oglethorpe's comparison of the value of labor of 100 men, 100 women, and 100 children in London and Georgia (43).

[146] Ibid., 45–6.   [147] On this point, see Simmel, *Philosophy of Money*, 362.

[148] Eltis, "Seventeenth-Century Migration and the Slave Trade," esp. 106–107.

knowing, the techniques of thinking through money had helped them to do so.

CIRCULATION AND THE PRICING OF PEOPLE

The comparative domain of the anthropologist allows for a valuable perspective on the fundamental characteristics of money, whether seen as attached to migrating persons or associated with social relations in general. Pointing to the Chinese character for currency, Thomas Crump noted that its original meaning was "a spring," which calls to mind the properties of money related to "the idea of fluidity and ubiquity."[149] The word *currency* itself carries the connotation of movement through flowing, and it accords with the more modern sense of money as a vehicle for mobility and personal freedom. Yet money seldom, if ever, operates without restraints. The actual life of money as something that circulates among people and enables individuals to purchase goods and services flourishes within a delimited context; no society allows perfect freedom of exchange or movement. Money as a fluid medium of economic life often functions in tandem with systems that restrict or regulate its flow.

Mary Douglas has elaborated on this paradox in an essay on the idea of rationing and the control of money in nonwestern exchange systems. Starting from the more realistic premise that a free flow of money may threaten to destroy an ordered plan to conserve a limited resource, Douglas set out to investigate the lines of similarity between primitive currencies and our more modern efforts to "earmark" or block the flow of money. "It is in the nature of money to flow freely, to be like water, to permeate," she pointed out. "This capacity that money has for flowing freely in all directions can be a great nuisance," she added.[150] The use of raffia cloth as a medium of exchange among the Lele of the Congo offered a useful point of comparison. As a primitive form of money, Douglas theorized, bundles of fabric functioned more precisely as coupons, not currency: "they were standardized entitlements to a series of social prerogatives," enabling men to marry, establish standing in

---

[149] *Phenomenon of Money* (London, 1981), 17; see also Douglas, "Primitive Rationing," 121.

[150] She adds, "There are some who read their bank statement without astonishment, but they must be exceptions." "Primitive Rationing," 121, 139. For the meaning of modern instances of earmarking, see Viviana A. Zelizer, *The Social Meaning of Money* (New York, 1994), 25–7, 201–4.

their villages, or protect themselves against insults.[151] Such control devices are revealing in their relationship to the ancillary functions that money can perform. The restriction in the movement of coupon money reveals how goods are similarly restricted in their circulation according to status: "a specified group of valuables" might "serve as a coupon for obtaining a specified status." In another instance, primitive money may perform the role of licensing systems, which "create monopoly advantages for those who issue licences and for those who receive them. Both parties become bound in a patron-client relation sustained by the strong interests of each in the continuance of the system."[152] Thus, our contemporary view of money as "an instrument of freedom" must be seen more accurately as only one use among a variety of possibilities. In communities using coupons, money may become allied with inducements to adhere to, rather than depart from, one's social context. It is in the interest of all societies to insert "coupon" or monetary payments into many areas of life in order to nourish vested interests in maintaining the social order.[153]

Douglas's meditation on the tendency of societies to involve money in more than just economic activity offers a useful means of appreciating the complex connections between money and the circulation of people across eighteenth-century England. The regulation of migration, perceived as a responsibility of the state, varied as poor law policies sought to address problems of employment and relief over the course of the first half-century. Attached to a system of monetary rewards (or their equivalent form of certificates), vagrancy law contributed to a broad tendency to associate prices with persons of a disenfranchised social stratum. And as the law attempted to regulate the free movement of the laboring population, it generated ever more ways of attaching money to those without property. Resorting to the profit motive had the obvious effect of commodifying human beings as the vagrant poor were swept into the path of beadles with craven ambition and contractors with entrepreneurial designs. At its best, the system of certificates authorized by local justices upheld a peculiar method of enabling geographical mobility, which many of the poor did not hesitate to use.[154]

By the first half of the eighteenth century, citizens at every level of society had learned the rules of the game. A brisk trade in certificates and passes insured that the resourceful migrant might obtain a

---

[151] Douglas, "Primitive Rationing," 119, 131–2.   [152] Ibid., 130–1.   [153] Ibid., 119–20.
[154] Thomas Sokoll, ed., *Essex Pauper Letters, 1731–1837* (Oxford, 2001).

necessary document for a few shillings, and punishment for such forgery was meted out accordingly by justices.[155] This does not erase the fact that the structure within which the game was played offered considerable risks to the common player, who was posed against power, property, and authority and the chance of imprisonment or exile. Yet the system harbored resemblances to market exchange, with similar promises of material reward: on the one hand, mercenary opportunism enabled beadles and contractors to squeeze personal profit from a process of social regulation; on the other, citizens eagerly bought off their responsibilities to the parish by turning in criminals. Even migrants themselves learned to exploit the techniques of a monetary regimen, creating their own certificates in order to facilitate mobility. By setting these practices alongside similar activities involving prices applied to people in the early eighteenth century, we can achieve a wider frame of incidence that may shed light on how the self-interest of contemporaries overlapped with regulatory meanings.

---

[155] *Old Bailey Sessions Papers*, 13–15 May 1725, Trial of Michael Fennel, is one example of many in which a laborer held a forged certificate, in this case, one that claimed he was a "Ship-wreck'd Sailor going home to Biddesford." Richard Burn includes an amusing ironic description of the manipulation of the finer points of the law by migrants across the countryside: *History of the Poor Laws*, 117–19; Slack, "Vagrants and Vagrancy," 54.

CHAPTER 7

The Price of People: Rethinking Money and Power in the Seventeenth and Eighteenth Centuries

William Warburton, Bishop of Gloucester and a controversial theologian, recorded the following exchange, which probably took place around 1720, with trademark candor:

> Mr. Pope was with Sir Godfrey Kneller one day, when his nephew, a Guinea trader, came in. 'Nephew, (said Sir Godfrey,) you have the honour of seeing the two greatest men in the world'. 'I don't know how great you may be (said the Guinea-man), but I don't like your looks: I have often bought a man, much better than both of you together, all muscles and bones, for ten guineas'.[1]

In its brazen insouciance, the encounter showed a swaggering young merchant confronting two celebrities with a reminder of their corporeal insignificance. Yet the conversation revealed more than simply the antics of great men: its relaxed tone, along with its irony, signaled a sense of how monetary values informed social discourse in the early eighteenth century. The tendency to create equivalencies between people and prices was a recognized feature of the age, part of a complex psychological involvement with money very different from our own.[2]

As we have seen, English culture supported a longstanding relationship between money and persons, revitalized by the rewards system and vagrancy law in the eighteenth century. As the previous chapter

---

[1] Rev. Joseph Spence, *Anecdotes, Observations, and Characters, of Books and Men*, 2nd. ed. (1756; repr., London, 1858), 281; also cited in the definition of "guinea-man" in the *Oxford English Dictionary*.

[2] Warburton eventually took a public stance against slavery; see his *Sermon Preached before the Incorporated Society for the Propagation of the Gospel in Foreign Parts* (London, 1766). Kneller died in 1723, so it is possible that Pope related this anecdote to Warburton, a close friend, after the fact.

made clear, these practices constituted a means of regulating individuals without property within a legal framework attached to the English state. Now we must assess monetary prices set on people in light of the larger social context of England in the seventeenth and eighteenth centuries. The objective of this chapter is twofold: to identify the scope of an early modern predisposition to apply monetary thinking to social relations through rhetorical means, in speech concerning the "worth" of people and through language that objectified them as commodities for sale; and secondly, to locate several points at which monetary discourse called attention to a literal transaction involving people, not just rhetorically, but as part of an economically motivated activity in which individuals were moved across distances or transferred from one proprietor to another. More than just social class or race was involved in an understanding of who might fall into the category of "priced": besides the obvious instance of African slaves, legal definitions of dependents rendered women, children, servants, and apprentices subject to such status, making it possible to conceive of certain categories of persons as private possessions over whom certain individuals (usually property-owning men) claimed authority. The condition of being priced brought with it a concatenation of opportunities and risks associated with economic developments at the end of the seventeenth century. And because it overlapped with social categories of dependency, the state of being measured according to monetary value appeared normative and sometimes even desirable to contemporaries.

The willingness to regard people in monetary terms and, more to the point, to trade in human beings, presents a peculiar anomaly on the eve of the enlightenment. Most English people of the late seventeenth century would not have honored a sharp distinction that placed human beings, apart from things, in a separable and unique category. In fact, as the following chapter will argue, the notion of property in persons, a fundamental part of English law and a mainstay of the slave trade, sustained the use of monetary measurements across many different kinds of relationships that were likely to be confused. Further complicating this picture was the assignment of absolute authority to household heads, whose patriarchal powers extended over servants as well as family members. As Susan Amussen has pointed out, the dependency that characterized the condition of servants under masters highlighted one of the problematic ambiguities in early modern social relations, as masters were capable of overstepping reasonable limits of their role by claiming the right to enforce discipline through the use of violence. Thus, monetary rhetoric and physical force could forge powerful connections between dependent persons and objectified status.[3]

The dating of this form of monetary thinking must be imprecise, as many of the social structures from which it sprang, such as indentured service and apprenticeship, preceded the late seventeenth century. The examples of wife sale and marriage settlements drew conceptual apparatus from partriarchal thinking of centuries-long provenance. Yet the question can be reframed fruitfully by asking how institutional and political developments following the Glorious Revolution may have created an environment which exposed and validated thinking about people in terms of money. From the 1690s, English people participated in a revolution in state finance and private investment, when new institutional structures fostered the creation of private wealth alongside the rise of the "fiscal-military state." The period was also one of unregulated financial experimentation, which culminated in the debacle of the South Sea Bubble, and public lotteries and novel insurance practices offered additional ways in which this "age of wagers" invited permissiveness with money.[4] Previously established social uses of money became newly visible as they occurred across a broad map that included London's urban landscape and colonial North America. The tendency to enlist money as a vehicle for comprehending and regulating social relations can be understood best against this variegated backdrop: an era extending from the last decade of the seventeenth century through the antislavery campaigns of the last decades of the eighteenth century, which called for a correction in the tendency in its most extreme form.

Certain individuals did recognize the significance of maintaining a boundary between people and things, inspiring them to register objections to slavery as early as the seventeenth century. They derived their insight from a religious understanding of the universality of the human soul, which recoiled from the denial of Christian baptism to slaves and the infliction of cruelties upon them. Significant to our purposes, they believed that the root of the problem was the destructive agency of money and its false god, Mammon. Not only dissenters grasped this tenet, despite the impression given by historiography on the subject.

---

[3] Susan Dwyer Amussen, "Punishment, Discipline, and Power: The Social Meanings of Violence in Early Modern England," *Journal of British Studies* 34 (1995): 17–18; Douglas Hay and Paul Craven, eds., *Masters, Servants, and Magistrates in Britain and the Empire, 1562–1955* (Chapel Hill, 2004).

[4] The phrase is P. G. M. Dickson's: *The Financial Revolution: A Study in the Development of Public Credit, 1688–1756* (Aldershot, 1993), 45.

Voices from across a religious spectrum spoke out against the mercenary motives behind colonial slavery.[5] From the pulpit of the Church
of England, Morgan Godwyn denounced North American planters in
a sermon aptly entitled *Trade Preferr'd Before Religion, and Christ made
to give place to Mammon* in 1680. Leaving their slaves in ignorance of
Christianity, such men resisted the attempts of others to baptize and protect Africans living in heinous subjection on English soil. These "wicked
Mammonists" wrongfully assumed that "whatever conduceth to the getting of Mony, and carrying on of Trade, must certainly be lawful." On
the subject of avarice, Godwyn exhibited exemplary zeal, proving that
a minister of the Church was capable of sectarian-style fury. He condemned all those "who *do account their Life here to be but a Market for gain*,
and that resolve *they must be getting*, tho it be with the ruine of their own,
and *their Peoples Souls*." "*Thirst* after *filthy Lucre*" knew no bounds, and
so Godwyn extended his attack to all unscrupulous actions at home in
England, including those against English servants. Agents of planters
were known for "trapanning and spiriting Men out of *England*, with
sugar Promises of large kindness to be exhibited to them at their arrival
in those Parts: whilst at the very instant they intend nothing else but to
expose them to sale, and to make *Slaves* of them, at least for some term of
Years." (Godwyn seemed unconcerned, unlike some twentieth-century
historians, about drawing a distinction between indentured labor and
slavery.) The effacement of the inviolable boundary around human
beings inspired his warning to righteous English people. Remember the
words of St. Peter, Godwyn inveighed, for he rightly cautioned against
those "who through Covetousness, with fained words, should make
Merchandise of us[.]"[6] His vocabulary drew as much ammunition from
a sense of the contemporary practice of making money out of men as
from invocations of Biblical rhetoric.

Another seventeenth-century defense of freedom from servitude
came from Thomas Tryon, author of advice books on health and a
pioneer voice in the construction of a humanitarian perspective. His
Friendly Advice to the Gentelmen-Planters [sic] of the East and West Indies

---

[5] Nicholas Hudson, "'Britons Never Will be Slaves': National Myth, Conservatism, and
the Beginnings of British Antislavery," *Eighteenth-Century Studies* 34, no. 4 (2001): 559–
76; Philippe Rosenberg, "Thomas Tryon and the Seventeenth-Century Dimensions of
Antislavery," *William and Mary Quarterly*, 3rd ser., 61, no. 4 (October 2004): 609–42;
Seymour Drescher, *Capitalism and Antislavery: British Mobilization in Comparative
Perspective* (New York, 1987), 16–17.

[6] Morgan Godwyn, *Trade preferr'd before Religion, and Christ made to give place to Mammon:
Represented in a Sermon Relating to the Plantations* (London, 1685), 6, 10–11.

(1684) offered an impassioned critique of the inhumanity of the plantation system. Ventriloquizing for the slave, Tryon produced an imaginary African's homily against covetousness, denouncing masters as "*swaggering Christians*" who "grow fat with our Blood and Sweat, gormandizing with the fruits procured by our *Slavery* and sore *Labour*[.]" His argument expanded on the universality of human beings, "alike in all particulars," based on a Biblical notion of equality. Like Aphra Benn, whose *Oroonoko* appeared four years later, Tryon presented an enslaved African in command of a complex subjectivity, in this instance, a powerful voice capable of critiquing the economic and class system that upheld the trade in human beings. The desire to make money from the need for labor in colonial ventures was self-evident, and Tryon, like Dickens in a later century, had an eye for trenchant detail. In a final dialogue, the slave registered a plea for greater allowances of food, arguing that its beneficial effects on the "Vigour" of labor would ultimately benefit the slaveowner. "And our Ill is your Loss," the slave asserted, adding, "are we not your *Money*?"[7]

Tryon's bold equation between slaves and money, a rhetorical gesture packed with meaning, calls attention to the distance between the mental world of the late seventeenth century and a hundred years later, when antislavery agitation gathered strength. It was the notion of slaves as property that captured the public imagination in the later period, but this earlier and different indictment of planter greed was entirely in keeping with the imaginative tendencies of the age. As later readers of Defoe would recognize, the trope of people as money could be translated positively into fictional accounts of persons on the make, such as the indomitable Moll Flanders, or negatively, as the biographies of transported labor and apprehended vagrants testified. For Tryon, an illicit love of money was at the heart of slavery, but perhaps he understood that mobilizing public opinion against this problem was a project destined to fail in Restoration England. The strategy of *Friendly Advice* focused instead on the excessive violence used by planters to intimidate

---

[7] Thomas Tryon, *Friendly Advcie [sic] to the Gentelmen-Planters [sic] of the East and West Indies* (London, 1684), 84, 96, 120–1, 214. Aphra Benn may have read Tryon's *Friendly Advice*. She owned a copy of his more popular work, *The Way to Health* (1683), and on the flyleaf, she composed an ode to him. Virginia Smith, "Tryon, Thomas (1634–1703)," *Oxford Dictionary of National Biography* (Oxford, 2004). [http://www.oxforddnb.com/view/article/27783.] On Aphra Benn, see Moira Ferguson, *Subject to Others: British Women Writers and Colonial Slavery, 1670–1834* (London, 1992), 27–49; Laura Brown, "The Romance of Empire: *Oroonoko* and the Trade in Slaves," in *The New Eighteenth Century*, ed. Felicity Nussbaum and Laura Brown (London, 1987).

the slave populations of plantations.[8] Historians who have been unable to make sense of contradictions within Tryon's arguments have also overlooked the salience of many forms of paternalistic social relationships, besides slavery, that entailed subservience to patriarchal authority. The mediating role of money often intruded into these relationships, as in the cases of apprenticeship and indentured labor.[9] Contemporary attitudes toward this fact may help to explain why, as G. R. Searle has shown, late eighteenth-century reformers had to work so hard to drive home the point that "selling people is wrong."[10]

The sale of unfree labor and wives offers an opportunity to examine this era of ambiguous exchange more closely. In the cases of indentured servitude and transported criminals, the subjection of labor to monetary signification illuminates a peculiar moment in the social history of colonial capitalism, when the tension between freedom and subjection was unmasked in a startlingly visible way. Subordinated labor was usually understood in the context of older paternalistic discourses, but the appearance of contractors who handled involuntary migrants as part of larger commercial ventures added a new dimension of monetized identity to the subjectivity of servants. In these cases, money rendered laborers fungible, at one moment, translating them into abstract units, at another, likening them to transferable possessions.

The sale of wives presents further evidence of the hybrid nature of monetary transactions involving people in the eighteenth century. Here, the hegemony of market strategies in the wider culture penetrated the plebeian world of marriage negotiation to the point of creating a peculiar form of divorce that made chattel out of women through a public spectacle of sale and purchase. The ambivalent potential of money becomes clear in the way it enabled individuals without sufficient money or status to maneuver within the confines of the law at a time when legitimate divorce would have been too costly or simply unavailable. Yet, as in the case of unfree labor, monetary transactions nevertheless reinforced hierarchies: the ritual of wife sale, as a literal enactment of female chattel status, highlighted the subjection of women and exposed distasteful elements of market transactions of people. As an exploration

---

[8] Until recently, the pre-history of the late-eighteenth-century antislavery movement has been overlooked or misunderstood; on this point, see Rosenberg, "Thomas Tryon," 610–13.

[9] As Philippe Rosenberg has pointed out, one of the problematic inconsistencies of Tryon's arguments against slavery is that he believed "that slaves should be considered as servants." "Thomas Tryon and Antislavery," 633.

[10] G. R. Searle, *Morality and the Market in Victorian Britain* (Oxford, 1998), 48–76.

of the ambiguities attached to monetary usages, the following discussion investigates the risks involved in enlisting money as a vehicle of self-help.

MONEY AS RHETORIC: POWER SIGNIFIED THROUGH A LANGUAGE OF MONETARY VALUE

Significations of power were conveyed through both language and social relations in early modern England. This dual force becomes apparent through discussions of personal worth, often expressed in monetary terms. From the vantage point of the 1770s, Adam Smith indicated the peculiar way in which money values served as a means of describing and ranking persons across society. "In consequence of [money] being the measure of value, we estimate that of all other commodities by the quantity of money that they will exchange for," he wrote in *The Wealth of Nations*. Without further explanation, he added, "We say of a rich man that he is worth a great deal, and of a poor man that he is worth very little money." Smith thus demonstrated the idiomatic practice of eliding the distinction between matters of exchange and the status of people.[11]

Despite the variety of models of society employing such measurements, monetary rhetoric provided a persistent means of creating hierarchy. Ben Jonson's *Bartholomew Fair* offered up a popular metaphor of the marketplace, which invited all comers to the *theatrum mundi*, compromised symbolically by the social categories of ticket entry prices "that every person here have his or their free-will of censure, to like or dislike at their own charge . . . to judge his six pen'orth, his twelve pen'orth, so to his eighteen pence, two shillings, half a crown, to the value of his place[.]"[12] In a society accustomed to commerce and consumption, money enforced distinctions of class even while broadening the arena of exchange. "[Mankind] is better distinguished by what he wants, than what he enjoys," Nicholas Barbon observed in his *Discourse*

---

[11] *An Inquiry into the Nature and Causes of the Wealth of Nations*, ed. Edwin Cannan (Chicago, 1976), 1:450. For an elaboration of the growth of the conviction that money merely stood in for other estimations of wealth, see Joyce Oldham Appleby, *Economic Thought and Ideology in Seventeenth-Century England* (Princeton, 1978), 226–7.

[12] *Bartholomew Fair*, ed. Michael Jamieson (1631; Harmondsworth, 1966), 333. For a complex reading of this play, its *theatrum mundi*, and contemporary notions of money and avarice, see Jean-Christophe Agnew, *Worlds Apart: The Market and the Theater in Anglo-American Thought, 1550–1750* (Cambridge, 1986), 47, 119–21.

Concerning Coining the New Money Lighter (1696). "A Poor Man wants a Pound, a Rich Man an Hundred, others Thousands, and a Prince Hundreds of Thousands."[13] The tendency to measure self-worth according to monetary amounts permeated society: this was Sarah Scott's point in *Millenium Hall*, when she described the ranking of physically deformed people who ultimately took refuge in the utopian community. These individuals fell into a clear hierarchy according to "the money their [former] keepers had gained in exhibiting them."[14]

While commerce and finance unsettled old hierarchies, customary social discourse understood wealth as capital measured in monetary amounts attributed to an individual, a fact reflected in habits of speech at least from the seventeenth century.[15] No firmer proof is needed than the colloquial terms in which contemporaries discussed suitable marriage partners. Young men were sized up according to their annual income in pounds, while prospective brides could be assessed, quite literally, in terms of financial assets, often artfully combined according to the latest investment opportunities. (The point becomes even clearer if we compare measurements of English landowners in monetary amounts with their Habsburg contemporaries, who were measured according to the number of villages they possessed.[16]) The notion of personal worth was not only a manner of speech, but a tag facilitating the transferal of family fortunes, and contemporaries did not hesitate to evaluate marriage alliances in such terms. On occasion, publications advertised the names, addresses, "reputed fortunes" and stock investments of eligible women and men in London. *A Master-Key to the Rich Ladies Treasury*, published in 1742 by "a younger brother," ran to thirty-two pages and circulated among a list of subscribers.[17]

Discussions of marriage settlements and dowries, entwined with evolving financial institutions and legal instruments, absorbed the vocabulary and conceptual framework of the market. "[O]ur Marriages are made, just like other common Bargains and Sales, by the meer

---

[13] *Discourse Concerning Coining the New Money Lighter* (1696), 3.

[14] *Millenium Hall*, ed., Gary Kelly (1762; Peterborough, Ontario, 1995), 74.

[15] Robert W. Gordon, "Paradoxical Property," in, *Early Modern Conceptions of Property*, ed. John Brewer and Susan Staves (London, 1996), 107, discusses the power of the trope of absolute dominion.

[16] I owe thanks to Professor István Deák for this analogy.

[17] Its subtitle was *The Widower and Batchelor's [sic] Directory*. Thanks to Amy Froide and Herb Sloan for bringing this publication to my attention. For another example, see *M – c L – n's Cabinet Broke Open; or, his private list of all the duchess dowagers, countesses, widow ladies, maiden ladies*[.] (1750).

Consideration of Interest and Gain," Sir William Temple lamented in 1731. "Yet this Custom is of no ancient Date in *England*, and I think I remember, within less than fifty Years, the first Noble Families that married into the City for downright Money, and thereby introduced by degrees this publick Grievance[.]"[18] Lawrence Stone has shown how "the period 1680 to 1710 was one of acute crisis in many propertied families," when strategies aimed at making advantageous matches among elites led to extortionate and even scandalous behavior. While his evidence was restricted to a limited sample of propertied families, his findings corroborate Temple's anxious dating of this otherwise timeless strategy.[19] As Stone puts it, "this was a period when fortune-hunting male, and occasionally female, predators and impostors were both peculiarly common and peculiarly ruthless in their tactics."[20] The somewhat ironic outcome of so much maneuvering in the marriage market was a firming up of parental power over the process. Hardwicke's Marriage Act of 1753 required parental permission for marriage and the public posting of banns in advance of an exchange of vows, thus ensuring that "paternal and male control of marriage" would be enforced by law. Parliamentary support for the bill indicated that "landowners and power-brokers" viewed marriage "primarily as a way of achieving material or political advantage."[21]

Patriarchal control of marriage inscribed women and their dowries as the objects, not the subjects, of property law.[22] Though the temper of the times would give testimony to a belief in romantic attachment, a gendered hierarchy within propertied patriarchy asserted itself when parties were faced with an impending marriage contract. Lady Mary Wortley Montagu's observations on marriage in this era underscored the point. "I never knew a lover that would not willingly secure his interest as well as his mistress," she reflected in a letter to her prospective

---

[18] Quoted in David Lemmings, "Marriage and the Law in the Eighteenth Century: Hardwicke's Marriage Act of 1753," *Historical Journal* 39, no. 2 (1996): 339–40.

[19] Lawrence Stone, *Uncertain Unions: Marriage in England, 1660–1753* (New York, 1992), 12; Olwen Hufton, *The Prospect Before Her: A History of Women in Western Europe, Volume One, 1500–1800* (London, 1995), 64–6.

[20] Stone, *Uncertain Unions*, 13.

[21] Lemmings, "Marriage and the Law," 357, 359; but see also R. B. Outhwaite, *Clandestine Marriage in England, 1500—1850* (London, 1995).

[22] As Susan Staves has argued persuasively, "A principle feature of these deeper patriarchal structures was that women functioned to transmit wealth from one generation of men to the next generation of men." *Married Women's Separate Property in England, 1660–1833* (Cambridge, MA, 1990), 4.

Figure 5. William Hogarth, "The Denunciation, or A Woman Swearing a Child to a Grave Citizen," 1729. Reproduced by permission of the National Gallery of Ireland, Dublin.

husband around 1710, "or, if one must be abandoned, had not the prudence (among all his distractions) to consider, that a woman was but a woman, and money was a thing of more real merit than the whole sex put together." The subject of money repeatedly surfaced in her correspondence, and though it never displaced the importance of property, it clearly held its own as a fact of aristocratic life in the eighteenth century.[23]

This fact did not preclude women as mothers from operating as energetic brokers, empowered to secure the future welfare of their daughters. The letters of Mary Jepp Clarke (1656[?]–1705[?]) reveal the degree of scrupulous attention that a determined woman might devote to settling a daughter in an advantageous match, a project of considerable financial complexity that extended, in this case, over two years. "[T]he pain of the

[23] Letter from Lady Mary Pierrepont Wortley Montagu to Edward Wortley Montagu, in *The Letters and Works of Lady Mary Wortley Montagu*, ed. Lord Wharncliffe, 3 vols. (London, 1837), 1:160.

body in bringing [children] into the world everybody will allow to be great and dangerous," she noted querulously at one point in the negotiations, "but I think the pain of the mind in disposing of them for the best is equall to it[.]"[24] As a Member for Somerset, her husband was absent for part of the year, leaving the delicate business of surmising the true worth of her daughter's suitor to her solo efforts. Letters to her husband indicate a bold command of financial expertise and abundant diplomatic skills. Confronted with a suitor's estate value that was rather less than she first comprehended, she cautioned her husband against borrowing from another daughter's settlement to make up the difference. "I beleve Mrs Ann notwithstanding her great favor and frendshipp for Mr Jones from the first acquaintance to this minnitt, would be loth to part with any share of her fortune towards the purchissing him for her brother-in-law," she advised.[25] The language of the marketplace was not misplaced in describing the nature of such dealings. Once the marriage was finalized and – months later – the financial arrangements complete, Mary Jepp Clarke expressed her relief in having emerged successfully from so many difficult transactions. "[M]y daughters fortune was all pd doune upon the naile a night since and the intrest of it offered from the day the bond was made soe poor Mr Edward is now out of danger and my sonne Jones likewise whether Mr Clarke lives or dyes," she wrote to a friend. Her abiding interest in money matters promptly prepared to flow in another direction, as she added, "and I wish there was as good an occation for the payment of Nannyes and Mollyes fortunes likewise."[26]

Even among the laboring classes, money arrangements exposed the tensions and inequalities that existed between genders, as abandoned pregnant women were enabled by law to swear their unborn children to men they named as responsible, and justices thereby extracted money payments from errant suitors. In Hogarth's "The Denunciation, or A Woman Swearing a Child to a Grave Citizen," (1729), satire immortalized a moment at which parochial care for unwed mothers had shifted to a new key. Having given up on shaming punishments, the objective of justice was, to paraphrase Stone, "money not morals." Monetary machinations with regard to matrimony, on public display in

---

[24] Letter from Mary Jepp Clarke to Edward Clarke, December 29, 1702, in *Clarke Family Letters*, British and Irish Women's Letters and Diaries, electronic source (http://www.alexanderstreet2.com), Alexandra Street Press, 2002, [1].
[25] Letter from Mary Jepp Clarke to Edward Clarke, May 20, 1704, Ibid., [1].
[26] Letter from Mary Jepp Clarke to John Spreat, December 2, 1704, Ibid., [1].

many of Hogarth's works, occupied a fair cross-section of eighteenth-century society.[27]

The use of a rhetoric of money in matters of marriage may not, in itself, indicate a literal commodification of persons in early modern English society, but language nevertheless reflects a persistent association between personal monetary interests and marital relations that was normative in the eighteenth century. Money was the stuff of every step of betrothal, from legal settlements to the emollient of relations with servants and neighbors attending the ceremony. If the journal of Walter Calverley, recorded in the years 1706 to 1707, is a reliable testimony, gifts of guineas (as well as gloves) and fees paid in cash punctuated the days surrounding his wedding with astonishing frequency. Though his wife's settlement had called forth the labors of at least three legal counsels already, a fourth received three guineas for simply perusing and amending the papers; added to this were the itemized payments for the clergyman, a new coach, liveries, wedding clothes, and expensive earrings and plate for the bride. Calverley's accounts, though rather obsessive, underscored the considerable ritual involving money required of an honorable marriage at the turn of the century. No couple, high or low, could enter into wedlock without a surplus of all types of ready coin.[28]

PROPERTY IN PERSONS: LEGAL CATEGORY MEETS SOCIAL SUBORDINATION

The legal category of the early modern person was bounded by multiple realms of proprietorship, and for those without property (technically, those without a visible means of support), any claim to being autonomous was highly compromised. The notion of persons as property emerged from a tangled web of legal principles and customary arrangements based upon master-servant relations.[29] Several forms

---

[27] Stone, *Uncertain Unions*, 83; Amy Louise Erickson, "Common Law versus Common Practice: The Use of Marriage Settlements in Early Modern England," *Economic History Review*, new series, 43, no. 1 (February 1990): 21–39. For Hogarth, see Ronald Paulson, *Hogarth: The "Modern Moral Subject," 1697–1732* (New Brunswick, 1991), 81; Bernadette Fort and Angela Rosenthal, eds., *The Other Hogarth: Aesthetics of Difference* (Princeton, 2001).

[28] "Walter Calverley's Marriage, 1706–7," in *English Family Life, 1576–1716*, ed. Ralph Houlbrooke (Oxford, 1988), 43–6.

[29] Hilary Beckles, "The Concept of 'White Slavery' in the English Caribbean During the Early Seventeenth Century," in *Early Modern Conceptions of Property*, ed. John Brewer and Susan Staves (London, 1996), 572–84; Richard B. Morris, *Government and Labor in Early America* (New York, 1946), pt. 2.

of compulsory labor retained a firm regulatory dimension in the late seventeenth century, including apprenticeship, at least on the books, which assigned a great deal of power to masters.[30] Children, whether as apprentices or simply as dependents, existed in a nebulous region of personhood, with few grounds on which their rights could be defended against their proprietors. Their lack of a clearly defined identity allowed for odd contradictions in the law. Though stealing a horse was an offense punishable by death, kidnapping was a misdemeanor with much lighter penalties, resisting recognition until the early nineteenth century, after a signal campaign on behalf of climbing boys that took place alongside agitation against slavery.[31] Such loopholes in the regulation of servant labor would lead to noticeable irregularities in an age of contractors, when renegade entrepreneurs were in charge of moving people from one place to another.

The rough-and-tumble commerce of street life in eighteenth-century London churned up a characteristically mercenary approach to the struggle for survival, and so generated numerous spectacles of the laboring and vagrant classes engaged in monetary transactions. From volumes of urban travelogues, one can discover references to venal activities offering human beings and their offspring as objects for exchange. Though these were as much a literary genre as an accurate portrayal of London life, their scope of imagination suggests a world of circulating people. In *A Trip from St. James's to the Royal-Exchange* (1744), the reader is introduced to "a Place call'd the *Infant Office*, where young Children stand at Livery, and are lett out by the Day to the Town-Mendicants":

> A Woman of above 50 would needs hire a Baby that was sucking at the Breast; and another, who had a Complexion as sallow as a Portuguese Sailor, must forsooth be accommodated with a Child as fair as a smock-faced Parson. One Woman hired no less than four for the Day, two she pack'd up behind her like a Scotch Pedlar's Budget.... A beggar Woman, who was vastly in Arrear for the Lett of Children, being refused any longer Credit till she had paid off the old Score[.][32]

---

[30] Robert Steinfeld, *The Invention of Free Labor: The Employment Relation in English and American Law and Culture, 1350–1870* (Chapel Hill, 1991), 16–23.

[31] John Wareing, "Preventive and Punitive Regulation in Seventeenth-Century Social Policy: Conflicts of Interest and the Failure to Make 'Stealing and Transporting Children, and Other Persons' a Felony, 1645–73," *Social History* 27, no. 3 (October 2002): 288–91.

[32] [Anon.], *A Trip from St. James' to the Royal-Exchange, with Remarks Serious and Diverting, on the Manners, Customs, and Amusements of the Inhabitants of London and Westminster* (1744), 25–6.

Later in the century, the same practice came to the attention of the German traveler, Johann Wilhelm von Archenholz, who registered his distaste for negotiations that established a pecking order among poor women and babies alike. "The female beggars hire children from other women, poorer still than themselves," he reported. Prices varied for infants, "according as it is more or less likely to excite compassion. A child that is shockingly deformed, is worth four shillings a-day, and even more." As one particularly mercenary woman reckoned, "monsters" marked the far end of the scale.[33]

The prevalence of false beggars led many contemporaries to complain vehemently against their aggressive tactics. Thrusting ingeniously embellished sores under the noses of dignified persons in passing coaches, some were masters at inveigling a daily living in coin. Not unlike the celebrated itinerants of the literature of roguery, these imposters understood that almost anything could be purchased or sold.[34] Roger North believed that "the False hath an Advantage" because they demonstrated their poverty "with Art and Address," compared to the more traditional supplicant.[35] Such "frightful Beggars," according to magistrate Sir John Fielding, were now "so common in the Streets, so offensive to Passengers in general, and so dangerous to pregnant Women."[36] Defoe provided an imaginative account of contemporary methods of chicanery: in *Captain Singleton*, for example, young Bob is spirited away from his mother at the age of two, then "disposed of to a Beggar-Woman that wanted a pretty Child to set out her Case, and after that to a Gypsey," who "continually dragged [him] about with her." "I called her Mother; tho' she told me at last, she was not my Mother, but that she bought me for Twelve Shillings of another Woman." Defoe sets his character in constant motion, from parish to parish, and then to sea, and calls him "not *Robert*, but plain *Bob*." By no coincidence, his lost identity is replaced by that stamped upon him by the "Strolling Trade," the cant term for a "Shop-lift's Comerade." Or perhaps Defoe meant his

---

[33] J. W. von Archenholz, *A Picture of England* (1797), 114.

[34] The popularity of *The Life and Adventures of Bampfylde-Moore Carew* (1745) testified to a public fascination with a world replete with such negotiations.

[35] Roger North, *A Discourse of the Poor* (1753), 15. This work was published posthumously.

[36] Sir John Fielding, *Extracts from Such of the Penal Laws, as Particularly Relate to the Peace and Good Order of this Metropolis*, new edition (London, 1768), 92; see also Joshua Gee, *Trade and Navigation of Great-Britain Considered* (London, 1729), 38–9, on "nauseous Sights" used to "terrify People, and force them to give Money to get rid of them" in London.

character to represent the condition of being "bobb'd," meaning cheated or tricked.[37]

The sale of children, a more general problem highlighted by underworld tactics, returns us to the questions raised by the pricing of people: to what extent was this practice part of a larger codified realm of commercialized social relations? Or were such transactions akin to the legally legitimate transferal of rights of control over people, in this case, persons without full legal status? If parents (or masters) possessed rights over children, what was the nature of this sort of "property," or possession? Blackstone's *Commentaries*, as well as philanthropic opinion, grappled at great length with these issues, though they do not offer an accurate indicator of what people actually thought and did with regard to children. Not until the second half of the eighteenth century, according to Ludmilla Jordanova, did a campaign of any sort against the unrestricted use of children as sources of income appear in print, indicating that childhood was not recognized as a category of entitlement, at least not across a class divide. It was no coincidence that the discourse of humanitarianism related to child labor and child abduction developed alongside growing sensitivity to the inhumanity of the slave trade.[38]

Whatever the nature of sentiment regarding children and apprenticeship, securing indentures for children led to an insertion of money into the process of placing the young within the social hierarchy of work. Such payments, or premiums, according to Defoe, originated in the seventeenth century, when optional gifts for the master's wife were converted into cash, but he is probably incorrect with regard to dating, given that merchants had been accepting cash premiums by the middle of the sixteenth century. Seventeenth-century guild records indicate the levying of such fees, and the practice was widespread enough to warrant taxing premiums through the Stamp Act of 1709.[39] The significance

---

[37] *The Life, Adventures, & Pyracies of Captain Singleton* (Oxford, 1720), 1–2; *A New Canting Dictionary* (London, 1725), 23–4. "Single-Ten" was the term applied to "a very foolish, silly fellow." (108) "Bob" did not apply to a shilling, according to the OED, until 1812.

[38] Jonas Hanway's *Sentimental History of Chimney Sweepers* (1785) provides one of the benchmarks of sentimental constructions of childhood, along with Ann Alexander, *Facts Relative to the State of Children Who are Employed by Chimney Sweepers as Climbing Boys*, 2nd ed. (York, 1817). Ludmilla Jordanova, "Conceptualizing Childhood in the Eighteenth Century: The Problem of Child Labour," *British Journal of Eighteenth-Century Studies* 10, no. 2 (1987): 189–99; Wareing, "Preventive and Punitive Regulation," 288–308. I also owe thanks to Leonore Davidoff for her insights into this topic.

[39] *The Complete English Tradesman* (1738), 147, quoted in Joan Lane, *Apprenticeship in England, 1600–1914* (London, 1996), 19–20.

of such payment as a gifting ritual indicated the hope on the part of parents that the master and his family would assume the responsibilities, including the subjective aspects of care, that the role of surrogate parents suggested. It is true that indentures employed terms of commodification, speaking of "good Usage" and the "sale" of a child to a trade or a particular master, and the escape of an apprentice could provoke the use of advertisements offering rewards.[40] But these were terms that resembled the formulations of bridewealth, indicating the transferal of rights over the subordinate person, and not commercial sale in a technical sense. Moreover, the statutory basis of apprenticeship ensured a complex legal relationship between master and servant. The master claimed rights to the labor of the apprentice, but his authority was *in loco parentis*, and not absolute. The move to regularizing and registering premiums signified a continuing shift from custom to contract, reflected in legal contests over apprenticeship, some of which were brought to light through court action when a master or a servant was negligent of duties or, more frequently, when an apprentice ran away.[41]

The intrusion of cash payments into the contractual relationship between master and apprentice nevertheless introduced hierarchical thinking, an effect of the regime of money, into the process of finding places for children. Higher money premiums served as markers for certain employments, not only reflecting, but also helping to generate the status of the trade. While the expense of a position in a company of merchant adventurers was predictably high, thereby setting a threshold for children of middling ranks, trades of a more vague status might gain reputation by high premiums. Mandeville inveighed against the crush of parents pressing to engage their children in higher-priced trades, while other lines of employment attracted less interest. According to Defoe, who reported premiums as high as a thousand pounds to "a *Turkey-Merchant*," but more commonly, £200 to £300 to shopkeepers in the 1720s, such apprentices were really "Gentlemen" and not to be deemed servants at all, but rather, "Lodgers."[42] Defoe believed that the source of such an inflation lay in the "unreasonable fondness and partiality of

---

[40] Lane, *Apprenticeship*, 10–11.

[41] Ilana Krausman Ben-Amos, *Adolescence and Youth in Early Modern England* (New Haven, 1994), 84–5, 105–6; Robert J. Steinfeld, *The Invention of Free Labor: The Employment Relation in English and American Law and Culture, 1350–1870* (Chapel Hill, 1991), 22–6.

[42] Bernard Mandeville, *The Fable of the Bees: Or, Private Vices, Public Benefits*, ed. F. B. Kaye, 2 vols. (Oxford, 1924), 1:58–9; *The Great Law of Subordination Consider'd* (London, 1724), 10–11. Mandeville quotes the price of "Three or Four Hundred Pounds" as the price of an apprenticeship with a merchant.

parents for their children," who strove to exempt offspring from demeaning tasks and living conditions. Larger premiums, he claimed, were stipulated so that "sons shall not eat with the other servants, but be allowed to sit at table with their masters and mistresses." Money, he reckoned, could secure privilege and subvert customary power relations between master and servant.[43]

Defoe was aware of the locus, if not the exact nature of a significant shift in social and class relations. Recent research has confirmed his report of inflated premiums in London, and as Ilana Ben-Amos has indicated, "the large distributive trades were far beyond the reach of youngsters who came from low and modest origins."[44] Christopher Brooks has shown that the terms of apprenticeship reflected the fact that "more gentry recruits came forward" in the seventeenth century, putting pressure on fewer places available within guilds, and as retailing and wholesale trades further down the scale rose in value, those premiums were also on the rise. Demographic changes helped fuel these changes, but so did the increasing prevalence of commerce across England: the abundance of goods in the inventories of the middling sort was also evidence of increasing commercial activity across the economy during these years. As the squirearchy "consolidated a dominance of landed property" and "lesser members of this group" (such as Ralph Josselin) chose to send sons into apprenticeship, the social class of the better sort of trades rose in accordance. Defoe was not imagining the fact that young gentlemen were occupying posts in trade; their higher premiums acted like flags announcing their arrival.[45]

FROM RHETORIC TO REALITY: INDENTURED SERVICE AND THE PRICING OF PEOPLE

Indentured service evolved from an arrangement resembling apprenticeship to contractual relations attached to varied exchanges of money, depending on the neediness of the migrant and the financial means of

---

[43] *The Complete English Tradesman*, 2 vols. (London, 1745), 1:114. Over time, such conditions led to a shift in the balance of power, a pet complaint of Defoe, who claimed it was a sign of declension, much to be lamented.

[44] Ben-Amos, *Adolescence*, 216–17.

[45] Christopher Brooks, "Apprenticeship, Social Mobility and the Middling Sort, 1550–1800," in *The Middling Sort of People: Culture, Society and Politics in England, 1550–1800*, ed. Jonathan Barry and Christopher Brooks (Basingstoke, 1994), 70–1; Margaret R. Hunt, *The Middling Sort: Commerce, Gender and the Family in England, 1680–1780* (Berkeley, CA, 1996).

the agent.[46] The project of filling out passenger lists of ships bound for the colonies once again highlighted the ambiguity of the status of the servant in English history. Without ready money, some migrants exchanged their future labor for passage to the New World; in the words of one historian, they became "human merchandise at no financial charge to themselves."[47] In most cases, servants signed away whatever personal agency and freedom they might have had to begin with. Given the restrictions on free movement from one locality to another in England, along with the customary practice of hiring servants for one-year contracts, this was not much. Being "free" often meant being unemployed, and the prospect of managing to find work in distant parts without assistance presented its own set of legal and financial difficulties.

Yet the subordination entailed in indentured status, when forced through a web of commercial transactions, could lead to a unique form of human commodification. Masters acquired some servants on credit, or exchanged them, like property, with other masters. Early colonial inventories might refer to servants alongside livestock, their value translated into the current market value of goods such as cotton.[48] Some servants were exchanged for "colonial produce" or auctioned off, as in the case of ships landing in Virginia and Barbados in 1636 and 1637, for prices measured in pounds of tobacco.[49] Unlike slaves, white women servants might be bought out of servitude by prospective husbands. Yet their skin color did not prevent them from being set in scales and sold per pound, as in Barbados in the 1640s.[50] The similitude to slavery was apt in the case of the Irish: England had flirted with the use of slavery as

---

[46] David W. Galenson, *White Servitude in Colonial America: An Economic Analysis* (Cambridge, 1981); A. E. Smith, *Colonists in Bondage: White Servitude and Convict Labor in America 1607–1776* (1947; Gloucester, MA, 1965); C. L. Alderman, *Colonists for Sale: The Story of Indentured Servants in America* (New York, 1975).

[47] David Cressy, *Coming Over: Migration and Communication Between England and New England in the Seventeenth Century* (Cambridge, 1987), 53; see also Galenson's discussion of "human capital" in *White Servitude in Colonial America*, 97–99. Galenson calls indentured servitude "a credit system under which human labor was leased," 97.

[48] Robin Blackburn cites a list of "goods and Chattels" of one Captain Hawley in 1640, valuing "28 servants (26 males, 2 females) 7,350 lbs of cotton." *The Making of New World Slavery: From the Baroque to the Modern 1492–1800* (London, 1997), 242–3.

[49] Galenson, *White Servitude in Colonial America*, 98, 100. Wareing cites a case of an apprentice hauled off to "the Barbadoes," where he was allegedly sold "for a slave for sixteene hundred poundes waight of suger." "Preventive and Punitive Regulation," 297.

[50] Beckles, "Concept," 576. Beckles was citing the account of Richard Ligon from 1657; see also idem., "The Colours of Property: Brown, White and Black Chattels and Their Responses on the Caribbean Frontier," in *Unfree Labour in the Development of the Atlantic World*, ed. Paul E. Lovejoy and Nicholas Rogers (Essex, 1994), 36–51.

punishment for vagrancy in the sixteenth century,[51] and during the Civil War, inhibitions were set aside. Around one thousand Irish were sold as slaves to Sweden in 1610, and during the 1650s, around eight thousand men were sent on penal contracts as prisoners of war to American colonies.[52]

This hybrid approach to dealing with labor, blending entrepreneurial calculation with paternalistic entitlements, led to illicit practices when it came to locating candidates for employment in the New World. The high demand for labor and the business of transporting it ultimately mirrored trafficking in slaves.[53] In his study of Bristol's Atlantic economy, David Harris Sacks emphasized the distinction between kidnapping and spiriting: through the latter method, "countless men and women in the mid-seventeenth century were 'enticed' or 'seduced' into bonds of servitude in the plantations." He also noted that "[t]he Middlesex County Records abound with references" to spiriting.[54] The practice met with disapproval, yet it proved persistent in the record of colonial history. As procedures for registering emigrants became more formalized after the middle of the seventeenth century, reports of spiriting declined. But at a time when state management of migration was yet in its infant stages, the law allowed for illegal varieties of contract labor to slip through administrative loopholes.[55] Ambiguities abounded and problems in filling out the numbers in ships' holds persisted, so that as late as the 1770s, the problem of kidnapping was not fully eradicated.[56]

---

[51] R. H. Tawney and Eileen Power, eds. *Tudor Economic Documents*, 3 vols. (London, 1965), 1:325–30.

[52] Blackburn, *Making of New World Slavery*, 316–7; Peter Linebaugh and Marcus Rediker, *The Many-Headed Hydra: Sailors, Slaves, Commoners and the Hidden History of the Revolutionary Atlantic* (Boston, 2000), 123.

[53] Historical debate has fastened on this issue, insisting that students of the subject should not mistake the exception for the rule: "the majority" of indentured servants "were emphatically not the victims of the grasping few [large-scale operators] who appear in the mythology surrounding the subject." David Souden, "'Rogues, Whores and Vagabonds'? Indentured Servant Emigrants to North America, and the Case of Mid-Seventeenth-Century Bristol," *Social History* 3 (January 1978): 35.

[54] *The Widening Gate: Bristol and the Atlantic Economy, 1450–1700* (Berkeley, 1991), 253, 417n.

[55] Smith, *Colonists in Bondage*, esp. Chap. 4; see also Sacks, *The Widening Gate*, Chap. 8, on the origins of the Bristol *Register of Servants to Foreign Plantations* in 1654.

[56] See the case of Elizabeth Brickleband, discussed in the next chapter. Kidnapping as a violation of personal and human rights appears as a subject of debate in discussions of children in the early nineteenth century. See Ann Alexander, *Facts Relative to the State of Children Who are Employed by Chimney Sweepers as Climbing Boys*, 2nd ed. (York, 1817).

What sort of person was carried off to the colonies? A careful analysis of the traffic in indentured servants contradicted the stereotypic image of "rogues, whores and vagabonds"; in fact, even spirited servants resembled typical labor of the seventeenth-century urban population.[57] In trying to persuade the crown to regulate the passage of legitimate servants through a system of registration, merchants complained that "[t]he generality of volunteers for transportation are the scruffe and scumme of the people, whose slothe, debauchery and prodigality brings them under those circumstances and if they were not transported to the Plantations it is to be feared many will probably go to Tyburn."[58] The unembarrassed approach of the Common Council and Lord Mayor of London in 1618 captured the reality of seventeenth-century discomfort with the unsupervised and often homeless condition of their charges. They contracted to supply the Virginia Company with one hundred vagrant children from the streets of the city, as they were "burdensome to the parish where they live" and a potential threat to the peace. Historians' mistaken blanket generalizations have reflected the categorization of labor as it was described at the time. The convergence of colonial demand and local supply created a timely opportunity on both sides to categorize and transport them.[59]

Even during the first decades of the eighteenth century, attitudes toward the undisciplined poor very nearly matched perceptions of indigent freedmen and slaves, as Edmund S. Morgan has shown in his classic study of freedom in colonial Virginia. According to contemporaries, the lowest rungs of society were seemingly overstocked with the "vicious, idle, dissolute" and "the vile and brutish part of mankind."[60] Within these ranks, laborers of all kinds fell into a category of subordination characterized by general, not particular, features. Planters made little distinction between types of laborers in the field, whether the person had entered voluntarily into contract labor, or come to the colony by

[57] The phrase was used by Smith, 5. See also David Souden, "'Rogues, whores and vagabonds.'"

[58] PRO *State Papers, Colonial*, Charles II, CO 1/50, 52–3, quoted in Wareing, "Preventive and Punitive Regulation," 300.

[59] Robert C. Johnson, "The Transportation of Vagrant Children from London to Virginia, 1618–1622," in *Early Stuart Studies: Essays in Honor of David Harris Willson*, ed. Howard S. Reinmuth, Jr. (Minneapolis, 1970), 137–51, esp. 149.

[60] Edmund S. Morgan, *American Slavery – American Freedom* (New York, 1975), 319–26. The quotations are from *An Enquiry into the Causes of the Encrease and Miseries of the Poor of England* (London, 1738), 9, and C. S. Hall, ed., *The Economic Writings of Sir William Petty* (Cambridge, 1899), 1:275.

way of the punishment of transportation. Ambrose Barcroft, of Bucks County, Pennsylvania, writing to his father in England in 1722, offered terse demonstration of his inability to discriminate:

> I had 4 servants. The woman I sold, she were not worth keeping. One run away, I have heard of him in Maryland, but I am afraid he'll get to England, that I shall not catch him; two I have still. I have been in an humour to sell one of them the next Summer (for there is no danger of his running in the winter). He is a good hand and can be a good Servant, that if I were sure he would stay with me, I would not part with him on any account, but being a convict for 7 years I am afraid he'll run.[61]

Barcroft's world of labor was prescriptive, bounded by assigned stations of master and servant, though the possibility of escape introduced an element of instability to the subject status of servants.[62]

The colonial world introduced elements of unpredictability into this picture, particularly through geographical mobility, but also as a result of the peculiar financial arrangements associated with settlements in the New World. Monetary considerations often determined how colonial laborers circulated within a world of risky opportunities and relatively interchangeable roles. Early immigrants to the American colony of Virginia, for example, intermingled with investors, or "adventurers," who had bought stock in the Company from its inception in 1606; such settlers were understood to have a stake in the project of settlement in the form of their "persons." Others gained land grants for transporting servants to the colony, thus delivering persons as a way of gaining propertied wealth.[63] Immigrants to America were able to recognize significant differences in rank among themselves, of course, quite apart from the financial means that each had brought to the project of overseas settlement. Far below the merchant and landed adventurers of means were the numerous individuals, recognized only as servants, who set out under various agreements in order to make a fresh start. Yet the condition of being penniless could be visited upon even the better sort. Some indentured servants, such as John Harrower, who left Scotland as

---

[61] Walter Hart Blumenthal, *Brides from Bridewell: Female Felons Sent to Colonial America* (Rutland, VT, 1962), 39.

[62] On runaway labor, see Jonathan Prude, "To Look upon the 'Lower Sort': Runaway Ads and the Appearance of Unfree Laborers in America, 1750–1800," *Journal of American History* 78, no. 1 (June 1991): 124–59.

[63] Annie Lash Jester, ed., *Adventurers of Purse and Person: Virginia, 1607–1625* (Princeton, 1956), 339, regarding the career of John Utie.

late as 1773, boasted education and social status; yet a candid account of his circumstances suggests that his sole claim to fortune may have been the small change in his pocket.[64]

The same condition of reduced identity was true of convict labor, which developed into another form of trafficking in humans with the inception of transportation as a punishment for an increasing number of crimes. From the passage of the Transportation Act of 1718, English courts exiled men and women to North America and committed them to forced labor for fourteen years for capital offences and seven years for felony. Together, officers of the Crown, prison keepers, and merchants quickly constructed elaborate machinery around the Act and set about emptying prisons for allotted payments, initially set at £3 per head.

The manner in which convicts were handled at the other end of the voyage only accentuated the commodity aspect of their status. Factors bought and sold convicts, worrying about their marketability alongside numbers of indentured servants and immigrants from economically distressed areas such as Ireland. The business promised to be lucrative, not to mention more economical than the slave trade, as it required less capital and fewer operating costs. The first "Contractor for Transports to the Government," Jonathan Forward, boasted experience in the American tobacco and slave trade, and so, in the words of one historian, "was well versed in the management of human cargoes." Within a year, he obtained what amounted to a monopoly in the business and demanded more per head for the transport of felons from county jails to make up for losses incurred through disease and pirating.[65] The similitude to slavery was not lost on critics of the system, who inveighed against forced servitude in remote places that would spare English people the offensive sight of "Slaves on *English* Land."[66]

Casting oneself (or being cast) into the netherworld of transport between England and other parts of the globe had a great deal to do with the fluid constitution of authority that was exercised over priced people such as indentured servants and convicts. As Peter Linebaugh

---

[64] "Diary of John Harrower, 1773–1776," *American Historical Review* 6 (October 1900): 65–107; David Galenson, "'Middling People' or 'Common Sort?': The Social Origins of Some Early Americans Reexamined," *William and Mary Quarterly* 35 (July 1978): 499–525.

[65] Peter Wilson Coldham, *Emigrants in Chains: A Social History of Forced Emigration to the Americas, 1607–1776* (Stroud, 1992), 61–7.

[66] A. Roger Ekirch, *Bound for America: The Transportation of British Convicts to the Colonies 1718–1775* (Oxford, 1987), 18, 76–77; "Verus," *Gentleman's Magazine*, 1738, 288, quoted in Ekirch, 21.

and Marcus Rediker have shown in striking form, transatlantic traffic literally generated new social formations, prompting the application of power by homogenizing a diverse population of laborers within a contained environment that had as its objective specified commercial purposes.[67] The expression "to take the King's shilling," which represented enlistment in military forces, appears to have come into being in the early eighteenth century, and not without a certain irony. As the state developed its financial and administrative machinery, the symbolic coin joined other rhetorical invocations of money, whether arising from mercenary or less reputable relations.[68]

The factor of money repeatedly intrudes as a key to the operation of these methods of dealing with people. Rather than rendering people as objects, the system transformed them into financial abstractions, a limbo of personal identity peculiar to the age. In the case of indentured servitude, laws and procedures borrowed at least part of their form from the practices of money-lending. Because the indenture functioned as "a credit mechanism by which the servant . . . borrowed against the future returns from his labor," the servant himself or herself became, in effect, "the security on the loan."[69] Money was thus imbricated within a distinct universe involving the exchange of servants. Contemporaries referred to the many "bargains," "contracts," "trade," and "sales" that were part of daily life,[70] though not with a sense of free dealing. Rather, monetary payments worked to facilitate movement and seal agreements; contemporaries seemed to be planning for risks within a realm of limited options. Galenson cites several seventeenth-century opinions on the subject of colonial indentures, including an anonymous account comparing the system with service in husbandry: 'Let no man be troubled at the thoughts of being a Servant for 4 or 5 years, for I can assure you, that many men [in England] give mony with their children to serve 7 years, to take more pains and serve nothing so well as the Servants in this Plantation will do."[71] Money introduced a certain degree of hopeful investment, it seems, into an otherwise risky exchange of one kind of servitude for another.

---

[67] Peter Linebaugh and Marcus Rediker, *The Many-Headed Hydra: Sailors, Slaves, Commoners, and the Hidden History of the Revolutionary Atlantic* (Boston, 2000).

[68] The *Oxford English Dictionary* gives 1707 as its first use; see also Linebaugh and Rediker, *Many-Headed Hydra*, esp. 214–21 on resistance to impressment; Nicholas Rogers, "Vagrancy, Impressment and the Regulation of Labour in Eighteenth-Century Britain," *Unfree Labour*, 102–13.

[69] Galenson, *White Servitude*, 8.   [70] Ibid., 10.

[71] From *A Brief Description of the Province of Carolina on the Coasts of Floreda [sic]* (London, 1666), 9, cited in Ibid., 10.

Figure 6. Matthias Finucane, "Sale of a Wife in Smithfield Market," 1797. Reproduced by permission of the Guildhall Library, Corporation of London.

THE SALE OF WIVES

As an "informal institution" documented since medieval times in Britain, the sale of wives seems to have occurred with greater frequency from the 1740s and was "particularly noticeable in the period 1785–1845." Though the practice was not unique to Britain, French observers viewed the phenomenon as peculiarly English.[72] Wife sale probably provided "a form ... flexible enough to carry many different messages": the need for an inexpensive method of divorce among common people, the desire to shame badly behaved spouses, and the provision of "street-theatre" of a socially preservative kind.[73] An exchange of money was often involved in plebeian marriage negotiations, which were managed

---

[72] Samuel Pyeatt Menefee, *Wives For Sale: An Ethnographic Study of British Popular Divorce* (New York, 1981), 34, 47. In a later contribution that responds, in part, to Menefee, E. P. Thompson provided what may be considered a more definitive historical account of the practice: "The Sale of Wives" in *Customs in Common* (New York, 1991). Thompson noted that "together we have collected some four hundred examples," 408.

[73] Thompson, "Sale," 447.

independently of justices and courts. Coins and other forms of wealth were included in a general effort to return gifts in the case of a withdrawn betrothal, or a release from one person before entering into obligations to another.[74] Given all the financial considerations of marriage under any circumstances, wife sale has escaped particular notice amidst abundant plebeian practices boasting the vocabulary and techniques of market transactions.

The earliest accounts of wife sale appear obliquely through the historical record: as churchwardens' presentments of penance completed by offending husbands in the late sixteenth century, or as anecdotal accounts in local histories. Ecclesiastical courts were alert to such occurrences through the end of the seventeenth century; thereafter, a burgeoning number of newspapers made note of the events as local curiosities, despite their regularity. Fragmentary evidence of the earlier period has eluded analysis (Thompson, for example, discounted incidents that were not fully ritualized), such as the case of Oxfordshire churchwardens who found a couple "cohabiting unlawfully" in 1696 after one Thomas Heath had bought the wife of George Fuller "at $2\frac{1}{4}$d the pound."[75] Gillis pointed out that Hardwicke's Marriage Act would have made second marriages more difficult for everyone, not just the upper classes, thus encouraging the resort to wife sale after 1753, which may explain the increase noted by Menefee at mid-century. It is impossible to know for sure, as accounts of the practice depended on public notice and also on contemporary attitudes. That the sale of wives was decried by a writer of the 1790s may not indicate the widespread incidence so much as the changing moral temperament of the times. The end of the Napoleonic Wars quite likely brought on a greater number of severed marriages, however. Each wave must be analyzed in its own context.[76]

English chroniclers were convinced that the custom was practiced mainly by "the lowest of our Vulgar,"[77] mostly proto-industrial workers

---

[74] John R. Gillis, *For Better, For Worse: British Marriages, 1600 to the Present* (New York, 1985), 51, 211.

[75] Cited in Keith Thomas, "The Double Standard," *Journal of the History of Ideas* 20, no. 2 (April 1959): 213, drawn from *The Churchwardens' Presentments in the Oxfordshire Peculiars of Dorchester, Thame and Banbury*, ed. S. A. Peyton (Oxford, 1828), 184.

[76] On shifting attitudes toward marriage, domesticity, and divorce, see Randolph Trumbach, *Sex and the Gender Revolution, Volume One: Heterosexuality and the Third Gender in Enlightenment London* (Chicago, 1998), 267, 377; Lawrence Stone, *Road to Divorce: England 1530–1987* (Oxford, 1990), 143–8; Gillis, *For Better*, 212.

[77] John Brand, *Observations on Popular Antiquities*, rev. ed. (1813) 2: 37, quoted in Thompson, "Sale," 411, 413.

or plebeians. Research has confirmed what one might expect: men in artisanal trades and those without property, lacking the means required for any other form of divorce, were most likely to engage in the custom.[78] These were individuals, it should be added, schooled in the requisite methods of the marketplace. More genteel examples have surfaced, too; among them is Sir Godfrey Kneller, who was reported to have purchased his wife from a Quaker.[79] The practice persisted well into the nineteenth century, memorialized (and in large part, misrepresented) in Thomas Hardy's *The Mayor of Casterbridge* (1886). A travesty to later sensibilities, the sale of wives met with disapproval from middle-class Victorians, who denounced it as a desecration of the state of matrimony.

As David D. Gilmore has argued in an anthropological analysis of misogyny, scholars have not rushed to analyze the ritual humiliation of women because they feel it is somehow self-explanatory and per-petual, even if it seems abhorrent.[80] Unconvinced by the moralistic response, E. P. Thompson discovered himself caught on the horns of a social historian's dilemma: he hoped to move beyond an interpreta-tion that seemed painfully obvious – the demonstration of the subjec-tion of women to chattel status – and an equally superficial assump-tion that marital relations among the poor were barbaric.[81] The axis of interpretation that focused on the question of oppression or agency imposed its own limitations: gathering a sufficiently large data base of sold wives, he finally argued, "far more often the reports suggest their independence and their sexual vitality."[82] Late-eighteenth-century satir-ical prints of the ritual project a somewhat similar profile of wives in the marketplace, portraying them as lusty, buxom, and overpowering beside their callow or diminutive husbands. The fact that the parties involved often reached mutual agreement before engaging in the act of sale seemed to endorse this point of view. As a result, scholarly dis-cussion continued to turn on the nature of consent, leaving the con-nections between wife sale and its implication in monetary practices unexplored.

Menefee's anthropological attempt to rescue wife-selling from the category of the extraordinary provided some help, but not enough to break out of such conceptual limits. By placing the practice in a larger

[78] Thompson, "Sale," 413–15; Gillis, *For Better*, 218.   [79] Menefee, *Wives*, 54, 213.

[80] David D. Gilmore, *Misogyny: The Male Malady* (Philadelphia, 2000).

[81] Thus, his essay appeared after the book-length anthropological study of Menafee. Thompson, "Sale," 406.

[82] Ibid., 461.

pattern of self-regulating communal rituals, his functional explanation achieved the ironic effect of making the sale of wives appear normative and almost timeless in character, diminishing the sense of any contextual specificity. Likewise, according to Erin Ihde, "Wife sales can be seen as one of those British customs that made the journey to Australia, and survived relatively intact." Like Thompson, Ihde asserted that wife sale "did not necessarily entail the degradation of women, but could in fact be a positive event in which the women were frequently willing participants." His evidence fit the model of positivistic functionalism far less comfortably: he cited several particularly horrific accounts involving the stripping and sexual abuse of women, which appeared to be sales of women as "servants" (or, as another historian more accurately described them, slaves, exploited prisoners, or prostitutes), rather than as matrimonial partners.[83]

The most significant aspect of our current knowledge of wife sale may be its apparent emergence as ritual, which Thompson dated with significant numbers from the 1760s. A set of prescribed actions constituted what he called "'true' ritual wife sale": location in a public forum, ideally, a marketplace; public announcement of the transaction; the act of leading the wife by means of a halter to the established location; the auctioneering of the wife to the highest bidder; the "passage of money" confirming the act of selling; and a "solemn transfer" of ownership, entailing possibly "the passing of the rope" or the "public declaration" of renunciation, and perhaps even the return of wedding rings. Evidence also reveals a less frequently used method of wife sale that relied on drawing up a paper contract with witnesses in a private location, thus relinquishing the role of public carnival in favor of a more private legal arrangement between individuals. What distinguished true wife sale from other varieties, according to Thompson, was the degree of involvement of the community, enlisted in place of established legal authority, in affirming the transferal of the wife from one "owner" to another.[84]

Such willingness to make the sale of wives normative, however misguided, opens up another interpretive avenue, however: that putting

---

[83] Erin Ihde, "'So Gross a Violation of Decency': A Note on Wife Sales in Colonial Australia," *Journal of the Royal Australian Historical Society* 84 (June 1998): 26–7. Ihde refers the reader to Robert Hughes's conflicting accounts of the same evidence; Hughes directly compares the sale of women to that of slaves and makes no mention of "wife sale." *The Fatal Shore: An Epic of Australia's Founding* (New York, 1986), 244–64.

[84] Thompson, "Sale," 416–26.

prices on women agreed with other, similarly ordinary assumptions about dealing with certain classes of people. Neither Menefee nor Thompson denied the troubling and ultimately unresolvable nature of wife sale, with its objectification of human beings through money and the marketplace: the fact that the ritual was marked by the use of a halter, a vivid symbol of dehumanization, makes the point quite clearly.[85] That wives for sale resembled cattle in the marketplace was, of course, no accident; many of the sales recorded in newspapers indicate Smithfield Market, London's cattle and horse market, as a favored place for the transaction. The expression "Smithfield Bargain," drawn from a proverb indicating "a roguish bargain," also carried the meaning "a marriage of interest," and the phrase acquired yet a third meaning through its use in connection to wife sale.[86] Cattle horns were also recognized symbols of cuckoldry in charivari rituals of the early modern period. The term "cow" or "cattle" when applied to women could also mean "whore" in vernacular terms in both English and French.[87] Menefee pointed to parallels within the market-oriented culture of late eighteenth-century England, reminding the reader that contemporaries sold children (as prostitutes and chimneysweeps) and corpses. But he resisted pursuing the similitude between wife-selling and slave-selling; this parallel, in his view, only indicated that both forms "could be ascribed to general market practices."[88] Visual evidence from a broadside dated around 1832 indicated the connection to cattle, showing a woman tied to gate, behind which several beasts are on display. One man offers a bag of money; the others display raucous, grinning faces.[89]

Linguistic connections lead to the most obvious deep meaning of wife sale, the link between wives and chattel, which underscored a woman's condition of subordination in common legal terms. As Menefee pointed out, wife sale differed from bridewealth because it was not used to secure alliances between two families, but rather, two individuals; and so the European and British incidence of *selling* a wife remains

---

[85] Thompson noted the regular mention of halters in accounts of wife sale date from 1740, an important aid in contextualizing the more local aspects of the ritual.

[86] *Oxford Dictionary of English Proverbs*, 2nd ed., comp. William George Smith (Oxford, 1948), 600.

[87] Menefee, *Wives*, 152–3.

[88] Ibid., 160. Menefee seems to interpret the notion of marketing quite literally, pointing out that "slave sales were more strictly economic than their domestic counterparts," 160.

[89] British Library, Pressmark LR 271, A.2, 4, no. 290, featured in Gillis, *For Better*, 212.

singular in nature.[90] In this peculiarly commercial social transaction, money played an important role. Inserted into a transaction that had no basis in written law, money imbued wife sale with an aura of legitimacy in several different senses. Lacking financial (and civil) resources to purchase legal means of divorce, the opposing parties sought the next best thing: the passage of coin, in the midst of the marketplace, invoked the normative process of property transferal, and thus confirmed the passage of a possessed person from one master to another. The amount of money applied to the transaction was irrelevant, for its symbolic significance was at issue.[91] By using a shilling, the parallel with enlistment was probably deliberate, as wives' obedience to husbands replicated the duty of soldier to the king.[92] Part of the money involved in wife sale might also be returned as "luck money," and here, an analogy to the sale of cattle and horses was explicit and deliberate: the custom supposedly provided financial compensation for future risk involved. Once again, the terms of the ritual reasserted the hierarchical place of the husband and the objectified identity of the wife. As a master of a person without full legal status, he engaged in a commercial transaction that was actually more a transferal of patriarchal rights into which money had intruded. The woman in question was reduced to the property of the auctioneering man.[93]

In the "nearest we can get to a thick description"[94] of ritual wife sale, two aspects become salient, and we can assume, with caution, that both would have been present in early eighteenth-century instances of the phenomenon. The original husband, in his performance before a crowd of villagers, called "to yer notice, a very handsome young ooman, and a nice little baby wot either belongs to me or to somebody else." Though the remark drew "a general laugh" and "good humour," the point provides us with our first significant assertion of ownership, albeit over an ambiguous circumstance. The mastery of men over women was understood as a form of possession, and the existence of a baby called up the same vocabulary of identity, understood by the law as property in

---

[90] Menefee, *Wives*, 154–5; see also Emmanuel Leroy Ladurie, *Love, Death and Money in the Pays d'Oc* (Harmondsworth, 1984), 138–40.

[91] Often the coin was a shilling, but both Thompson and Menefee provide much evidence of a wide variety of prices paid for wives, along with ironic commentary on the fact. Thompson, "Sale," 423–4; Menefee, *Wives*, 53.

[92] Menefee, *Wives*, 173.　　[93] Thompson, "Sale," 423–4.

[94] The account is from Frederick W. Hackwood, *Staffordshire Customs, Superstitions and Folkore* (Lichfield, 1924), 71–3, and is reproduced by Thompson in "Sale," 463–6.

persons within master-servant law. In fact, the entire ceremony alternated between each side of the duality, as the speaker referred to both the character of the woman on the block and the quality of her performance in terms of labor and sexual relations. A further remark indicated what is so obvious as to be overlooked: "It's all right," he reportedly proclaimed, "accordin' to the law." The man was providing reassurance of the transaction, as onlookers had urged him to "get on wi' it!" after the woman broke down in tears. The witness recalled the claim of legitimacy, as the ritual lurched through its expected paces, however unsavory, as a literal sale of property in the shape of a person.[95]

The historian needn't emphasize "victimhood" in order to bring the weight of interpretation to bear on the market aspects of wife sale. Attention needs to be focused on the willingness of English people, according to records dating from the 1690s and continuing through the eighteenth century into the nineteenth century, to utilize the techniques of the market in order to adjudicate rights over women as wives. That the practice of wife sale was coterminous with the financial revolution, a contemporary upheaval in marriage arrangements (at least until mid-century), and a colonial trade in persons and slaves deserves emphasis. That the practice illustrates the efflorescence of an enduring form of male hegemony seems obvious. The significant historical point may be that "wife selling in its ritual form is a creation of the very late seventeenth and the eighteenth centuries."[96] The existence of the practice may also reveal the inadequacy of marriage reform provided by Hardwicke's Act of 1753. If so, then its chronology reinforces the larger argument presented throughout these pages: the regime of money exerted a magnetism all its own during a period when the institutions of English society enhanced its attractiveness and enforced its power.

TRAFFIC IN PEOPLE: AN EARLY MODERN ANOMALY?

Though historians have uncovered evidence of the pricing of people in the eighteenth century, most analyses have been confined to the history of slavery or to discrete areas of research. Some historians of crime, for

---

[95] "Sale," 465–6.
[96] Thompson, "Sale," citing Martin Ingram, *Church Courts, Sex and Marriage in England, 1570–1640* (Cambridge, 1987), 207.

example, see the traffic in transported felons as part of a larger renovation of the law mainly through numerous statutes aimed at violators of many kinds of property law. Others have pointed out that transportation provided a merciful option when compared to the sentence of death by hanging.[97] The business of contracting for the "removal" of convicts thus appears as a secondary issue, subject to a wholly different standard of assessment. To Roger Ekirch, for example, the system was "a major advance over the haphazard methods of past years." Using a Weberian yardstick, he placed the statutes relating to transportation in the context of an evolving penal bureaucracy: they rendered uniform the procedures for dealing with categories of felons across London, Middlesex, Buckinghamshire, and the Home Counties. In those places, the Treasury subsidized the passage of convicts at the rate of three pounds sterling per head; other courts were required to make their own arrangements with merchants. The cost, rather than the system of calculating it, struck Ekirch as remarkable. "Maybe the country's 'financial revolution' made transportation possible," Ekirch posited.[98]

Sidney and Beatrice Webb were among the first historians to call attention to the trade in vagrants, discussed in the previous chapter, which developed from statutes dating from the last years of the seventeenth century. The rewards system, they contended, bred corruption and only perpetuated the problems of migration and poverty that vagrancy laws had set out to solve. The laws also brought about the unintended consequence of encouraging vagrants to offer themselves up to the "regular trade" of contractors, who passed wanderers from one place to another.[99] Criticizing the Webbs for their reckless zeal in condemning the old Poor Law, historians have also subjected their treatment of the rewards system to scrutiny. Calculating the proportion of rewards

---

[97] J. M. Beattie, *Policing and Punishment in London, 1660–1750* (Oxford, 2001). The literature on this debate is voluminous; see, for example, Douglas Hay, Peter Linebaugh, John G. Rule, E. P. Thompson and Cal Winslow, *Albion's Fatal Tree: Crime and Society in Eighteenth-Century England* (New York, 1975).

[98] *Bound for America: The Transportation of British Convicts to the Colonies, 1718–1775* (Oxford, 1987), 18. The system of pricing convicts generated bureaucratic red tape with problems of its own. Ekirch cited a western assize clerk's complaint to the keeper of the Wiltshire gaol: "Nothing will be done" without the payment of "a Guinea for each Persons Certificate," 88.

[99] Sidney and Beatrice Webb, *English Local Government: English Poor Law History: Part I. The Old Poor Law*, 3 vols. (London, 1927), 1: 370–3. The words "regular trade" come from a Report of the Select Committee of the House of Commons on Vagrancy, 1821. The Webbs point out that this secondary effect of the law developed later in the eighteenth century, when physical punishments for vagrancy had ceased (372).

to apprehensions, which ran at "rarely more than 20 percent," Nicholas Rogers argued that authorities found other, more effective ways of dealing with vagrancy. By mid-century, justices were cognizant of the pitfalls of such a system, warning against the "too liberal distribution" of such payments. Yet this judicial "admonition" need not be seen only as a sign of administrative efficiency; one might also interpret it as a measure of how widely acknowledged the expectation of rewards seemed to be.[100] As noted above, Rogers cast rewards within the larger context of a "regulatory regime" consonant with the exercise of civil authority. But why this aspect of regulation took the form of putting prices on heads remains unexplained.[101]

Contemporaries occasionally expressed moral outrage against trafficking in people, though of a sort that registered more against the venal age than the act of pricing people. Horace Walpole's reaction to the Roundhouse incident offers the perfect example: the "mercenary" round-up of "honest labouring women," discussed in the previous chapter, was the work of unscrupulous watchmen, constables, and magistrates. "[T]here is no tyranny they do not exercise, no villany of which they do not partake," he wrote, and his standpoint was faithfully reproduced by W. E. Lecky.[102] In the context of a history of crime in the metropolis, he focused solely on the potential for corruption built into the rewards system. If people tended to indulge in a covert trade in people, then this was largely the failing of individual morality in an imperfectly governed society.

Twentieth-century historians have been too inclined to see the trade in people in light of simplistic economic models. Economic historians have superimposed modern expectations on evidence relating to indentures, insisting on interpreting migration to America as a sign of enterprising spirit. The lure of transatlantic migration was sufficiently strong, according to one account, to persuade emigrants to "voluntarily [sell] some of their future labor, this being the only other asset at their disposal."

---

[100] "Policing the Poor in Eighteenth-Century London: The Vagrancy Laws and Their Administration," *Histoire sociale – Social History* 24, no. 47 (May 1991): 128–30.

[101] Rogers, "Vagrancy," 102–13. Historians of poverty have been sensitive to the fact that vagrants were sometimes lumped together with convicts and shipped to the colonies in similar fashion; the confusion of categories, not the particular method of measuring numbers by prices per head, is the point they have wondered about.

[102] Letter to Sir Horace Mann, ca. Wednesday 21 July 1742, in *Horace Walpole's Correspondence with Sir Horace Mann*, ed. W. S. Lewis, Warren Hunting Smith and George L. Lam (New Haven, 1954), 1:503–4; W. E. Lecky, *A History of England in the Eighteenth Century*, 3rd ed., 4 vols. (London, 1883), 1:483–4.

But the conceptual apparatus of free-market economics hardly seems to apply to those who faced few or no options in England, or had in fact been added to the pool of servants through coercion. Yet in the interest of constructing a narrative with the advantage of hindsight, this account allows theoretical speculation of a modern sort to intervene:

> These institutions of immigrant servitude were the private market's solution to financing the voyage of those who could not pay in advance. It gave the poorer part of the population the ability to finance moving from low-productivity areas to high-productivity areas thereby improving their own welfare as well as the overall welfare of society. Without these labor markets it is unlikely that pre-19th century America would have been populated as fast or grown as rapidly as it did.[103]

The overall function of indentured servitude therefore takes center stage, where it is made to serve the long-range goals of economic growth. While acknowledging that the mercantile economy was not "free" in a modern sense, historians have assumed that decision-making was nevertheless rational and progressive. The only exception to this approach has occurred in the study of child labor, where historians have recognized the full extent of unfree labor in a literal "market for children in early America."[104]

And yet, to assume that indentured service was similar to the "ancient institution of apprenticeship" in England leads to misapprehensions of a different sort.[105] Contemporaries seem to have regarded the two systems of labor as the same, but David Galenson has convincingly demonstrated otherwise. Even though the system of indentures in the colonies held much in common with service in husbandry, the treatment of colonial labor departed significantly from the less restrictive arrangements of rural England. According to Galenson, the American "adaptations produced a fundamental change in the institution, as the rigidity introduced as a result of economic imperatives destroyed relationships basic to the English system of service in husbandry, and resulted in a system in which men were traded and sold as objects." Terms of labor were

---

[103] Farley Grubb, "The Incidence of Servitude in Trans-Atlantic Migration, 1771–1804," *Explorations in Economic History* 22 (1985): 317.

[104] John E. Murray and Ruth Wallis Herndon, "Markets for Children in Early America: A Political Economy of Pauper Apprenticeship," *Journal of Economic History* 62, no. 2 (June 2002): 356–82.

[105] This is the view of Abbot Emerson Smith in his definitive *Colonists in Bondage: White Servitude and Convict Labor in America, 1607–1776* (Chapel Hill, 1947), 8; quoted also in Galenson, *White Servitude,* 6.

longer than the customary one-year contracts of service in husbandry, and restrictions upon the movement of indentured servants were common. Because servants in America were likely to be tempted to run away before serving their time, colonists passed laws aiming to discourage desertion. A system of passes evolved, which functioned to monitor the travel of servants; such measures most likely added to an adversarial atmosphere surrounding relations between masters and servants.[106]

Setting prices on people suggests an obvious parallel with slavery, and it is instructive to reconsider the distinction between free and slave labor. Though the racial oppression that was part of colonial slavery was unique, similarities existed among forms of "unfree" labor. As David Eltis observed, "It is more useful to regard slave and non-slave labour as part of a continuum than as polar opposites."[107] In the interest of examining the larger Atlantic world, Hilary Beckles and others have cast unfree labor into a comparative framework, highlighting the growing power of capitalist economies as they were integrated with the continents of Africa and Asia. Beckles has argued that "a highly developed market-oriented conception of labour" brought about several different categories of laborer, which were treated as interchangeable forms of capital. "A range of domestic apprenticeship/ indentureship systems . . . required at best a little fine tuning for direct application to colonial circumstances," and created similar circumstances for Amerindian peoples, African slaves, white indentured servants, and Irish prisoners. Beckles has shown that "West Indian planters freely bought, sold, gambled away, mortgaged, taxed as property and alienated in wills their white indentured servants, African slaves and Amerindian bondsman." Within this system, property rights in persons performed an important function, enabling planters to transfer labor to locations where it was needed or most valuable.[108]

Individuals without property at the bottom of the social scale, those who may have entered into unfree relations of labor, fell into a separable social category. Stanley L. Engerman aptly summarized the general status applying to a wide spectrum of people on the lowest rung of the social ladder: "The presumption was that anyone who labored for another lacked full property in himself and was 'free' only in a restricted

[106] Galenson, *White Servitude*, 7–8; Smith, *Colonists in Bondage*, Chap. 11.
[107] David Eltis, "Labour and Coercion in the English Atlantic World from the Seventeenth to the Early Twentieth Century," in *Wages of Slavery: From Chattel Slavery to Wage Labour in Africa, the Caribbean and England*, ed. Michael Twaddle (London, 1993), 207.
[108] Hilary Beckles, "The Colours of Property," 39, 37.

sense."[109] In the history of political economy, the link between free-dom of individual choice and maximum productivity is a relatively modern idea; people without property or skills in the early modern period were believed to be under an obligation (thus, coerced) to labor by their bodily needs and lack of means.[110] When we think of laborers unattached to the social relations of employment – between "situations," so to speak – we must consider their vulnerability to coercion of some form. One is reminded of Moses Finley's assertion that "in the context of universal history, free labor, wage labor, is *the* peculiar institution."[111] Thus distinguished more by degree than by absolute difference, a large category of people, including migrating servants in husbandry, inden-tured servants, and convicts, existed within a relatively indeterminate social realm.

In his *Second Treatise of Government*, John Locke argued that an individ-ual owned his capacity to labor and was in charge of determining how that capacity would be used. But Locke's greater attention to the task of defining authorized citizens of property resulted in a rather dismis-sive treatment of the freedom assigned to people of lower rank, whose "property" consisted of the labor of their hands. Locke recognized that "life was still sacred and inalienable" for such individuals, but some might still be forced to sign over their capacities to a master and, in other words, to alienate their property in themselves. "[A] Free-man makes himself a Servant to another, by selling him for a certain time, the Service he undertakes to do, in exchange for Wages he is to receive[.]" Locke chose to portray this as a temporary *"Contract* between 'em",[112] even

---

[109] "Coerced and Free Labor: Property Rights and the Development of the Labor Force," *Explorations in Economic History* 29 (1992): 3.

[110] Engerman, "Coerced and Free Labor," 5; A. W. Coats, "Changing Attitudes to Labour in the Mid-Eighteenth Century," *Economic History Review*, 2nd ser., 11, no. 1 (August 1958): 35–51 and "The Relief of Poverty, Attitudes to Labour, and Economic Change in England, 1660–1782," *International Review of Social History* 21 (1976): 98–115.

[111] "A Peculiar Institution?" *Times Literary Supplement* 3877 (2 July 1976): 819, quoted in Engerman, 1n. As Engerman points out, the reasons for the eventual endorsement of "free labor ideology" were "not only on the obvious moral grounds," but also on account of the aim to increase output. This was, after all, Adam Smith's argument in *The Wealth of Nations*. See also Eric Foner, *Free Soil, Free Labor, Free Men: The Ideology of the Republican Party Before the Civil War* (New York, 1970); David Brion Davis, *The Problem of Slavery in the Age of Revolution, 1770–1823* (Ithaca, 1975).

[112] John Locke, *Two Treatises of Government*, ed. Peter Laslett (Cambridge, 1988), 322. He adds, "But there is another sort of Servants, which by a peculiar Name we call *Slaves*, who being Captives taken in a just War, are by the Right of Nature subjected to the Absolute Dominion and Arbitrary Power of their Masters (322–3)."

though the condition of being under contract may have persisted for a laborer's lifetime. Those who were dependent on others, as "servants" (i.e., laborers) or as receivers of alms, were thus disenfranchised because their participation in the political realm would be compromised by their vulnerability to the will of their masters. In this way, social and economic circumstances ultimately excluded many people from civil status, and consequently, from the benefits of Locke's universal freedom.[113]

The transferal of unlimited rights over the life of another individual gradually came to be seen as a violation of natural religion and natural rights. But relatively few early enlightenment figures were concerned with the contradictions of slavery, and it was not until arguments were made from the basis of property law that reformers found one of their strongest arguments. The disabilities stemming from the condition of being owned disqualified a man from assuming the duties of a fully endowed male citizen. "It is necessary that all *property* should be inferior to its *possessor*," Thomas Clarkson argued in 1785, pointing out that a male slave lost his claim to "authority as a parent, and his duty as a son." By the end of the century, natural rights claims, as well as religious principles, would be applied to the condition of all slaves, including women, as their degraded state was couched in general terms: subjection to others signified a loss of dignity unacceptable to all human creatures.[114] But at the beginning of the century, this vocabulary of universal entitlement had not yet found expression in the general public sphere.

The seventeenth and eighteenth centuries thus constituted a transitional period during which a traditional notion of the individual as embedded in social relationships of obligation came into conflict with a new definition of the individual as severed from ties of dependency. "Property in oneself" became more widely established as a principle of significant import, as late seventeenth-century thinkers embraced a more liberal, modern notion of freedom. Yet the fact that a system of slavery expanded in the American colonies while Europeans trumpeted the ideal of freedom constitutes one of the paradoxes of intellectual history during this time. Studies of labor and slavery indicate that political theory was far in advance of legal and social changes. As Douglas Hay has shown, employers exercised prerogatives, spelled out in master and

---

[113] C. B. Macpherson, *The Political Theory of Possessive Individualism* (New York, 1962), 231.

[114] *An Essay on the Slavery and Commerce of the Human Species* (London, 1785), 69, 70, 243–4, 248, quoted in Searle, *Morality and the Market*, 50. On women defined as subjects generally, see Ferguson, *Subject to Others*.

servant law, enabling them to physically punish, humiliate, and imprison workers for misbehavior well into the nineteenth century.[115] Nevertheless, as the next chapter will argue, enlightened thinking about the self converged with practices involving money, welding the medium to self-advancement and autonomy in the latter half of the eighteenth century.

---

[115] Douglas Hay, "Patronage, Paternalism, and Welfare: Masters, Workers, and Magistrates in Eighteenth-Century England," *International Labor and Working-Class History* 53 (Spring 1998): 27–48; Douglas Hay and Paul Craven, eds., *Masters, Servants, and Magistrates in Britain and the Empire, 1562–1955* (Chapel Hill, 2004).

CHAPTER 8

Money Makes Masteries: The Triumph of the Monetary Self in the Long Eighteenth Century

The first half of the eighteenth century fostered an open recognition of the power of money, along with a continuing effort to comprehend its meanings. Money acted as more than a medium of exchange: it functioned as a measure of status marking people according to their ownership of property and as an incentive in a system of checking the movement of vagrants. Mediated by the state, the involvement of money in social relations contributed to its authorization as a normative aspect of culture. Over time, conveyed by overlapping discourses of proprietorship and commercial profit-seeking, a paradoxical but distinctively new attitude toward the use of money emerged. People situated their sense of selfhood within the hierarchies and reversals revealed through money, incorporating the medium into experiences of personal achievement and autonomy. This chapter is intended as a suggestive, if partial, account of how these themes fared in the second half of the eighteenth century. Though the tensions created by the "heads" and "tales" of money were never resolved, the social life of money after 1750 demonstrated the virtues and pitfalls of a universal instrument of personal agency.

THE DETOXIFICATION OF MONEY IN THE AGE OF ENLIGHTENMENT

> I was this day thro' Cheapside, the Change & cc and cou'd not help imediately reflecting, that the sole cause of that vast concourse of people, of the Hurry & bustle they were in, & the eagerness that appeard in their countenances, was getting of Money, & whatever some Divines would teach to the contrary, this is true in fact that it is the main business of the life of Man[.]
>
> Letter from Jedediah Strutt to Elizabeth Strutt, 1765.[1]

---

[1] Quoted in R. S. Fitton and A. P. Wadsworth, *The Strutts and the Arkwrights, 1758–1830* (Manchester, 1958), 109–110.

Viewing the spectacle of the financial world of London at work, factory magnate Jedediah Strutt registered its brisk energy through provincial eyes. His observations were faintly reminiscent of the ruminations of Bunyan's pilgrim in the presence of Mr. Money-love, but with a reformation of attitude with regard to "the main business" of life. In truth, Strutt shared more with these metropolitan contemporaries than with seventeenth-century Dissenters on the subject of money. Reassuring his wife in the same letter, he continued, "& thou knowest not how solicitous I am while life, & youth, & opportunity last to acquire something [so] that you & I, should we live so long, may not have the two great calamities of Human Life, poverty & Old Age, come upon us together." Like Ralph Josselin, Strutt strove to multiply his monetary wealth for the sake of his family's well-being, a purpose that helped him to preserve a sense of moral integrity amidst worldly concerns. For Strutt and other influential people of means in the second half of the eighteenth century, money, allied with this worthy objective, enjoyed a life of redemption.

John Wesley granted the same capacious role to money in his sermon on its use in the 1760s. While carrying on the tradition of cataloguing the perilous allurements of lucre, Wesley made a distinction that Puritan divines would not have countenanced. "It has indeed been the manner of poets, orators, and philosophers, in almost all ages and nations," he pointed out, "to rail at this the grand corrupter of the world, the bane of virtue, the pest of human society." He continued, "But is not all this mere empty rant?"

> For let the world be as corrupt as it will, is gold or silver to blame? 'The love of money', we know, 'is the root of all evil'; but not the thing itself. The fault does not lie in the money, but in them that use it. It may be used ill; and what may not? But it may likewise be used well; it is full as applicable to the best as to the worst uses. It is of unspeakable service to all civilized nations in the common affairs of life. It is a most compendious instrument of transacting all manner of business and . . . of doing all manner of good.[2]

Wesley demonstrated how the terms of discussion with regard to this thorny issue of moral virtue had shifted to the subject of individual character and agency, away from a wariness of the object of temptation.

---

[2] "The Use of Money," in *John Wesley's Sermons: An Anthology*, ed. Albert C. Outler and Richard P. Heitzenrater (Nashville, 1991), 349.

An ability to master the threat posed by money rested on a powerful, new notion of the self, the product of an age of enlightenment that had advanced a sense of enriched interiority, as well as a hopeful attitude toward human perfectibility. In this latter quest, pious individuals were just as likely to enlist money as they were to shun it. As Wesley famously advised his followers, "Gain all you can," "Save all you can," and "[G]ive all you can." Money thus rendered beneficial continually circulated, replicating the organic nourishment of the social body envisioned by early modern thinkers, but in substantially greater proportions.[3]

Wesley and Strutt imagined an identification with money that favored mutuality over self-interest, suggestive of the social relations of gifting. Family fortunes and philanthropy aimed to neutralize the noxious aspects of money once attached to the vice of avarice. For many propertied people in the latter half of the eighteenth century, their sense of a monetary self was tied to a private vow to concentrate on its distribution, rather than its accumulation. "I have not enough of the miser, to love treasures hidden and buried," confided Elizabeth Robinson Montagu in a letter to her husband, as she catalogued the different faces of money at mid-century: "Money is convertible to credit and pleasure; useful in the hands of the prudent; noble in the hands of the generous; pernicious with the bad; ridiculous with the prodigal; and contemptible with the miser."[4] The challenge, she understood, was to lay out money with reason and moderation.

The moralism implied by Montagu's cautionary words did not rule out an open recognition of the pleasure of spending money, which eighteenth-century elite women expressed with relish for all of their class. In correspondence between friends, candor won over more polite rhetoric concerning money, as writer Elizabeth Carter demonstrated in a letter to Elizabeth Robinson Montagu. "I am glad you have such good accounts from your colliery; indeed, whatever you may think about it, nobody loves money better than I do, both for my friends and myself."[5]

---

[3] Ibid., 350, 353, 355.

[4] Letter from Elizabeth Robinson Montagu to Edward Montagu, August 30, 1751, in *The Letters of Mrs. E. Montagu, With Some of the Letters of Her Correspondents*, 4 vols. (London, 1813), 3: 165–6.

[5] Letter from Elizabeth Carter to Elizabeth Robinson Montagu, July 2, 1771 in Elizabeth Carter, *Letters from Mrs. Elizabeth Carter to Mrs. Montagu, between the Years 1755 and 1800*, 3 vols. (London, 1817), 2:368.

Mary Granville Pendarves Delaney echoed these sentiments in a letter to her sister, referring to an impending court decision that would affect her household finances. "You know . . . that though I do *not* love money *for its own sake*, that I *love to spend it!*"[6] The association between women and spending was a persistent trope for luxury and moral degeneracy, though in a later century, women would adroitly exercise their own authority in refiguring this image to positive ends.[7]

Didactic literature and visual evidence communicated a similar reconciliation with money, often placing coins and bills within a circumscribed universe of charity and paternal supervision. This form of circulation differed greatly from the extravagant gestures of largesse pictured in an earlier era, in which a beneficent monarch might shower coins upon his subjects as they gathered to pay him homage. As Jean Starobinski has argued, by the eighteenth century, images of charitable giving that show a more deferential, devout poor in receipt of monetary alms from the rich replace depictions of indiscriminate largesse. At the same time, enlightenment philosophy elevated the charitable gift to a level of abstraction, donated "for the love of humanity" and severed from the particular interests that had governed the social relations of money in an earlier era.[8] Sir William Beechey's "Portrait of Sir Francis Ford's Children Giving a Coin to a Beggar," exhibited in 1793, displayed this social dynamic by assigning the role of almsgiver to two children, a girl and a boy, who exude adult-like decorum as they extend monetary succor to a barefoot boy who is probably older, though with eyes downcast in suitable deference. The pair are exercising capacious sensibility, demonstrating an enlightened education assimilated with obvious success. Describing this development in art, David H. Solkin highlighted how "the moral scope of a conversational imagery expanded to embrace the dimension of 'humanity'."[9]

---

[6] Letter from Mary Granville Pendarves Delany to Anne Granville Dewes, November 4, 1752, in *The Autobiography and Correspondence of Mrs. Delany*, rev. from Lady Llanover's edition, ed. by Sarah Chauncey Woolsey (Boston, MA, 1879), 1:421.

[7] Lisa Tiersten, *Marianne in the Market: Envisioning Consumer Society in fin-de-siecle France* (Berkeley, 2001).

[8] Jean Starobinski uses "The Liberality of Titus (Allegory of the Liberality of Louis XIII and Cardinal Richelieu)," ca. 1637–1638, by Jacques Stella, as a prime example of an image of largesse in his *Largesse*, trans. by Jane Marie Todd (Chicago, 1997), 89, 94; see also David H. Solkin, *Painting for Money: The Visual Arts and the Public Sphere in Eighteenth-Century England* (Yale, 1992), esp. Chap. 5.

[9] Solkin, *Painting*, 200.

Figure 7. Sir William Beechey. "Portrait of Sir Francis Ford's Children Giving a Coin to a Beggar Boy," 1793. Reproduced with permission of the Tate Gallery, London/Art Resource, NY.

For Jedediah Strutt, redistribution of wealth in a general sense translated into a paternalistic plan to address the needs of his workforce, demonstrated in the early factory owner's efforts to offer housing, provisions, and schooling to factory families. Yet a careful assessment of his distribution of literal money, that is, specie, suggests a qualified view of the generosity of paternalism. According to surviving account books, wages allotted to a female reeler working a seventy-two-hour week were 2s., to cite just one example, yet in reality, workers were paid mostly in kind and in truck. Ironically, the Strutts labeled the fraction of their workers' wages paid in cash – which amounted to one-sixth of the total – as "quarterly gift money," and this outlay was whittled away by deductions made for disciplinary infractions. Within the tightly circumscribed universe of wealth defined by factory own-ers, money payments acquired the aura of "gift" simply because they were exceptional to the inflexible allotments ordinarily doled out to workers.[10]

Until changes in coinage law, early factory industrialism enhanced the power of paternalism by diminishing the monetary capability of the working population.[11] The situation was chronic across England, as the shortage of coin, heightened by periodic wars, made the distribution of wages difficult, forcing early factory owners to resort to makeshift plans to distribute whatever specie they could cobble together. For Strutt, this might consist of a mélange of Spanish dollars, a variety of silver, gold, and copper pieces, and tokens made up from miscellaneous coins countermarked for specific workforces. At Samuel Oldknow's factory at Mellor, workers literally starving for cash in 1793 finally consented to a stopgap measure, which used the only available money to buy oatmeal for general distribution with potatoes and beef as part of their overdue wages.[12] The alternative to these measures, a resort to privately issued tokens, offered more flexibility than payment in kind, but nevertheless circumscribed the spending of workers to the microcosm of their locali-ties, consumer worlds served by quaint symbols of local production or, in some cases, the literal "heads" of factory masters. Beloved by twenty-first-century collectors, the genre of trade tokens inspired a broad vari-ety of inscriptions that responded in their own way to the absence of small coin. The classic example of this is the token produced by

---

[10] Records of the amounts of this "gift money" also list the amounts of cash deducted for disciplinary infractions. Fitton and Wadsworth, *Strutts*, 237, 244.

[11] This is argued from a different standpoint, from different kinds of evidence, by William M. Reddy, *Money and Liberty in Modern Europe: A Critique of Historical Understanding* (Cambridge, 1987), 93–4, 165ff.

[12] The account of Oldknow's predicament is from a letter from Dr. James Currie to William Wilberforce, quoted in Fitton and Wadsworth, *Strutts*, 241; on the collection of coinage used to pay factory workers, see 242–4.

John Wilkinson, the renowned iron master, whose half-penny pictured a magisterial profile satirized by the *Gentleman's Magazine* in 1787: "So Wilkinson, from this example/Gives of himself a matchless sample... Which shows his modesty and sense/And how and where, he made his pence."[13] Among the most eloquent was the creation of radical Thomas Spence, which featured a line from Oliver Goldsmith's "Deserted Village," "One only master grasps the whole domain," curling around an image of a humble cottage.[14]

As an early chapter argued, the failure to provide small change to the public at large, based on a fundamental loyalty to intrinsic value, had the effect of obstructing the circulation of monetary wealth among those without property. Given the needs of a burgeoning modern economy, this should have presented a serious obstacle to British economic growth. Yet the early phase of a consumer revolution proceeded in spite of this fact, depending on credit relations for much ordinary spending. Such coin-starved conditions contributed to the persistence of an aura of gifting, along with the supervision and control that accompanied such exchange relations, well into the nineteenth century.[15]

Token manufacture, a prime example of autonomous fashioning of money media, laid the groundwork for a modern system of state coinage. The invention of Boulton's steam press in 1787 made possible mass-produced, high-quality coins, but nearly thirty years passed before Britain officially came to terms with the monetary implications of such technology. The first state to take advantage of this new opportunity to produce small coin for popular use was the Russian government, which purchased Boulton's machinery in 1799. While other governments endeavored to manage monetary systems that included currency of representative rather than intrinsic value, the English state contracted with Boulton to produce copper coins at "full-bodied" value, resulting in pennies of one ounce each in 1797.[16] Only after the persistent

---

[13] Peter Mathias and A. C. Barrington-Brown, *English Trade Tokens: The Industrial Revolution Illustrated* (London, 1962), 54–56; F. D. Klingender, "Eighteenth-century Pence and Ha'pence," *Architectural Review* 93 (February 1943): 40–6.

[14] Ibid., 33–34; see also Peter Mathias, "The People's Money in the Eighteenth Century: The Royal Mint, Trade Tokens and the Economy," *The Transformation of England: Essays in the Economic and Social History of England in the Eighteenth Century* (London, 1979), 190–208.

[15] See Margot C. Finn, *The Character of Credit: Personal Debt in English Culture, 1740–1914* (Cambridge, 2003).

[16] Thomas J. Sargent and Francois R. Velde, *The Big Problem of Small Change* (Princeton, 2002), 61–3.

Figure 8. Half-penny issued by John Wilkinson, 1788. © Copyright The Trustees of The British Museum.

Figure 9. Coin issued by Thomas Spence, 1795. © Copyright The Trustees of the British Museum.

production of "convertible token coins" by private firms could the government finally recognize, through such practical success, the benefit of relinquishing an attachment to intrinsic value for all exchange media. The Coinage Act of 1816 thus put into place the components of a modern system of small change, providing more abundant coinage of copper and silver of mere representative value.[17]

[17] Ibid., 303–4.

THE LASTING MARRIAGE OF MONEY AND FREEDOM

Another variety of individualism, one that rested on a positive identification with the power of money as a vehicle of personal freedom
and expression, flourished alongside these developments as the eighteenth century progressed. Imagined identification with money persisted as a powerful trope in literature. Moll Flanders, Robinson Crusoe,
Humphrey Clinker, Roderick Random, and many other characters
emerged from fiction to pursue the fantasies of travel and migration once
imagined by Taylor's Twelve-pence and Addison's Shilling.[18] Money on
the move demonstrated the proverbial truth – "money makes a man free
everywhere" – and offered the possibility of social relations drained of
obligation and deference, free of the dependency so reviled by enlightenment promoters of personal liberty.

Autobiographical accounts of actual experiences of adventurous
travel, such as that of Charlotte Charke, the intrepid, cross-dressing
actress, suggest that women with extraordinary determination might
make the migratory "monetary" life their own. As a veritable embodiment of Moll Flanders in resourcefulness and pluck, Charke succeeded
in determining her own movements and professional activities without
interference from others. In truth, no such venture could succeed without alternations between earnings and the random receipt of gifts and
credit, dutifully noted by the itinerant actress.[19] Yet Charke saliently
punctuated her narrative with the steady recording of her dealings with
money, each amount registered with an assiduousness that suggests that
she saw coins (and occasional windfalls of notes) as the very instruments
of her progress. Avoiding credit relations that would have hindered her
freedom, she managed to get by on "a solitary Shilling" in London, and
to travel from "Devizes in Wiltshire, to Rumsey in Hampshire," a "Full
forty Miles," with four shillings obtained from selling "a few trifling
Things." "My projecting Brain was forced again to set itself to work,"
she recorded after another itinerant round of employment, using the
language of a character sprung from the polemics of Defoe, "to find
fresh Means of Subsistence."[20] Perhaps her greatest expense was paid
out in the form of the compromised value of her appearance and virtue,
which were repeatedly altered to suit circumstances so that she could

---

[18] On "Fictions of Social Circulation," see Deidre S. Lynch, *Economy of Character: Novels,
Market Culture, and the Business of Inner Meaning* (Chicago, 1998), 80–119.

[19] Charlotte Charke, *A Narrative of the Life of Mrs. Charlotte Charke* [1755], ed. Robert Rehder
(London, 1999), 49–50, 53, 70.

[20] Ibid., 68, 70, 135.

continue on her way. Charke's remarkable testament, one of the earliest female autobiographies of its kind, nevertheless gives proof of the involvement of money in the construction of independent character, constantly mobile and fungible, like money itself.

As William Reddy has argued, the association between liberty and money formed one of the main currents of enlightenment thought, a point of contestation on every level of society.[21] "I love liberty," Jean-Jacques Rousseau wrote in his *Confessions*. "So long as the money lasts in my purse, it assures me of independence and relieves me of the need of plotting to obtain more, a need which has always appalled me." Identifying with the power behind money, Rousseau was also aware of its negative dimension. He added, "money [that]one pursues is the instrument of servitude. That is why I hold fast to what I have, but covet no more."[22] Its association with freedom and autonomy at times overshadowed the more subtle ways in which money maintained social ties and affirmed hierarchies. Many aspects of the social life of money described in the preceding chapters – its attachment to the subordinate status of people who owned no property, its descriptive value in relation to propertied persons, and its vast rhetorical power – continued to inform its use in the eighteenth century. But considerations of a new era enhanced the power of the self, which set these elements in a different perspective. Contemporaries expounded on and enthused over the pleasures wrought by money, sealing its compartmentalization with an exaltation of freedom, while other elements of the life of money remained associated with customs of the past. To enlightenment thinkers, money appeared directly tied to an individual state of happiness, competing with virtue as a guiding notion of personal imperatives.[23]

A diminished sense of the embeddedness of money was a prerequisite of a later phase of its identity, when it was reincarnated as a key component of a critique of capitalist social relations in nineteenth-century social thought.[24] The alienated, fungible character of money lay at the

---

[21] Reddy, *Money*, esp. 73–81.   [22] Quoted in Reddy, *Money*, vi.

[23] The "individuals" of this "modern world," in Sylvana Tomaselli's words, now "conceived of happiness as the pursuit of private interest, not the public good, however much they unintentionally secured the latter by devoting themselves to the former." "The Death and Rebirth of Character in the Eighteenth Century," in *Rewriting the Self: Histories from the Renaissance to the Present*, ed. Roy Porter (London, 1997), 92.

[24] The impoverished sense of social relations noted by Durkheim as he critiqued English liberalism, the abstract sense of freedom presented by Simmel in his classic work on money, and the notion of reification in the work of Lukács were also inheritors of this outlook. See Margaret Jane Radin, *Contested Commodities* (Cambridge, MA, 1996), Chap. 6.

heart of capitalist relations of production and exchange for Karl Marx. In his analysis of production, he described an all-encompassing panorama of exchange, which relied principally on money as the representative of disembodied value, torn from its human origins. This was part of "the magic of money": "Men are henceforth related to each other in their social process of production in a purely atomistic way," he wrote in *Capital*. In a frequently quoted passage, he pursued the metaphor of enchantment:

> Since money does not reveal what has been transformed into it, everything, commodity or not, is convertible into money. Everything becomes saleable and purchaseable. Circulation becomes the great social retort into which everything is thrown, to come out again as money crystal. Nothing is immune from this alchemy, the bones of the saints cannot withstand it[.]

Marx credited the ancients with an understanding of the true extent of money's supernatural power,[25] which he enshrined in the concept of fetishism. He also elaborated on the cause of its deracinated condition, which he located in the phenomenon of circulation. This activity, not production, was responsible for transforming the manufactured product into the special category of "commodity."[26] Marx's theory of commodification under industrial capitalism thus mirrored the circulation of people without property in the late seventeenth and eighteenth centuries. Not surprisingly, as a voracious reader of early English political economy, Marx had spent many of his months in the Reading Room of the British Museum plumbing this critical period of history.[27]

ESTABLISHING LIMITS FOR THE SOCIAL LIFE OF MONEY

It is no accident that a paradoxical development occurred at the end of the eighteenth century with regard to the social life of money: from the 1760s, enlightened voices began to protest the unbounded

---

[25] *Capital*, Vol. 1, trans. Ben Fowkes (New York, 1977), Book 1, pt. 1, 187, 229. R. H. Tawney, in turn, credited Marx as the last defender of the moral perspective of Aristotle and the Schoolmen.

[26] "This locational moment – the bringing of the product to market, which is a necessary condition of its circulation, except when the point of production is itself a market – could more precisely be regarded as the transformation of the product *into a commodity*." *Grundrisse: Foundations of the Critique of Political Economy*, trans. Martin Nicolaus (Harmondsworth, 1973), 534.

[27] See Ibid., 229–32, 870–1; also *Capital*, Chap. 3, "Money, or the Circulation of Commodities," 188–244, shows the full array of Marx's readings in early tracts on political economy.

migration of monetary measurements into so many aspects of human identity. The association between money and a unique sense of self proceeded alongside a growing discomfort with monetary measurements of people. Opposition to colonial slavery inspired a call for drawing lines demarcating what we might recognize as a modern social life of money. A notion of the individual as the carrier of an inviolable human identity, preserved from objectified status associated with monetary prices and the market, took shape in antislavery discourses in America, France, and England.[28] Though the concept of liberty drew from diverse sources, it was the contradictions within paternalistic social relations that prompted true engagement with the issue of individual freedom. While older forms of proprietorial relations, such as labor indentures and vagrant apprehensions, had authorized the use of monetary measurements, abuses of authority called attention to the dangers of enlisting such incentives within the social relations of duty. The example of slavery stood as the supreme example of the regime of money gone awry, proof that the rhetoric of monetary thinking, replete with its power to commodify whatever it measured, could, in fact, debase human beings by objectifying them. The abolition of the slave trade in 1807 indicated that a new sensibility opposing the application of prices to people was beginning to make its mark through legislative efforts. The reform of law regulating child labor in 1819 denoted the same wish to set apart areas of human identity from the commodifying presence of prices.[29]

The ramifications of these important debates are beyond the chronology and scope of this book, but they nevertheless suggest a denouement of the tendencies that have been traced from the mid-1600s to the middle of the eighteenth century in this study. The aim of this partial examination of the involvement of money in the social life of English people

---

[28] Historians differ in their placement of the beginning of antislavery activity in the Anglo-American world: Philip Gould, *Barbaric Traffic: Commerce and Anti-Slavery in the Eighteenth-Century Atlantic World* (Cambridge, MA, 2002); Robin Blackburn, *The Overthrow of Colonial Slavery, 1776–1848* (London, 1988); Seymour Drescher, *Capitalism and Antislavery: British Mobilization in Comparative Perspective* (Oxford, 1986); David Brion Davis, *The Problem of Slavery in Western Culture* (Oxford, 1966), pt. 3.

[29] Ludmilla Jordanova, "Conceptualizing Childhood in the Eighteenth Century: The Problem of Child Labour," *British Journal of Eighteenth-Century Studies* 10, no. 2 (1987): 189–99; John Wareing, "Preventive and Punitive Regulation in Seventeenth-Century Social Policy: Conflicts of Interest and the Failure to Make 'Stealing and Transporting Children, and Other Persons' a Felony, 1645–73," *Social History* 27, no. 3 (October 2002): 288, 304; "'Violently taken away or cheatingly duckoyed'. The illicit recruitment in London of indentured servants for the American colonies, 1645–1718," *London Journal* 26 (2001): 1–22.

has been twofold: to illuminate changes in attitudes toward the use of money during a period of considerable instability with regard to its definition; and to identify the broad range of power relations associated with the use of money in early modern England. It is clear that these developments did not usher in the triumph of individualism over older social values. The eighteenth century in fact reaffirmed the paradoxical nature of money's powers, shown in the way that monetary measurements were applied to people throughout the period. The medium of money also extended its virtual orbit through popular life and heightened its image as a democratic enabler. These might be seen as significant portents of changes to come. On balance, however, money continued to exert its trademark power to create hierarchies, especially as a marker of mastery over the vulnerable categories of gender and class.

The dualism of money would persist beyond the early modern period as long as money remained entwined with the means of subjecting people to the condition of being "priced." The medium also continued to convey the allurement of free movement to adventure-hungry individuals. A vivid example of its problematic implications emerges from an account of an abduction that occurred in June, 1775, when seventeen-year-old Elizabeth Brickleband joined a woman caller at her door, unknown to her mother, and stepped out without explanation, vanishing into the confusion of the London streets. Thus began a determined mother's search for a missing daughter that ended, frustrated, at the Old Bailey nearly a year later. The three convicted kidnappers, who ran a "lock-up house" that supplied indentured servants to the American colonies, received relatively light sentences.[30] Historian Dorothy George cited the case in her treatment of London's emigrants, lauding the fortitude of Elizabeth Brickleband's mother while acknowledging the survival of violations in the passage of labor to American colonies. Such methods resembled the business of "spiriting" that had been addressed and outlawed by Parliament in the seventeenth century.[31]

---

[30] *OBSP*, 17 April 1776, 246–8.

[31] M. Dorothy George, *London Life in the Eighteenth Century* (New York, 1965), 146. She points out that by 1770, "Maryland was the only colony which still regularly accepted convicts," 144. It is worth noting that Sarah Brickleband, Elizabeth's mother, demonstrated an often exercised capacity of ordinary women to utilize the legal means available to her. It is likely that she was a single mother who had been pregnant at the time of her marriage and later parted company with her husband. See Boyd's Marriage Index, Marylebone (St. Mary Le Bone), Middlesex, for 1769.

It is easy to register the incident simply as the manipulation and treachery it is, particularly when one considers the way in which the abduction of a female teenager could be categorized as part of a broader exploitation of women in an underworld of colonial labor.[32] Yet the court account included a number of disputed points which challenge this monolithic narrative and also call to mind the multiple dimensions of transactions involving money. Was Elizabeth Brickleband an agent, at least in part, in her own disappearance? For example, did she know the caller at her door, ominously attired in black crape? Initially, in response to what must have been her mother's inquiry, Elizabeth denied recognizing her, but the woman, who gave her name as Mary M'Kenneller, had information that succeeded in drawing Elizabeth out of the house and down the street. The same M'Kenneller later led Mrs. Brickleband to the place where the indenturing business was carried on, managed by a couple, Jane and John Dennison. A friend of Mrs. Brickleband came forward in court to corroborate the account of the aggrieved mother, and related information that shed new light on Elizabeth's abduction. She recounted the words of the Dennisons' son, who was present at the time of Mrs. Brickleband's visit to the lock-up house: "you old 'Caddameran, what do you do here again about your whore of a daughter? I debauched her at school; and I took her on board the ship, and there I debauched her again, and gave her a flogging," he reportedly cried out to her.

None of this was necessarily true, but it did suggest that Elizabeth might have been drawn into the arrangement by some sort of romantic inducement. How seriously are we to take two witnesses, brought in from a public house? They reported that Elizabeth had waited at the King's Arms "for a young man to call for her" to take her to America with him. When one of the men drinking at the public house predicted dangers ahead – "you will repent of it before you get to the Downs" – she allegedly protested in a similar stock fashion: "she said she did not care, she would go to the farthest part of the world with him." Were they telling the truth? Or were they paid off in a web of underworld intrigue?

Perhaps Elizabeth was consenting to the arrangement in some way. According to Mrs. Brickleband, Elizabeth's entry was unlike those of the rest of the women on the passenger list of the *Nancy*. Most were

---

[32] On this point, see Walter Hart Blumenthal, *Brides from Bridewell: Female Felons Sent to Colonial America* (Rutland, 1962).

committed for four years of labor; Elizabeth was entered "*twenty-one free*," suggesting that some special accommodation had been made for her. Historian and genealogist Peter Wilson Coldham's list of emigrants to Baltimore, Maryland, lists one Elizabeth Brittlebank, age 21, not 17, departing exactly as poor Mrs. Brickleband stated, on the week of June 12th, 1775. How and why was Elizabeth added to the bottom of the list (Mrs. Brickleband noted this in her comments to the court, and it is indeed true, save one Thomas Eldridge, a carpenter from Kent), incorrectly?[33]

The case gives us plentiful evidence of the distinctive confluence of eighteenth-century sensibilities: the self-interested drive for money and love; the desire for freedom from confining ties; an imaginative capability and the capacity to act on a powerful impulse; an awareness of the contemporary transatlantic world and the possibilities it held; the defense of family ties by a valiant mother; the wish to see justice done in an urban world ridden with venality and vice. All of the players in this drama understood that money was a medium of circulation, used to promote or inhibit freedom, easily inserted into equations involving the value of human life. They understood that money flowed through boundary walls: family ties, religious principles, and the law itself, but also geographical boundaries, as it connected London to the world at large. Prices thus were placed on human heads: the Dennison operation reportedly produced "near an hundred servants for £91. 7s. 6d." Mrs. Brickleband went to Gravesend, ready to pay the required sum to obtain her daughter's release, but the ship had left the harbor; the Dennisons supposedly offered Mrs. Brickleband £500 as hush money. She retorted, "Do you think I will sell my child's blood[?]"[34]

The court sentenced John and Jane Dennison to three months' imprisonment, with security for good behavior for two years, while their accomplice received a lighter sentence of one month and one year's security.[35] Given that stealing a horse would have carried a sentence of death, the trial demonstrated how the laws regarding property and persons remained unreformed and contradictory. Efforts to make child-stealing a felony resumed, after a 130-year interval, in 1808, but a law was not passed until 1814. Coincidentally, "blood money" was also debated in Parliament at this time, and parliamentary rewards ultimately were abolished by law in 1818. Thus, prices placed on people

---

[33] Peter Wilson Coldham, *The Complete Book of Emigrants, 1751–1776* (Baltimore, 1993), 271.

[34] *OBSP*, 17 April 1776, 247.   [35] Ibid., 248.

were gaining recognition as an inducement to illegal and immoral behavior.[36]

What became of Elizabeth Brickleband remains something of a mystery. According to the ship's records, the passengers were redemptioners, a variable category open to abuse. Once landed, such persons were responsible for finding their own employers, from whom they would obtain the passage money that was still owed to the ship's master – hence, they could become "redeemed". In fact, few passengers were given the chance to do so, and instead, many fell into some form of bound servitude, advertised for sale under the pretence of being convicts or some sort of fugitives. Treatment meted out to them was judged to be harsh.[37] Neither Elizabeth Brickleband nor "Elizabeth Brittlebank" surfaces in Maryland census records after her landing in Baltimore.[38] If she was, in fact, "free" upon arrival, it is possible that she soon married someone other than the Dennison son, or that she found passage on another ship, perhaps destined for another colonial haven or back to London. We might at least imagine that an originating impulse toward independence could have meshed momentarily with the means provided by circumstance.

The more likely outcome of Brickleband's adventure, unfortunately, is suggested by the conditions surrounding the landing of any ship of indentured servants in the port of Baltimore in 1775. This year marked the last period in which loads of labor arrived under these arrangements, with mechanisms in place for funneling servants to employers eager to absorb them. Such was the iron works and Hampton plantation owned by the wealthy Ridgely family, which received a large number of alleged convicts in the 1760s and 1770s: their hunger for labor meant that they received "regular announcements of incoming groups." In 1769, Captain Charles Ridgley also managed to buy and resell at least 15 men and women for profit.[39] Perhaps one of his agents met the *Nancy* when it arrived at port in the summer of 1775, forcing Elizabeth Brickleband into yet another channel of migration.

Not every servant sold from these shipments was a convict, but if part of a roster included transported labor, then an entire group might

---

[36] Wareing, "Preventive and Punitive Regulation," 304. Leon Radzinowicz, *A History of English Criminal Law and its Administration from 1750: Vol. 2, The Clash Between Private Initiative and Public Interest in the Enforcement of the Law* (London, 1956), 79–80.

[37] George, *London Life*, 147.   [38] I owe thanks to Seth Rockman for this information.

[39] R. Kent Lancaster, "Almost Chattel: The Lives of Indentured Servants at Hampton-Northampton, Baltimore County," *Maryland Historical Magazine* 94, no. 3 (Fall 1999): 341–2.

be categorized as such. Abusive treatment of convict and servile labor established a climate of coercion in the colony, graphically illustrated by advertisements in the *Maryland Gazette.* "Run away from the Subscribers, on the 20th of May last, two Servant-Men, one of them White, the other a Negro," read one example from 1745, offering "Forty Shillings Reward" for their capture. Another described the escape of "an English Convict Servant Woman" marked by "a large Scar on each Side of the Ancle," no doubt from manacles applied at an earlier point in her career.[40] Ridgley registered an advertisement in 1775, seeking the return of an escaped carpenter and sawyer named Francis Barrett, who could be identified by his iron collar, a remnant from one of his four previous escapes to freedom.[41] A letter from a female servant describes ceaseless labor, scanty provisions, and insufficient clothing.[42] If Elizabeth Brickleband was thrust into this environment, it is unlikely that she enjoyed a happier fate than that offered by her life in London. We can only speculate about the conclusion of her story.

The involvement of people with money is more complicated than our modern sensibilities wish to admit, particularly when we encounter examples of individual agency involved in market exchange. The mechanisms of market transactions may lead to a confusion between persons and commodities, so that priced people become fungible and thus "understood instrumentally, as means to satisfy the owner's needs and desires."[43] Yet the mechanisms of market thinking also lead to ideologically bound narratives, sometimes shaped by wishful thinking. Advocates of rational choice theory construct possibilities navigated by ideal agents who are committed to implicit and therefore ambiguous moral principles; a nominal equality equips them for success in a universe governed by law. Such conditions hardly match the more fragile and compromised conditions of real life. Seventeenth- and eighteenth-century English life, markedly different from such a theoretical model, illustrates how dealings with money led to power relations inherently fraught with risk. As G. R. Searle has argued for the period that followed, market-oriented thinking continued to violate boundaries of common sense and decency. Not until 1788, for example, was corpse-stealing made a misdemeanor in an attempt to redress regular

---

[40] *Maryland Gazette*, June 21, 1745.   [41] Lancaster, "Almost Chattel," 345–6.
[42] See "Letter from Elizabeth Springs to Her Father," in *Colonial Captivities, Marches, and Journeys*, ed. Isabel Calder (New York, 1935), 151–52.
[43] Radin, *Contested Commodities*, 59.

violations of gravesites for the sake of selling bodies to anatomy schools; even then, the practice continued, as prices rose in response to pressure on supplies.[44] Not surprisingly, given the vulnerability of those without property, pauper bodies were most likely to be pilfered.[45] Our interpretation of data must take into account the compromises imposed on theoretical models by early modern inequalities of power, along with the abuses that followed from them.

An optimist might argue that once these abuses were recognized, positive advances followed in the form of legal protection. Over the past two centuries, modern societies have marked out personal property that is "morally connected to the self" as exempt from free exchange and protected within "specific contexts...requisite for human flourishing."[46] Sexual and reproductive identities fall within this category, along with commodities such as blood and breastmilk. Legal scholar Margaret Radin has explained this sensitivity as belonging to a "thick theory of the self," which limits the number of aspects of the person that can be alienated through market relations. In the case of a "thin theory of the self," too many aspects of the self become fungible, saleable, and thus alienable. The consequences of this condition, she admits, can result in the loss of personal freedom and moral integrity.[47] For our own times, Radin recommends a middle way through such difficulties, a path designated as "incomplete commodification." Human flourishing, she argues, requires both "context-embeddedness and the need for context-transcendence." An individual may steer clear of extreme examples of these two options, yet retain the advantages of both in order to achieve personal satisfaction from a relatively free interaction with a market order. In other words, when opportunities arise to advance oneself through "selling" one's own products or skills, if the conditions are acceptable, then one should be able to take full advantage.[48]

This study of the English past concludes with a cautious regard for the possibilities emanating from the use of money. The eighteenth century witnessed a period of history when the identification between people

---

[44] G. R. Searle, *Morality and the Market in Victorian Britain* (Oxford, 1998), 71–2.

[45] Thomas W. Laqueur, "Bodies, Death and Pauper Funerals," *Representations* 1, no. 1 (1983): 109–31.

[46] Radin, *Contested Commodities*, 57, 60.

[47] Nowhere are the risks more evident than in Third World nations today, where men and women enter into employment which, in all but name, constitutes slavery. See Kevin Bales, *Disposable People: New Slavery in the Global Economy*, rev. ed. (Berkeley, 2004).

[48] Radin, *Contested Commodities*, 62, 113–14.

and money was a complex affair. Through its powers of transformation and circulation, money mediated and redefined social relationships, at times remaking the very identities of its users. I have traced a developing sense of mastery over the problematic qualities of money as the age rearranged its categories and rules to accommodate the volatile effects of this powerful medium; but the more recent history of the social life of money offers no such closure. The tensions highlighted by this segment of the past are still present, evident in countless signs of sovereignty and servitude across a global economy.

Bibliography

ARCHIVAL DOCUMENTS

British Library, London

Add. MS. 40,883. Nehemiah Wallington. Spiritual Diary, 1641–1643.
Add. MS. 21,935. Nehemiah Wallington. Historical Notes and Meditations.
Sloane MS. 922. Nehemiah Wallington. Letters.
Sloane MS. 1457. Nehemiah Wallington. Memorial of God's Judgment Against the Rebels.
Proclamation Books, 1680–1785.

Corporation of London Record Office

City of London, Court of Common Council. Repertories.
Miscellaneous Manuscripts.
Vagrant Books, 1738–1742.

Greater London Record Office, London

Middlesex Sessions Papers, 1711–1712, 1717, 1750–1751, 1756–1758, 1760, 1767–1768.
Certificates for Prosecuting Felons ("Tyburn Tickets"), 1730–1786.

Vagrant Removal Orders

Westminster Sessions Papers, Vagrant Settlement Examinations, 1705–1830.
Westminster Parish Exams, 1708–1709, 1752–1753, 1773–1786.

Folger Shakespeare Library, Washington, D.C.

Nehemiah Wallington. Writing book, 1654.

Friends House Library

Letter. MS. Vol. 101.115
Memorandum. MS. Vol. 101.114.

Guildhall Library, London
Journal of Nehemiah Wallington. MS. 204.

Harvard Law School Library
Old Bailey Sessions Papers, 1670–1780.

NEWSPAPERS

Evening Advertiser, 1757.
London Daily Post, 1734–1735, 1740–1741.
London Evening Post, 1727–1729, 1745, 1748–1767.
London Gazette, 1665–1712, 1715, 1732.
London Morning Advertiser, 1741–1743.

PRIMARY PRINTED SOURCES

Addison, Joseph. "Dialogues upon the Usefulness of Ancient Medals (1726)." In *The Miscellaneous Works of Joseph Addison*. 2 vols. Ed. A. C. Guthkelch. London, 1914.
      The Spectator. 5 vols. Ed. Donald F. Bond. Oxford, 1965.
Addison, Joseph, and Richard Steele. *The Tatler*. Ed. Lewis Gibbs. London, 1953.
Alexander, Ann. *Facts Relative to the State of Children Who Are Employed by Chimney Sweepers as Climbing Boys*. 2nd ed. York, 1817.
[Anon.] *A Discourse of Money*. London, 1696.
[Anon.] *The English Man's Two Wishes: . . . History of the Travels, and Various Turns of Fortune of a Shilling*. London, [1728?].
[Anon.] *The Hunting after Money*. [1709?].
[Anon.] *The Last Speech, Confession, and Dying Words, of A Queen Ann's Guinea*. [1774?].
[Anon.] *The Laws Concerning the Poor*. 1705.
[Anon.] *A New Canting Dictionary*. 1725.
[Anon.] *A Trip from St. James' to the Royal-Exchange, with Remarks Serious and Diverting, on the Manners, Customs, and Amusements of the Inhabitants of London and Westminster*. London, 1744.
[Anon.] *Use and Abuse of Money*. 1671.
[Anon.] *The Widower and Batchelor's [sic] Directory*.
Barbon, Nicholas. *A Discourse Concerning Coining the New Money [L]ighter* (London, 1696).
Bellers, John. *Essays About the Poor*. London, 1699.
      Proposals for Raising a Colledge of Industry. London, 1695.
Bohn, Henry G. *A Hand-Book of Proverbs Comprising an Entire Republication of Ray's Collection of English Proverbs*. London, 1855.
Briscoe, John. *A Discourse of Money*. London, 1696.
Bunyan, John. *The Pilgrim's Progress*. Ed. Roger Sharrock. Baltimore, 1965.
Burn, Richard. *The History of the Poor Laws*. London, 1764.
      Justice of the Peace and Parish Officer. London, 1755.

Carew, Bampfylde-Moore. "The Life and Adventures of Bampfylde-Moore Carew." In *King of the Beggars, Bampfylde-Moore Carew*. Ed. C. H. Wilkinson. Oxford, 1931.

Carter, Elizabeth. *Letters to Mrs. Montagu, Between the Years 1755 and 1800*. 3 vols. London, 1817.

Charke, Charlotte. *A Narrative of the Life of Mrs. Charlotte Charke [1755]*. Ed. Robert Rehder. London, 1999.

Child, Josiah. *A New Discourse of Trade*. London, 1693.

Clarke Family Letters. Available at British and Irish Women's Letters and Diaries, from 1500–1900 [electronic resource]. Chicago, 2002.

Creole. *The Fortunate Transport; or, the Secret History of the Life and Adventures of the Celebrated Polly Haycock. . . .* London, [1750?].

Cullen, William Henry. *The Life, Adventures, and Serious Remonstrances of a Scotch Guinea Note*. Edinburgh, 1826.

Defoe, Daniel. *The Complete English Tradesman*. 2 vols. London, 1726.
> *An Essay upon Projects*. Ed. Joyce D. Kennedy, *et al*. New York, 1999.
> *The Great Law of Subordination Consider'd*. London, 1724.
> *The Life, Adventures, & Pyracies of the Famous Captain Singleton*. Ed. Shiv K. Kumar. Oxford, 1969.
> *Moll Flanders [1722]*. Ed. Edward Kelly. New York, 1973.
> *Robinson Crusoe*. Ed. Angus Ross. Harmondsworth, 1965.
> *The True and Genuine Account of the Life and Action of the Late Jonathan Wild*. London, 1725.

Delaney, Mary. *The Autobiography and Correspondence of Mrs. Delany, Rev. from Lady Llanover's Edition*. 2 vols. Ed. Sarah Chauncey Woolsey. Boston, MA, 1879.

Dunton, John. *An Essay on Death-Bed-Charity, Exemplify'd in the Life of Mr. Thomas Guy, Late bookseller in Lombard-Street, Madam Jane Nicholas, of St. Albans. And Mr. Francis Bancroft, Late of London Draper*. London, 1728.

Durkheim, Emile, and Marcel Mauss. *Primitive Classification. 1903*. Chicago, 1963.

Dykes, Oswald. *English Proverbs with Moral Reflexions; [In Imitation of Sir Roger L'Estrange's Aesop]*. London, 1709.

E. B. *A New Dictionary of the Terms Ancient and Modern of the Canting Crew, In its several Tribes, of Gypsies, Beggers, Thieves, Cheats, & C*. London, 1699.

Evelyn, John. *Numismata: A Discourse of Medals, Antient and Modern*. London, 1697.

Fielding, Henry. *An Enquiry into the Late Increase of Robbers [1751]*. Wesleyan Edition of the Works of Henry Fielding. Middletown, 1988.
> *Jonathan Wild*. Ed. David Nokes. Harmondsworth, 1982.

Fielding, Sir John. *Extracts from Such of the Penal Laws, as Particularly Relate to the Peace and Good Order of this Metropolis*. New edition. London, 1768.

Fuller, Thomas. *Gnomologia: Adagies and Proverbs*. London, 1732.

Gee, Joshua. *The Trade and Navigation of Great-Britain Considered*. London, 1729.

Godwyn, Morgan. *Trade Preferr'd Before Religion, and Christ Made to Give Place to Mammon: Represented in a Sermon Relating to the Plantations*. London, 1685.

Great Britain. "House of Lords." In *The Manuscripts of the House of Lords, 1692–1693*. London, 1894.

Jacob, Giles. *The Complete Parish Officer*. London, 1734.

H., N. *The Pleasant Art of Money-catching, Newly and Fully Discover'd*. London, 1684.

Hale, Sir Matthew. *A Discourse Touching Provision for the Poor*. London, 1683.

Hanway, Jonas. *Sentimental History of Chimney Sweepers*. London, 1785.

Harrower, John. "Diary of John Harrower, 1773–1776." *American Historical Review* 6, no. 1 (October 1900): 65–107.

Hay, William. *Remarks on the Laws Relating to the Poor*. London, 1735.

Henry, Philip. *Diaries and Letters of Philip Henry, M.A.* Ed. Matthew Henry Lee. London, 1882.

Heywood, Rev. Oliver. *The Rev. Oliver Heywood, B.A., 1630–1702; His Autobiography, Diaries, Anedote and Event Books*. 4 vols. Ed. J. Horsfall Turner. Brighouse, 1882–1885.

Hobbes, Thomas. *Leviathan*. Ed. C. B. Macpherson. Harmondsworth, 1968.

Houstoun, James. *Some New and Accurate Observations Geographical, Natural and Historical*. London, 1725.

Howell, James. *Paroimiographia. Proverbs*. London, 1659.

[Johnston, Charles]. *Chrysal; or the Adventures of a Guinea*. London, 1760.

Jonson, Ben. *Bartholomew Fair*. Ed. Michael Jamieson. Harmondsworth, 1966.

Josselin, Ralph. *The Diary of Ralph Josselin, 1616–1683*. Ed. Alan Macfarlane. London, 1976.

King, Gregory. "Natural and Political Observations and Conclusions upon the State and Condition of England." In *Two Tracts by Gregory King*. Ed. George E. Barnett. Baltimore, 1936.

Lecky, W. E. H. *A History of England in the Eighteenth Century*. 3rd ed. 4 vols. London, 1883.

Locke, John. *An Essay Concerning Human Understanding*. Ed. Roger Woolhouse. London, 1997.

    Further Considerations concerning the Value of Money. London, 1695.

    "Political Essays." [see original]

    Some Considerations of the Consequences of Lowering the Interest and Raising the Value of Money. London, 1692.

Mandeville, Bernard. *By a Society of Ladies: Essays in The Female Tatler*. Ed. M. M. Goldsmith. Bristol, 1999.

    The Fable of the Bees: Or Private Vices, Publick Benefits. 2 vols. Ed. F. B. Kaye. Oxford, 1924.

Marx, Karl. *Capital: A Critique of Political Economy*. Trans. Ben Fowkes. New York, 1976.

    Grundrisse. Foundations of the Critique of Political Economy. Trans. Martin Nicolaus. Harmondsworth, 1973.

    "The Power of Money in Bourgeois Society," *Economic and Philosophic Manuscripts of 1844*. In *The Marx-Engels Reader*. 2nd ed. Ed. Robert C. Tucker. New York, 1978.

Mauss, Marcel. *The Gift: The Form and Reason for Exchange in Archaic Societies*. Trans. W. D. Halls. New York, 1990.

Montagu, Mary Wortley. "Lady." In *The Letters and Works of Lady Mary Wortley Montagu*. 2 vols. Ed. Lord Wharncliffe. London, 1813.

North, Roger. *A Discourse of the Poor*. London, 1753.

[Oglethorpe, James]. *A New and Accurate Account of the Provinces of South-Carolina and Georgia*. London, 1733.

Palmer, Samuel. *Moral Essays on Some of the Most Curious and Significant English, Scotch and Foreign Proverbs*. London, 1710.

Peacham, Henry. *The Art of Living in London [1642]*. Folger Documents of Tudor and Stuart Civilization. Ed. Virgil B. Heltzel. Ithaca, 1962.

    Peacham's Compleat Gentleman, 1634. Oxford, 1906.

    The Worth of a Peny, or A Caution to Keep Money (1641).

Pepys, Samuel. *The Diary of Samuel Pepys*. Ed. Robert Latham and William Matthews. 11 vols. Berkeley, 1970–1983.

Petty, Sir William. *The Economic Writings of Sir William Petty*. Ed. C. S. Williams. Cambridge, 1899.

Philips, John. "The Splendid Shilling: An Imitation of Milton." In *The New Oxford Book of Eighteenth-Century Verse*. Ed. Roger Lonsdale. Oxford, 1984.

Potter, William. *The Tradesman's Jewel (1650)*.

Quarles, Francis. *Emblemes (1635)*. Hildesheim: Emblematisches Cabinet, 1993. Roxburghe Ballad Collection.

[Quarles, Francis]. *Wisdom's Better Than Money, Or the Whole Art of Knowledge, and the Art to know Men*. London, 1698.

Scott, Sarah. *Millenium Hall*. Ed. Gary Kelly. Peterborough, Ontario, 1995.

Smith, Adam. *An Inquiry into the Nature and the Causes of the Wealth of Nations*. Ed. Edwin Cannan. Chicago, 1976.

Snelgrave, William. *A New Account of Some Parts of Guinea, and the Slave-Trade*. London, 1734.

Spence, Joseph. *Anecdotes, Observations, and Characters, of Books and Men*. 2nd ed. London, 1858.

Stafford, J. Martin, ed. *Private Vices, Publick Benefits? The Contemporary Reception of Bernard Mandeville*. Solihull, 1997.

Tryon, Thomas. *Friendly Advcie [sic] to the Gentelmen-Planters [sic] of the East and West Indies*. London, 1684.

Tawney, R. H., and Eileen Power, eds. *Tudor Economic Documents*. 3 vols. London, 1965.

Taylor, John. *All the Workes of John Taylor the Water-Poet. Being Sixty and Three in Number. Collected into One Volume by the Author: With sundry Additions, Corrected, Revised, and Newly Imprinted*. London, 1630.

    A Shilling or, Travailes of Twelve-Pence. London, 1621.

Turner, Thomas. *The Diary of Thomas Turner, 1754–1765*. Ed. David Vaisey. Oxford, 1985.

Vanderlint, Jacob. *Money Answers All Things*. London, 1734.

Vaughan, Rice. *A Discourse of Coin and Coinage*. London, 1675. In *Old and Scarce Tracts on Money*. Ed. J. R. McCulloch. New edition. London, 1933.

Von Archenholz, J. W. *A Picture of England*. London, 1797.

Wallington, Nehemiah. *Historical Notices of Events Occurring Chiefly in the Reign of Charles I*. 2 vols. Ed. from the original mss. (by R. Webb). London, 1869.

Walpole, Horace. *Horace Walpole's Correspondence with Sir Horace Mann*. Ed. W. S. Lewis, Warren Hunting Smith, and George L. Lam. New Haven, 1954.

Ward, Edward. *The London-Spy*. 2 vols. London, 1703.

The Miracles Perform'd by Money; A Poem. London, 1692.

Wesley, John. "The Use of Money." In *John Wesley's Sermons: An Anthology*. Ed. Albert C. Outler and Richard P. Heitzenrater. Nashville, 1991.

[Winstanley, William]. *A Hue and Cry After Money*. London, 1689.

Poor Robin's Hue and Cry After Good-Housekeeping. London, 1687.

SECONDARY SOURCES

Agnew, Jean-Christophe. *Worlds Apart: The Market and the Theater in Anglo-American Thought, 1550–1750*. Cambridge, 1986.

Altman, Ida, and James Horn, eds. *"To Make America": European Emigration in the Early Modern Period*. Berkeley, 1991.

Amussen, Susan Dwyer. *An Ordered Society: Gender and Class in Early Modern England, 1560–1725*. Oxford, 1988.

"Punishment, Discipline, and Power: The Social Meanings of Violence in Early Modern England." *Journal of British Studies* 34, no. 1 (January 1995): 1–34.

Amussen, Susan, and Mark Kishlansky, eds. *Political Culture and Cultural Politics in Early Modern England*. Manchester, 1995.

Andrew, Donna. *Philanthropy and Police: London Charity in the Eighteenth Century*. Princeton, 1989.

Appadurai, Arjun, ed. *The Social Life of Things: Commodities in Cultural Perspective*. Cambridge, 1986.

Apperson, G. L. *English Proverbs and Proverbial Phrases: An Historical Dictionary*. London and Toronto, 1929.

Appleby, Joyce Oldham. "Consumption in Early Modern Thought." In *Consumption and the World of Goods*. Ed. John Brewer and Roy Porter. London, 1993.

Economic Thought and Ideology in Seventeenth-Century England. Princeton, 1978.

"Locke, Liberalism and the Natural Law of Money." *P & P*, no. 71 (1976): 43–69.

Arendt, Hannah. *The Human Condition*. Chicago, 1958.

Armitage, David. "Greater Britain: A Useful Category of Historical Analysis?" *AHR* 104, no. 2 (April 1999): 427–45.

Aston, T. H., and C. H. E. Philpin, eds. *The Brenner Debate: Agrarian Class Structure and Economic Development in Pre-Industrial Europe*. Cambridge, 1985.

Attenborough, F. L., ed. and trans. *The Laws of the Earliest English Kings*. Cambridge, 1922.

Bailyn, Bernard, and Philip D. Morgan, eds. *Strangers Within the Realm: Cultural Margins of the First British Empire*. Chapel Hill, NC, 1991.

Barry, Jonathan, and Christopher Brooks, eds. *The Middling Sort of People: Culture, Society and Politics in England, 1550–1800*. Basingstoke, 1994.

Baudrillard, Jean. *The Mirror of Production*. St. Louis, 1975.

Beattie, J. M. *Crime and the Courts in England, 1660–1800*. Princeton, 1986.

 Policing and Punishment in London, 1660–1750. Oxford, 2001.

Beckerman, John S. "Adding Insult to *Iniuria*: Affronts to Honor and the Origins of Trespass." In *On the Laws and Customs of England: Essays in Honor of Samuel E. Thorne*. Eds. Morris S. Arnold, *et al*. Chapel Hill, 1981.

Beckles, Hilary. "The Colours of Property: Brown, White and Black Chattels and Their Responses on the Caribbean Frontier." In *Unfree Labour in the Development of the Atlantic World*. Ed. Paul E. Lovejoy and Nicholas Rogers. Essex, 1994.

 "The Concept of 'White Slavery' in the English Caribbean During the Early Seventeenth Century." In *Early Modern Conceptions of Property*. Ed. John Brewer and Susan Staves. London, 1996.

Beier, A. L. *Masterless Men: The Vagrancy Problem in England, 1560–1640*. London, 1985.

Beier, A. L., and Roger Finlay, eds. *London, 1500–1700: The Making of the Metropolis*. London, 1986.

Bellamy, Liz. *Commerce, Morality, and the Eighteenth-Century Novel*. Cambridge, 1998.

Ben-Amos, Ilana Krausman. *Adolescence and Youth in Early Modern England*. New Haven, 1994.

Benson, John, and Laura Ugolini, eds. *A Nation of Shopkeepers: Five Centuries of British Retailing*. London, 2003.

Blackburn, Robin. *The Making of New World Slavery: From the Baroque to the Modern 1492–1800*. London, 1997.

Blackwell Dictionary of Twentieth-Century Social Thought. 2nd ed. Ed. William Outhwaite and Tom Bottomore. Oxford, 1993.

Bloch, Maurice, and Jonathan Parry, eds. *Money and the Morality of Exchange*. Cambridge, 1989.

Blumenthal, Walter Hart. *Brides from Bridewell: Female Felons Sent to Colonial America*. Rutland, VT, 1962.

Bond, Donald F. "English Legal Proverbs." *PMLA* 51 (December 1936): 921–35.

Bowles, Samuel. "Endogenous Preferences: The Cultural Consequences of Markets and Other Economic Institutions." *Journal of Economic Literature* 36 (March 1998): 75–111.

Braddick, Michael J. *The Nerves of State: Taxation and the Financing of the English State, 1558–1714*. Manchester, 1996.

Braithwaite, William C. *The Second Period of Quakerism*. London, 1919.

Braudel, Fernand. *The Structures of Everyday Life: The Limits of the Possible*. Trans. Sian Reynolds. New York, 1981.

Brewer, John. *The Sinews of Power: War, Money and the English State, 1688–1783*. London, 1989.

Brewer, John, and Roy Porter, eds. *Consumption and the World of Goods*. London, 1993.

Brewer, John, and Susan Staves, eds. *Early Modern Conceptions of Property*. London, 1995.

Britnell, R. H. *The Commercialisation of English Society, 1000–1500.* 2nd ed. Manchester, 1996.

Brooks, Christopher. "Apprenticeship, Social Mobility and the Middling Sort, 1550–1800." In *The Middling Sort of People: Culture, Society and Politics in England, 1550–1800.* Ed. Jonathan Barry and Christopher Brooks. Basingstoke, 1994.

Brooks, Christopher, and Michael Lobban, eds. *Communities and Courts in Britain, 1150–1900.* London, 1997.

Burtt, Shelley. *Virtue Transformed: Political Argument in England, 1688–1740.* Cambridge, 1992.

Caffentzis, Constantine George. *Clipped Coins, Abused Words and Civil Government: John Locke's Philosophy of Money.* New York, 1989.

———. *Exciting the Industry of Mankind: George Berkeley's Philosophy of Money.* Dordrecht, 2000.

Cannan, E., *et al.* "Who Said 'Barren Metal'? A Symposium." *Economica* no. 5 (June 1922): 105–11.

Capp, Bernard. *The World of John Taylor the Water-Poet, 1578–1653.* Oxford, 1994.

Carrier, James G. *Gifts and Commodities: Exchange and Western Capitalism Since 1700.* London, 1995.

Carrier, James G., ed. *Meanings of the Market: The Free Market in Western Culture.* Oxford, 1997.

Carruthers, Bruce G. *City of Capital: Politics and Markets in the English Financial Revolution.* Princeton, 1996.

Chalmers, Robert. *A History of Currency in the British Colonies.* London, 1893.

Clark, Geoffrey. *Betting on Lives: The Culture of Life Insurance in England, 1695–1775.* Manchester, 1999.

———. "Life Insurance in the Society and Culture of London, 1700–75." *Urban History* 24, pt. 1 (1997): 17–36.

Clark, Peter, and David Souden, eds. *Migration and Society in Early Modern England.* London, 1987.

Clarke, George, ed. *John Bellers: His Life, Times and Writings.* London, 1987.

Coats, A. W. "Changing Attitudes to Labour in the Mid-Eighteenth Century." *Economic History Review,* 2nd ser., 11, no. 1 (August 1958): 35–51.

———. "The Relief of Poverty, Attitudes to Labour and Economic Change in England, 1660–1782." *International Review of Social History* 21 (1976): 98–115.

Coldham, Peter Wilson. *Emigrants in Chains: A Social History of Forced Emigration to the Americas, 1607–1776.* Stroud, Gloucs, 1992.

Colie, Rosalie. *The Resources of Kind: Genre Theory in the Renaissance.* Berkeley, 1973.

Copeland, Edward. *Women Writing About Money: Women's Fiction in England, 1790–1820.* Cambridge, 1995.

Craig, Sir John. *The Mint: A History of the London Mint from A.D. 287 to 1948.* Cambridge, 1953.

———. *Newton at the Mint.* Cambridge, 1946.

Cressy, David. *Coming Over: Migration and Communication Between England and New England in the Seventeenth Century.* Cambridge, 1987.

Crump, Thomas. *The Phenomenon of Money.* London, 1981.

Davies, Owen. *Cunning-Folk: Popular Magic in English History*. London, 2003.

Davison, Lee, and Tim Hitchcock, Tim Keirn, and Robert B. Shoemaker, eds. *Stilling the Grumbling Hive: The Response to Social and Economic Problems in England, 1689–1750*. Stroud, 1992.

Davis, David Brion. *The Problem of Slavery in the Age of Revolution, 1770–1823*. Ithaca, 1975.

Davis, Natalie Zemon. *The Gift in Sixteenth-Century France*. Madison, 2000.

De Roover, Raymond. *Business, Banking and Economic Thought in Late Medieval and Early Modern Europe*. Ed. Julius Kirshner. Chicago, 1974.

De Vries, Jan. "Between Purchasing Power and the World of Goods: Understanding the Household Economy in Early Modern Europe." In *Consumption and the World of Goods*. Ed. John Brewer and Roy Porter. London, 1993.

Dickson, P. G. M. *The Financial Revolution: A Study in the Development of Public Credit, 1688–1756*. Aldershot, 1993.

Drescher, Seymour. *Capitalism and Antislavery: British Mobilization in Comparative Perspective*. New York, 1987.

Dyer, Alan W. "Making Semiotic Sense of Money as a Medium of Exchange," *Journal of Economic Issues* 23, no. 2 (June 1989): 503–10.

Earle, Peter. *The Making of the English Middle Class: Business, Society and Family Life in London, 1660–1730*. Berkeley, 1989.

Einaudi, Luigi. "The Theory of Imaginary Money from Charlemagne to the French Revolution." In *Enterprise and Secular Change*. Ed. Frederic C. Lane and Jelle C. Riemersma. Homewood, Illinois, 1953.

Einzig, Paul. *Primitive Money in its Ethnological, Historical, and Economic Aspects*. 2nd ed. Oxford, 1966.

Ekirch, A. Roger. *Bound for America: The Transportation of British Convicts to the Colonies 1718–1775*. Oxford, 1987.

Ellul, Jacques. *Money and Power*. Trans. LaVonne Neff. Downers Grove, 1979.

Eltis, David. *Economic Growth and the Ending of the Transatlantic Slave Trade*. Oxford, 1987.

"Labour and Coercion in the English Atlantic World from the seventeenth to the Early Twentieth Century." In *The Wages of Slavery: From Chattel Slavery to Wage Labour in Africa, the Caribbean, and England*. Ed. Michael Twaddle. London, 1993.

The Rise of African Slavery in the Americas. Cambridge, 2000.

"Seventeenth Century Migration and the Slave Trade: The English Case in Comparative Perspective." In *Migration, Migration History, History*. Eds. Jan Lucassen and Leo Lucassen. Bern, 1997.

Engell, James. "Wealth and Words: Pope's *Epistle to Bathurst*," *Modern Philology* 85, no. 4 (1988): 433–46.

Engerman, Stanley L. "Coerced and Free Labor: Property Rights and the Development of the Labor Force." *Explorations in Economic History* 29 (1992): 1–29.

Erickson, Amy Louise. "Common Law versus Common Practice: The Use of Marriage Settlements in Early Modern England." *EHR*, n.s., 43, no. 1 (February 1990): 21–39.

Feaveryear, A. E. *The Pound Sterling: A History of English Money*. London, 1931.

Ferber, Marianne A., and Julie A. Nelson, eds. *Beyond Economic Man: Feminist Theory and Economics*. Chicago, 1993.

Ferguson, Moira. *Subject to Others: British Women Writers and Colonial Slavery, 1670–1834*. London, 1992.

Fifoot, C. H. S. *History and Sources of the Common Law: Tort and Contract*. London, 1949.

Finlay, Roger. *Population and Metropolis: The Demography of London, 1580–1650*. Cambridge, 1981.

Finkelstein, Andrea. *Harmony and the Balance: An Intellectual History of Seventeenth-Century English Economic Thought*. Ann Arbor, 2000.

Finn, Margot C. *The Character of Credit: Personal Debt in English Culture, 1740–1914*. Cambridge, 2003.

Firth, Raymond, ed. *Themes in Economic Anthropology*. London, 1967.

Fitton, R. S., and A. P. Wadsworth. *The Strutts and the Arkwrights, 1758–1830*. Manchester, 1958.

Flint, Christopher. "Speaking Objects: The Circulation of Stories in Eighteenth-Century Prose Fiction." *PMLA* 113, no. 2 (March 1998): 212–26.

Fort, Bernadette, and Angela Rosenthal, eds. *The Other Hogarth: Aesthetics of Difference*. Princeton, 2001.

Foucault, Michel. *Madness and Civilization*. Trans. Richard Howard. New York, 1973.

Fox, Adam. *Oral and Literate Culture 1500–1700*. Oxford, 2000.

Friedland, Roger, and A. F. Robertson, eds. *Beyond the Marketplace: Rethinking Economy and Society*. New York, 1990.

Fry, A. Ruth. *John Bellers, 1654–1725: Quaker. Economist and Social Reformer*. London, 1935.

Furniss, Edgar. *Position of the Laborer in a System of Nationalism*. New York, 1965.

Galbraith, John Kenneth. *Money: Whence It Came, Where it Went*. Rev. ed. Boston, 1995.

Galenson, David. *White Servitude in Colonial America: An Economic Analysis*. Cambridge, 1981.

Gallagher, Catherine. *Nobody's Story: The Vanishing Acts of Women Writers in the Marketplace, 1670–1820*. Berkeley, 1994.

Games, Alison. *Migration and the Origins of the English Atlantic World*. Cambridge, MA, 1999.

Gaskill, Malcolm. *Crime and Mentalities in Early Modern England*. Cambridge, 2000.

George, M. Dorothy. *London Life in the Eighteenth Century*. New York, 1965.

Geyer, Jane I., ed. *Money Matters: Instability, Values and Social Payments in the Modern History of West African Communities*. Portsmouth, NH, 1995.

Gillis, John R. *For Better, For Worse: British Marriages, 1600 to the Present*. New York, 1985.

Goldsmith, M. M. *Private Vices, Public Benefits: Bernard Mandeville's Social and Political Thought*. Cambridge, 1985.

Goody, Jack, and S. J. Tambiah. *Bridewealth and Dowry*. Cambridge, 1973.

Gordon, Robert W. "Paradoxical Property." In *Early Modern Conceptions of Property*. Ed. John Brewer and Susan Staves. London, 1996.

Goux, Jean-Joseph. *Symbolic Economies: After Marx and Freud*. Ithaca, 1990.

Grassby, Richard. *The Business Community of Seventeenth-century England*. Cambridge, 1995.

Graves, Robert. *The English Ballad: A Short Critical Survey*. London, 1927.

Greene, Thomas. "The Flexibility of the Self in Renaissance Literature." In *The Disciplines of Criticism*. Ed. Peter Demetz, Thomas Greene, and Lowry Nelson, Jr. New Haven, 1968.

Griffiths, Paul, Adam Fox, and Steve Hindle, eds. *The Experience of Authority in Early Modern England*. Basingstoke, 1996.

Grubb, Isabel. *Quakerism and Industry Before 1800*. London, 1930.

Guest, Harriet. *Small Change: Women, Learning, Patriotism, 1750–1810*. Chicago, 2000.

Gunn, J. A. W. "'Interest Will Not Lie': A Seventeenth-Century Political Maxim." *Journal of the History of Ideas* 29 (October–December 1968): 551–64.

Guth, Delloyd J. "The Age of Debt, the Reformation and English Law." In *Tudor Rule and Revolution: Essays for G. R. Elton from His American Friends*. Ed. Delloyd J. Guth and John W. McKenna. Cambridge, 1982.

Hanagan, Michael P. "Labor History and the New Migration History: A Review Essay." *International Labor and Working-Class History* 54 (Fall 1998): 57–79.

Harding, Vanessa. "The Population of London, 1550–1700: A Review of the Published Evidence." *London Journal* 15 (1990): 111–28.

Hart, Keith. "Heads or Tails? Two Sides of the Coin." *Man* 21 (December 1986): 643–7.

———. "On Commoditization." In *From Craft to Industry: The Ethnography of Proto-industrial Cloth Production*. Ed. Esther N. Goody. Cambridge, 1982.

Haskell, Thomas L., and Richard F. Teichgraeber III, eds. *The Culture of the Market: Historical Essays*. Cambridge, 1993.

Hay, Douglas. "Patronage, Paternalism, and Welfare: Masters, Workers, and Magistrates in Eighteenth-Century England." *International Labor and Working-Class History* 53 (Spring 1998): 27–48.

Hay, Douglas, and Paul Craven, eds. *Masters, Servants, and Magistrates in Britain and the Empire, 1562–1955*. Chapel Hill, 2004.

Hay, Douglas, and Francis Snyder, eds. *Policing and Prosecution in Britain, 1750–1850*. Oxford, 1989.

Hayton, David. "Moral Reform and Country Politics in the Late Seventeenth-Century House of Commons," *P & P*, no. 128 (1990): 48–89.

Heal, Felicity. *Hospitality in Early Modern England*. Oxford, 1990.

Helgason, Agnar, and Gisli Palsson. "Contested Commodities: The Moral Landscape of Modernist Regimes." *Journal of the Royal Anthropological Institute*, n.s., 3, no. 3 (September 1997): 451–71.

Helleiner, Eric. *The Making of National Money: Territorial Currencies in Historical Perspective*. Ithaca, 2003.

Henderson, Tony. *Disorderly Women in Eighteenth-Century London: Prostitution and Control in the Metropolis, 1730–1830*. London, 1999.

Herbert, Christopher. *Culture and Anomie*. Chicago, 1991.

Herrup, Cynthia. *The Common Peace: Participation and the Criminal Law in Seventeenth-Century England*. Cambridge, 1987.

Hilton, Rodney, *et al. The Transition from Feudalism to Capitalism.* London, 1976.

Hindle, Steve. "Power, Poor Relief, and Social Relations in Holland Fen, c. 1600–1800." *HJ* 41, no. 1 (March 1998): 67–96.

Hirschman, Albert O. *The Passions and the Interests: Political Arguments for Capitalism Before Its Triumph.* Repr. Princeton, 1997.
    Rival Views of Market Society and Other Recent Essays. Cambridge, MA, 1992.

Hitchcock, Timothy V., ed. *Richard Hutton's Complaints Book: The Notebook of the Steward of the Quaker Workhouse at Clerkenwell, 1711–1737.* Vol. 24. London: London Record Society, 1987.

Hitchcock, Tim, Peter King, and Pamela Sharpe, eds. *Chronicling Poverty: The Voices and Strategies of the English Poor, 1640–1840.* Basingstoke, 1997.

Hitchcock, Tim, and Heather Shore, eds. *The Streets of London: From the Great Fire to the Great Stink.* London, 2003.

Hobsbawm, Eric. *On History.* London, 1997.

Hoerder, Dirk, and Jorg Nagler, eds. *People in Transit: German Migrations in Comparative Perspective, 1820–1930.* Cambridge, 1995.

Holdsworth, Sir William. *A History of English Law,* 16 vols. 1938–1952. Repr. London, 1982.

Holmes, Geoffrey. *The Making of a Great Power: Late Stuart and Early Georgian Britain, 1660–1722.* London, 1993.

Holton, Robert J. *Economy and Society.* London, 1992.

Hoppit, Julian. "The Use and Abuse of Credit in Eighteenth-Century England." In *Business Life and Public Policy: Essays in Honor of D. C. Coleman.* Ed. Neil McKendrick and R. B. Outhwaite. Cambridge, 1986.

Hont, Istvan, and Michael Ignatieff, eds. *Wealth and Virtue: The Shaping of Political Economy in the Scottish Enlightenment.* Cambridge, 1983.

Horne, Thomas A. *Property Rights and Poverty: Political Argument in Britain, 1605–1834.* Chapel Hill, 1990.

Horsefield, J. Keith. *British Monetary Experiments.* Cambridge, MA, 1960.

Houlbrooke, Ralph, ed. *English Family Life, 1576–1716.* Oxford, 1988.

Hudson, Nicholas. " 'Britons Never Will be Slaves': National Myth, Conservatism, and the Beginnings of British Antislavery." *Eighteenth-Century Studies* 34, no. 4 (2001): 559–76.

Hufton, Olwen. *The Prospect Before Her: A History of Women in Western Europe, Volume One, 1500–1800.* London, 1995.

Hundert, E. G. *The Enlightenment's Fable: Bernard Mandeville and the Discovery of Society.* Cambridge, 1994.

Hunt, Margaret R. *The Middling Sort: Commerce, Gender and the Family in England, 1680–1780.* Berkeley, 1996.

Hutchison, Terence. *Before Adam Smith: The Emergence of Political Economy, 1662–1776.* Oxford, 1988.

Ihde, Erin. " 'So Gross a Violation of Decency': A Note on Wife Sales in Colonial Australia." *Journal of the Royal Australian Historical Society* 84 (June 1998): 26–37.

Ingham, Geoffrey. "On the Underdevelopment of the 'Sociology of Money'." *Acta Sociologica* 41, no. 1 (1998): 3–18.

Innes, Joanna. "The 'Mixed Economy of Welfare' in Early Modern England: Assessments of the Options from Hale to Malthus (c. 1683–1803)." In *Charity, Self-Interest and Welfare in the English Past*. Ed. Martin Daunton. London, 1996.

———. "Prisons for the Poor: English Bridewells, 1555–1800." *Labour. Law, and Crime: An Historical Perspective*. Ed. Francis Snyder and Douglas Hay. London, 1987.

Jackson, Kevin, ed. *The Oxford Book of Money*. Oxford, 1995.

Jester, Annie Lash, ed. *Adventurers of Purse and Person: Virginia, 1607–1625*. Princeton, 1956.

Johnson, Robert C. "The Transportation of Vagrant Children from London to Virginia, 1618–1622." In *Early Stuart Studies: Essays in Honor of David Harris Willson*. Ed. Howard S. Reinmuth, Jr. Minneapolis, 1970.

Jordanova, Ludmilla. "Conceptualizing Childhood in the Eighteenth Century: The Problem of Child Labour." *British Journal of Eighteenth-Century Studies* 10, no. 2 (1987): 189–99.

Jutte, Robert. *Poverty and Deviance in Early Modern Europe*. Cambridge, 1994.

Kapferer, Bruce, ed. *Transaction and Meaning: Directions in the Anthropology of Exchange and Symbolic Behavior*. Philadelphia, 1976.

Kaye, Joel. *Economy and Nature in the Fourteenth Century: Money, Market Exchange and the Emergence of Scientific Thought*. Cambridge, 1998.

Kelley, Donald R. *The Human Measure: Social Thought in the Western Legal Tradition*. Cambridge, 1990.

Kelly, Patrick Hyde, ed. *Locke on Money*. 2 vols. Oxford, 1991.

King, Peter. "Punishing Assault: The Transformation of Attitudes in the English Courts." *Journal of Interdisciplinary History* 27 (Summer 1996): 43–74.

Klingender, F. D. "Eighteenth-century Pence and Ha'pence." *Architectural Review* 93 (February 1943): 40–6.

Kowaleski, Maryanne. *Local Markets and Regional Trade in Medieval Exeter*. Cambridge, 1995.

Klamer, Arjo, and Thomas C. Leonard. "So What's an Economic Metaphor?" In *Natural Images in Economic Thought: "Markets Read in Tooth and Claw."* Ed. Philip Mirowski. Cambridge, 1994.

Kohler, Charles *A Quartet of Quakers*. London, 1978.

Kopytoff, Igor. "The Cultural Biography of Things: Commoditization as Process." In *The Social Life of Things: Commodities in Cultural Perspective*. Ed. Arjun Appadurai. Cambridge, 1986.

Kuper, Adam. *Wives for Cattle: Bridewealth and Marriage in Southern Africa*. Boston, 1982.

Lancaster, R. Kent. "Almost Chattel: The Lives of Indentured Servants at Hampton-Northampton, Baltimore County." *Maryland Historical Magazine* 94, no. 3 (Fall 1999): 341–62.

Lane, Joan. *Apprenticeship in England, 1600–1914*. London, 1996.

Laqueur, Thomas W. "Bodies, Death and Pauper Funerals." *Representations* 1, no. 1 (1983): 109–31.

———. *Solitary Sex: A Cultural History of Masturbation*. New York, 2003.

Laslett, Peter. "John Locke, the Great Recoinage, and the Origins of the Board of Trade," *William and Mary Quarterly* 14 (1957): 368–402.

Lees, Lynn Hollen. *The Solidarities of Strangers: The English Poor Laws and the People, 1700–1948.* Cambridge, 1998.

Lemmings, David. "Marriage and the Law in the Eighteenth Century: Hardwicke's Marriage Act of 1753." *HJ* 39, no. 2 (1996): 339–40.

Lester, Richard A. *Monetary Experiments: Early American and Recent Scandinavian.* Princeton, 1939.

Letwin, William. *The Origins of Scientific Economics: English Economic Thought, 1660–1776.* Westport, 1963.

Lewis, Jayne Elizabeth. *The English Fable: Aesop and Literary Culture, 1651–1740.* Cambridge, 1996.

Linebaugh, Peter. *The London Hanged: Crime and Civil Society in the Eighteenth Century.* Cambridge, 1992.

Linebaugh, Peter, and Marcus Rediker. *The Many-Headed Hydra: Sailors, Slaves, Commoners and the Hidden History of the Revolutionary Atlantic.* Boston, 2000.

Little, Lester K. *Religious Poverty and the Profit Economy in Medieval Europe.* Ithaca, 1978.

Lucassen, Jan, and Leo Lucassen, eds. *Migration, Migration History, History.* Bern, 1997.

Lynch, Deidre Shauna. *The Economy of Character: Novels, Market Culture, and the Business of Inner Meaning.* Chicago, 1998.

    "Person Effects and Sentimental Fictions." *Eighteenth-Century Fiction* 12 (January–April 2000): 345–68.

Macfarlane, Alan. *The Family Life of Ralph Josselin: A Seventeenth-Century Clergyman.* New York, 1970.

    The Origins of English Individualism: The Family, Property and Social Transition. Oxford, 1978.

Macfarlane, Stephen. "Social Policy and the Poor in the Later Seventeenth Century." In *London, 1500–1700.* Ed. A. L. Beier, and Roger Finlay. London, 1986.

MacIntyre, Alasdair. *A Short History of Ethics.* New York, 1996.

Macpherson, C. B. *The Political Theory of Possessive Individualism: Hobbes to Locke.* Oxford, 1962.

Mascuch, Michael. *Origins of the Individualist Self: Autobiography and Self-Identity in England, 1591–1791.* Cambridge, 1997.

    "Social Mobility and Middling Self-Identity: The Ethos of British Autobiographers, 1600–1750." *Social History* 20, no. 1 (1995): 45–61.

Mathias, Peter. *The Transformation of England: Essays in the Economic and Social History of England in the Eighteenth Century.* London, 1979.

McCloskey, Deirdre N. *The Rhetoric of Economics.* 2nd ed. Madison, 1998.

McKeon, Michael. "Historicizing Patriarchy: The Emergence of Gender Difference in England, 1660–1760." *Eighteenth-Century Studies* 28, no. 3 (1995): 295–322.

    The Origins of the English Novel, 1600–1740. Baltimore, 1987.

Meadows, Andrew, and Kirsty Shipton, eds. *Money and Its Uses in the Ancient Greek World.* Oxford, 2001.

Menefee, Samuel Pyeatt. *Wives for Sale: An Ethnographic Study of British Popular Divorce*. New York, 1981.

Merry, Sally Engle. "Hegemony and Culture in Historical Anthropology: A Review Essay on Jean and John L. Comaroff's *Of Revelation and Revolution*." *American Historical Review* 108, no. 2 (April 2003): 466–7.

Mieder, Wolfgang. *Proverbs Are Never Out of Season: Popular Wisdom in the Modern Age*. New York, 1993.

Mieder, Wolfgang, and Alan Dundes, eds. *The Wisdom of Many: Essays on the Proverb*. New York, 1981.

Mirowski, Philip, ed. *Natural Images in Economic Thought: "Markets Read in Tooth and Claw."* Cambridge, 1994.

Miskimin, H. A. *Cash, Credit and Crisis in Europe, 1300–1600*. London, 1989.

Morgan, Edmund S. *American Slavery – American Freedom*. New York, 1975.

Morgan, K. *Slavery and Servitude in North America, 1607–1800*. Edinburgh, 2000.

Morris, Richard B. *Government and Labor in Early America*. New York, 1946.

Moxey, Keith. "The Criticism of Avarice in Sixteenth-Century Netherlandish Painting." In *Northern Mannerism*. Ed. G. Cavalli-Bjorkman. Stockholm, 1985.

Muldrew, Craig. *The Economy of Obligation: The Culture of Credit and Social Relations in Early Modern England*. Basingstoke, 1998.

——— "'Hard Food for Midas': Cash and its Social Value in Early Modern England." *P & P*, no. 170 (February 2001): 78–120.

——— "Interpreting the Market: The Ethics of Credit and Community Relations in Early Modern England." *Social History* 18, no. 2 (1993): 163–8.

Murphy, Antoin. *John Law: Economic Theorist and Policy Maker*. Oxford, 1997.

Murray, John E., and Ruth Wallis Herndon. "Markets for Children in Early America: A Political Economy of Pauper Apprenticeship." *JEH* 62, no. 2 (June 2002): 356–82.

Neal, Larry. *The Rise of Financial Capitalism: International Capital Markets in the Age of Reason*. Cambridge, 1990.

Nelson, Julie A. "Abstraction, Reality and the Gender of 'Economic Man'." In *Virtualism: A New Political Economy*. Ed. James G. Carrier and Daniel Miller. Oxford, 1998.

Newhauser, Richard. *The Early History of Greed: The Sin of Avarice in Early Medieval Thought and Literature*. Cambridge, 2000.

New Palgrave Dictionary of Money and Finance, 3 vols. Ed. Peter Newman, Murray Milgate and John Eatwell. London, 1992.

Nussbaum, Felicity and Laura Brown, eds. *The New Eighteenth Century*. London, 1987.

Oakley, Thomas P. *English Penitential Discipline and Anglo-Saxon Law in Their Joint Influence*. Columbia University Studies in History, Economics and Public Law, vol. 107. New York, 1923.

Obelkevich, James. "Proverbs and Social History." In *The Social History of Language*. Ed. Peter Burke and Roy Porter. Cambridge, 1987.

O'Brien, P. K. "The Political Economy of British Taxation, 1660–1815." *EHR*, n.s., 41, no. 1 (1988): 1–32.

Ong, Walter J. "Oral Residue in Tudor Prose Style." *PMLA* 53, no. 3 (1965): *Oxford Dictionary of English Proverbs*. 2nd ed. Comp. William George Smith. Oxford, 1948.

Paley, Ruth. "Thief-takers in London in the Age of the McDaniel Gang, ca. 1745–1754." In *Policing and Prosecution in Britain, 1750–1850*. Ed. Douglas Hay and Francis Snyder. Oxford, 1989.

Patterson, Annette. *Fables of Power: Aesopian Writing and Political History*. Durham, 1991.

Patterson, Orlando. *Slavery and Social Death*. Cambridge, MA, 1982.

Paulson, Ronald. *Hogarth: The "Modern Moral Subject," 1697–1732*. New Brunswick, 1991.

Pocock, J. G. A. *The Machiavellian Moment: Florentine Political Thought and the Atlantic Republican Tradition*. Princeton, 1975.

Pollock, Sir Frederick, and Frederic William Maitland. *The History of English Law Before the Time of Edward I*. 2nd ed. 2 vols. Cambridge, 1968.

Polyani, Karl. *The Great Transformation*. Boston, 1957.

Pooley, Colin G., and Ian D. Whyte. *Migrants, Emigrants and Immigrants: A Social History of Migration*. London, 1991.

Porter, Roy, ed. *Rewriting the Self: Histories from the Renaissance to the Present*. London, 1997.

Prude, Jonathan. "To Look upon the 'Lower Sort': Runaway Ads and the Appearance of Unfree Laborers in America, 1750–1800." *Journal of American History* 78, no. 1 (June 1991): 124–59.

Radcliffe-Brown, A. R. "Bride-Price, Earnest or Indemnity." *Man* 29 (July 1929): 131–2.

Radin, Margaret Jane. *Contested Commodities*. Cambridge, MA, 1996.

Radzinowicz, Leon. *A History of English Criminal Law and Its Administration from 1750, Vol. 2: The Clash Between Private Initiative and Public Interest in the Enforcement of the Law*. London, 1956.

Reddy, William M. *Money and Liberty in Modern Europe: A Critique of Historical Understanding*. Cambridge, 1987.

Reddy, William M. *The Rise of Market Culture: The Textile Trade and French Society, 1750–1900*. Cambridge, 1984.

Ribton-Turner, Charles J. *A History of Vagrants and Vagrancy, Beggars and Begging*. London, 1887.

Roberts, Richard, and David Kynaston, eds. *The Bank of England: Money, Power and Influence, 1694–1994*. Oxford, 1995.

Rogers, Nicholas. "Policing the Poor in Eighteenth-Century London: The Vagrancy Laws and Their Administration." *Histoire sociale – Social History* 24 (May 1991): 127–47.

    "Vagrancy, Impressment and the Regulation of Labour in Eighteenth-Century Britain." In *Unfree Labour in the Development of the Atlantic World*. Ed. Paul E. Lovejoy and Nicholas Rogers. London, 1994.

Rosenberg, Philippe. "Thomas Tryon and the Seventeenth-Century Dimensions of Antislavery." *William and Mary Quarterly*, 3rd ser., 61, no. 4 (October 2004): 609–42.

Rothschild, Emma. *Economic Sentiments: Adam Smith, Condorcet, and the Enlightenment*. Cambridge, MA, 2001.

Sacks, David Harris. *The Widening Gate: Bristol and the Atlantic Economy, 1450–1700*. Berkeley, 1991.

Sargent, Thomas J., and Francois R. Velde. *The Big Problem of Small Change*. Princeton, 2002.

Schaps, David M. *The Invention of Coinage and the Monetization of Ancient Greece*. Ann Arbor, 2004.

Scribner, Robert W. "The Reformation, Popular Magic, and the 'Disenchantment of the World'." *Journal of Interdisciplinary History* 23, no. 3 (Winter 1993): 475–94.

Searle, G. R. *Morality and the Market in Victorian Britain*. Oxford, 1998.

Seaver, Paul S. *Wallington's World: A Puritan Artisan in Seventeenth-Century London*. Stanford, 1985.

Shammas, Carole. "Changes in English and Anglo-American Consumption from 1550 to 1800." In *Consumption and the World of Goods*. Ed. John Brewer and Roy Porter. Oxford, 1993.

    The Pre-Industrial Consumer in England and America. Oxford, 1990.

Sharpe, Kevin. *Reading Revolutions: The Politics of Reading in Early Modern England*. Yale, 2000.

Shell, Marc. *Money, Language and Thought: Literary and Philosophical Economies from the Medieval to the Modern Era*. Berkeley, 1982.

Sherman, Sandra. *Finance and Fictionality: Accounting for Defoe*. Cambridge, 1996.

    Imagining Poverty: Quantification and the Decline of Paternalism. Columbus, 2001.

Simmel, Georg. *The Philosophy of Money*. Trans. Tom Bottomore and David Frisby. Boston, 1978.

Simpson, A. W. B. "The Laws of Ethelbert." In *On the Laws and Customs of England: Essays in Honor of Samuel E. Thorne*. Ed. Morris S. Arnold, *et al.* Chapel Hill, 1981.

Slack, Paul. *The English Poor Law, 1531–1782*. Cambridge, 1995.

    From Reformation to Improvement: Public Welfare in Early Modern England. Oxford, 1999.

Smelser, Neil J., and Richard Swedberg, eds. *The Handbook of Economic Sociology*. 2nd ed. Princeton, 2005.

Smelser, Neil J. *Poverty and Policy in Tudor and Stuart England*. London, 1987.

Snell, K. D. M. *Annals of the Labouring Poor: Social Change and Agrarian England, 1660–1900*. Cambridge, 1985.

    "Pauper Settlement and the Right to Poor Relief in England and Wales." *Continuity and Change* 6, no. 3 (1991): 375–415.

Sokoll, Thomas, ed. *Essex Pauper Letters, 1731–1837*. Oxford, 2001.

Sokoll, Thomas. "Old Age in Poverty: The Record of Essex Pauper Letters, 1780–1834." In *Chronicling Poverty: The Voices and Strategies of the English Poor, 1640–1840*. Ed. Tim Hitchcock, Peter King, and Pamela Sharpe. Basingstoke, 1997.

Solkin, David H. *Painting for Money: The Visual Arts and the Public Sphere in Eighteenth-Century England*. New Haven, 1992.

  "Samaritan or Scrooge? The Contested Image of Thomas Guy in Eighteenth-Century England." *Art Bulletin* 78, no. 3 (September 1996): 467–84.

Souden, David. " 'Rogues, Whores and Vagabonds'? Indentured Servant Emigrants to North America, and the Case of Mid-Seventeenth-Century Bristol." *SH* 3 (January 1978): 23–41.

Spufford, Peter. *Money and Its Use in Medieval Europe*. Cambridge, 1988.

Starobinski, Jean. *Largesse*. Trans. Jane Marie Todd. Chicago, 1997.

Staves, Susan. *Married Women's Separate Property in England, 1660–1833*. Cambridge, MA, 1990.

Steinfeld, Robert. *The Invention of Free Labor: The Employment Relation in English and American Law and Culture, 1350–1870*. Chapel Hill, 1991.

Stone, Lawrence. *Uncertain Unions: Marriage in England, 1660–1753*. New York, 1992.

Supple, B. E. "Currency and Commerce in the Early Seventeenth Century." *EHR*, 2nd ser., 10 (1957): 239–55.

Taylor, James Stephen. *Poverty, Migration and Settlement in the Industrial Revolution: Sojourners' Narratives*. Palo Alto, CA, 1989.

Tawney, R. H. *Religion and the Rise of Capitalism, 1926*. Harmondsworth, 1984.

Thirsk, Joan. *Economic Policy and Projects: The Development of a Consumer Culture in Early Modern England*. Oxford, 1978.

Thomas, Keith. *Religion and the Decline of Magic*. Harmondsworth, 1971.

  "The Social Origins of Hobbes's Political Thought." In *Hobbes Studies*. Ed. K. C. Brown. Cambridge, MA, 1965.

Thompson, E. P. *Customs in Common*. New York, 1991.

Thompson, James. *Models of Value: Eighteenth-Century Political Economy and the Novel*. Durham, 1996.

Tiersten, Lisa. *Marianne in the Market: Envisioning Consumer Society in fin-de-siecle France*. Berkeley, 2001.

Tilley, Morris Palmer. *A Dictionary of the Proverbs in England in the Sixteenth and Seventeenth Centuries*. Ann Arbor. 1950.

Valenze, Deborah. "Custom, Charity, and Humanity: Attitudes Towards the Poor in Eighteenth-Century England." In *Revival and Religion since 1700: Essays for John Walsh*. Ed. Jane Garnett and Colin Matthew. London, 1993.

Vickers, Douglas. *Studies in the Theory of Money, 1690–1776*. Philadelphia, 1959.

Vilar, Pierre. *A History of Gold and Money, 1450–1920*. Trans. Judith White. 1969; London, 1976.

Viner, Jacob. "Introduction to Bernard Mandeville, *A Letter to Dion* (1732)." In *The Long View and the Short: Studies in Economic Theory and Policy*. Glencoe, 1958.

Walsh, John. "John Wesley and the Community of Goods." In *Protestant Evangelicalism: Britain, Ireland, Germany, and America, c. 1750–c. 1950: Essays in Honour of W. R. Ward*. Ed. Keith Robbins. Oxford, 1990.

Wareing, John. "Preventive and Punitive Regulation in Seventeenth-Century Social Policy: Conflicts of Interest and the Failure to Make Stealing and

Transporting Children, and Other Persons' a Felony, 1645–73." *Social History* 27, no. 3 (October 2002): 288–308.

"'Violently Taken Away or Cheatingly Duckoyed'. The Illicit Recruitment in London of Indentured Servants for the American Colonies, 1645–1718." *London Journal* 26 (2001): 1–22.

Webb, Sidney, and Beatrice Webb. *English Local Government: English Poor Law History: Part I. The Old Poor Law.* 3 vols. London, 1927.

Weiner, Annette B. *Inalienable Possessions: The Paradox of Keeping-While-Giving.* Berkeley, 1992.

Weintraub, E. Roy, ed. *The Future of the History of Economics.* Durham, NC, 2002.

Wennerlind, Carl. "Credit-Money as the Philosopher's Stone: Alchemy and the Coinage Problem in Seventeenth-Century England." In *Oeconomies in the Age of Newton.* Ed. Margaret Schabas and Neil De Marchi. *History of Political Economy,* Suppl. no. 35 (2003): 235–62.

"The Death Penalty as Monetary Policy: The Practice and Punishment of Monetary Crime, 1690–1830." *History of Political Economy* 36, no. 1 (2004): 131–61.

"Money Talks, But What Is It Saying? Semiotics of Money and Social Control." *Journal of Economic Issues* 35, no. 3 (September 2001): 557–74.

Whiting, Bartlett Jere. *When Evensong and Morrowsong Accord: Three Essays on the Proverb.* Ed. Joseph Harris and Wolfgang Mieder. Cambridge, MA, 1994.

Whiting, J. R. S. *Trade Tokens: A Social and Economic History.* Newton Abbot, 1971.

Williams, Jonathan, ed. *Money: A History.* London, 1997.

Williamson, George C. *Trade Tokens Issued in the Seventeenth Century in England, Wales, and Ireland, by Corporations, Merchants, Tradesmen, Etc., A New and Revised Edition of William Boyne's Work.* 2 vols. London, 1889.

Wilson, Charles. *England's Apprenticeship, 1603–1763.* 2nd ed. London, 1984.

Winch, Donald, and Patrick K. O'Brien, eds. *The Political Economy of British Historical Experience, 1688–1914.* Oxford, 2002.

Wormald, Patrick. *Legal Culture in the Early Medieval West: Law as Text, Image and Experience.* London, 1999.

Wrightson, Keith. *Earthly Necessities: Economic Lives in Early Modern Britain.* New Haven, 2000.

Würzbach, Natascha. *The Rise of the English Street Ballad, 1550–1650.* Trans. Gayna Walls. Cambridge, 1990.

Yamey, Basil S. *Art and Accounting.* New Haven, 1989.

Zelizer, Viviana. "Human Values and the Market: The Case of Life Insurance and Death in 19th-Century America." In *The Sociology of Economic Life.* Ed. Mark Granovetter and Richard Swedberg. Boulder, 1992.

The Social Meaning of Money. New York, 1994.

Index

www.ingramcontent.com/pod-product-compliance
Ingram Content Group UK Ltd.
Pitfield, Milton Keynes, MK11 3LW, UK
UKHW020451010325
455719UK00015B/525